Introducing Phonology

This accessible textbook provides a clear and practical introduction
to phonology, the study of sound patterns in language. Designed for
undergraduates with only a basic knowledge of linguistics, it teaches in a
step-by-step fashion the logical techniques of phonological analysis and
the fundamental theories that underpin it. Through over sixty graded
exercises, students are encouraged to make their own analyses of
phonological patterns and processes, based on extensive data and
problem sets from a wide variety of languages. *Introducing Phonology*
equips students with the essential analytical skills needed for further
study in the field, such as how to think critically and discover
generalizations about data, how to formulate hypotheses, and how to
test them. Providing a solid foundation in both the theory and practice
of phonology, it is set to become the leading text for any introductory
course, and will be invaluable to all students beginning to study the
discipline.

DAVID ODDEN is Professor in the Department of Linguistics, Ohio State
University, having previously held positions at Yale University, the
University of Tromsø and the University of Durham. He is the author
of *The Phonology and Morphology of Kimatuumbi* (1996), and has contributed
to many journals such as *Phonology, Language, Linguistic Inquiry, Linguistic
Analysis, Journal of African Languages and Linguistics* and *Studies in African
Linguistics,* of which he is the editor.

Cambridge Introductions to Language and Linguistics

This new textbook series provides students and their teachers with accessible introductions to the major subjects encountered within the study of language and linguistics. Assuming no prior knowledge of the subject, each book is written and designed for ease of use in the classroom or seminar, and is ideal for adoption on a modular course as the core recommended textbook. Each book offers the ideal introductory materials for each subject, presenting students with an overview of the main topics encountered in their course, and features a glossary of useful terms, chapter previews and summaries, suggestions for further reading, and helpful exercises. Each book is accompanied by a supporting website.

Books published in the series
Introducing Phonology David Odden
Introducing Speech and Language Processing John Coleman

Forthcoming:
Introducing Phonetic Science John Maidment and Michael Ashby
Introducing Sociolinguistics Miriam Meyerhoff
Introducing Morphology Maggie Tallerman and S. J. Hannahs
Introducing Historical Linguistics Brian Joseph
Introducing Second Language Acquisition Muriel Saville-Troike
Introducing Language Bert Vaux

Introducing Phonology

DAVID ODDEN
Department of Linguistics
Ohio State University

CAMBRIDGE
UNIVERSITY PRESS

PUBLISHED BY THE PRESS SYNDICATE OF THE UNIVERSITY OF CAMBRIDGE
The Pitt Building, Trumpington Street, Cambridge, United Kingdom

CAMBRIDGE UNIVERSITY PRESS
The Edinburgh Building, Cambridge, CB2 2RU, UK
40 West 20th Street, New York, NY 10011–4211, USA
477 Williamstown Road, Port Melbourne, VIC 3207, Australia
Ruiz de Alarcón 13, 28014 Madrid, Spain
Dock House, The Waterfront, Cape Town 8001, South Africa

http://www.cambridge.org

First published 2005

Printed in the United Kingdom at the University Press, Cambridge

Typeface Swift 9/12 pt   *System* Quark Express™   [TB]

A catalogue record for this book is available from the British Library

Library of Congress Cataloguing in Publication data

Odden, David Arnold, 1954–
Introducing phonology / David Odden.
    p.   cm. — (Cambridge introductions to language and linguistics)
Includes bibliographical references and index.
ISBN 0 521 82669 1 (hardback) – ISBN 0 521 53404 6 (paperback)
1. Grammar, Comparative and general – Phonology.   I. Title.   II. Series.
P217.03   2005
414–dc22   2004051884

ISBN 0 521 82669 1 hardback
ISBN 0 521 53404 6 paperback

Contents

About this book

This is an introductory textbook on phonological analysis, and does not assume any prior exposure to phonological concepts. The core of the book is intended to be used in a first course in phonology, and the chapters which focus specifically on analysis can easily be covered during a ten-week quarter. Insofar as it is a textbook in phonology, it is not a textbook in phonetics (though it does include the minimum coverage of phonetics required to do basic phonology), and if used in a combined phonetics and phonology course, a supplement to cover more details of acoustics, anatomy and articulation should be sought: Ladefoged 2001a would be an appropriate phonetics companion in such a course.

The main emphasis of this book is developing the foundational skills needed to analyze phonological data, especially systems of phonological alternations. For this reason, there is sig-nificantly less emphasis on presenting the various theoretical positions which phonologists have taken over the years. Theory cannot be entirely avoided, indeed it is impossible to state generalizations about a particular language without a theory which gives you a basis for postulating general rules. The very question of what the raw data are must be interpreted in the context of a theory, thus analysis needs theory. Equally, theories are formal models which impose structure on data – theories are theories *about* data – so theories need data, hence analysis. The theoretical issues that are discussed herein are chosen because they represent issues which have come up many times in phonology, because they are fundamental issues, and especially because they allow exploration of the deeper philosophical issues involved in theory construction and testing.

Acknowledgments

A number of colleagues have read and commented on versions of this book. I would like to thank Lee Bickmore, Patrik Bye, Chet Creider, Lisa Dobrin, Kathleen Currie Hall, Sharon Hargus, Tsan Huang, Beth Hume, Keith Johnson, Ellen Kaisse, Susannah Levi, Marcelino Liphola, Mary Paster, Charles Reiss, Richard Wright, and especially Mary Bradshaw for their valuable comments on earlier drafts. Andrew Winnard and Juliet Davis-Berry have also provided valuable comments during the stage of final revisions, and Heather Curtis provided assistance in the production of the drawings. I would also like to thank students at the University of Western Ontario, University of Washington, University of Tromsø, Ohio State University, Kyungpook National University, Concordia University, and the 2003 LSA Summer Institute at MSU, for serving as a sounding board for various parts of this book.

Data from my own field notes provide the basis for a number of the examples, and I would like to thank my many language consultants for the data which they have provided me, including Tamwakat Gofwen (Angas), Bassey Irele (Efik), Edward Amo (Gã), John Mtenge and the late Margaret Fivawo (Hehe), Beatrice Mulala (Kamba), Oben Ako (Kenyang), Deo Tungaraza (Kerewe), Emmanuel Manday (Kimatuumbi), Matthew Kirui (Kipsigis), Habi (Kotoko), Patrick Bamwine (Nkore), David Mndolwa (Shambaa), Kokerai Rugara (Shona), Udin Saud (Sundanese) and Nawang Nornang (Tibetan).

I would like to thank a number of professional colleagues for providing or otherwise helping me with data used in this book, including Charles Marfo (Akan), Grover Hudson (Amharic), Bert Vaux (Armenian), David Payne (Axininca Campa), Hamza Al-Mozainy (Bedouin Hijazi Arabic), Nasiombe Mutonyi (Bukusu), Anders Holmberg (Finnish), Georgios Tserdanelis (Modern Greek), Lou Hohulin (Keley-i), Younghee Chung, Noju Kim, and Misun Seo (Korean), Chacha Nyaigotti Chacha (Kuria), Marcelino Liphola (Makonde), Karin Michelson (Mohawk), Ove Lorentz (Norwegian), Berit Anne Bals (Saami), Nadya Vinokurova (Sakha/Yakut), and Wayles Browne, Svetlana Godjevac and Andrea Sims (Serbo-Croatian), all of whom are blameless for any misuse I have made of their languages and data.

Finally, I would like to acknowledge my debt to authors of various source books, in particular Whitley 1978, Halle and Clements 1983, and especially Kenstowicz and Kisseberth 1979.

A note on languages

The languages which provided data for this book are listed below. The name of the language is given, followed by the genetic affiliation and location of the language, finally the source of the data ("FN" indicates that the data come from my own field notes). Genetic affiliation typically gives the lowest level of the language tree which is likely to be widely known, so Bantu languages will be cited as "Bantu," and Tiv will be cited as "Benue-Congo," even though "Bantu" is a part of Benue-Congo and "Tiv" is a specific language in the Tivoid group of the Southern languages in Bantoid. Locations will generally list one country but sometimes more; since language boundaries rarely respect national boundaries, it is to be understood that the listed country (or countries) is the primary location where the language is spoken, especially the particular dialect used; or this may be the country the language historically originates from (the Yiddish-speaking population of the US appears to be larger than that of any one country in Eastern Europe, due to recent population movements).

Akan [Volta-Congo; Ghana]: Dolphyne 1988; Charles Marfo p.c.

Amharic [Semitic; Ethiopia]: Whitley 1978; Grover Hudson p.c.

Angas [Chadic; Nigeria]: FN.

Arabela [Zaparoan; Peru]: Rich 1963.

Aramaic (Azerbaijani) [Semitic; Azerbaijan]: Hoberman 1988.

Araucanian [Araucanian; Argentina, Chile]: Echeverría and Contreras 1965; Hayes 1995.

Armenian [Indo-European; Armenia, Iran, Turkey]: Vaux 1998 and p.c.

Axininca Campa [Arawakan; Peru]: Payne 1981 and p.c.

Bedouin Hijazi Arabic [Semitic; Saudi Arabia]: Al-Mozainy 1981 and p.c.

Bukusu [Bantu; Kenya]: Nasiombe Mutonyi p.c.

Catalan [Romance; Spain]: Lleo 1970, Kenstowicz and Kisseberth 1979; Wheeler 1979; Hualde 1992.

Chamorro [Austronesian; Guam]. Topping 1968; Topping and Dungca 1973; Kenstowicz and Kisseberth 1979; Chung 1983.

Chukchi [Chukotko-Kamchatkan; Russia]: Krauss 1981.

Digo [Bantu; Kenya and Tanzania]: Kisseberth 1984.

Efik [Benue-Congo; Nigeria]: FN.

Eggon [Benue-Congo; Nigeria]: Ladefoged and Maddieson 1996.

Evenki [Tungusic; Russia]: Konstantinova 1964; Nedjalkov 1997; Bulatova and Grenoble 1999.

Ewe (Anlo) [Volta-Congo; Benin]: Clements 1978.

Farsi [Indo-European; Iran]: Obolensky, Panah and Nouri 1963; Cowan and Rakušan 1998.

Finnish. [Uralic; Finland, Russia]: Whitney 1956; Lehtinen 1963; Anders Holmberg p.c.

Fula [West Atlantic; West Africa]: Paradis 1992.

Gã [Volta-Congo; Ghana]: FN in collaboration with Mary Paster.

Luganda [Bantu; Uganda]: Cole 1967; Snoxall 1967.

Gen [Kwa; Togo]: FN.

Greek [Indo-European; Greece]: Georgios Tserdanelis p.c.

Hebrew [Semitic; Israel]: Kenstowicz and Kisseberth 1979.

Hehe [Bantu; Tanzania]: FN in collaboration with Mary Odden.

Holoholo [Bantu; Congo]: Coupez 1955.

Hungarian [Uralic; Hungary]: Vago 1980, Kenesei, Vago and Fenyvesi 1998, 2000.

Icelandic [Germanic; Iceland]: Einarsson 1945; Jónsson 1966; Oresnik 1985.

Japanese [Japanese; Japan]: Martin 1975.

Jita [Bantu; Tanzania]: Downing 1996.

Kamba [Bantu; Kenya]: FN in collaboration with Ruth Roberts-Kohno.

Karok [Hokan; USA]; Bright 1957, Kenstowicz
    and Kisseberth 1979.
Keley-i [Austronesian; Phillipines]: Kenstowicz
    and Kisseberth 1979; Lou Hohulin p.c.
Kenyang [Bantu; Cameroun]: FN.
Kera [Chadic; Chad]: Ebert 1975; Kenstowicz
    and Kisseberth 1979.
Kerewe [Bantu; Tanzania]: FN.
Kikuyu [Bantu; Kenya]: Clements 1984.
Kimatuumbi [Bantu; Tanzania]: FN.
Kipsigis [Nilotic; Kenya]: FN.
Klamath [Penutian; USA]: Barker 1963, 1964.
Koasati [Muskogean; Louisiana]: Kimball 1991.
Kolami [Dravidian; India]: Emeneau 1961.
Korean [Korean; Korea]: Martin 1992; Younghee
    Chung, Noju Kim and Misun Seo p.c.
Koromfe [Gur; Bourkina Fasso]: Rennison 1997.
Kotoko [Chadic; Cameroun]: FN.
Krachi [Kwa; Ghana]: Snider 1990.
Kuria [Bantu; Kenya]: FN.
Lamba [Bantu; Zambia]: Doke 1938, Kenstowicz
    and Kisseberth 1979.
Lardil [Pama-Nyungan; Australia]: Klokeid
    1976.
Latin [Indo-European; Italy]: Allen and
    Greenough 1983; Hale and Buck 1966.
Lithuanian [Indo-European; Lithuania]:
    Dambriunas et al. 1966; Ambrazas 1997;
    Mathiassen 1996.
Lomongo [Bantu; Congo]: Hulstaert 1961.
Lulubo [Nilo-Saharan; Sudan]: Andersen 1987.
Makonde [Bantu; Mozambique]: Marcelino
    Liphola p.c.
Maltese [Semitic; Malta]: Aquilina 1965; Borg
    and Azzopardi-Alexandre 1997; Brame 1972;
    Hume 1996.
Manipuri [Sino-Tibetan; India, Myanmar,
    Bangaladesh]: Bhat and Ningomba 1997.
Maranungku [Australian: Australia]: Tryon
    1970; Hayes 1995.
Margyi [Chadic; Nigeria]: Hoffmann 1963.
Mende [Mande; Liberia, Sierra Leone]: Leben
    1978.
Mixtec [Mixtecan; Mexico]: Pike 1948;
    Goldsmith 1990.
Mohawk [Hokan; USA]: Postal 1968; Beatty
    1974; Michelson 1988 and p.c.
Mongolian [Altaic; Mongolia]: Hangin 1968.

Nkore [Bantu; Uganda]: FN in collaboration
    with Robert Poletto.
Norwegian [Germanic; Norway]: Ove Lorentz p.c.
Osage [Siouan; Oklahoma]: Gleason 1955.
Ossetic [Indo-European; Georgia, Russia]: Abaev
    1964; Whitley 1978.
Palauan [Austronesian; Palau]: Josephs 1975;
    Flora 1974.
Polish [Slavic; Poland]: Kenstowicz and
    Kisseberth 1979.
Quechua (Cuzco) [Quechua; Peru]: Bills et al.
    1969; Cusihuamán 1976, 1978.
Saami [Uralic; Sápmi (Norway, Sweden,
    Finland, Russia)]: FN in collaboration with
    Curt Rice and Berit Anne Bals.
Sakha (Yakhut) [Altaic; Russia]: Krueger 1962;
    Nadezhda Vinokurova p.c.
Samoan [Austronesian; Samoa]: Milner 1966.
Serbo-Croatian [Slavic; Yugoslavia] Kenstowicz
    and Kisseberth 1979; Wayles Browne,
    Svetlana Godjevac and Andrea Sims p.c.
Setswana [Bantu; Botswana]: Cole 1955,
    Snyman, Shole and Le Roux 1990.
Shambaa [Bantu; Tanzania]: FN.
Shona [Bantu; Zimbabwe]: FN.
Swati [Bantu; Swaziland]: FN.
Slave [Athapaskan; Canada]. Rice 1989.
Slovak [Slavic; Slovakia]: Kenstowicz 1972;
    Rubach 1993.
Somali [Cushitic; Somalia]: Andrzejewski
    1964; Kenstowicz 1994; Saeed 1993, 1999
Sundanese [Austronesian; Indonesia]: FN.
Syrian Arabic [Semitic; Syria]: Cowell 1964.
Tera [Chadic; Nigeria]: Newman.
Thai [Daic; Thailand]: Halle and Clements 1983.
Tibetan [Sino-Tibetan; Tibet]: FN.
Tiv [Benue-Congo; Nigeria]: Arnott 1964;
    Goldsmith 1976.
Tohono 'O'odham (Papago) [Uto-Aztecan; USA]:
    Saxton 1963, Saxton and Saxton 1969,
    Whitley 1978.
Tonkawa [Coahuiltecan; USA]: Hoijer 1933.
Turkish [Altaic; Turkey] Lees 1961, Foster 1969,
    Halle and Clements 1983.
Ukrainian (Sadžava, Standard) [Slavic; Ukraine]:
    Carlton 1971; Kenstowicz and Kisseberth
    1979; Press and Pugh 1994 (Standard);
    Popova 1972 (Sadžava).

Vata [Kru; Côte d'Ivoire]: Kaye 1982.

Votic [Uralic; Russia]: Ariste 1968.

Warao [Warao; Venezuela] Osborn 1966, Hayes 1995.

Weri [Goilalan: New Guinea]: Boxwell and Boxwell 1966; Hayes 1995.

Wintu [Penutian; USA]: Pitkin 1984.

Woleaian [Austronesia; Micronesia]: Sohn 1975.

Yawelmani [Penutian; USA]: Newman 1944; Kenstowicz and Kisseberth 1979.

Yekhee (Etsako) [Edoid; Nigeria]: Elimelech 1978.

Yiddish [Germanic; Eastern Europe]: Neil Jacobs p.c.

Yoruba [Kwa; Nigeria]: Akinlabi 1984.

Abbreviations

abl	ablative	masc	masculine
acc	accusative	ms(c)	millisecond
ant	anterior	nas	nasal
ATR	advanced tongue root	neut	neuter
bk	back	nom	nominative
c.g.	constricted glottis	obj	object
cl	class	pl	plural
cons	consonantal	poss	possessive
cont	continuant	pres	present
cor	coronal	rd	round
dat	dative	sg, sing	singular
dB	decibel	s.g.	spread glottis
del.rel	delayed release	son	sonorant
dim	diminutive	sp	species
distr	distributed	strid	strident
e.o.	each other	syl	syllabic
fem	feminine	tns	tense
gen	genitive	tr	transitive
hi	high	vcd	voiced
Hz	Hertz	vcls	voiceless
imp	imperative	voi	voice
intr	intransitive	1	first person
lat	lateral	2	second person
lo	low	3	third person
loc	locative		

CHAPTER

1 What is phonology?

PREVIEW

This chapter introduces phonology, the study of the sound systems of language. Its key objective is to:

◆ introduce the notion of phonological rule
◆ explain the nature of sound as a physical phenomenon
◆ highlight the tradeoff between accuracy and usefulness in representing sound
◆ distinguish between phonetics and phonology
◆ contrast the continuous and discrete aspects of linguistic sounds
◆ introduce the notion of "sound as cognitive symbol"

Phonology is one of the core fields that composes the discipline of linguistics, which is defined as the scientific study of language structure. One way to understand what the subject matter of phonology is, is to contrast it with other fields within linguistics. A very brief explanation is that phonology is the study of sound structure in language, which is different from the study of sentence structure (syntax) or word structure (morphology), or how languages change over time (historical linguistics). This definition is very simple, and also inadequate. An important feature of the structure of a sentence is how it is pronounced – its sound structure. The pronunciation of a given word is also a fundamental part of the structure of the word. And certainly the principles of pronunciation in a language are subject to change over time. So the study of phonology eventually touches on other domains of linguistics.

An important question is how phonology differs from the closely related discipline of phonetics. Making a principled separation between phonetics and phonology is difficult – just as it is difficult to make a principled separation between physics and chemistry, or sociology and anthropology. A common characterization of the difference between phonetics and phonology is that phonetics deals with "actual" physical sounds as they are manifested in human speech, and concentrates on acoustic waveforms, formant values, measurements of duration measured in milliseconds, of amplitude and frequency, or in the physical principles underlying the production of sounds, which involves the study of resonances and the study of the muscles and other articulatory structures used to produce physical sounds. On the other hand, phonology, it is said, is an abstract cognitive system dealing with rules in a mental grammar: principles of subconscious "thought" as they relate to language sound. Yet once we look into the central questions of phonology in greater depth, we will find that the boundaries between the disciplines of phonetics and phonology are not entirely clear-cut. As research in both of these fields has progressed, it has become apparent that a better understanding of many issues in phonology requires that you bring phonetics into consideration, just as a phonological analysis is a prerequisite for any phonetic study of language.

1.1 Concerns of phonology

As a step towards understanding what phonology is, and especially how it differs from phonetics, we will consider some specific aspects of sound structure that would be part of a phonological analysis. The point which is most important to appreciate at this moment is that the "sounds" which phonology is concerned with are symbolic sounds – they are cognitive abstractions, which represent but are not the same as physical sounds.

The sounds of a language.   One aspect of phonology considers what the "sounds" of a language are. We would want to take note in a description of the phonology of English that we lack a particular vowel that exists in German in words like *schön* 'beautiful,' a vowel which is also found in French (spelled *eu,* as in *jeune* 'young'), or Norwegian (*øl* 'beer'). Similarly, the consonant spelled *th* in English *thing, path* does exist in English (as well as in Icelandic where it is spelled with the letter *þ,* or Modern Greek where it is spelled with *θ,* or Saami where it is spelled *đ*), but this sound does not occur in German or French, and it is not used in Latin American Spanish, although it does occur in Continental Spanish in words such as *cerveza* 'beer,' where by the spelling conventions of Spanish, the letters *c* and *z* represent the same sound as the one spelled *θ* (in Greek) or *th* (in English).

Rules for combining sounds.   Another aspect of language sound which a phonological analysis would take account of is that in any given language, certain combinations of sounds are allowed, but other combinations are systematically impossible. The fact that English has the words *brick, break, bridge, bread* is a clear indication that there is no restriction against having words begin with the consonant sequence *br*; besides these words, one can think of many more words beginning with *br* such as *bribe, brow* and so on. Similarly, there are many words which begin with *bl,* such as *blue, blatant, blast, blend, blink,* showing that there is no rule against words beginning with *bl.* It is also a fact that there is no word **blick*[1] in English, even though the similar words *blink, brick* do exist. The question is, why is there no word **blick* in English? The best explanation for the nonexistence of this word is simply that it is an accidental gap – not every logically possible combination of sounds which follows the rules of English phonology is found as an actual word of the language.

Native speakers of English have the intuition that while *blick* is not actually a word of English, it is a theoretically possible word of English, and such a word might easily enter the language, for example via the introduction of a new brand of detergent. Fifty years ago the English language did not have any word pronounced *bick,* but based on the existence of words like *big* and *pick,* that word would certainly have been included in the set of nonexistent but theoretically allowed words of English. Contemporary English, of course, actually does contain that word – spelled *Bic* – which is a type of pen.

While the nonexistence of *blick* in English is accidental, the exclusion from English of many other imaginable but nonexistent words is based on a principled restriction of the language. While there are words that begin with *sn* like *snake, snip* and *snort,* there are no words beginning with *bn,* and thus **bnick, *bnark, *bniddle* are not words of English. There simply are no words in English which begin with *bn.* Moreover, native speakers of English have a clear intuition that hypothetical **bnick, *bnark, *bniddle* could not be words of English. Similarly, there are no words in English which are pronounced with *pn* at the beginning, a fact which is not only demonstrated by the systematic lack of words such as **pnark, *pnig, *pnilge,*

---

1 The asterisk is used to indicate that a given word is non-existent or wrong.

but also by the fact that the word spelled *pneumonia* which derives from Ancient Greek (a language which does allow such consonant combinations) is pronounced without *p*. A description of the phonology of English would then provide a basis for characterizing such restrictions on sequences of sounds.

Variations in pronunciation.   In addition to providing an account of possible versus impossible words in a language, a phonological analysis will explain other general patterns in the pronunciation of words. For example, there is a very general rule of English phonology which dictates that the plural suffix on nouns will be pronounced as [ɨz], represented in spelling as *es*, when the preceding consonant is one of a certain set of consonants including [š] (spelled *sh*) as in bushes, [č] (spelled as *ch*) as in *churches*, and [ǰ] (spelled *j*, *ge*, *dge*) as in *cages*, *bridges*. This pattern of pronunciation is not limited to the plural, so despite the difference in spelling, the possessive suffix *s*[2] is also subject to the same rules of pronunciation: thus, plural *bushes* is pronounced the same as the possessive *bush's*, and plural *churches* is pronounced the same as possessive *church's*.

This is the sense in which phonology is about the sounds of language. From the phonological perspective, a "sound" is a specific unit which combines with other such specific units, and which represent physical sounds.

1.2 Phonetics – what is physical sound?

Phonetics, on the other hand, is about the concrete, instrumentally measurable physical properties and production of these cognitive speech sounds. That being the case, we must ask a very basic question about phonetics (one which we also raise about phonology). Given that phonetics and phonology both study "sound" in language, what *are* sounds, and how does one *represent* the sounds of languages? The question of the physical reality of an object, and how to represent the object, is central in any science. If we have no understanding of the physical reality, we have no way of talking meaningfully about it. Before deciding *how* to represent a sound, we need to first consider *what* a sound is. To answer this question, we will look at two basic aspects of speech sounds as they are studied in phonetics, namely acoustics which is the study of the properties of the physical sound wave that we hear, and articulation, which is the study of how to modify the shape of the vocal tract, thereby producing a certain acoustic output (sound).

1.2.1 Acoustics

A "sound" is a complex pattern of rapid variations in air pressure, traveling from a sound source and striking the ear, which causes a series of neural signals to be received in the brain: this is true of speech, music and random noises.

---

2 This is the "apostrophe *s*" suffix found in *The child's shoe*, meaning 'the shoe owned by the child.'

Waveforms. A concrete way to visually represent a sound is with an acoustic waveform. A number of computer programs allow one to record sound into a file and display the result on the screen. This means one can visually inspect a representation of the physical pattern of the variation in air pressure. Figure 1 gives the waveforms of a particular instance of the English words *seed* and *Sid*.

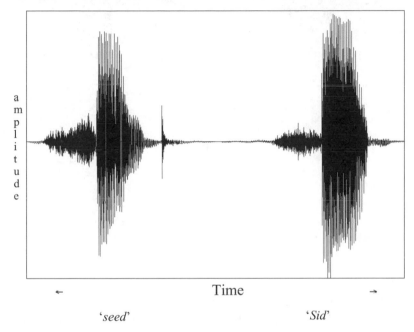

Time

'*seed*'　　　　　'*Sid*'

FIGURE 1
Waveforms of speech

The horizontal axis represents time, with the beginning of each word at the left and the end of the word at the right. The vertical axis represents displacement of air particles and correlates with the variations in atmospheric pressure that affect the ear. Positions with little variation from the vertical center of the graph represent smaller displacements of air particles, such as the portion that almost seems to be a straight horizontal line at the right side of each graph. Such minimal displacements from the center correspond to lower amplitude sounds. The portion in the middle where there is much greater vertical movement in the graph indicates that the sound at that point in time has higher amplitude. While such a direct representation of sounds is extremely accurate, it is also fairly uninformative.

The difference between these words lies in their vowels (*ee* versus *i*), which is the part in the middle where the fluctuations in the graph are greatest. It is difficult to see a consistent difference just looking at these pictures – though since these two vowels *are* systematically distinguished in English, it cannot be impossible. It is also very difficult to see similarities looking at actual waveforms. Consider figure 2 which gives different repetitions of these same words by the same speaker.

Absolute accuracy is impossible, both in recording and measurement. Scientific instruments discard information: microphones have limits on what they can capture, as do recording or digitizing devices. Any representation of a sound is a measurement, which is an idealization about an actual physical event.

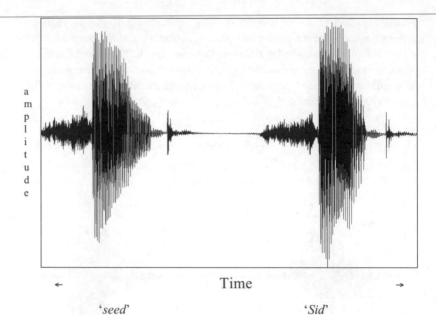

amplitude

Time

→

'seed'   'Sid'

FIGURE 2
Different repetitions of
words

Visual inspection gives you no reason to think that these sets of graphs are
the same words said on different occasions. The problem is that while a
physical waveform is a very accurate representation of a word, it provides
so much information that we cannot tell what is important and what
is not.

Since we are interested in the part which makes these two words
sound different, we might get a clearer picture of the physical difference by expanding the scale and looking just at a part of the vowel.
Vowels are periodic, which means that the pattern of their waveform repeats over time. The display in figure 3 gives a portion of the

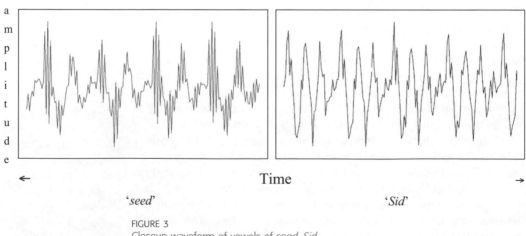

amplitude

Time

'seed'   'Sid'

FIGURE 3
Closeup waveform of vowels of *seed*, *Sid*

vowels from the middle of the words *seed* and *Sid*, involving around 30 milliseconds (ms) of each of the words (the entire word in each of these two examples actually lasts approximately 600 ms, so this is a small part of the entire word). We can indeed see that there is a pattern which is repeated (although successive repetitions are not perfect reproductions).

Though there are visible differences between the waveforms, the basis for distinguishing these vowels remains unclear.

Sound spectra.   We need a better analytical technique than just looking at raw sound, to be able to talk precisely about properties of these sounds. We therefore need to understand some basic properties of physical sounds. All sound waves are definable in terms of three properties that characterize a sine wave familiar from trigonometry, namely frequency measured in cycles per second also known as Hertz (Hz), amplitude measured in decibels (dB), and phase measured in the angular measure radians. These characteristics suffice to define any sine wave, which is the analytic basis of sounds. The property phase, which describes how far into the infinite cycle of repetition a particular sine wave is, turns out to be unimportant for the study of speech sounds, so it can be ignored. Simple sine waves (termed "pure tones" when speaking of sounds) made up of a single frequency are not commonly encountered in the real world, but can be created by a tuning fork or by electronic equipment.

Speech sounds (indeed all sounds) are complex waveforms which are virtually impossible to describe with intuitive descriptions of what they "look like." Fortunately, a complex waveform can be mathematically related to a series of simple waves which have different amplitudes at different frequencies, so that we can say that a complex waveform is "built from" a set of simple waves. Figure 4 shows a complex wave on the left which is constructed mathematically by just adding together the three simple waveforms of different frequencies and amplitudes that you see on the right.

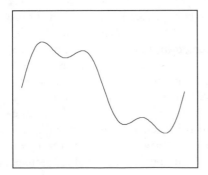 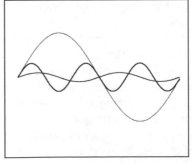

FIGURE 4
Complex wave and the component simple waves defining it

The complex wave on the left is made from simple sine waves at 100, 200, and 300Hz, and the individual components defining the complex wave are graphed on the right. The most prominent component (the one with the highest amplitude) is the one at 100 Hz, the thinnest line which makes one cycle in the chart: it has an amplitude of 60 dB. By comparison, the component at 200 Hz (graphed with a medium-weight line, which makes two cycles in the chart on the right) has the lowest amplitude, 40 dB. The 300 Hz component, graphed with the thickest line, has an intermediate amplitude of 50 dB. It is the amplitudes of the individual components which determine the overall shape of the resulting complex wave.

Now we will see what happens when we change this artificial sound to make the 200 Hz component be the most prominent component and the 100 Hz one be less prominent – if we simply switch the amplitudes of the 100 Hz and 200 Hz components, we get the wave shown in figure 5.

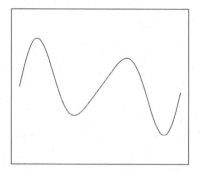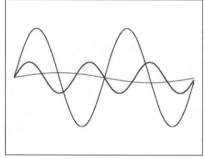

FIGURE 5
Effect of changing
component amplitude

Changing the amplitude of one such component changes the overall character of the waveform. A complex wave is mathematically equivalent to a corresponding series of sine wave components, so describing a complex wave directly is equivalent to describing the individual components. If we see two differently shaped complex waves and we can't describe their differences directly in terms of the complex waves, we can instead focus on the equivalent series of sine wave components, and describe the differences in terms of very simple information about component frequency and amplitude.

Just as a single complex waveform can be constructed from a series of simple waves at different frequencies and amplitudes, a single complex waveform can also be mathematically broken down into a series of components which have different frequencies and amplitudes. Rather than graph the full shape of each specific sine wave component – which becomes very hard to understand if there are more than a handful of components – we can simply graph the two important values for each of the component sine waves, the amplitude and frequency. This is known as a spectrum: it is the defining frequency and amplitude components of a complex waveform, over a fixed period of time. The spectrum of the waveform in figure 4 is plotted in figure 6, where the horizontal axis corresponds to frequency from 0 to 7,000 Hz and the vertical axis corresponds to amplitude from 0 to 60 dB. Note that in this display, time is not represented: the spectrum simply describes amplitude and frequency, and information about how long a particular complex waveform lasts would have to be represented somewhere else.

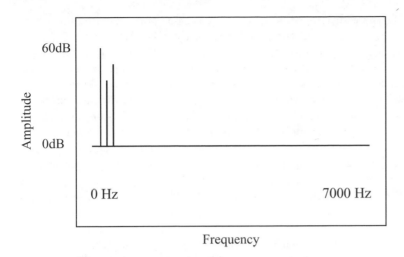

FIGURE 6
Spectrum

This is a very simple spectrum, representing an artificially constructed sound containing only three components. Naturally occurring sounds have many more components than this.

Since complex sounds can be mathematically broken down into a series of simple components, we can use this very useful tool to look at the vowel sounds of *seed* and *Sid*: we look at the physical properties of the component frequencies that define the two vowels that we were interested in. Figure 7 provides the spectrum of the portion from the middle of the vowels of *Sid* and *seed* which we looked at in figure 3. The horizontal axis again represents frequency, ranging from 0 to 7000 Hz, and the vertical axis represents amplitude in decibels. Here, the spectrum is represented as a continuous set of amplitude values for all frequencies in this frequency range, and not just three discrete frequencies as seen in the constructed sound of figure 6.

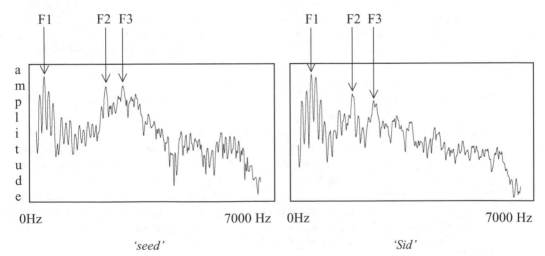

FIGURE 7
Spectrum of the vowels of *seed*, *Sid*

Inaccuracy in spectral data has three main sources. Half of the information in the original signal, phase, has been discarded. Frequency information is only approximate and is related to how much speech is analyzed. Finally, a spectrum assumes that sound properties are constant during the period being analyzed. If too large a piece of speech is taken for analysis, a misrepresentative blending of a continuously changing signal results.

In these spectra, certain frequency regions are more prominent than others, due to resonances in the vocal tract. Resonances are frequency regions where sound amplitude is enhanced. These frequencies are perceptually more prominent than other lower-amplitude frequencies. The frequencies at which these resonances occur are related to the length of various parts of the vocal tract (ultimately related to the position of the tongue and lips as specific sounds are made). The relation between size and frequency is simple and familiar: a large bottle has a low-resonance frequency and a small bottle has a higher-resonance frequency. The first three of these prominent frequency regions, called formants, are indicated with pointed vertical lines in the graphs. You can see that in the spectrum for *seed* on the left, the first formant (F1) occurs at a lower frequency than the first formant of the vowel in *Sid*. However, the second and third formants (F2, F3) of *seed* occur at somewhat higher frequencies than F2 and F3 of *Sid*. By comparing the frequencies at which these formants occur, one can begin to systematically describe the physical properties of the vowels in *seed* and *Sid*. One of the most important properties which allows a listener to distinguish speech sounds, such as the vowels of *seed* versus *Sid*, is the frequencies of these formants.

Viewing the waveform versus the spectrum of a sound involves a trade-off between accuracy and usefulness. While the spectrum is more informative since it allows us to focus on certain specific properties (formant frequencies), it is a less accurate representation of reality than the original waveform. Another very significant limitation of this type of spectral display is that it only characterizes a single brief moment in the utterance: speech is made up of more than just little 30 millisecond bits of steady sound. We need to include information about changes over time in a sound.

A spectrogram can be made by a mechanical spectrograph, which uses an adjustable filter to select different frequency ranges and display the changes in amplitude at each frequency range; or, it can be created by a computer program, which uses Fourier analysis to determine these component amplitudes.

Spectrograms.   Another display, the spectrogram, shows both frequency and amplitude properties as they change over time, by adding a third dimension of information to the display. Figure 8 provides spectrograms of the entirety of the two words *seed* and *Sid*. In this display, the horizontal axis represents the time dimension: the utterance begins at the left and ends at the right. The vertical axis represents frequency information, lower frequencies appearing at the bottom and higher frequencies at the top. Amplitude is represented as darkness: higher amplitudes are darker and lower amplitudes are lighter.

The initial portion of the spectrogram between the arrows represents the consonant *s*, and the second portion with the series of minute vertical striations represents the vowel (the consonant *d* is visible as the light horizontal band at the bottom of the graph, beginning at around 500 ms). The formants which characterize the vowels of *seed* and *Sid* are represented as dark bands, the first formant being the darker lower band and the second and third formants being the two somewhat lighter bands appearing approximately one-third of the way up the display.

Looking at these spectrograms, we learn two other things about these vowels that we would not have suspected from looking at the spectrum in

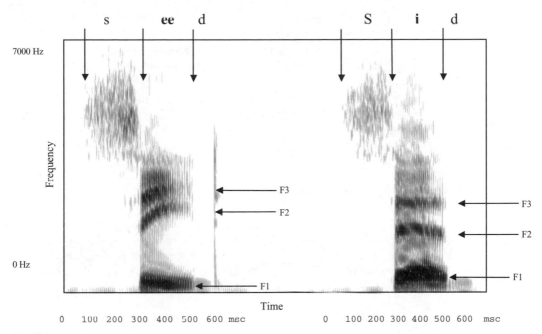

FIGURE 8
Spectrograms

figure 7 taken from a single point in time. First, notice that the vowel portion of *seed* is longer than in *Sid*. Second, the frequencies of the formants
change over time, so in *seed* the first two formants start out much closer
together than they do in *Sid*, and then in *seed* the second formant rises
over the first half of the vowel whereas in *Sid* the second formant falls.

A spectrogram is a reasonably informative and accurate display of properties of sound. It is less accurate than the spectrum at a single point, such
as figure 7. A spectrogram is nothing more than a series of such spectra,
where the more detailed amplitude information represented on the vertical axis in figure 7 is simplified to a less detailed and less reliable visual
difference in darkness. It is also inefficient as a representation of the
sound in two ways. First, as represented on a computer, it is bulky in comparison to a waveform, so that the above spectrogram is around eight
times the size of the original waveform. Second, it is still difficult to interpret. While you can learn how to read a spectrogram of a word in a familiar language, and be fairly certain from inspecting certain properties of
the display what word the spectrogram represents, even the most skilled
of spectrogram readers require tens of seconds to interpret the display;
the average person who has learned the basics of spectrogram reading
would require a number of minutes and may not be able to correctly identify the utterance at all. Spectrograms are created either by special
machinery or specialized computer programs, which are not always available. It is therefore quite impractical and also unnecessary to base the scientific study of language sound systems exclusively on spectrograms.

1.2.2 Articulation

Another way to analyze speech sounds is in terms of the arrangement of articulators – the lips, tongue and other organs of the vocal tract required to produce a particular speech sound. By appropriate positioning of articulators, the shape of the vocal tract can be changed, and consequently the sound which emerges from the vocal tract can be changed (much as different sized bottles produce different tones when you blow across the top). For the purpose of studying the production of speech, the most important articulators are the lips, teeth, tongue, palate, velum, pharynx and larynx.

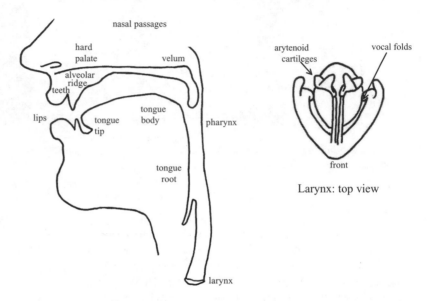

FIGURE 9
Speech anatomy

Figure 9 illustrates the anatomical landmarks which are most important for the study of speech production.

Because sound production involves the manipulation of airflow, production of speech generally begins with the lungs which drive the air coming out of our mouths. Air is forced out of the lungs through the vocal folds, which act as a valve that goes through a repeated cycle of blocking and allowing air to pass from the lungs to the vocal tract. This repeated movement of air would produce a waveform that looks something like figure 10, which represents airflow through the vocal folds when a voiced sound (such as a vowel) is produced.

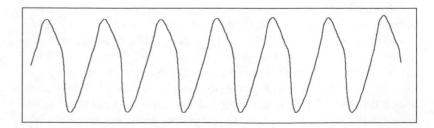

FIGURE 10
Airflow through glottis

This wave is further shaped by the geometry of the vocal tract, which emphasizes certain frequencies and suppresses others. Thus the particular tongue shape that is characteristic of the vowel in *seed* – a higher and fronter position of the tongue – is responsible for the acoustic difference between that vowel and the vowel of *Sid*.

It is a fact of physics that a longer tube has a lower resonance frequency than a shorter one. The vocal tract can be treated as a series of tubes, where the resonance frequencies of different tubes correspond to different frequencies of formants. By placing the tongue in various positions or by protruding the lips, sections of the vocal tract are lengthened or shortened, and thus their resonances – formant frequencies – are lowered or raised. For example, the length of the vocal tract in front of the constriction formed with the tongue determines the frequency of the second formant. When the tongue is advanced as it is for the vowel in *seed*, the portion of the vocal tract in front of the tongue is rather short, and therefore this front part of the vocal tract has a high resonance frequency: and thus the vowel has a high value for F2. On the other hand, the vowel in *pool* is produced with the tongue positioned further back, which means that the part of the vocal tract in front of the tongue is relatively long – it is made even longer because when [u] is produced, the lips are also protruded, which lengthens the entire vocal tract. The effect of lengthening the front part of the vocal tract is that the resonance frequency is lowered, and thus the vowel in *pool* has a very low value of F2.

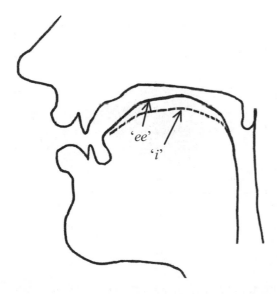

FIGURE 11
Tongue position differences between *ee* and *i*

How vocal tract shape determines the acoustic output is the domain of phonetics. While the acoustic and articulatory properties of speech are important in understanding phonology, indeed constitute the foundation on which phonology is built, it is just that – the foundation. Phonology

looks at how these physical aspects of manifested speech are represented
as part of the mental entity "language."

1.3 The symbolic representation of speech

The English word *ground* is composed of six letters, and by happy coincidence, six distinct phonological sounds or, as they are called by phonologists, segments. But an inspection of what we can measure objectively in
the acoustic signal, such as found in a spectrogram, shows no physical
boundaries in the stream of sound pointing to exactly six distinct sound
events. Instead, we find a continuously changing sound pattern, with the
amplitude of the signal being stronger at a given time at certain frequencies than at others – corresponding to formant frequencies – where the
frequencies of these peaks are constantly changing. For example, looking
at the spectrogram in figure 12, one can see a sliver of a darker area in the
lower quarter at the very left edge of the spectrogram, which is followed
by a light area, and then a pattern of closely spaced vertical striations.
Below the spectrogram, you can see points that provide approximate indi-
cations where each segment begins and ends, and this initial dark sliver
followed by a light sliver constitutes the acoustic energy of the initial
consonant [g]. While there seems to be a relatively clear break between the
initial [g] and the following [r], the same cannot be said for any of the
other adjacent sounds in this word.

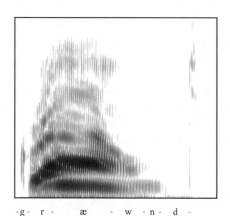

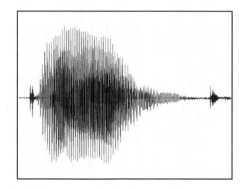

ˆgˆ   r   ˆ   æ   ˆ   w   ˆn ˆ d ˆ

FIGURE 12
Spectrogram   acoustic waveform

This points to one of the most basic properties of phonology, and clar-
ifies another essential difference between phonetics and phonology.
Phonetics studies language sound as a continuous property. A phonological analysis relies on an important idealization of language sound,
that the continuous speech signal can be analyzed as a series of discrete

segments with constant properties. It is evident, looking at the portion of the spectrogram corresponding to *r*, that the physical properties of the *r* change continuously over time – this is true of the entire spectrogram. Yet the transcription simply indicated a single unit *r*, implying a clear beginning and end, and not suggesting that there is time-varying structure within *r*.

Both phonetics and phonology involve representations of sound. A phonetic representation can be given as a series of numbers, representing the three acoustic essentials – amplitude, frequency and time – or as an analogous description of the complex and continuously changing internal geometry of the vocal tract. Such a representation would be highly accurate, and is appropriate if the goal is to understand the fine-grained details of speech sounds as physical entities. For the purposes of grammar, physical sound contains way too much information to allow us to make meaningful and general statements about language sound, and we require a way to represent just the essentials of language sounds. A phonological representation of an utterance reduces this great mass of phonetic information to a cognitively based minimum, a sequence of discrete segments.

The basic tool behind this conversion of the continuous stream of speech sound into units is the phonetic transcription. The philosophy behind a transcription is that one can adequately represent all of the linguistically important details of an utterance by symbols whose interpretation is predefined. Phonology then can be defined as the study of higher- level patterns of language sound, conceived in terms of discrete mental symbols, whereas phonetics can be defined as the study of how those mental symbols are manifested as continuous muscular contractions and acoustic waveforms.

By way of introduction to the nature of a symbolic transcription, let us take the case of the word *ground* given above. The spelling *ground* is a poor representation of the pronunciation of the word, for scientific purposes. If you were to follow rules for pronunciation in other languages such as Portuguese, Spanish or Italian, you might think that the word spelled *ground* would be pronounced like *groaned*. The problem with spelling is that the letter sequence *ou* is pronounced one way in Portuguese, another way in French (the word would be pronounced more like *grooned* if French pronunciation rules were followed), and a third way according to English rules. We need a system for representing sounds, one which is neutral with respect to the choice of language being studied – a system which could be used to discuss not only languages with a long written history like Greek or Chinese, but also languages like Ekoti (a Bantu language spoken in Mozambique) which remains to this day largely unwritten.

In addition, English spelling is imprecise in many cases. The consonant in the middle of *ether* is not the same as the one in the middle of the word *either* (if it were, these words would be pronounced the same, and they are not). English has two distinct kinds of *th* sound, but both are represented the same way in spelling. Linguists adopt special symbols which are better suited to accurately representing speech in an objective manner, so that anyone who knows the pronunciation of the symbols could pronounce a word of English (or Portuguese, Chinese, or Ekoti) written with those symbols with a high degree of accuracy. Thus, we would represent the word *ground* (as spoken by this author) as [græwnd], where [æ] represents the vowel found in *hat*.

The goal of phonology is not to provide accurate symbolic representations of speech. Rather, the goal is to understand the linguistic rules which operate on sounds mentally represented as symbols, and the transcription is our means of representing the data which we discuss. As it happens, the transcription [græwnd] does not really tell the scientist everything they need to know, in order to pronounce this word the same way as in figure 12. A transcription is, essentially, a measurement of a physical phenomenon, and like all measurements can be made with greater or less precision. This particular transcription is quite sufficient for most purposes (such as a phonetic dictionary of English, where knowledge of the systematic principles of the language's sound system might be taken for granted). A more precise transcription such as [kɹʷæ̃ːw̃nd] could be required for another purpose, such as conveying information about pronunciation that is independent of general knowledge of rules of phonetic realization that exist in English.

The very idea of trying to render a highly information-rich structure such as an acoustic waveform in terms of a rather small repertoire of discrete symbols is based on a very important assumption, one which has proven to have immeasurable utility in phonological research, namely that there are systematic limits on what constitutes a possible speech sound in human language. Some such limitations may be explained in terms of physical limits on the vocal tract, so humans are not physically capable of producing the sound emitted by a dentist's high-speed drill, nor can humans produce the sound of a ton of dynamite exploding, but even restricting our attention to sounds which can be produced by the human vocal tract, there are very many sounds which humans can produce which are nevertheless not part of language. The basis for this limitation on speech sounds will be taken up in more detail in later chapters.

Interestingly, humans (especially standup comics) are capable of producing sounds which we understand as representing non-human sounds, even though they are not the actual sounds themselves. Even such sounds-representing-sounds are not part of the set of human speech sounds.

Summary

Phonetics and phonology both study language sound. Phonology examines language sound as a mental unit, encapsulated symbolically for example as [æ] or [g], and focuses on how these units function in grammars. Phonetics examines how symbolic sound is manifested as a continuous physical object. The conversion from physically continuous event to symbolic representation requires focusing on the information that is important, which is possible because not all physical properties of speech sounds are cognitively important. One of the goals of phonology is then to to discover exactly what these cognitively important properties are, and how they function in expressing regularities about languages.

Exercises

These exercises are intended to be a framework for discussion of the points made in this chapter, rather than being a test of knowledge and technical skills.

1. Examine the following true statements and decide if each best falls into the realm of phonetics or phonology.
    a. The sounds in the word *frame* change continuously.
    b. The word *frame* is composed of four segments.
    c. Towards the end of the word *frame*, the velum is lowered.
    d. The last consonant in the word *frame* is a bilabial nasal.
2. Explain what a "symbol" is; how is a symbol different from a letter?
3. Give four rules of the phonological system of English, other than the ones already discussed in this chapter. Important: these should be rules about segments in English and not about spelling rules.
4. How many segments (not letters) are there in the following words (in actual pronunciation)?

sit	trap	fish
bite	ball	up
ox	through	often

5. Why would it be undesirable to use the most accurate representation of a spoken word that can be created under current technology in discussing rules of phonology?

Further reading

Fry 1979; Johnson 1997; Kelly and Local 1989; Ladefoged 2001; Levelt 1989; Liberman 1983; Stevens 1998; Zemlin 1981.

2 Phonetic transcriptions

PREVIEW

This chapter gives an overview of phonetic transcriptions. It:

- gives the important transcriptional symbols
- introduces the two major schemes of phonetic transcriptions
- presents the main articulatory classifications of sounds
- surveys the main variations in phonetic properties exploited by languages
- further develops the relevance of phonetics for the study of phonology

KEY TERMS

transcription
vowels
consonants
place and manner of articulation

In phonetic transcription, speech is represented by a small set of symbols with a standard interpretation. This chapter looks at the different systems for phonetic transcription. There are two major schemes, the informal American scheme used especially in North America, sometimes known as APA (American Phonetic Alphabet), and the IPA (International Phonetic Alphabet), promulgated by the International Phonetic Association. The primary difference between these systems is that in certain cases the American scheme uses a regular letter plus a diacritic where IPA tends to use separate special characters. Thus the sound spelled <sh> at the beginning of *ship* would be transcribed as [š] in the American system, but with the separate letter [ʃ] in IPA. There are relatively few differences between the two systems, and you should become familiar with both systems (actively with one and passively with the other). This text uses APA: the distinctly IPA symbols are given in section 2.3. In this chapter, we will aim for a general overview of transcription and articulation. The goal is not to have a complete account of these topics, but rather to mention the important phonetic symbols, so that the student has a working knowledge of basic transcription, as well as an introduction to the articulatory basis for speech sounds which will be referred to in discussing phonological processes.

> *Angled brackets, e.g. <sh>, represent spelling and square brackets, e.g. [šɪp], are for phonetic representation. Underlying forms, found in later chapters, are placed in slanted brackets, e.g. /šɪp/.*

2.1 Vowels: their symbols and properties

Conventionally, the first division in speech sounds is made between vowels and consonants. Symbols for vowels will be considered first, because there are fewer vowels than consonants. American English has a fairly rich vowel inventory, so we can illustrate most of the vowel symbols with English words.

(1) | Symbol | English equivalent |
|---|---|
| i | beat [biyt] |
| ι or I | bit [bɪt] |
| e | bait [beyt] |
| ɛ | bet [bɛt] |
| æ | bat [bæt] |
| a | cot [kat] |
| ɔ | caught [kɔt] |
| o | coat [kowt] |
| ʊ or U | could [kʊd] |
| u | cooed [kuwd] |
| ʌ | cud [kʌd] |
| ə | (unstressed vowel in) 'array' [əréy] |

The glides *y* and *w* in the transcription of tense vowels in English reflect the phonetic diphthongal quality of these vowels, which is especially evident when one compares the pronunciation of English *say* and Spanish *se*. There are different ways of transcribing that vowel, e.g. [se], [se:], [sei], [seɪ], [seⁱ] and [sey]. Transcriptions like [se] or [se:] are much broader, that is, reveal less of the phonetic details of English because they suppress the information that this is phonetically a diphthong – which can be predicted by a rule – whereas [sei], [seɪ], [seʲ] and [sey] report this phonetic property. There is little scientific basis for picking a specific one of these latter four transcriptions as a representation of how the word is pronounced, and you are likely to encounter all of them in one source or another.

Some dialects of English make no distinction in the pronunciation of the words *cot* and *caught*; even among speakers who distinguish the pronunciation of *cot* and *caught*, the precise pronunciation of the two vowels differs considerably. An important point developed in this book is that transcriptional symbols are approximations representing a range of similar values, and that symbols do not always have absolute universal phonetic values.

Tongue and lip position in vowels. Values of phonetic symbols are defined in terms of a variety of primarily articulatorily defined phonetic dimensions as in (2).

> *A diphthong is a sequence of vowel-like elements – vowels and glides – in one syllable.*

(2)
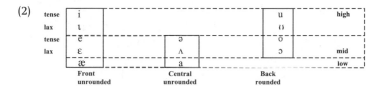

The three most important properties for defining vowels are height, backness, and roundness. The height of a vowel refers to the fact that the tongue is higher when producing the vowel [i] than when producing [e] (which is higher than that used for [æ]), and the same holds for the relation between [u], [o] and [a].

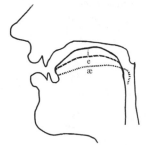
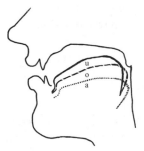

FIGURE 13
Tongue position of vowels

Three primary heights are generally recognized, namely high, mid and low, with secondary distinctions introduced either under the name tense ~ lax or close ~ open to distinguish vowel pairs such as [i] (*seed*) vs. [ɪ] (*Sid*), [e] (*late*) vs. [ɛ] (*let*) or [u] (*food*) vs. [ʊ] (*foot*), where [ieu] are tense (close) and [ɪɛʊ] are lax (open). Tense vowels are higher and often less centralized compared to their lax counterparts.

Independent of height, vowels can differ in relative frontness of the tongue. The vowel [i] is produced with a front tongue position, whereas [u] is produced with a back tongue position. In addition, [u] is produced with rounding of the lips: it is common but by no means universal for back vowels to also be produced with lip rounding. Three phonetic degrees of horizontal tongue positioning are generally recognized: front, central and back. Finally, any vowel can be pronounced with protrusion (rounding) of the lips, and thus [o], [u] are rounded vowels whereas [i], [æ] are unrounded vowels.

With these independently controllable phonetic parameters – five degrees of height, three degrees of fronting, and rounding versus non-rounding – one predicts the possibility of up to thirty vowels, which is many more vowels than are found in English. Many of these vowels are lacking in English, but can be found in other languages. Here are a few examples:

(3) ü   high front round vowel (found in German, French, Turkish)

ʊ̈   lax high front round vowel (found in Icelandic)

ö   mid front round vowel (found in German, French, Turkish)

ɔ̈   lax mid front round vowel (found in Swiss German)

œ   low front round vowel (found in French)

ɨ, ɯ   central (or back) unrounded vowel (found in Turkish, Russian)

All of these vowels can be characterized in terms of the three basic vowel properties of height, backness and rounding. A more complete listing of vowel symbols is given below. It should be borne in mind that the exact phonetic definitions of certain symbols, especially those for low vowels, central vowels, and back unrounded vowels, can vary in usage. Therefore, the symbol <a> might be used to denote a back vowel rather than a central vowel in many published sources; it may also be used for a low front vowel, one which is phonetically lower than [æ].

(4)   *Nonround vowels*

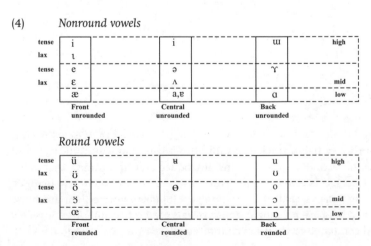

	Front unrounded	Central unrounded	Back unrounded	
tense	i	i	ɯ	high
lax	ɪ			
tense	e	ə	ɤ	
lax	ɛ	ʌ		mid
	æ	a, ɐ	ɑ	low

Round vowels

	Front rounded	Central rounded	Back rounded	
tense	ü	ʉ	u	high
lax	ʊ̈		ʊ	
tense	ö	ɵ	o	
lax	ɔ̈		ɔ	mid
	œ		ɒ	low

While this yields a fairly symmetrical system of symbols and articulatory classifications, there are gaps such as the lack of tense/lax distinctions among low vowels or central vowels except for the [ʌ] ~ [ə] distinction.

These properties of tongue and lip position are the ones most commonly exploited for making vowels, but there are a number of other phonetic properties that play a role in defining vowels, and we turn to those properties next.

Nasalization. Typical vowels are produced with air flowing from the lungs through the mouth, but any vowel can be produced with nasalization, where air flows through the nose as well as through the mouth, by lowering the velum. Nasalized vowels occur in French, Portuguese, Hindi and other languages. Rather than representing each nasalized vowel with its own symbol, the property of nasalization is symbolized with a tilde diacritic [˜] placed over the vowel, so the phonetic transcription of French *bon* would be [bõ].

Length. Vowels (as well as consonants) may also be either long or short, that is, produced with relatively greater versus lesser duration, and length can be represented with a colon [ː], a macron [ˉ], a raised dot [·] or a pair of points which resemble a colon [ː] placed after the appropriate symbol. Thus a long version of the vowel [a] may be symbolized as [aː], [ā], [a·] or [aː]. Equally common is the practice of doubling the vowel or consonant symbol, so long [a] could be represented as [aa]. Examples of languages which systematically exploit the difference between long and short vowels include Japanese ([go] '5', [goo] 'issue') and the Tanzanian Bantu language Kikerewe ([ihuna] 'owl' versus [ihuuna] 'hut'). Languages with long and short consonants include Japanese ([ita] 'was' versus [itta] 'went') and Saami (Arctic Europe) as in the pairs [miella] 'intention (nominative)' versus [miela] 'intention (accusative)'.

Stress. The marking of stress generally encompasses the distinction between primary stress, notated with an acute accent [ˊ], and secondary stress, marked with a grave accent [ˋ]; alternatively, raised and lowered ticks [ˈ, ˌ] may be placed before the initial consonants of a stressed syllable. The first syllable of the English word *telegraphic* has a secondary stress and the third syllable has the primary stress: thus the word could be transcribed either as [tèləgrǽfɪk] or as [ˌtɛləˈgræfɪk]. It is notoriously difficult to give any simple definition of the acoustics or articulation of stress, and indeed the phonetic realization of stress seems to vary considerably across languages, being expressed in terms of amplitude, pitch, duration, vowel quality, as well as a host of other properties. Typically, though, stressed syllables have higher pitch and greater duration and amplitude.

Tone. Tone differences, as found in many Asian, American and African languages, and in addition a few European languages such as Norwegian and Swedish, are also typically transcribed with accent marks. The articulatory basis for producing tone is the rate of vocal fold vibration, which we perceive in terms of *pitch*, so that the vocal folds might vibrate at the rate of 120 cycles per second (120 Hertz, abbreviated Hz) for the production of a low-pitched vowel and at the rate of 170 Hz for the production of a high-pitched vowel. The actual frequency of vibration of a given tone varies from language to language, and also varies from speaker to speaker (depending on age, size and gender inter alia), and even varies within a speaker depending on mood, emphasis and so on. Thus tones do not represent specific frequency values, but are defined relative to a given pitch range used at the moment. A high tone is relatively high within the range that a speaker is using, and if the physical range is raised or lowered, the actual pitch of a high tone is raised or lowered. The traditions for marking tone are rather varied. Accents are generally used to mark tones, and the following examples illustrate the most common usages. As many as five distinct levels are distinguished, arranged in (5) from highest to lowest in pitch.

(5)   a̋   superhigh toned [a]
      á   high toned [a]
      ā or a̍   mid toned [a]
      à   low toned [a]
      ȁ   superlow toned [a]

The characteristic property of a contour-toned vowel is that pitch changes during the vowel, and we can characterize the contour in terms of the tonal values at the beginning and ending points. The diacritic for rising tone is a "hacek," as in [ǎ], which combines the low tone mark grave accent (as in [à]) followed by the high tone mark acute accent (as in [á]), reflecting the fact that a rising tone begins low and ends high. Falling tone is analogously symbolized with a circumflex, as in [â], since it starts high (acute accent) and ends low (grave accent). Many other combinations are possible, for example a mid-to-high rising tone which combines the accents for mid and high, as in [ā́]: you can see that rather than defining a large number of special symbols to indicate the twenty possible contour tones, it is simpler to define symbols for specific levels and describe contours as movement between levels. Another convention for marking tones is to write a superscripted number referring to the pitch level, e.g. ta^3, and combinations of numbers to mark contours e.g. ta^{31}. Traditions for languages in different parts of the world, such as Africa versus Asia or Mexico, differ as to whether 1 refers to the highest or lowest pitch level.

Another pitch property of importance to phonological analysis is downstep and upstep, which are the systematic lowering and raising of the overall pitch space for lexical and grammatical purposes. When a downstep occurs (symbolized by a raised exclamation mark as in (6)), it indicates that all subsequent tones are produced with the upper and lower values of the pitch range decreased. An example comes from Akan, a language of Ghana. Phonologically, each vowel after the first syllable [mè] has a high tone. However, as indicated by the downstep marker, the actual pitch level of a high tone is lower on the third vowel than it is on the second vowel; the pitch of the sixth high-toned vowel is lower than that of the fifth, and so on – in principle, this process can continue infinitely, the only limit being the speaker's ability to actually produce lower pitches.

(6) mè kó'fíɛ́'dɔ́ á'bóá dá'déɛ́ m̄'pá

 [‾ ‾ ‾‾ ‾‾ ‾‾ ‾ ‾‾‾ _]   'My Kofi's love's pet iron bed'

Analogous to downstep, upstep involves raising the pitch range. Upstep, symbolized with a raised inverted exclamation mark, is rare in comparison to downstep, but is found in Krachi, another language of Ghana: the upstep appears between the third and fourth vowels.

(7) àlí kɔ́'tʊ́'ná   'our mat'
  [_ ‾‾ ‾ ‾]

Downstep and upstep may also be symbolized with downward and upward arrows, viz. [á'pá] = [á↓pá], [á'pá] = [á↑pá].

Phonation type.   A number of languages such as Ju/'hoansi (Namibia), Dinka (Sudan), Hmong (SE Asia) and Mazateco (Mexico) employ distinctive patterns of vocal fold vibration or phonation in the production of vowels. One such phonation, known as creaky voicing or laryngealization, is produced by closing the vocal folds abruptly, and gives vowels a particularly "sharp" sound which is notated by placing a tilde beneath the vowel. The other type of phonation, known as breathy voice, is produced by more gradual and even incomplete closure of the vocal folds giving vowels a "soft" quality, and is marked with two dots below the vowel.

(8) a̰ creaky [a]
   a̤ breathy [a]

These modes of phonation are probably familiar to most people (but the labels assigned to these phonations are unfamiliar), since some individuals systematically speak with a creaky quality to their voice (for example, the actor Edward G. Robinson), or with a breathy quality (Marilyn Monroe). What is special about these phonations in languages such as Ju/'hoansi is that they can be used as a meaningful property of specific words realized on single segments, not just as general voice quality properties of all sounds coming from a particular speaker.

Glides.   Standing between consonants and vowels in terms of their phonological function and phonetic properties are the glides, also known as semi-vowels. The typical glides are [y] and [w] as in English *yes*, *wet*, termed "palatal" and "labial" or "labiovelar." These glides are very similar to the high vowels [i], [u], but are shorter and have a greater

degree of constriction than the corresponding vowels. It is often very difficult to distinguish glides and vowels based solely on what they sound
like, and one often has to consider the rules of the language in order to
decide whether to transcribe e.g. [kau] or [kaw], [tua] or [twa]. In addition, some languages such as French, Chinese and Kotoko (Central
Africa) have a "labiopalatal" glide, with the tongue position of [y] and
the lip position of [w], transcribed as [ẅ]: an example from French is *huit*
'eight,' transcribed [ẅit]. Like vowels, glides may also be nasalized,
breathy, or creaky.

2.2 Consonants: their symbols and properties

There are many more consonants than vowels. English only has a fraction
of the full range of possible consonants, so illustration of many of these
symbols involves more extensive consideration of languages other than
English. Most English dialects systematically use the following consonants:

(9) p   **p**ig   b   **b**ig
     m   **m**ug   f   **f**og
     v   **v**armint   θ   **th**ing
     ð   **th**is   t   **t**op
     s   **s**op   d   **d**og
     n   **n**og   č   **ch**uck
     š   **sh**uck   ǰ   **j**ug
     ž   mea**s**ure   k   **c**ot
     g   **g**ot   ŋ   ha**ng**
     h   **h**orse

Other segments used in English include *r, l, z, h*: this is only a partial list.
There are a few additional phonetic segments found in English which,
because they only arise due to general rules of the type to be discussed in
the next chapter, are not immediately obvious:

(10) φ   voiceless bilabial fricative; variant of *p* found in words like
          rasps in casual speech.
      x   variant of *k* found in words like *masks* in casual speech; also
          found in German, Russian, Greek, Scots (English).
      ɱ   labiodental nasal; variant of *m* found before [f] and [v] as in
          comfort.
      t̪   dental *t*. Found in English before [θ]: the word *width* is actually
          pronounced [wɪt̪θ]. Also how *t* is pronounced in French.
      n̪   dental *n*; found in English before [θ] as in *panther*.
      ʔ   glottal stop; found in most dialects of American English
          (except in certain parts of the American south, such as Texas)
          as the pronunciation of *t* before syllabic *n*, i.e. *button*. Also
          stereotypical of British "Cockney" pronunciation *bottle*,
          coulda.
      ɾ   flapped *t* in American English *water*.

Some other consonants found in European languages, for instance, are the following.

(11) p^f, t^s voiceless labiodental and alveolar affricates found in German (<Pfanne> [p^{f}anə] 'pan', <Zeit> [t^{s}ait] 'time')

β   voiced bilabial fricative, found phonetically in Spanish (<huevo> [weβo] 'egg')

γ   voiced velar fricative, found in Modern Greek ([aγapo] 'love') and Spanish (<fuego> [fweγo] 'fire')

Many consonants are only encountered in typically unfamiliar languages, such as retroflex consonants (ṭ, etc.) found in Hindi, Tamil and Ekoti, or uvulars and pharyngeals such as q, χ, ħ found in Arabic.

Consonant symbols are traditionally given in tabular form, treating the place of articulation where the major constriction occurs as one axis, and treating properties such as voicing, being a continuant, or nasality as the other axis. Eleven places of articulation for consonants are usually recognized: bilabial, labiodental, dental, alveolar, alveopalatal, retroflex, palatal, velar, uvular, pharyngeal and laryngeal, an arrangement which proceeds from the furthest forward to furthest back points of the vocal tract: see figure 9 of chapter 1 for anatomical landmarks. Manner of articulation refers to the way in which a consonant at a certain place of articulation is produced, indicating how airflow is controlled: the standard manners include stops, fricatives, nasals and affricates. A further property typically represented in these charts is whether the sound is voiced or voiceless. The following table of consonants illustrates some of the consonants found in various languages, organized along those lines.[1]

(12) *Consonant symbols*

Place of articulation	Consonant manner and voicing						
	vcls stop	vcls affricate	vcls fricative	vcd stop	vcd affricate	vcd fricative	nasal
bilabial	p	(p^φ)	φ	b	(b^β)	β	m
labiodental		p^f	f		b^v	v	ɱ
dental	t̪	t^θ	θ	d̪	d^ð	ð	n̪
alveolar	t	t^s	s	d	d^z	z	n
alveopalatal		č, t^š	š		ǰ, d^ž	ž	ñ
retroflex	ṭ	t^s	ṣ	ḍ	d^z	ẓ	ṇ
palatal	c	(c^c)	ç	ɟ	ɟ^j	j	ñ
velar	k	k^x	x	g	g^γ	γ	ŋ
uvular	q	q^χ	χ	ɢ	ɢ^γ, ɢ^ʁ	γ, ʁ	ŋ̣, N
pharyngeal			ħ		ʕ		
laryngeal~ glottal	ʔ		h			ɦ	

1. Except for č, ǰ, affricates are symbolized by combining the relevant stop and fricative component. Some theoretically expected affricates have not been observed and are placed in parentheses.

2.2.1 Place of articulation

The place of articulation of consonants is divided into primary place of articulation – something that every consonant has – and secondary place of articulation – something that some consonants may add to a primary place of articulation. We begin with primary place. Proceeding from the furthest-forward articulation (the top row of (12)) to the furthest-back articulation (the bottom row of (12)), the bilabial consonants such as *m* have a constriction of both lips. This closure of the lips is not just a property of *m*, it is a defining characteristic of the whole bilabial row *p*, *p*ᵠ, φ, *b*, *b*ᵝ, β and *m*. A labiodental constriction as found in *f* is formed with a constriction between the lower lip and the upper teeth.

Lingual consonants. The tip or blade of the tongue is the active (moveable) articulator in the production of many consonants, including dental, alveolar, alveopalatal, retroflex and palatal consonants. These consonants form a constriction involving the tongue and an appropriate place on the teeth, or hard or soft palate. The contact is with the teeth in the case of dentals, on the hard palate behind the teeth in the case of alveolars, behind the alveolar ridge in the case of alveopalatals and retroflex consonants, and with the blade of the tongue at the boundary between the hard and soft palate in the case of palatals. In many traditional organizations of segments, retroflex consonants are classified as a separate place of articulation from alveolars and alveopalatals. This traditional concept of "place of articulation" combines properties of both active (moveable) articulators and a passive articulator – the target towards which an active articulator moves. What unifies the various kinds of retroflex consonants across languages is not the specific location of the constriction on the hard palate, but rather the manner in which just the tongue tip approaches the palate.

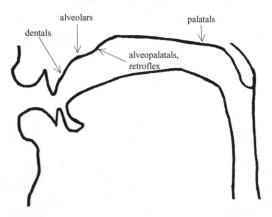

FIGURE 14
Lingual places of
articulation

The terminology used for "palatal" sounds may be particularly confusing. Alveopalatals (sometimes termed "palatoalveolars") are exemplified by the English consonants [š ž č ǰ] (*sheep*, *measure*, *watch*, *judge*), and ("true") palatals are found in Norwegian *kjøpe* [çö:pe] 'buy' and German *ich* [iç] 'I.' The term "palatalized" refers to a secondary articulation (discussed below), but in some linguistic traditions such consonants may also be called "palatals." In addition, alveopalatals may be palatalized or not: the Russian fricatives <ж ш> [ž š] are nonpalatalized whereas the affricate <ч> [čʸ] is a palatalized alveopalatal.

"Back" consonants. The body of the tongue can also be positioned in a number of places in the back of the vocal tract to form a constriction, so if the tongue is retracted and raised a velar consonant such as *k* (*cool*) is formed; if the tongue is retracted but not raised and thus approaches the uvula, a uvular such as *q* is formed, and if the back of the tongue is retracted and lowered toward the pharynx, a pharyngeal such as ʕ is formed. Finally, a consonant can be formed with no constriction above the glottis, when the constriction is made with the vocal folds as in the case of the laryngeal consonants *h, ʔ*.

Secondary articulations. Consonants may have more than one point of constriction: generally, one of these constrictions is the major (most radical) constriction and the other constrictions are less radical – more vowel-like in nature. The most common of these secondary constrictions are given in (13). Secondary articulations are notated by combining the appropriate symbol for the primary place with the symbol representing a kind of glide at the secondary place of articulation.

(13)

		Secondary articulation	Example language
p	t	(none)	English
pʸ	tʸ	palatalized	Russian
pʷ	tʷ	rounded	Nupe (Nigeria)
pᵚ, pˠ, pˣ, ᵽ	tᵚ, tˠ, tˣ, ł	velarized	Marshallese (Marshall Island)
pˤ	tˤ	pharyngealized	Arabic
pʷ̈	tʷ̈	rounded and fronted	Baulé (Ivory Coast)

Plain consonants are those produced with only a single, narrow constriction. Palatalized consonants are formed by combining the basic constriction of the consonant with a less radical vowel-like constriction of the kind that is found in the glide *y* or the vowel *i*; secondarily articulated consonants sound essentially like combinations of consonant plus a glide *y*, *w*. Rounded consonants analogously involve a protrusion of the lips (as do round vowels and the glide *w*). Velarized consonants are produced by combining the narrower primary articulation of a consonant with a raised, retracted tongue position which is similar to the back unrounded vowel [ɯ] or the velar fricative [ɣ], and pharyngealized consonants combine a consonantal constriction with a retracted and lowered tongue position, appropriate for a pharyngeal consonant such as [ʕ]. Rounding of the lips and fronting of the tongue can be combined simultaneously in a secondary articulation, e.g. [tʷ].

Consonants formed with two major constrictions. In a number of languages of Africa (Yoruba, Nupe, Konni, Kuku and others), as well as some languages of New Guinea (Amele), there are consonants typically transcribed as *kp*, *gb*, *ŋm*, which are phonologically single consonants produced with two (virtually) simultaneous complete constrictions, one at the lips and the other formed by raising the body of the tongue to the soft palate, as in the production of a velar. Occasionally, to make clear that this is a single consonant, a "tie" character is written over the two components, viz. k͡p, g͡b. This would be especially necessary in a language like Eggon, which phonetically distinguishes the consonant cluster *k+p*, *g+b* from single consonants with simultaneous labial and velar constrictions, for example [k͡pu] 'die' with a single consonant at the beginning versus [kpu] 'kneel' with a cluster; [g͡bu] 'arrive' with a labiovelar, and [gba] 'divide' with a cluster of a velar followed by a labial.

If consonants can be formed by simultaneously combining both complete labial and velar constrictions, one would reasonably expect there to exist other such consonants with lingual and velar constrictions, or lingual and labial constrictions. In fact, clicks such as lateral [ǁ], alveolar [!], palatoalveolar [ǂ] or dental [ǀ] which are found in Khoisan language such as !Xõo and Khoekhoe (Namibia) or southern Bantu languages such as Zulu and Xhosa (South Africa) are exactly such lingual-velar consonants. These consonants are formed by raising the back of the tongue to form a constriction at the velar place of articulation, and raising the tip or blade of the tongue to make an appropriate constriction on the palate. The middle of the tongue is lowered, creating a vacuum. When the lingual constriction is released, a very loud noise results, which is the typical sound of a click. Finally, lingual-labial consonants, i.e. t͡p, which involve simultaneous complete constrictions with the tongue and lips, are found in the New Guinean language Yeletnye.

2.2.2 Manner of articulation

Stops, fricatives and affricates. Largely independent of the place where a consonant's constriction is formed, the manner in which the constriction is formed can be manipulated in various ways. If a constriction is formed which completely blocks the flow of air, the resulting sound, such as *t*, is called a stop. A consonant can also be produced by forming a narrow constriction which still allows air to pass through the vocal tract, resulting in noise at the constriction, and such consonants, for example *s* and *v*, are called fricatives. A combination of complete constriction followed by a period of partial constriction is termed an affricate, as in *č*. From a phonetic perspective, such consonants can generally be thought of as a sequence of a stop plus a fricative at the same place of articulation (a *homorganic* sequence). From a phonological perspective, they function as single-stop consonants, and are considered to be a particular kind of stop consonant, one with an affricated release. Even from a phonetic perspective, the characterization of affricates as sequence of stop plus fricative is not completely adequate, since there are cases where there is a phonetic difference between stop plus fricative, versus affricate. The most well-known case of this type is Polish, which contrasts the affricate [č] versus the stop-plus-fricative sequence [tš] in the words [či] 'whether' versus [tši] 'three'.

Liquids, glides and approximants. Additionally, languages typically have some kind of liquid consonants, a class of consonants involving the blade or tip of the tongue in their production. The typical examples of liquids are [r] and [l]. The symbol [r] is generally used to refer to "trilled r" as found in Italian. The variety of *r* used in American English is, phonetically speaking, a glide or approximant, which is a segment involving very little constriction in the vocal tract, and would be transcribed as [ɹ]. Some languages also have a type of *r* which is produced by quickly tapping the tongue against the alveolar ridge: this flapped *r* would be transcribed as [ɾ]. English actually has this segment, which is a phonetic variant of /t/ and /d/ in words such as *motto* which is phonetically [mɔɾow]. The flapped variant of /t, d/ is also often transcribed as [ɒ]. The uvular *r* found in French, German and the Bergen dialect of Norwegian is transcribed as [ʀ]. Vowels, liquids, glides and nasals are usually grouped together as sonorants. Chapter 6 discusses the physical basis for that grouping.

> *The concept "approximant," which is not widely used in the phonological literature, is a broader category that includes glides and liquids. The phonetic literature tends not to use the term "glide."*

Laterals. Consonants produced with the blade of the tongue may be produced in such a way that air flows over the sides of the teeth, and such consonants are referred to as *laterals*. English *l* is an archetypical example of a lateral; languages can have lateral fricatives such as voiceless [ɬ] (also transcribed [ɫ]) which appears in Welsh, Lushootseed, Zulu and Xhosa, and voiced [ɮ] found in Zulu and Xhosa, affricates such as [λ] (also transcribed [tˡ]) found in many languages of the Pacific Northwest, and lateral clicks such as [ǁ].

Nasalization. There are other phonetic properties which relate to the manner in which consonants are produced, apart from the location of the constriction. One such modification, which we have already considered since it is applicable to vowels, is nasalization. Consonants such as [m,n,ñ,ŋ] are the archetypical nasals; however, one can produce other nasal consonants (or "nasalized" consonants) by lowering the velum during the production of the consonant. Such nasalized consonants are rare, due to the fact that it is quite difficult to distinguish them from their oral counterparts, but nasalized versions of fricatives and approximants such as [h], [β], [v], [ɣ], [r], [l] do exist in the world's languages. Nasalized fricatives are extremely rare, but the fricative [ṽ] is attested in the Angolan Bantu language Umbundu (Schadeberg 1982), and voiceless nasal fricatives are found in Coatzospan Mixtec of Mexico (Gerfen 1999). It is also claimed that various languages have "prenasalized" consonants, transcribed ᵐb, ⁿd, ᵑg, but it is controversial whether these are truly single segments, and not just clusters of nasal plus consonant, i.e. *mb, nd, ŋg*.

2.2.3 Laryngeal properties

Different actions of the larynx result in a considerable number of consonantal distinctions. The following examples illustrate the major consonant differences which are due to the action of the larynx.

(14)	p	t	k	unaspirated voiceless
	b	d	g	unaspirated voiced
	pʰ	tʰ	kʰ	aspirated voiceless
	bʰ~bɦ~b̤ɦ	dʰ~dɦ~d̤ɦ	gʰ~gɦ~g̤ɦ	aspirated voiced
	p'	t'	k'	ejective
	ɓ	ɗ	ɠ	implosive

Voiced stops are produced with vibration of the vocal folds during their production, whereas voiceless stops are produced with no such vocal fold vibration. Voiceless aspirated stops differ from voiceless unaspirated stops by the presence, in aspirated stops, of a significant delay between the moment when the constriction for the consonant is released and the moment when voicing begins. Such sounds are typically perceived as having a "puff of air" at their release, due to the high volume of air flow during their production. Voiced aspirated consonants, on the other hand, maintain vocal fold vibration, but also are produced with spread vocal folds, resulting in high air flow and a "murmured" quality. Implosives and ejectives are produced by one basic glottal gesture, but they are differentiated in terms of supplementary laryngeal actions. In the case of ejectives, the glottis is first constricted, then the larynx is raised resulting in high pressure in the vocal tract behind the main consonantal constriction; when that constriction is released, a loud high-pitched popping sound results. In the case of implosives, the glottis is also constricted, but is then lowered resulting in a vacuum within the oral cavity. When the constriction is released, a dull, lower-pitched resonance results.

A final property of stop consonants, partially related to laryngeal activity, is the property of release. In some languages, stop consonants in certain positions (before other consonants or at the end of a word) are produced without audibly releasing the consonantal constriction. This property of consonants is notated with the symbol [̚]. In American English, voiceless consonants, especially *t*, are often unreleased at the end of the word, and thus *hit* may be realized phonetically as [hɪt̚]. This generally involves cutting off the flow of air at the glottis during or somewhat before the time when the consonant closure is made. When pronounced with release, as [hɪt], there is a brief burst of noise as the consonant constriction is released and air begins to flow again, which sounds like aspiration.

2.2.4 Syllabicity

A further phonetic property of consonants that may be transcribed is whether the consonant is *syllabic*. There is a phonetic difference between the *n* of American English *cotton* and that of *con*: the *n* of *cotton* is syllabic, whereas the *n* of *con* is nonsyllabic. A syllabic consonant is indicated by placing a vertical tick under the consonant, so *cotton* is transcribed [kaʔn̩] and *con* is transcribed [kan]. There is no simple definition of "syllabic consonant" versus "nonsyllabic consonant," save that a syllabic consonant forms the peak of a syllable and a nonsyllabic consonant does not. Given that *cotton* has two syllables, and taking it for the moment to be a principle that every syllable has a peak, then *n* must be the peak of the second syllable in *cotton*. The main phonetic correlate of the distinction between syllabic and nonsyllabic consonant is duration, where syllabic consonants are generally longer than their nonsyllabic counterparts. Especially in tone languages, syllabic consonants can have distinctive tone, for example Hehe (Tanzania) [ńdage] 'chase me!'.

Because the concept "syllabic consonant" depends on the notion "syllable," we also need to consider the syllable itself, and how to indicate it in a transcription. It is generally agreed that in English, the words *spring, sixths* and *Mike* have one syllable, and *osprey, happy* and *allow* have two. The syllable is made up of a contiguous sequence of segments, so the main issue regarding syllables is where the syllable begins and ends. The conventional symbol for marking the beginning and end of a syllable is a period, which can be unambiguously assigned in the monosyllabic words [.sprɪŋ.], [.sɪksθs.] and [.mayk.]. There is also no problem in deciding where the syllable breaks are in [.ə.lǽw.]. However, in dealing with words having certain clusters of consonants or certain stress patterns, the question becomes more complicated. It would be reasonable to transcribe *osprey* either as [.ás.pri.] or [.á.spri.] (whereas *[.ásp.ri.] would almost certainly be wrong for any speaker of English), and research on the organization of syllables has in fact proposed both [.hǽ.pi.] and [.hǽp.i.] as transcriptions for the word *happy*. Determining syllable boundaries is thus not trivial.

A number of sonorant consonants of English can be syllabic: [baɒl̩] 'bottle', [fr̩] 'fur', [lɛsn̩] 'lesson.' There is even a special phonetic symbol for syllabic [r̩], written either as [ɚ] or [ɝ]. Syllabic sonorants also exist in other languages, such as Sanskrit, Serbo-Croatian, and many African languages. Generally, one finds syllabic sonorants only between consonants, or between a consonant and the beginning or end of a word. Thus in English, final [r] is nonsyllabic when it is preceded by a vowel, as in [kar] 'car,' and syllabic when preceded by a consonant, as in [kapr̩] 'copper.' One can almost completely predict the difference between syllabic and nonsyllabic sonorant in English from surrounding segments. However, in normal speech American English [təreyn] *terrain* is pronounced as [tr̩eyn] distinct from *train* which is [treyn], and [pəlayt] *polite* is pronounced as [pl̩ayt] which is different from [playt] *plight*. Still, the syllabic consonants can be predicted by a rule in English. In some languages this is not possible: in Serbo-Croatian the word *groze* 'fear (genitive)' has a nonsyllabic [r] before a vowel and *groce* 'little throat; larynx' has syllabic [r] in the same context. In Swahili, the word [mbuni] 'ostrich' has a nonsyllabic [m], and [m̩buni] 'coffee plant' has a syllabic [m] in the same position.

2.2.5 Symmetry in consonants

There would be gaps in an otherwise symmetrical universal table of consonants, were we to list all of the consonants found in human languages. In some instances, the gap reflects physiological impossibility, such as the fact that one cannot produce a nasal pharyngeal, analogous to velar nasal [ŋ] but at a pharyngeal place of articulation. A nasal involves making a complete obstruction at a given point of articulation and also requires air to flow through the velum. In order to make a pharyngeal nasal, it would be necessary to make a complete constriction at the pharynx. But since the pharynx lies below the velum, no air can flow through the nasal passages if the pharynx is totally constricted. However a nasalized pharyngeal continuant, i.e. the consonant [ʕ̃] produced with simultaneous nasal airflow, would not be a physical impossibility, since that consonant does not require complete constriction of the pharynx. In other cases, the gap indicates that no such sound has been found, but there is no immutable physical reason for such a sound not to exist. Thus bilabial affricates do not seem to be attested, nor do plain nonaffricated alveopalatal stops, nor do nasalized pharyngeal fricatives. Similarly, while pharyngealized consonants exist, and rounded consonants exist, there are apparently no cases of consonants which are both rounded and pharyngealized, though such segments are not logically impossible. These lacunae may be an indication of a deeper constraint on sound systems; however, it is also possible that these segments do exist in some language which has not been studied yet, since there are many languages in the world which remain uninvestigated.

> *This does not mean that it is impossible to lower the velum and make a complete pharyngeal constriction at the same time. It means that the air will not flow through the nose, which is a defining property of a nasal consonant, so you could not tell from the sound itself whether it is nasalized.*

2.3 IPA symbols

The main difference between the preceding system of transcription and the International Phonetic Alphabet (IPA) lies in differences in the symbols used to transcribe vowels. The IPA system for transcribing vowels can be described in terms of the following chart (when vowels are presented in pairs, the first vowel in the pair is unrounded and the second is rounded).

> *IPA requires close adherence to the graphic design of letters. The IPA symbol for a voiced velar stop is specifically [ɡ] not [g], and the voiced velar fricative is [ɣ] not [γ]. Such fine distinctions in letter shape are irrelevant in APA tradition.*

(15) VOWELS

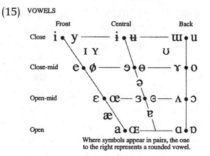

Where symbols appear in pairs, the one to the right represents a rounded vowel.

The most important differences between the vowels of the two systems are the following.

(16)

IPA	APA	
ø	ö	mid front rounded vowel
œ	œ or ɔ̈	open-mid front rounded vowel (in APA, œ tends to imply a low vowel whereas ɔ̈ represents a lax mid vowel)
ʏ	ö or ʏ	lax front rounded vowel
y	ü	front round vowel

In the American tradition, fewer vowel distinctions are generally made, so where IPA treats the members of the following sets as different vowels, APA usage tends to treat these as notational variants of a single vowel. If a distinction needs to be made in some language between nonback unrounded vowels or low vowels, the appropriate IPA symbol will be called upon. APA usage tends to treat [ɯ], [ɨ] and [ï] as graphic variants, whereas in IPA they have distinct interpretations.

(17) ɯ = high back unrounded
      ɨ = high central unrounded
      ï = high centralized unrounded (between i and ɨ)

Where IPA systematically distinguishes the use of the symbols [æ a ɐ ɑ ɒ], APA usage typically only distinguishes front [æ] and nonfront [a].

(18) æ = not fully open front unrounded
      a = low front unrounded
      ɐ = not fully open central unrounded
      ɑ = low back unrounded
      ɒ = low back rounded vowel
      (usually all of these are represented as [a] in American usage
      except for [æ] which represents front low unrounded vowels)

Another more significant difference between the two systems is the difference in terminology for classifying vowels: note that a three-way division into high, mid and low vowels is assumed in the American system, with subdivisions into tense and lax sets, whereas in the IPA, a basic four-way division into close, close-mid, open-mid and open vowels is adopted, where the distinction between close-mid [e] and open-mid [ɛ] is treated as being on a par with the distinction between high [i] and close-mid [e]. High lax vowels are not treated as having a distinct descriptive category, but are treated as being variants within the category of high vowels.

IPA consonant symbols.   The following IPA symbols, which are the most important differences between IPA and APA symbols for consonants, should be noted:

(19)	**IPA**	**APA**	
	j	y	palatal glide
	ɥ	ẅ	front rounded glide
	dʒ	ǰ	voiced alveopalatal affricate; <j> is also used
	tʃ	č	voiceless alveopalatal affricate
	ʃ	š	voiceless alveopalatal fricative
	ʒ	ž	voiced alveopalatal fricative
	ɲ	ñ	palatal nasal
	ṣ, ẓ, ṛ, ḷ, ṇ, ḍ, ṭ	ṣ, ẓ, ṛ, ḷ, ṇ, ḍ, ṭ	retroflex s, z, r, l, n, d, t
	ɾ	ř, D	voiced alveolar flap

ɬ	ɬ, ꞁ	voiceless lateral fricative
ł	I, ɫ	velarized l
c	kʸ	voiceless palatal stop
ç	xʸ	voiceless palatal fricative
dl	λ	voiced lateral affricate
tl	ƛ	voiceless lateral affricate

This represents the current IPA standard. The IPA has developed over a period of more than a hundred years, and has been subject to numerous revisions. For example, in the 1900 version of the IPA, the symbols <ü ï ö ë ꭓ ä> indicated central vowels, as opposed to their contemporary counterparts <ʉ ɨ ɵ ə ɞ ɐ> (the diacritic [¨] is still used to represent a vowel variant that is closer to the center). The letters [ꞵ] and [ʊ] were used for the voiceless and voiced bilabial fricatives, in contrast to contemporary [φ] and [β] (or [Φ] and [β], using the officially sanctioned letter shapes). In the 1914 version, the fricative trill (found in Czech) was transcribed as [ř], in 1947 this was replaced with [r̝], and in contemporary useage, [r̝] is used. The high lax vowels have been transcribed with the symbols <ɩ, ɪ> and <ʊ, ʋ, ꭒ> in the history of the IPA. In reading older works with phonetic transcriptions, the student may thus encounter unfamiliar symbols or unfamiliar uses of familiar symbols. The best solution to uncertainty regarding symbols is to consult a reference source such as Pullum and Ladusaw 1986.

2.4 Illustrations with English transcription

To further illustrate these symbols, we consider the transcription of some words of English, using a broad phonetic transcription, that is, one which does not include a lot of predictable phonetic detail – the issue of predictable features of speech will be taken up in more detail in subsequent chapters. Consider first the transcription of the words [kʌt] *cut*, [siys] *cease* and [sɪk] *sick*. These examples show that phonetic [s] may be spelled in a number of ways, and that the letter <c> in spelling may have a number of phonetic realizations. The example [baks] *box* further makes the point that one has to be careful of not inadvertently importing English orthography into phonetic transcriptions. A transcription such as [bax] might be appropriate for the name of the composer *Bach* (since many people do pronounce the name with a velar fricative, as it is pronounced in German), but otherwise (barring careful transcriptions of casual speech where *k* is actually pronounced as the fricative [x] in some contexts), [x] does not occur in (standard American) English – it would be appropriate for transcribing Scots *Loch* [lɔx].

Examples like [sɪŋ] *sing*, [sɪŋgyəlr̩] *singular*, [ʌngluwd] *unglued*, [sɪŋk] *sink* and [dɪŋiy] *dinghy* show that <ng> may represent a single segment [ŋ] or a sequence [ŋg] or [ng], and that [ŋ] need not be spelled <ng>. In the word [fənɛDɪk] *phonetic*, there may be some temptation to transcribe the word with the full vowel [o] in the first syllable. This is (almost always) a spelling pronunciation – the first unstressed vowel is pronounced as schwa ([ə]) in American English.

The vowel [e] in words such as *same* in English is noticeably different from the pronunciation of [e] in French, Spanish, Italian, or German. In English, the "pure" vowels [e], [o], [i] and [u] do not exist by themselves, and are always combined with a glide of similar phonetic quality, forming what is referred to as a *diphthong*. Thus the transcriptions [seym] *same*, [town] *tone*, [tiym] *team* and [tuwn] *tune* are more phonetically accurate characterizations of the pronunciations of these words. These diphthongs are sometimes also written as [ei], [ou], or [eɪ], [oʊ]. The glide element is also frequently omitted, since it can be predicted by a rule, and thus these words might also be transcribed as [sem], [ton], [tim], and [tun]. However, in [tæwn] (or [tawn], depending on which dialect you speak) *town*, [taym] *time* and [ʊoyl] *toil*, the glide element of the diphthong is not predictable by rule and must be included in any transcription.

In the words [riyɒɪŋ] *reading* and [skeyɒɪŋ] *skating*, both orthographic <t> and <d> are pronounced the same, with the flap [ɒ]. Some dialects of English maintain a phonetic difference between *riding* and *writing*, either via a difference in vowel length ([raːyɒɪŋ] *riding* vs. [rayɒɪŋ] *writing*) and/or by a vowel quality difference ([rʌyɒɪŋ] *riding* vs. [rayɒɪŋ] *writing*).

The word [hr̩t] *hurt* has a "vowel" – a syllable peak – which is essentially equivalent to the consonant [r]. Sonorant consonants can function as vowels, thus this "vowel" is referred to as "syllabic r," as indicated by a tick under the consonant. The IPA provides a separate symbol for this particular sound: [ɚ]. Similarly, English has syllabic [l̩] as in [pæʊl̩] *puddle*, syllabic [n̩] as in [bʌʔn̩] *button*, and syllabic [m̩] as in [skɪzm̩] *schism* (which have no separate IPA symbols). Sometimes the syllabic sonorants are transcribed as the combination of schwa plus a consonant, as in [hərt], [pædəl], [bʌʔən] and [skɪzəm]. It is possible that there are some dialects of English where these words are actually pronounced with a real schwa followed by a sonorant, but in most dialects of American English, they are not pronounced in this way (this is particularly clear if you compare the pronunciation of such English words with that of other languages which do have clear phonetic [ən], [ər] sequences). In addition, as we will discover when we discuss the rule for glottal stop in English, the presence of glottal stop in [bʌʔn̩] can only be explained if there is no schwa before the sonorant.

Summary

Because phonology views speech sounds symbolically, knowledge of the system of symbols for representing speech is a prerequisite to doing a phonological analysis. It is also vital to know the phonetic parameters for describing the sounds of human languages which have been presented here. The main characteristics of vowels involve fronting of the tongue (*front*, *central* and *back*), *rounding*, and vowel height (*high*, *mid* and *low*, with *tense* and *lax* variants of high and mid vowels). Other properties of vowels include stress, tone (including *downstep* and *upstep*) and the phonation types creaky and breathy voice. Primary consonantal places of articulation include *bilabial*, *labiodental*, *dental*, *alveolar*, *alveopalatal*, *retroflex*, *palatal*, *velar*, *uvular*, *pharyngeal* and *laryngeal*. These may be supplemented by vowel-like secondary articulations including palatalization, velarization, pharyngealization and rounding. Consonants may be produced with a number of constriction and release types, and may be stops, fricatives or nasals, and stop consonants may be unreleased or released, the latter type allowing plain versus affricate release. Differences in the laryngeal component for consonants include voicing and aspiration, and the distinction between ejectives and implosives. Vowels and consonants may also exploit differences in nasalization and length.

Appendix 1: Phonetic symbols (APA)

Vowels

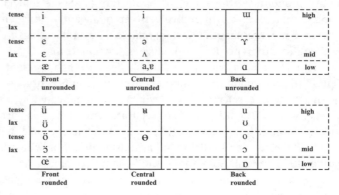

	Front unrounded	Central unrounded	Back unrounded	
tense	i	ɨ	ɯ	high
lax	ɪ			
tense	e	ə	ɤ	
lax	ɛ	ʌ		mid
	æ	a, ɐ	ɑ	low

	Front rounded	Central rounded	Back rounded	
tense	ü	ʉ	u	high
lax	ü̈		ʊ	
tense	ö	ɵ	o	
lax	ɜ̹		ɔ	mid
	œ		ɒ	low

Vowel diacritics

ã	nasalized	ā, a̍,	mid tone	á	high tone
a̰	creaky	a:	long	à	low tone
á, ˈa	primary stress	a̤	breathy	ȁ	superlow tone
a̋	superhigh tone	à, ˌa	secondary stress		

Consonants

	vcls stop	vcls affricate	vcls fricative	vcd stop	vcd affricate	vcd fricative	nasal
bilabial	p	(pᶲ)	φ	b	(bᵝ)	β	m
labiodental		pᶠ	f		bᵛ	v	ɱ
dental	t̪	tᶿ	θ	d̪	dᵟ	ð	n̪
alveolar	t	tˢ	s	d	dᶻ	z	n
alveopalatal		č	š		ǰ	ž	ñ
retroflex	ṭ	ṭˢ	ṣ	ḍ	ḍᶻ	ẓ	ṇ
palatal	c	(cᶜ)	ç	ɟ	(ɟʲ)	ʝ	ñ
velar	k	kˣ	x	g	gˠ	γ	ŋ
uvular	q	qˣ	χ	ɢ	ɢˠ, ɢʁ	ɣ, ʁ	ŋ̣, N
pharyngeal			ħ			ʕ	
laryngeal	ʔ		h			ɦ	

clicks:	ʘ	labial		ǀ	dental
	ǁ	lateral		!	alveolar
	ǂ	postalveolar			

implosives: ɓ   ɗ   ɠ

liquids:	r	trill or tap	ɾ, ᴅ	flap	ɹ	approximant
	ɫ	voiceless lateral spirant	ɮ	voiced lateral spirant	l	lateral approximant
	ʎ	palatal lateral	λ	lateral affricate		

glides:	w	labiovelar	y	palatal	ɥ̈	labiopalatal

Consonant diacritics

p^y	palatalized	p^w	rounded
p^ɯ	velarized	p^ʕ	pharyngealized
p^ẅ	rounded and fronted	ṭ	retroflex
p^h	aspirated voiceless	b^h~b^ɦ	aspirated voiced
p'	ejective	p$^˥$	unreleased
m̩	syllabic	m̥	voiceless

Appendix 2: IPA symbols

Vowels

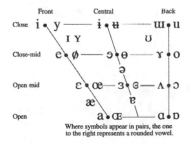

Where symbols appear in pairs, the one to the right represents a rounded vowel.

Consonants

	Bilabial	Labiodental	Dental	Alveolar	Postalveolar	Retroflex	Palatal	Velar	Uvular	Pharyngeal	Glottal
Plosive	p b			t d		ʈ ɖ	c ɟ	k ɡ	q ɢ		ʔ
Nasal	m	ɱ		n		ɳ	ɲ	ŋ	N		
Trill	ʙ			r					R		
Tap or Flap				ɾ		ɽ					
Fricative	ɸ β	f v	θ ð	s z	ʃ ʒ	ʂ ʐ	ç ʝ	x ɣ	χ ʁ	ħ ʕ	h ɦ
Lateral fricative				ɬ ɮ							
Approximant		ʋ		ɹ		ɻ	j	ɰ			
Lateral approximant				l		ɭ	ʎ	ʟ			

Where symbols appear in pairs, the one to the right represents a voiced consonant. Shaded areas denote articulations judged impossible.

Exercises

1. Give the phonetic symbols for the following segments:

   voiceless alveopalatal affricate
   voiceless dental fricative
   front lax high unrounded vowel
   central mid lax unrounded vowel
   voiced velar fricative
   front unrounded low vowel
   voiced dental fricative
   high front rounded tense vowel
   front mid lax unrounded vowel
   voiced alveolar stop
   voiceless laryngeal fricative

2. Give words in English containing the following sounds

   (a) ǰ   (b) ɾ   (c) ŋ
   (d) š   (e) θ   (f) ɛ

3. Transcribe the following words phonetically. If you are a fluent first-
   language speaker of English, represent your own pronunciation.
   Otherwise, use the pronunciation of someone else who is a fluent
   first-language speaker of English.

   push   alphabet   collapse
   punish   Jurassic   salmonella
   diphthong   women   flood

4. From the following pairs of symbols, select the symbol which matches
   the articulatory description.

   ɯ   ɨ   high central unrounded vowel
   ã   a̰   creaky [a]
   ɢ   g   voiced uvular stop
   ɪ   i   lax front high vowel
   ʕ   ʔ   glottal stop
   œ   ö   low front round vowel
   θ   tᶿ   dental affricate
   ž   ǰ   alveopalatal fricative
   á   à   low-toned [a]

5. Provide the phonetic symbols for the following sounds.

   voiced bilabial fricative
   high back unrounded vowel
   voiceless uvular ejective stop
   front round mid oral tense vowel
   voiceless labiodental fricative
   rounded voiceless dental stop
   low front unrounded vowel
   alveolar nasal
   voiced retroflex stop
   voiced pharyngeal fricative
   voiceless alveolar stop
   back low unrounded vowel

6. Provide the articulatory description of the following segments (assume the Americanist system of transcription in cases where the symbol is ambiguous between the two systems). Example:

    i. θ   voiceless interdental fricative
   ii. ɔ   _____
  iii. ə   _____
  iv. a   _____
   v. ɱ   _____
  vi. ḏ   _____
 vii. ʊ   _____
viii. ü   _____
  ix. æ   _____
   x. œ   _____
  xi. tˢ   _____
  xii. č   _____
 xiii. ṣ   _____
 xiv. ɬ   _____
  xv. kˣ   _____
 xvi. x   _____
xvii. ɩ   _____
xviii. φ   _____
 xix. bˠ   _____
  xx. gʷ   _____
 xxi. gˠ   _____
xxii. ʔ   _____

7. Transcribe the following English words phonetically.

listen	[ ]	pleasure	[ ]
unique	[ ]	who	[ ]
attack	[ ]	geriatric	[ ]
significant	[ ]	sample	[ ]
contagious	[ ]	journal	[ ]
resident	[ ]	philosophy	[ ]
pile	[ ]	resign	[ ]
attic	[ ]	punishment	[ ]

Further reading

International Phonetic Association 1999; Ladefoged and Maddieson 1996; Ladefoged 2001a, b; Pike 1947; Pullum and Ladusaw 1986; Smalley 1964.

3 Allophonic relations

PREVIEW

KEY TERMS

allophone

phoneme

complementary distribution

contrast

distinctiveness

This chapter begins the analysis of phonological processes. You will:

◆ learn of predictable variants of basic sounds in English

◆ learn about the concepts "phoneme" and "allophone"

◆ discover that similar relations between sounds exist in other languages

◆ begin to learn the general technique for inducing phonological rules from data that come from a language which you do not know

◆ be introduced to the formalization of phonological rules

While a phonetically accurate representation of pronunciation is useful to phonology, the focus of phonology is not transcription of words, but is rather the mental rules which govern the pronunciation of words in a given language. Certain facts about pronunciation simply cannot be predicted by rule, for example that in English the word *sick* is pronounced [sɪk] and *sip* is pronounced [sɪp]. Hence one fundamental component of a language is a lexicon, a list of words (or morphemes – parts of words), which must provide any information which cannot be predicted by rules of the language. However, much about the pronunciation of words can be predicted. For example, in the word *tick* the initial voiceless consonant *t* is phonetically aspirated, and is phonetically transcribed [tʰɪk]. This aspiration can be demonstrated visually by dangling a tissue in front of the mouth when saying the word: notice that when you pronounce *t*, the tissue is blown forward. In comparison, *t* in the word *stick* is not aspirated (thus, the tissue is not blown forward), so this word is transcribed as [stɪk]. This fact can be predicted by rule, and we now consider how this is done.

3.1 English consonantal allophones

While the physical difference between *t* and *tʰ* in English is just as real as the difference between *t* and *d*, there is a fundamental linguistic difference between these two relationships. The selection of *t* versus *d* may constitute the sole difference between many different words in English: such words, where two words are differentiated exclusively by a choice between one of two segments, are referred to as minimal pairs.

(1)

[d]	[t]	[d]	[t]
dire	tire	do	two
Dick	tick	had	hat
said	set	bend	bent

The difference between [t] and [d] is contrastive (also termed distinctive) in English, since this difference – voicing – forms the sole basis for distinguishing different words (and thus, [t] and [d] contrast).

The choice of a voiceless aspirated stop such as [tʰ] versus a voiceless unaspirated stop such as [t], on the other hand, never defines the sole basis for differentiating words in English. The occurrence of [t] versus [tʰ] (also [k] versus [kʰ], and [p] versus [pʰ]) follows a rule that aspirated stops are used in one phonological context, and unaspirated stops are used in all other contexts. In English, [t] and [tʰ] are predictable variants of a single abstract segment, a phoneme, which we represent as /t/. Predictable variants are termed allophones – the sounds are in complementary distribution because the context where one variant appears is the complement of the context where the other sound appears. As we have emphasized, one concern of phonology is determining valid relations between surface phonetic segments and the abstract mental constructs, the phonemes, which represent the unity behind observed [t]~[tʰ] etc. The implicit claim is that despite physical differences, [t] and [tʰ] (also [k] and [kʰ], [p] and [pʰ]) are in a fundamental sense "the same thing": reducing physically realized [t tʰ k kʰ p pʰ] to /t k p/ and supplying the information "realised as [t] vs. [tʰ]" recognizes these regularities.

3.1.1 Aspiration

We will turn our attention to rules of pronunciation in English, starting with aspiration, to see what some of these regularities are. In the first set of words below, the phonemes /p, t, k/ are aspirated whereas they are not aspirated in the second set of words.

(2) *Aspirated stops*

pool	[pʰuwl]	tooth	[tʰuwθ]	coop	[kʰuwp]
pit	[pʰɪt]	tin	[tʰɪn]	kill	[kʰɪl]
apply	[əpʰlay]	atomic	[ətʰamɪk]	account	[əkʰæwnt]
prawn	[pʰran]	truth	[tʰruwθ]	crab	[kʰræb]
pueblo	[pʰwɛblow]	twine	[tʰwayn]	quill	[kʰwɪl]
play	[pʰley]			clay	[kʰley]
puce	[pʰyuws]			cube	[kʰyuwb]

(3) *Unaspirated stops*

spool	[spuwl]	stool	[stuwl]	school	[skuwl]
spit	[spɪt]	stick	[stɪk]	skid	[skɪd]
sap	[sæp]	sat	[sæt]	sack	[sæk]
spray	[sprey]	stray	[strey]	screw	[skruw]
split	[splɪt]			sclerosis	[sklərowsɪs]
spew	[spyuw]			skew	[skyuw]

The selection of an aspirated versus an unaspirated voiceless stop is determined by the context in which the stop appears. Aspirated stops appear at the beginning of a word, whereas unaspirated stops appear after [s]; aspirated stops appear before a vowel or a sonorant consonant, whereas unaspirated stops appear at the end of a word. This collection of contexts can be expressed succinctly by referring to the position of the consonant in the syllable: aspirated stops appear at the beginning of the syllable and unaspirated stops appear elsewhere.

We assume that the voiceless stops are basically unaspirated in English, and explain where aspirated segments appear by having a rule that assigns aspiration to voiceless stops, when the stop is at the beginning of the syllable: the rule can be stated as "voiceless stops become aspirated at the beginning of a syllable." We don't need a second special rule to derive unaspirated stops in other environments, because that follows directly from our assumption that the basic or underlying form of the voiceless stops in English is unaspirated, and they will therefore be pronounced as such unless they are specifically changed by a rule. We investigate the idea of underlying representations in greater detail in chapter 4.

Actually, the issue of aspiration in English is a bit more complex. Notice that in the following words, [p], [t] and [k] in the middle of the word are not aspirated, even though the consonant is between vowels or syllabic sonorants – between syllable peaks – and therefore is presumably at the beginning of a syllable.

(4) hǽpiy   happy   kʰǽmpɪŋ   camping   hɛ́lpɪŋ   helping
    lʌ́kiy   lucky   sʌ́kr̩   sucker   sáltiy   salty

Compare these words with seemingly analogous words where there is aspiration on the stop between vowels, such as [ətʰǽk] *attack*, [əkʰyúwmyəlèyt] *accumulate*, [léytʰɛ̀ks] *latex*, [əpʰɛ́ndɪks] *appendix*. The important difference in these words is the location of stress. In all of the words in (4), where a voiceless consonant is not aspirated in syllable-initial position, the consonant is followed by an unstressed vowel. In other words, these data force us to refine our statement of the rule for assignment of aspiration, to be "voiceless stops become aspirated at the beginning of a stressed syllablea."

Alternations involving aspiration. The dependence of aspiration on the location of stress leads to discovering further evidence for an aspiration rule. Certain word-formation processes in English change the location of stress, for example in 'atom' the stress is on the first syllable of the root and in the related adjective 'atomic' the stress is on the second syllable. The pairs of words in (5) further illustrate the property of stress shifting, where the verbs on the left have stress on the second syllable of the root but the nouns derived from these verbs on the right have no stress on the second syllable.

(5) [əpʰláy]   apply   [æpləkʰéyšn̩]   application
    [səpʰówz]   suppose   [sʌ̀pəzíšn̩]   supposition
    [əʰkwáyr]   acquire   [æ̀kwəzíšn̩]   acquisition

As predicted by our rule for aspiration, the phonetic presence or absence of aspiration on the medial stop of the root may alternate within a given root, according to where the stress appears in the root.

Another set of examples involves the word-formation process adding -*ee* to a verb, to form a noun referring to the direct object of the action. That suffix must be stressed, unlike the subject-nominalization suffix -*er*.

(6) *Verb*   *Subject noun*   *Object noun*
    [grǽnt]   [grǽntr̩]   [græ̀ntʰí]   grant
    [šíft]   [šíftr̩]   [šɪ̀ftʰí]   shift
    [hɛ́lp]   [hɛ́lpr̩]   [hɛ̀lpʰí]   help
    [čʰówk]   [čʰówkr̩]   [čʰòwkʰí]   choke
    [stráyk]   [stráykr̩]   [stràykʰí]   strike
    [ətʰǽk]   [ətʰǽkr̩]   [ətʰæ̀kʰí]   attack

Again, as our rule predicts, when the stress shifts to the suffix vowel, the pronunciation of the preceding consonant changes to become aspirated.

Pronunciation of novel utterances.   Not only does the existence of this aspiration rule explain why all voiceless stops are aspirated at the beginning of a stressed syllable in English words, it also explains facts of language behavior by English speakers outside the domain of pronouncing ordinary English words. First, when English speakers are faced with a new word which they have never heard before, for example one coming from a foreign language, voiceless consonants will be aspirated or unaspirated according to the general rule for the distribution of aspiration. The pronunciation of unfamiliar foreign place names provides one simple demonstration. The place names Stord (Norway) and Palma (Mozambique) will be pronounced by English speakers as [stɔrd] and [pʰalmə], as predicted by the aspiration rule. The name Stavanger (Norway) may be pronounced many ways – [stəvǽŋɹ], [stǽvənjɹ̩], [stəvǽnjɹ̩], [stǽvəŋɹ̩] and so on, but consistently throughout this variation, the /t/ will remain unaspirated because of its position in the syllable. In the English pronunciation of Rapallo (Italy), stress could either be in the first syllable in [rǽpəlo], with no aspiration because /p/ is at the beginning of an unstressed syllable, or on the second syllable as in [rəpʰálo] – again the choice of aspirated versus unaspirated consonant being determined by the rule of aspiration.

Second, when English speakers attempt to learn a language which does not have the same distribution of aspirated and unaspirated consonants as in English, they encounter difficulties in pronunciation that reflect the effect of the rule of aspiration. Hindi has both aspirated and unaspirated voiceless stops at the beginning of syllables, as well as after /s/. Words such as [pʰal] 'fruit' and [stan] 'breast' are not difficult for English speakers to pronounce; accurate pronunciation of [pal] 'want' and [stʰal] 'place' on the other hand are. This is due to the fact that the rule of aspiration from English interferes in the pronunciation of other languages.

Finally, even in native English words, unaspirated stops can show the effect of the aspiration rule in hyper-slow, syllable-by-syllable pronunciation. Notice that in the normal pronunciation of *happy* [hǽpiy], only the first syllable is stressed and therefore [p] remains unaspirated. However, if this word is pronounced very slowly, drawing out each vowel, then both syllables become stressed, and as predicted the stop *p* is aspirated – [hǽːː] . . . [pʰìːːy]. All of these facts are explained by one simple hypothesis, that in English the occurrence of aspiration on stops derives from applying a rule.

3.1.2 Flapping

We now turn to another rule. A phonetic characteristic of many North American dialects of English is "flapping," where /t/ and /d/ become the flap [ɾ] in certain contexts, for example in [wáɾɹ̩] *water*. It is clear that there is no contrast between the flap [ɾ] and any other consonant of English: there are no minimal pairs such as hypothetical [hɪt] and *[hɪɾ], or *[bətɹ̩] and [bəɾɹ̩], whose existence would establish that the flap is a distinct phoneme of English. Moreover, the contexts where the flap appears in English are quite restricted. In our previous examples of nonaspiration in the context v́Cv in (4) and (5), no examples included [t] as an intervocalic consonant. Now consider the following words:

> *Vowels and syllabic sonorants often function together in phonology, and we unify them with the term* **syllabic**.

(7) a.

wáɒɾ	water	wéyɒɾ	waiter; wader
ǽɒm̩	atom; Adam	ǽɒətʰùwd	attitude

b.

hít	hit	híɒɪŋ	hitting
pút	put	púɒɪŋ	putting
sét	set	séɒɪŋ	setting

In (7a) orthographic <t> is phonetically realized as the flap [ɒ] in the context V́_V, that is, when it is followed by a vowel or syllabic sonorant – represented as V – and preceded by a stressed vowel or syllabic sonorant. Maybe we have just uncovered an orthographic defect of English, since we have no letter for a flap (just as no letter represents /θ/ vs. /ð/) and some important distinctions in pronunciation are lost in spelling. The second set of examples show even more clearly that underlying *t* becomes a flap in this context. We can convince ourselves that the verbs [hɪt], [pʊt] and [sɛt] end in [t], simply by looking at the uninflected form of the verb, or the third-person-singular forms [hɪts], [pʊts] and [sɛts], where the consonant is pronounced as [t]. Then when we consider the gerund, which combines the root with the suffix -*ɪŋ*, we see that /t/ has become the flap [ɒ]. This provides direct evidence that there must be a rule deriving flaps from plain /t/, since the pronunciation of root morphemes may actually change, depending on whether or not the rule for flapping applies (which depends on whether a vowel follows the root).

> *The theory of distinctive features given in chapter 6 makes it easier to distinguish different notions of vowel and glide.*

There is analogous evidence for an underlying /t/ in the word [ǽɒm̩] *atom*, since, again, the alveolar consonant in this root may either appear as [tʰ] or [ɒ], depending on the phonetic context where the segment appears. Flapping only takes place before an unstressed vowel, and thus in /ætm̩/ the consonant /t/ is pronounced as [ɒ]; but in the related form [ətʰámɪk] where stress has shifted to the second syllable of the root, we can see that the underlying /t/ surfaces phonetically (as an aspirate, following the previously discussed rule of aspiration).

We may state the rule of flapping as follows: "an alveolar stop becomes a flap when it is followed by an unstressed syllabic and is preceded by a vowel or glide." It is again important to note that the notion of "vowel" used in this rule must include syllabic sonorants such as [ɾ] for the preceding segment, and [ɾ] or [m̩] for the following segment. Flapping is not limited to the voiceless alveolar stop /t/: underlying /d/ also becomes [ɒ] in this same context.

(8)

Base verbs	*'One who V-s'*	*'V-ing'*	
bíd	bíɒɾ	bíɒɪŋ	bid
háyd	háyɒɾ	háyɒɪŋ	hide
wéyd	wéyɒɾ	wéyɒɪŋ	wade

3.1.3 Glottal stop

There is one context where flapping of /t/ does not occur when preceded by a vowel and followed by an unstressed syllabic segment (vowel or syllabic sonorant), and that is when /t/ is followed by a syllabic [ṇ]. Consider, first, examples such as [bʌʔṇ] *button* and [káʔṇ] *cotton*. Instead of the flap that we expect, based on our understanding of the context where flapping takes place, we find glottal stop before syllabic [ṇ]. Consider the following pairs of words:

(9) [rat]   rot   [raʔṇ]   rotten
     [hayt]   height   [hayʔṇ]   heighten
     [layt]   light   [layʔṇ]   lighten
     [fæt]   fat   [fæʔṇ]   fatten

The bare roots on the left show the underlying /t/ which has not changed to glottal stop, and on the right, we observe that the addition of the suffix /ṇ/ conditions the change of /t/ to [ʔ] in the context V́_n, i.e. when *t* is preceded by a stressed vowel and followed by an alveolar nasal. Words like [ǽDm̩] *atom* show that the glottal stop rule does not apply before all nasals, just alveolar nasals.

Finally, notice that in casual speech, the gerundive suffix *-ıŋ* may be pronounced as [ṇ]. When the verb root ends in /t/, that /t/ becomes [ʔ] just in case the suffix becomes [ṇ], and thus provides the crucial context required for the glottal stop creation rule.

(10) *Base verb*   *Careful speech*   *Casual speech*
      hıs   hısıŋ   hısṇ
      rat   raDıŋ   raʔṇ
      flowt   flowDıŋ   flowʔṇ

> *Some speakers have [ʔ] only before syllabic [ṇ], so their rule is different. Not all American dialects have this rule – it is lacking in certain Southern dialects, and instead the flapping rule applies. Some British dialects have a rule which applies in a rather different context, e.g. [lɛʔə] letter.*

In the examples considered so far, the environment for appearance of glottal stop has been a following syllabic [ṇ]. Is it crucial that the triggering nasal segment be specifically a syllabic nasal? We also find glottal stop before nonsyllabic nasals in words such as *Whitney* [ʍıʔniy] and *fatness* [fæʔnəs], which shows that the *t*-glottalization rule does not care about the syllabicity of the following nasal. The presence of glottal stop in these examples can be explained by the existence of a rule which turns /t/ into glottal stop before [n] or [ṇ]. Notice that this rule applies before a set of segments, but not a random set: it applies before alveolar nasals, without mention of syllabicity. As we will repeatedly see, the conditioning context of phonological rules is stated in terms of phonetic properties.

3.2 Allophony in other languages

Allophonic rules of pronunciation are found in most human languages, if not indeed all languages. What constitutes a subtle contextual variation in one language may constitute a wholesale radical difference in phonemes in another. The difference between unaspirated and aspirated voiceless stops in English is a completely predictable, allophonic one which speakers are not aware of, but in Hindi the contrast between aspirated and unaspirated voiceless consonants forms the basis of phonemic contrasts, e.g. [pal] 'want', [pʰal] 'fruit.' Unlike the situation in English, aspiration in Hindi is an important, distinctive property of stops which cannot be supplied by a rule.

l and *d* in Setswana. The consonants [l] and [d] are clearly separate phonemes in English, given words such as *lie* and *die* or *mill* and *mid*. However, in Setswana (Botswana), there is no contrast between [l] and [d]. Phonetic [l] and [d] are contextually determined variants of a single phoneme: surface [l] appears before nonhigh vowels, and [d] appears before high vowels (neither consonant may come at the end of a word or before another consonant).

(11)

lefifi	'darkness'	loleme	'tongue'
selɛpɛ	'axe'	molɔmo	'mouth'
xobala	'to read'	mmadi	'reader'
lerumɔ	'spear'	xoɲala	'to marry'
loxadima	'lightning flash'	dijɔ	'food'
dumɛla	'greetings'	feedi	'sweeper'
lokwalɔ	'letter'	kʰudu	'tortoise'
mosadi	'woman'	podi	'goat'
badisa	'the herd'	hudi	'wild duck'

Setswana has a rule which can be stated as "/l/ becomes [d] before high vowels."

(12)   l → d / _high vowel

This statement introduces the standard formalism for giving rules which will be used in the book. Rules generally take the form "A→ B/C_D," where A, C, D are variables that stand for classes of sounds (single segments like [l] or [d], or phonetic classes such as "high vowel"), and B describes the nature of the change, either a phonetic parameter such as "voiceless" or "nasal," or simply a specific segment like [d]. The conditioning context might involve only a preceding element in which case "D" would be null, it might involve only a following element in which case "C" would be null, or the applicability of the rule might depend on both what precedes and what follows. The arrow means "becomes," the slash means "in the environment" where the context is what follows the slash. The dash indicates the position of the affected segment in the relevant environment, so the environment 'C_D' means "when the affected segment is preceded by C and followed by D." Thus, rule (12) says "*l* becomes *d* when it stands before a high vowel" (and it does not matter what precedes *l*, since the rule says nothing about what precedes).

An equally accurate and general statement of the distribution or [l] and [d] would be "/d/ becomes [l] before nonhigh vowels."

(13)   d → l / _ nonhigh vowel

There is no evidence to show whether the underlying segment is basically /l/ or /d/ in Setswana, so we would be equally justified in assuming either rule (12) or rule (13). Sometimes, a language does not provide enough evidence to allow us to decide which of two (or more) analyses in correct.

Tohono O'odham affricates.   In the language Tohono O'odham (formerly known as Papago: Arizona and Mexico), there is no contrast between [d] and [ǰ], or between [t] and [č]. The task is to inspect the examples in (14) and discover what factor governs the choice between plain alveolar [d, t] versus the alveopalatal affricates [ǰ, č]. In these examples, word-final sonorants are devoiced by a regular rule which we disregard, explaining the devoiced *m* in examples like [wahčum̥]

(14)	ǰihsk	'aunt'	dɔʔaʔk	'mountain'
	ču:li̥	'corner'	čɯwaʔgi̥	'clouds'
	wahčum̥	'drown'	taht	'foot'
	ǰuwɯhkɔh	'cut hair'	ʔahidaʔk	'year'
	tɔnɔm̥	'be thirsty'	hɯhtahspču̥	'make it 5'
	hɯǰuli̥	'self'	čihkpan̥	'work'
	stahtɔnɔm:ah	'thirsty times'	ʔi:dḁ	'this'
	muḍuḍam	'runner'	tɔhntɔ̥	'degenerate'
	tɔdsid	'frighten'	čuwɔsid	'brand'
	gahtwi̥	'to shoot'	čuhči̥	'name'
	gɯʔɯdtḁ	'get big'	ǰumali̥	'low'
	tobidk	'White Clay'	waʔǰiwih	'swim'
	spadmahkam̥	'lazy one'	ǰu:ʔw̥	'rabbits'

We do not know, at the outset, what factor conditions the choice of [t, d] versus [č, ǰ] (indeed, in the world of actual analysis we do not know in advance that there *is* any such relationship; but to make your task easier, we will at least start with the knowledge that there is a predictable relationship, and concentrate on discovering the rule governing that choice). To begin solving the problem, we explore two possibilities: the triggering context may be the segment which immediately precedes the consonant, or it may be the segment which immediately follows it.

Let us start with the hypothesis that it is the immediately preceding segment which determines how the consonant is pronounced. In order to organize the data so as to reveal what rule might be at work, we can simply list the preceding environments where stops versus affricates appear, so *h_* means "when [h] precedes" – here, the symbol '#' represents the beginning or end of a word. Looking at the examples in (14), and taking note of what comes immediately before any [t, d] versus [č, ǰ], we arrive at the following list of contexts:

(15)   [t, d]: # _, h _, ɯ _, i: _, s _, i _, n _, ɔ _
       [č, ǰ]: # _, h _, ɯ _, ʔ _, p _

Since both types of consonants appear at the beginning of the word, or when preceded by [h] or [ɯ], it is obvious that the preceding context cannot be the crucial determining factor. We therefore reject the idea that the preceding element determines how the phoneme is pronounced.

Focusing next on what follows the consonant, the list of contexts correlated with plain stops versus affricates is much simpler.

(16)   [t, d]: _ɔ, _a, _a̧, _#, _s, _t, _k, _m, _w
        [č, ǰ]: _i, _i̧, _u, _u̧, _ɯ

Only the vowels [i, u, ɯ] (and their devoiced counterparts) follow [č] and [ǰ], and the vowels [a, ɔ] follow [t] and [d]. Moreover, when no vowel follows, i.e. at the end of the word or before another consonant, the plain alveolar appears (*taht, tɔdsid*). The vowels [i, u, ɯ] have in common the property that they are high vowels, which allows us to state the context for this rule very simply: /t/ and /d/ become alveopalatal affricates before high vowels, i.e.

(17)   alveolar stop → alveopalatal affricate / _ high vowel

The retroflex consonant [ɖ] does not undergo this process, as seen in [muɖɯdaṃ].

This account of the distribution of alveolars versus alveopalatals assumes that underlyingly the consonants are alveolars, and that just in case a high vowel follows, the consonant becomes an alveopalatal affricate. It is important to also consider the competing hypothesis that underlyingly the consonants are alveopalatals and that they become alveolars in a context which is complementary to that stated in rule (17). The problem with that hypothesis is that there is no natural statement of that complementary context, which includes nonhigh vowels, consonants, and the end of the word.

(18)   alveopalatal affricate → alveolar stop / _ $\left\{ \begin{array}{c} \text{nonhigh V} \\ \text{C} \\ \text{\#} \end{array} \right\}$

The brace notation is a device used to force a disjunction of unrelated contexts into a single rule, so this rule states that alveopalatal affricates become alveolar stops when they are followed either by a nonhigh vowel, a consonant, or are at the end of the word, i.e. there is no coherent generalization. Since the alternative hypothesis that the consonants in question are underlyingly alveopalatals leads to a much more complicated and less enlightening statement of the distribution of the consonants, we reject the alternative hypothesis and assume that the consonants are underlyingly alveolar.

Obstruent voicing in Kipsigis.   In the Kipsigis language of Kenya, there is no phonemic contrast between voiced and voiceless obstruents as there is in English. No words are distinguished by the selection of voiced versus voiceless consonants: nevertheless, phonetic voiced obstruents do exist in the language.

(19)

kuur	'call!'	ke-guur	'to call'
ŋok-ta	'dog'	ŋog-iik	'dogs'
kɛ-tɛp	'request'	i-teb-e	'you are requesting'
ker	'look at!'	ke-ger	'to look at'
put	'break up!'	ke-but	'to break up'
poor	'thresh maize!'	ke-boor	'to thresh maize'
ŋelyep-ta	'tongue'	ŋelyeb-wek	'tongues'
kisipči	'to follow for'	iŋgurwet	'pig'
kipkirui	(name)	ke-baakpaak	'to strip repeatedly'
pʊnbʊn	'soft'	tilɑkse	'it is cuttable'
kirgit	'bull'	kagyam	'we ate'
taaptɛɛt	'flower type'	kebritɑmɛɛt	'to fall asleep'
kɪblaŋat	(name)	peečiŋge	'they are going for 'themselves'

In these examples, we can see that the labial and velar consonants become voiced when they are both preceded and followed by vowels, liquids, nasals and glides: these are all sounds which are voiced.

(20)   voiceless peripheral consonant → voiced / voiced _ voiced

In stating the context, we do not need to say "voiced vowel, liquid, nasal or glide," since, by saying "voiced" alone, we refer to the entire class of voiced segments. It is only when we need to specifically restrict the rule so that it applies just between voiced consonants, for example, that we would need to further specify the conditioning class of segments.

While you have been told that there is no contrast between [k] and [g] or between [p] and [b] in this language, children learning the language do not use explicit instructions, so an important question arises: how can you arrive at the conclusion that the choice [k, p] versus [g, b] is predictable? Two facts lead to this conclusion. First, analyzing the distribution of consonants in the language would lead to discovering the regularities that no word begins or ends in [b, g] and no word has [b, g] in combination with another consonant, except in combination with the voiced sonorants. We would also discover that [p, k] do not appear between vowels, or more generally between voiced segments. If there were no rule governing the distribution of consonants in this language, then the distribution is presumed to be random, which would mean that we should find examples of [b, g] at the beginning or end of words, or [p, k] between vowels.

Another very important clue in understanding the system is the fact that the pronunciation of morphemes will actually change according to the context that they appear in. Notice, for example, that the imperative form [kuur] 'call!' has a voiceless stop, but the same root is pronounced as [guur] in the infinitive [ke-guur] 'to call.' When learning words in the language, the child must resolve the changes in pronunciation of word-parts in order to know exactly what must be learned. Sometimes the root 'call' is [kuur], sometimes [guur] – when are you supposed to use the pronunciation [guur]? Similarly, in trying to figure out the root for the word 'dog,' a child will observe that in the singular the root portion of the word is pronounced [ŋok], and in the plural it is pronounced [ŋog]. From observing that there is an alternation between [k] and [g], or [p] and [b], it is a relatively simple matter to arrive at the hypothesis that there is a systematic relation between these sounds, which leads to an investigation of when [k, p] appear, versus [g, b].

Implosive and plain voiced stops in Kimatuumbi. The distinction between implosive and plain voiced consonants in Kimatuumbi (Tanzania) can be predicted by a rule.

(21)

ɓɛɓɛɛlu	'male goat'	ɗundumuka	'be scared'
ɓutuka	'flow'	ɗaala	'storage in roof'
kɔɓɔkwa	'unfold'	ɓwʊʊmɪ	'life'
kɔɔndwa	'dig clay'	ŋgaambalɛ	'fish sp.'
ɓalaka	'luck'	ɗʊlʊya	'drive fast'
lisɛɛŋgɛlɛ	'dowry'	ɓila	'without'
ɗɔlɔya	'straighten'	ɗuna	'murmur'
kiɓʊla	'towards Mecca'	kitʊʊmbɪ	'hill'
kyaaŋgi	'sand'	ɓɔmwaana	'destroy'
likʊʊŋgwa	'storage structure'	ɓʊʊka	'leave'
ɗɔɔmba	'shoot a gun'	ɗʊlʊka	'fly'
ɓalaaŋga	'count'	aliɓika	'be out of order'

Upon consideration of consonant distribution in these data, you will see that implosives appear in word-initial position and after vowels, whereas plain voiced consonants appear exclusively after nasals.

There is further clinching evidence that this generalization is valid. In this language, the first-person-singular form of the verb has a nasal consonant prefix (there is also a change in the final vowel, where you get -a in the infinitive and -ɛ in the "should" form, the second column below).

(22)

to V	I should V		
ɗʊlʊka	ŋgʊlʊkɛ	'fly'	
ɗɔɔmba	ŋgɔɔmbɛ	'shoot a gun'	
ɗɔlɔya	ŋgɔlɔyɛ	'straighten'	
ɗuna	ŋgunɛ	'murmur'	
ɓalaaŋga	mbalaaŋgɛ	'count'	
ɓutuka	mbutukɛ	'flow'	
ɓʊʊka	mbʊʊkɛ	'leave'	
ɗuumu	nduumu	'continue'	

Thus the pronunciation of the root for the word for 'fly' alternates between [ɗʊlʊk] and [gʊlʊk], depending on whether a nasal precedes.

Having determined that implosives and plain voiced stops are allophonically related in the grammar of Kimatuumbi, it remains to decide whether the language has basically only plain voiced consonants, with implosives appearing in a special environment; or should we assume that Kimatuumbi voiced stops are basically implosive, and plain voiced consonants appear only in a complementary environment. The matter boils down to the following question: is it easier to state the context where imposives appear, or is it easier to state the context where plain voiced consonants appear? We generally assume that the variant with the most easily stated distributional context is the variant derived by applying a rule. However, as we saw with the case of [l] and [d] in Setswana, a language may not provide empirical evidence which is the correct solution.

Now let us compare the two possible rules for Kimatuumbi: "implosives appear word initially and after a vowel":

(23) $C \rightarrow \text{implosive} \, / \begin{Bmatrix} V \\ \# \end{Bmatrix} -$

versus "plain consonants appear after a nasal":

(24) $C \rightarrow \text{nonimplosive} \, / \text{nasal} \, \_$

It is simpler to state the context where plain consonants appear, since their distribution requires a single context – after a nasal – whereas describing the process as replacement of plain consonants by implosives would require a more complex disjunction "either after a vowel, or in word-initial position." A concise description of contexts results if we assume that voiced consonants in Kimatuumbi are basically implosive, and that the nonimplosive variants which appear after nasals are derived by a simple rule: implosives become plain voiced consonants after nasals.

It is worth noting that another statement of the implosive-to-plain process is possible, since sequences of consonants are quite restricted in Kimatuumbi. Only a nasal may precede another "true" consonant, i.e. a consonant other than a glide. A different statement of the rule is that plain voiced consonants appear only after other consonants – due to the rules of consonant combination in the language, the first of two true consonants is necessarily a nasal, so it is unnecessary to explicitly state that the preceding consonant in the implosive-to-plain-C rule is a nasal. Phonological theory does not always give a single solution for any given data set, so we must accept that there are at least two ways of describing this pattern. One of the goals of the theory, towards which considerable research energy is being expended, is developing a principled basis for making a unique and correct choice in such cases where the data themselves cannot show which solution is right.

Velar and uvular stops in Kenyang.   In Kenyang (Cameroon), there is no contrast between the velar consonant *k* and uvular *q*.

(25)   enɔq   'tree'   enoq   'drum'
       eket   'house'   nčiku   'I am buying'

nek	'rope'	eywɑrek	'sweet potato'
ŋgɑq	'knife'	ekɑq	'leg'
mək	'dirt'	nɑq	'brother in law'
ndek	'European'	pɔbrik	'work project'
betək	'job'	bepək	'to capsize'
tiku	(name)	ku	'buy!'
ɑyuk	(name)	esikɔŋ	'pipe'
kebwep	'stammering'	ŋkɔq	'chicken'
ŋkɑp	'money'	kɔ	'walk!'

What determines the selection of k versus q is the nature of the vowel which precedes the consonant. The uvular consonant q is always preceded by one of the back nonhigh vowels o, $ɔ$ or a, whereas velar k appears anywhere else.

(26)   voiceless velar $\rightarrow$ uvular / back nonhigh vowel __

This relation between vowels and consonants is phonetically natural. The vowels triggering the change have a common place of articulation: they are produced at the lower back region of the pharynx, where q (as opposed to k) is articulated.

An alternative is that the underlying segment is a uvular, and velar consonants are derived by rule. But under that assumption, the rule which derives velars is very complex. Velars would be preceded by front or central vowels, by high back vowels, by a consonant ($ŋ$), or by a word boundary. We would then end up with a disjunction of contexts in our statement of the rule.

$$(27)\quad q \rightarrow k \;/ \left\{ \begin{array}{c} \text{front V} \\ \text{central V} \\ \text{high back V} \\ \text{C} \\ \text{\#} \end{array} \right\} \;-$$

The considerably more complex rule deriving velars from uvulars leads us to reject the hypothesis that these segments are underlyingly uvular. Again, we are faced with one way of capturing the generalization exploiting phonetically defined classes, and an alternative that involves a disjunctive list, where there is nothing that unifies the contexts: we select the alternative which allows a rule to be stated that refers to a simple, phonetically definable context. This decision reflects an important discovery regarding the nature of phonogical rules which will be discussed in greater detail in chapter 6, namely that phonological rules operate in terms of phonetic classes of segments.

Arabela nasalization.   Nasalization of vowels and glides is predictable in Arabela (Peru).

(28)   nẽẽkyææʔ   'lying on back'   mõnũʔ   'kill'
      tukuruʔ   'palm leaf'   šiyokwaʔ   'grease'
      nỹ̃æ̃æ̃riʔ   'he laid it down'   suroʔ   'monkey'
      nĩĩkyææʔ   'is pouring out'   suwakaʔ   'fish'
      posunã h̃ãʔ   'short person'   kuwɔxoʔ   'hole'
      nõõnũʔ   'be pained'   h̃ẽẽgiʔ   'termites'
      tæweʔ   'foreigner'   h̃ỹũũššænõʔ   'where I fished'
      nĩnỹũʔ   'to come'   mỹæ̃nũʔ   'swallow'
      nuẇaʔ   'partridge'   h̃ũw̃ãʔ   'a yellow bird'

Scanning the data in (28), we see nothing about the following phonetic context that explains occurrence of nasalization: both oral and nasal vowels precede glottal stop ([tæweʔ] 'foreigner' versus [nõõnũʔ] 'be pained'), [k] ([nĩĩkyææʔ] 'is pouring out' versus [šiyokwaʔ] 'grease') or [n] ([mỹæ̃nũʔ] 'swallow' versus [posunã h̃ãʔ] 'short person'). A regularity does emerge once we look at what precedes oral versus nasal vowels: when a vowel or glide is preceded by a nasal segment – be it a nasal consonant (including [h̃] which is always nasal in this language), vowel, or glide – then a vowel or glide becomes nasalized. The rule for nasalization can be stated as "a vowel or glide becomes nasalized after any nasal sound." We discuss how vowels and glides are unified in Chapter 6: for the moment, we will use the term vocoid to refer to the phonetic class of vowels and glides.

(29)   vocoid → nasal / nasal __

The naturalness of this rule should be obvious – the essential property that defines the conditioning class of segment, nasality, is the very property that is added to the vowel: such a process, where a segment becomes more like some neighboring segment, is known as an assimilation. Predictable nasalization of vowels almost always derives from a nasal consonant somewhere near the vowel.

Sundanese: a problem for the student to solve.   Bearing this suggestion in mind, where do nasalized vowels appear in Sundanese (Indonesia), given these data?

(30)   abot   'heavy'   agiŋ   'big'
      amĩs   'sweet'   anõm   'young'
      handap   'light'   luhur   'high'
      awon   'bad'   basir   'wet'
      konẽŋ   'yellow'   bɨrɨm   'red'
      eŋgal   'new'   gədde   'big'
      mãhĩr   'skillful'   mĩrɨ   'uncertain'
      mõhẽhẽd   'poor'   bumĩ   'house'
      mə̃rri   'duck'   mãhãsiswa   'student'

mãũŋ	'tiger'	mĩãsih	'true love'
mĩliar	'billion'	mĩñãk	'oil'
mũãra	'confluence'	pamõhãlan	'impossible'
mãẽn	'play'	mãõt	'die'
nãʔãs	'get worse'	mĩʔĩs	'leak'
mãʔãp	'excuse me'	mãhĩ	'enough'
nẽwak	'catch'	tiʔis	'cold'

Since the focus at the moment is on finding phonological regularities, and not on manipulating a particular formalism (which we have not yet presented completely), you should concentrate on expressing the generalization in clear English.

We can also predict the occurrence of long (double) consonants in Sundanese, using the above data supplemented with the data in (31).

(31)

abuabu	'grey'	bəddil	'gun'
gəttih	'blood'	akar	'root'
səddih	'sad'	jənnə̃ŋŋãn	'name'
bərrəkkah	'useful'	bagoŋ	'wild pig'
babi	'pig'	kinã	'quinine'
təbbih	'far'	bapa	'father'
bɨbɨr	'belt'	ŋə̃ppel	'sweep'
bənnər	'correct'	sɨkɨt	'sharp'
panãs	'hot'	mə̃ddəm	'dark'
hukum	'law'	sərrat	'letter'
kamẽ̌ja	'shirt'	pačul	'shovel'
bənnãŋ	'thread'	dada	'torso'
pəttis	'fish sauce'	ǰaŋkuŋ	'tall'
asəm	'tamarind'	wawəs	'tooth'

What rule determines the length of consonants in this language?

Vowel length in Mohawk. The context for predicting some variant of a phoneme may include more than one factor. There is no contrast between long and short vowels in Mohawk (North America): what is the generalization regarding where long versus short vowels appear (here, accent marks are used to indicate stressed vowels)?

(32)

ranahé:zʌ̃s	'he trusts her'	ragé:das	'he scrapes'
í:geks	'I eat it'	odá:we	'flea'
gadá:dis	'I talk'	ʌkhní:nũʔ	'I will buy it'
sdʌ̃:ha	'a little bit'	aplám	'Abram'
ʌgá:radeʔ	'I lay myself down'	dʌ́:gehgweʔ	'I'll lift it'
rayʌ́thos	'he plants'	yégreks	'I push it'
wísk	'five'	royóʔdeʔ	'he works'
aweryáhsa	'heart'	yágwaks	'they and I eat it'
ísgʌ̃s	'you (sg) see her'	gatgáhthos	'I look at it'
yokékhaʔ	'it's burning'	ʌgídyeʔ	'I will fly around'

One property which holds true of all long vowels is that they appear in stressed syllables: there are no unstressed long vowels. However, it would be incorrect to state the rule as lengthening all stressed vowels, because there are stressed short vowels as in [wísk]. We must find a further property which distinguishes those stressed vowels which become lengthened from those which do not. Looking only at stressed vowels, we can see that short vowels appear before two consonants and long vowels appear before a consonant-plus-vowel sequence. It is the combination of two factors, being stressed and being before the sequence CV, which conditions the appearance of long vowels: stressed vowels are lengthened if they precede CV, and vowels remain short otherwise. We hypothesize the following rule:

(33) $\acute{V} \rightarrow$ long | _ CV

Since there is no lexical contrast between long and short vowels in Mohawk, we assume that all vowels have the same underlying length: all long and shortened in one context, or all short and lengthened in the complementary context. One hypothesis about underlying forms in a given language results in simpler grammars which capture generalizations about the language more directly than do other hypotheses about underlying forms. If all vowels in Mohawk are underlyingly long, you must devise a rule to derive short vowels. No single generalization covers all contexts where supposed vowel shortening takes place, so your analysis would require two rules, one to shorten unstressed vowels, and another to shorten vowels followed by two consonants. In comparison, the single rule that stressed vowels lengthen before CV accounts for vowel length under the hypothesis that vowels in Mohawk are underlyingly short. No other rule is needed: short vowels appear everywhere that they are not lengthened.

Aspiration in Ossetic.   Aspiration of voiceless stops can be predicted in Ossetic (Caucasus).

(34)

t^{h}əχ	'strength'	k^{h}ɔttag	'linen'
χɔstɔg	'near'	ɔftən	'be added'
fadat^h	'possibility'	k^{h}astɔn	'I looked'
t^{sh}ɔst	'eye'	k^{h}ark^h	'hen'
akkag	'adequate'	dəkkag	'second'
t^{sh}əppar	'four'	t^{sh}ət^h	'honor'
t^{sh}əχt	'cheese'	k^{h}ɔm	'where'
fɔste	'behind'	k^{h}ɔm	'mouth'
p^{h}irən	'comb wool'	zaχta	'he told'
χɔskard	'scissors'	χɔstɔn	'military'
p^{h}ɔrrɔst	'fluttering'		

Since aspirated and plain consonants appear at the end of the word ([t^{sh}ɔst] 'eye,' [t^{sh}ət^h] 'honor'), the following context alone cannot govern aspiration. Focusing on what precedes the consonant, aspirates appear word initially, or when preceded by a vowel or [r] (i.e. a sonorant) at the end of the word; unaspirated consonants appear when before or after an obstruent. It is possible to start with unaspirated consonants (as we did for English) and predict aspiration, but a simpler description emerges if we start from the assumption that voiceless stops are basically aspirated in Ossetic, and deaspirate a consonant next to an obstruent. The relative simplicity of the resulting analysis should guide your decisions about underlying forms, and not the phonetic nature of the underlying segments that your analysis results in.

Optional rules.   Some rules of pronunciation are optional, often known as "free variation." In Makonde (Mozambique), the phoneme /š/ can be pronounced as either [s] or [š] by speakers of the language: the same speaker may use [s] one time and [š] another time. The verb 'read' is thus pronounced as *šoomya* or as *soomya*, and 'sell' is pronounced as *šuluuša* or as *suluusa*. We will indicate such variation in pronunciation by giving the examples as "*šuluuša ~ suluusa*," meaning that the word is pronounceable either as *šuluuša* or as *suluusa*, as the speaker chooses. Such apparently unconditioned fluctuations in pronunciation are the result of a rule in Makonde which turns /š/ into [s]: this rule is optional. The optional nature of the rule is indicated simply by writing "optional" to the side of the rule.

(35)   š → s   **optional**

Normally, any rule in the grammar always applies if its phonological conditions are satisfied. An optional rule may either apply or not, so for any optional rule at least two phonetic outcomes are possible: either the rule applies, or it does not apply. Assuming the underlying form /šoomya/, the pronunciation [soomya] results if the rule is not applied, and [soomya] results if the rule is applied.

Optional rules may have environmental conditions on them. In Kimatuumbi, as we have seen in (21), voiced stops are implosive except after a nasal. The voiced velar stop exhibits a further complication, that after a vowel (but not initially) underlying /ɠ/ optionally becomes a fricative [ɣ] (the symbol "~" indicates "may also be pronounced as").

(36)   ɓaɠana   ~   ɓaɣana   'divide'
       ɓiliɠana   ~   ɓiliɣana   'wrestle'
       ɓulaɠa   ~   ɓulaɣa   'kill'
       ɠalaambuka   ~   (*ɣalaambuka)   'change'

Hence the optional realization of /ɠ/ as [ɣ], but only after a vowel, can be explained by the following rule.

(37)   ɠ → ɣ / V _   (optional)

The factors determining which variant is selected are individual and sociological, reflecting age, ethnicity, gender, and geography, inter alia. Phonology does not try to explain why people make the choices they do:

that lies in the domain of sociolinguistics. We are also only concerned with systematic options. Some speakers of English vary between [æks] and [æsk] as their pronunciation of *ask*. This is a quirk of a particular word: no speaker says [mæks] for *mask*, or [fɪsk] for *fix*.

It would also be mistaken to think that there is one grammar for all speakers of English (or German, or Kimatuumbi) and that dialect variation is expressed via a number of optional rules. From the perspective of grammars as objects describing the linguistic competence of individuals, an optional rule is countenanced only if the speaker can actually pronounce words in multiple ways. In the case of Makonde, some speakers actually pronounce /šoomya/ in two different ways.

Summary

Contrastive aspects of pronunciation cannot be predicted by rule, but *allophonic* details can be. Allophonic changes are a type of rule-governed phonological behavior, and phonology is concerned with the study of rules. The practical concern of this chapter is understanding the method for discovering those rules. The linguist looks for regularities in the distribution of one sound versus others, and attempts to reduce multiple surface segments to one basic segment, a *phoneme*, where the related segments derive by applying a rule to the underlying phoneme in some context. Going beyond static distribution of sounds, you should look for cases where the pronunciation of morphemes changes, depending on the presence or absence of prefixes and suffixes.

Assuming that sounds are in complementary distribution, you need to determine which variant is the "basic" underlying one, and which derives by rule. The decision is made by comparing the consequences of alternative hypotheses. Sometimes, selecting underlying /X/ results in a very simple rule for deriving the surface variant [Y] whereas selecting underlying /Y/ results in very complex rules for deriving [X] from /Y/: in such a case, the choice of /X/ over /Y/ is well motivated. Sometimes, no definitive decision can be made.

Exercises
1 Kuria
Provide rules to explain the distribution of the consonants [β, r, ɣ] and [b, d, g] in the following data. (Note that [r] is a fricative consonant in this language.) Accents mark tone: acute is high tone and "hacek" [ˇ] is rising tone.

aβaánto	'people'	aβamúra	'young men'
amahííndi	'corn cobs'	amakɛ́ɛ́ndɔ	'date fruits'
eβǎ	'forget!'	eeŋgwé	'leopard'
eɣǎ	'learn!'	ekeβwɛ́	'fox'
hoorá	'thresh!'	iβiɣúrúβe	'small pigs'
iβirúúŋgúuri	'soft porridges'	uɣusíri	'huge rope'
βáinu	'you (pl)'	βoryó	'on the right'
ičiiŋgɛ́na	'grinding stones'	ičiiŋgúrúβe	'pig'

ɣaβǎ	'share!'	ičiiŋgúta	'walls'
βɛreká	'carry a child!'	iɣitúúmbe	'stool'
ɣúúká	'ancestor'	remǎ	'weed!'
rɛɛntá	'bring!'	oβoɣááká	'male adulthood'
oβotééndééru	'smoothness'	okoɣéémbá	'to cause rain'
okoómbára	'to count me'	okoβára	'to count'
okoóndɔ́ɣa	'to bewitch me'	okorɔ́ɣa	'to bewitch'
romǎ	'bite!'	teɣetá	'be late!'
ukuúmbuuryá	'to ask me'	uruɣúta	'wall'

2 Modern Greek

Determine whether the two segments [k] and [kʸ] are contrastive or are governed by rule; similarly, determine whether the difference between [x] and [xʸ] is contrastive or predictable. If the distribution is rule-governed, what is the rule and what do you assume to be the underlying consonants in these cases?

kano	'do'	kori	'daughter'
xano	'lose'	xori	'dances'
xʸino	'pour'	kʸino	'move'
krima	'shame'	xrima	'money'
xufta	'handful'	kufeta	'bonbons'
kali	'charms'	xali	'plight'
xʸeli	'eel'	kʸeri	'candle'
xʸeri	'hand'	oxʸi	'no'

3 Farsi

Describe the distribution of the trill [r̃] and the flap [ř].

ær̃teš	'army'	far̃si	'Persian'
qædr̃i	'a little bit'	r̃ah	'road'
r̃ast	'right'	r̃iš	'beard'
ahaɽ	'starch'	axær̃	'last'
hær̃towɽ	'however'	šiɽ	'lion'
ahaři	'starched'	bæřadæɽ	'brother'
čeřa	'why?'	dařid	'you have'
biřæng	'pale'	šiřini	'pastry'

4 Osage

What rule governs the distribution of [d] versus [ð] in the following data?

dábrī	'three'	áðikhǎžǎ	'he lay down'
dačpé	'to eat'	č?éðe	'he killed it'
dak?é	'to dig'	ðéze	'tongue'
dálï	'good'	ðíe	'you'
daštú	'to bite'	ðíški	'to wash'

5 Amharic

Is there a phonemic contrast between the vowels [ə] and [ɛ] in Amharic? If not, say what rule governs the distribution of these vowels, and what the underlying value of the vowel is.

| fərəs | 'horse' | tənəsa | 'stand up!' |
| yɛlïjlïj | 'grandchild' | mayɛt | 'see' |

gənzəb	'money'	jĕgna	'brave'
nəñ	'I am'	məwdəd	'to like'
mənnəsat	'get up'	məmkər	'advise'
žɛle	'unarmed'	yɛlləm	'no'
məč	'when'	məsťət	'give'
fəlləgə	'he wanted'	agəññɛ	'he found'
təməččɛ	'it got comfortable'	mokkərə	'he tried'
kʼažžɛ	'he talked in his sleep'	žɛmmərə	'he started'
laččʼɛ	'he shaved'	ašše	'he rubbed'
bəkkʼələ	'it germinated'	šɛməggələ	'he became old'

6 Gen

Determine the rule which accounts for the distribution of [r] and [l] in the following data.

agblɛ	'farm'	agoŋglo	'lizard'
aŋɔli	'ghost'	akplɔ	'spear'
sabulɛ	'onion'	sra	'strain'
alɔ	'hand'	atitrwɛ	'red billed wood dove'
avlɔ	'bait'	blafogbe	'pineapple'
drɛ	'stretch arms'	edrɔ	'dream'
exlɔ	'friend'	exle	'flea'
hlɛ	'read'	ŋlɔ	'write'
črɔ̃	'exterminate'	ñrã	'be ugly'
klɔ	'wash'	tre	'glue'
vlu	'stretch a rope'	lɔ	'like'
mla	'pound a drum'	pleplelu	'laughing dove'
wla	'hide'	zro	'fly'
esrɔ	'spouse'	etro	'scale'
eñrɔ̃	'spitting cobra'	jro	'hint'

7 Kishambaa

Describe the distribution of voiced versus voiceless nasals (voiceless nasals are written with a circle under the letter, as in m̥), and voiceless aspirated, voiceless unaspirated and voiced stops in Kishambaa.

tagi	'egg'	kitabu	'book'	paalika	'fly!'
ni	'it is'	ŋombe	'cow'	matagi	'eggs'
dodoa	'pick up'	goša	'sleep!'	babu	'skin'
ndimi	'tongues'	ŋgoto	'heart'	mbeu	'seed'
n̥tʰumbii	'monkey'	ŋ̥kʰuŋguni	'bedbug'	m̥pʰeho	'wind'

8 Thai

The obstruents of Thai are illustrated below. Determine what the obstruent phonemes of Thai are ([pˀ, tˀ and kˀ] are unreleased stops). Are [pˀ, tˀ, kˀ] distinct phonemes, or can they be treated as positional variants of some other phoneme? If so, which ones, and what evidence supports your decision? Note that no words begin with [g].

bil	'Bill'	müü	'hand'
rakˀ	'love'	baa	'crazy'
loŋ	'go down'	brüü	'extremely fast'

haa	'five'	plaa	'fish'
dii	'good'	čaan	'dish'
tʰee	'pour'	tʰruumɛɛn	'Truman'
kʰɛŋ	'hard'	panyaa	'brains'
ləəy	'pass'	pʰyaa	[title]
lüak˥	'choose'	klaaŋ	'middle'
čʰat˥	'clear'	traa	'stamp'
riip˥	'hurry'	ɔɔk˥	'exit'
pʰrɛɛ	'silk cloth'	kiə	'wooden shoes'
kʰwaa	'right side'	kɛɛ	'old'
dray	'drive (golf)'	düŋ	'pull'
kan	'ward off'	čuək˥	'pure white'
pʰleeŋ	'song'	čʰan	'me'
staaŋ	'money'	rap˥	'take'
yiisip˥	'twenty'	pʰaa	'cloth'
kʰaa	'kill'	dam	'black'
raay	'case'	tit˥	'get stuck'
sip˥	'ten'	pen	'alive'

9 Palauan

Analyse the distribution of ð, θ and *d* in the following data. Examples of the type 'X ~ Y' mean that the word can be pronounced either as X or as Y, in free variation.

kəðə	'we (inclusive)'	bəðuk	'my stone'
ðiak ~ diak	'negative verb'	maθ	'eye'
tŋoθ	'tattoo needle'	ðe:l ~ de:l	'nail'
ðiosəʔ ~ diosəʔ	'place to bathe'	ðik ~ dik	'wedge'
kuθ	'louse'	ʔoðiŋəl	'visit'
koaθ	'visit'	eaŋəθ	'sky'
ŋərarəðə	'a village'	baθ	'stone'
ieðl	'mango'	ʔəðip	'ant'
kəðeb	'short'	məðəŋei	'knew'
uðouθ	'money'	olðak	'put together'

10 Quechua (Cuzco dialect)

Describe the distribution of the following four sets of segments: k, x, q, χ; ŋ, N; i, e; u, o. Some pairs of these segments are allophones (positional variants) of a single segment. You should state which contrasts are phonemic (unpredictable) and which could be predicted by a rule. For segments which you think are positional variants of a single phoneme, state which phoneme you think is the underlying variant, and explain why you think so; provide a rule which accounts for all occurrences of the predictable variant. (Reminder: N is a uvular nasal.)

qori	'gold'	čoχlu	'corn on the cob'
qʼomir	'green'	niŋri	'ear'
moqo	'runt'	hoqʼara	'deaf'
pʰulʸu	'blanket'	yuyaŋ	'he recalls'
tulʸu	'bone'	api	'take'
suti	'name'	oNqoy	'be sick!'
čilwi	'baby chick'	čʰičiŋ	'he whispers'

čʰaɴqay	'granulate'	aɴqosay	'toast'
qečuŋ	'he disputes'	pʼisqo	'bird'
musoχ	'new'	čuŋka	'ten'
yaŋqaŋ	'for free'	čulʸu	'ice'
qʰelʸa	'lazy'	qʼeɴqo	'zigzagged'
čeqaŋ	'straight'	qaŋ	'you'
noqa	'I'	čaxra	'field'
čeχniŋ	'he hates'	soχta	'six'
aχna	'thus'	lʸixlʸa	'small shawl'
qosa	'husband'	qara	'skin'
alqo	'dog'	seɴqa	'nose'
karu	'far'	atoχ	'fox'
qaŋkuna	'you pl.'	pusaχ	'eight'
tʼeχway	'pluck'	čʼaki	'dry'
waleχ	'again'	aŋka	'eagle'
waχtay	'hit!'	haku	'let's go'
waqay	'tears'	kaŋka	'roasted'
wɔχča	'poor'	waleχ	'poor'
tʰakay	'drop'	reχsisqa	'known'

11 Lhasa Tibetan

There is no underlying contrast in this language between velars and uvulars, or between voiced or voiceless stops or fricatives (except /s/, which exists underlyingly). State what the underlying segments are, and give rules which account for the surface distribution of these consonant types. (Notational reminder: [ɢ] represents a voiced uvular stop.)

aŋgu	'pigeon'	aɳʈãã	'a number'	aŋba	'duck'
apsoo	'shaggy dog'	amčɔɔ	'ear'	tukʈüü	'poison snake'
amto	'a province'	iɣu	'uncle'	imči	'doctor'
uʈɨ	'hair'	uβʊ	'forehead'	eʁa	'bells'
embo	'deserted'	uʊtˢi	'oh-oh'	qa	'saddle'
qaʁa	'alphabet'	qaŋba	'foot'	qamba	'pliers'
qam	'to dry'	qamtoo	'overland'	sarβʊ	'steep'
kikʈɨ	'belch'	kiβu	'crawl'	kiiŋguu	'trip'
kik	'rubber'	kiʈuu	'student'	kʊcuu	'translator'
kʊrii	'roll over'	kiiɣuu	'window'	ku	'nine'
kupčɨ	'900'	kupčaa	'chair'	kɛnča	'contract'
kɛmbo	'headman'	keɣöö	'head monk'	kerβa	'aristrocrat'
qo	'head'	qomba	'monastery'	qɔr	'coat'
qɔɔʁɔɔ	'round'	čʰeʁa	'half'	čʰuɣum	'cheese'
topcaa	'stairs'	tʰoʁõõ	'tonight'	ʈaaʁãã	'post office'
ʈuɣɨ	'harbor'	ʈuɴɢo	'China'	nɛɴɢaa	'important'
paɴɢɔɔ	'chest'	pɛɛβãã	'frog'	simɢãã	'build a house'

Further reading
Cohn 1993; Halle 1959; Harris 1994; Kahn 1976; Sapir 1925.

4 Underlying representations

PREVIEW

KEY TERMS

alternation
neutralization
predictability

This chapter looks deeper into the nature of underlying forms by

- introducing contrast-neutralizing rules
- seeing how unpredictable information must be part of the underlying form
- learning what factors are most important in establishing an underlying representation
- understanding how underlying forms are different from actually pronounced words

A fundamental characteristic of the rules discussed up to this point is that they have been totally predictable allophonic processes, such as aspiration in English or vowel nasalization in Sundanese. For such rules, the question of the exact underlying form of a word has not been so crucial, and in some cases a clear decision could not be made. We saw that in Sundanese every vowel becomes nasalized after a nasal sound, and every phonetic nasal vowel appears after a nasal. Nasality of vowels can always be predicted by a rule in this language: all nasal vowels appear in one predictable context, and all vowels are predictably nasal in that context. It was therefore not crucial to indicate whether a given vowel is underlyingly nasal or underlyingly oral. If you assume that vowels are underlyingly oral you can write a rule to derive all of the nasal vowels, and if you contrarily assume that vowels are all underlyingly nasal you could write a rule to derive all of the oral vowels. The choice of underlying sound may make a considerable difference in terms of simplicity and elegance of the solution, and this is an important consideration in evaluating a phonological analysis, but it is possible to come up with rules which will grind out the correct forms no matter what one assumes about underlying representations in these cases. This is not always the case.

4.1 The importance of correct underlying forms

Neutralizing rules, on the other hand, are ones where two or more underlyingly distinct segments have the same phonetic realization in some context because a rule changes one phoneme into another – thus the distinction of sounds is neutralized. This means that if you look at a word in this neutralized context, you cannot tell what the underlying segment is. Such processes force you to pay close attention to maintaining appropriate distinctions in underlying forms.

Consider the following examples of nominative and genitive forms of nouns in Russian, focusing on the final consonant found in the nominative.

(1) *Nominative singular*   *Genitive singular*
     vagon   vagona   'wagon'
     avtomobil^y avtomobil^{y}a   'car'
     večer   večera   'evening'
     muš   muža   'husband'
     karandaš   karandaša   'pencil'
     glas   glaza   'eye'
     golos   golosa   'voice'
     ras   raza   'time'
     les   lesa   'forest'
     porok   poroga   'threshold'
     vrak   vraga   'enemy'
     urok   uroka   'lesson'
     porok   poroka   'vice'
     t^{s}vet   t^{s}veta   'color'

prut	pruda	'pond'
soldat	soldata	'soldier'
zavot	zavoda	'factory'
xlep	xleba	'bread'
grip	griba	'mushroom'
trup	trupa	'corpse'

To give an explanation for the phonological processes at work in these data, you must give a preliminary description of the morphology. While morphological analysis is not part of phonology per se, it is inescapable that a phonologist must do a morphological analysis of a language, to discover the underlying form.

In each of the examples above, the genitive form is nearly the same as the nominative, except that the genitive also has the vowel [a] which is the genitive singular suffix. We will therefore assume as our initial hypothesis that the bare root of the noun is used to form the nominative case, and the combination of a root plus the suffix -*a* forms the genitive. Nothing more needs to be said about examples such as *vagon* ~ *vagona*, *avtomobiľ* ~ *avtomobiľa*, or *večer* ~ *večera*, where, as it happens, the root ends with a sonorant consonant. The underlying forms of these noun stems are presumably /vagon/, /avtomobiľ/ and /večer/: no facts in the data suggest anything else. These underlying forms are thus identical to the nominative form. With the addition of the genitive suffix -*a* this will also give the correct form of the genitive.

There are stems where the part of the word corresponding to the root is the same: *karandaš* ~ *karandaša*, *golos* ~ *golosa*, *les* ~ *lesa*, *urok* ~ *uroka*, *porok* ~ *poroka*, *tˢvet* ~ *tˢveta*, *soldat* ~ *soldata* and *trup* ~ *trupa*. However, in some stems, there are differences in the final consonant of the root, depending on whether we are considering the nominative or the genitive. Thus, we find the differences *muš* ~ *muža*, *glas* ~ *glaza*, *porok* ~ *poroga*, *vrak* ~ *vraga*, *prut* ~ *pruda*, and *xlep* ~ *xleba*. Such variation in the phonetic content of a morpheme (such as a root) are known as alternations. We can easily recognize the phonetic relation between the consonant found in the nominative and the consonant found in the genitive as involving voicing: the consonant found in the nominative is the voiceless counterpart of the consonant found in the genitive. Not all noun stems have such an alternation, as we can see by pairs such as *karandaš* ~ *karandaša*, *les* ~ *lesa*, *urok* ~ *uroka*, *soldat* ~ *soldata* and *trup* ~ *trupa*. We have now identified a phonological problem to be solved: why does the final consonant of some stems alternate in voicing? And why do we find this alternation with some stems, but not others?

The next two steps in the analysis are intimately connected; we must devise a rule to explain the alternations in voicing, and we must set up appropriate underlying representations for these nouns. In order to determine the correct underlying forms, we will consider two competing hypotheses regarding the underlying form, and in comparing the predictions of those two hypotheses, we will see that one of those hypotheses is clearly wrong.

Suppose, first, that we decide that the form of the noun stem which we see in the nominative is also the underlying form. Such an assumption is reasonable (it is, also, not automatically correct), since the nominative is grammatically speaking a more "basic" form of a noun. In that case, we would assume the underlying stems /glas/ 'eye,' /golos/ 'voice,' /ras/ 'time' and /les/ 'forest.' The problem with this hypothesis is that we would have no way to explain the genitive forms *glaza, golosa, raza* and *lesa*: the combination of the assumed underlying roots plus the genitive suffix *-a* would give us **glasa, golosa, *rasa* and *lesa*, so we would be right only about half the time. The important step here is that we test the hypothesis by combining the supposed root and the affix in a very literal-minded way, whereupon we discover that the predicted forms and the actual forms are different.

We could hypothesize that there is also a rule voicing consonants between vowels (a rule like one which we have previously seen in Kipsigis, chapter 3):

(2)   C → voiced / V _ V

While applying this rule to the assumed underlying forms /glas-a/, /golos-a/, /ras-a/, and /les-a/ would give the correct forms *glaza* and *raza*, it would also give incorrect surface forms such as **goloza* and **leza*. Thus, not only is our first hypothesis about underlying forms wrong, it also cannot be fixed by positing a rule of consonant voicing.

You may be tempted to posit a rule that applies only in certain words, such as *eye*, *time* and so on, but not *voice*, *forest*, etc. This misconstrues the nature of phonological rules, which are general principles that apply to all words of a particular class – most generally, these classes are defined in terms of phonological properties, such as "obstruent," "in word-final position." Rules which are stated as "only applying in the following words" are almost always wrong.

The "nominative is underlying" hypothesis is fundamentally wrong: our failure to come up with an analysis is not because we cannot discern an obscure rule, but lies in the faulty assumption that we start with the nominative. That form has a consistent phonetic property, that any root-final obstruent (which is therefore word-final) is always voiceless, whereas in the genitive form there is no such consistency. If you look at the genitive column, the last consonant of the root portion of the word may be either voiced or voiceless.

We now consider a second hypothesis, where we set up underlying representations for roots which distinguish stems which have a final voiced obstruent in the genitive versus those with a final voiceless obstruent. We may instead assume the following underlying roots.

(3)   *Final voiced obstruent*   *Final voiceless obstruent*

/muž/	'husband'	/karandaš/	'pencil'
/glaz/	'eye'	/golos/	'voice'
/raz/	'time'	/les/	'forest'
/porog/	'threshold'	/porok/	'vice'

/vrag/	'enemy'	/urok/	'lesson'
/prud/	'pond'	/tsvet/	'color'
/zavod/	'factory'	/soldat/	'soldier'
/grib/	'mushroom'	/trup/	'corpse'
/xleb/	'bread'		

Under this hypothesis, the genitive form can be derived easily. The genitive form is the stem hypothesized in (3) followed by the suffix *-a*. No rule is required to derive voiced versus voiceless consonants in the genitive. That issue has been resolved by our choice of underlying representations where some stems end in voiced consonants and others end in voiceless consonants. By our hypothesis, the nominative form is simply the underlying form of the noun stem, with no suffix.

However, a phonological rule must apply to the nominative form, in order to derive the correct phonetic output. We have noted that no word in Russian ends phonetically with a voiced obstruent. This regular fact allows us to posit the following rule, which devoices any word-final obstruent.

(4) *Final devoicing*
       obstruent → voiceless / _#

By this rule, an obstruent is devoiced at the end of the word. As this example has shown, an important first step in doing a phonological analysis for phenomena such as word-final devoicing in Russian is to establish the correct underlying representations, which encode unpredictable information.

Whether a consonant is voiced cannot be predicted in English ([dɛd] *dead*, [tɛd] *Ted*, [dɛt] *debt*), and must be part of the underlying form. Similarly, in Russian since you cannot predict whether a given root ends in a voiced or a voiceless consonant in the genitive, that information must be part of the underlying form of the root. That is information about the root, which cannot always be determined by looking at the surface form of the word itself: it must be discovered by looking at the genitive form of the noun, where the distinction between voiced and voiceless final consonants is not eliminated.

4.2 Refining the concept of underlying form

It is important to understand what underlying forms are, and what they are not. The nature of underlying forms can be best appreciated in the context of the overall organization of a grammar, and how a given word is generated in a sentence. The structure of a grammar can be represented in terms of the standard block model.

(5)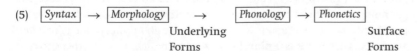

| | Syntax | → | Morphology | → | Phonology | → | Phonetics |

Underlying   Surface
Forms   Forms

This model implies that the output of one component forms the input to the next component, so the phonological component starts with whatever the morphological component gives it, and applies its own rules (which are then subject to principles of physical interpretation in the phonetic component). The output of the morphological component, which is the input to the phonology, is by definition the underlying form, so we need to know a little bit about what the morphological component does, to understand what is presented to the phonology.

The function of the morphological component is to assemble words, in the sense of stating how roots and affixes combine to form a particular word. Thus the morphological component is responsible for combining a noun root [dag] and a plural affix [z] in English to give the word *dog-s* (i.e. /dag-z/), or in Russian the morphology combines a noun root [vagon] with an inflectional ending [a] according to rules of inflection for Russian, to give the genitive word *vagon-a*. Each morpheme is assumed to have a single constant phonetically defined shape coming out of the morphology (there are a few exceptions such as the fact that the third-person-singular form of the verb *be* in English is [ɪz] and the first-person-singular form of that verb is [æm]). The phonetic realization of any morpheme is subject to rules of phonology, so while the morphology provides the plural morpheme *z* (spelled <s>), the application of phonological rules will make that that morpheme being pronounced as [s] as in *cats* or [ɪz] as in *bushes*.

It is very important to understand that the grammar does not formally derive one word from another. (Some languages seem to have special morphological processes, which we will not be discussing here, that derive one word from another – clipping such as *Sally* → *Sal* would be an example.) Rather, one word derives from a given abstract root plus whatever affixes are relevant, and a related word derives by adding a different set of affixes to the same abstract root. Accordingly, the plural of a noun in English does not derive from the singular, rather, both the singular *and* the plural forms derive from a common root: no suffix is added to the root in the singular, and the suffix /z/ is added to the root in the plural. The Russian genitive [vagona] also does not derive from the nominative, nor does the nominative derive from the genitive. Rather, both derive from the root /vagon/, where the nominative adds no affix and the genitive adds the affix -*a*.

The underlying form of a word is whatever comes out of the morphology and is fed into the phonology, before any phonological rules have applied. The underlying form of the word [kæts] is /kæt-z/, since that is what results in the morphology by applying the rule that combines a noun root such as *cat* with the plural suffix. The underlying form of the plural word [kæts] is *not* /kæt/, because the plural word has to have the plural morpheme. However, /kæt/ *is* the underlying form of the singular word [kæt]. There is no phonological rule which inserts *z* or *s* in order to form a plural. The principles for combining roots and affixes are not part of the phonology, and thus there is no need to include rules such as "insert [z] in the plural." Be explicit about what you assume about morphology in a language, i.e. that there is a plural suffix -*z* in English or a genitive suffix -*a* in Russian. As for the mechanics of phonological analysis, you should assume, for example, that the plural suffix is already present in the underlying form, and therefore do not write a rule to insert the plural suffix since that rule is part of morphology. A phonological analysis states the underlying forms of morphemes, and describes changes in the phonological shape of the root or suffix.

We have concluded that the underlying form of the Russian word [prut] 'pond' is /prud/. In arriving at that conclusion, we saw how important it is to distinguish the phonological concept of an underlying form from the morphological concept "basic form," where the singular form, or an uninflected nominative form would be the morphological "basic form." An underlying form is a strictly phonological concept and is not necessarily equivalent to an actually pronounced word (even disregarding the fundamental fact that underlying forms are discrete symbolic representations whereas actually pronounced words are acoustic waveforms). It is a representation that is the foundation for explaining the variety of actual pronounciations found in the morpheme, as determined by phonological context.

The morphologically basic form of the Russian word for pond is the unmarked nominative, [prut], composed of just the root with no inflectional ending. In contrast, the phonological underlying form is /prud/, for as we have seen, if we assume the underlying form to be */prut/, we cannot predict the genitive [pruda]. The word *[prud], with a voiced consonant at the end of the word, does not appear as such in the language, and thus the supposition that the underlying form is /prud/ is an abstraction, given that [prud] by itself is never found in the language – it must be inferred, in order to explain the actual data. The basis for that inference is the genitive form [pruda], which actually contains the hypothesized underlying form as a subpart. It is important to understand, however, that the underlying form of a root may not actually be directly attested in this way in any single word, and we will discuss this point in section 4.6.

4.3 Finding the underlying form

A similar problem arises in explaining the partitive and nominative forms of nouns in Finnish. The first step in understanding the phonological alternation seen here is to do a standard preliminary morphological analysis of the data, which involves identifying which parts of a word correlate with each aspect of word structure (such as root meaning or grammatical case). The following examples illustrate that the nominative singular suffix is Ø (i.e. there is no overt suffix in the nominative singular) and the partitive singular suffix is -æ, which alternates with -a if there is a back vowel somewhere before it in the word (we will not be concerned with that vowel alternation in the partitive suffix).

(6)   *Nominative sg*   *Partitive sg*
    a.   aamu   aamua   'morning'
        hopea   hopeaa   'silver'

katto	kattoa	'roof'
kello	kelloa	'clock'
kirya	kiryaa	'book'
külmæ	külmææ	'cold'
koulu	koulua	'school'
lintu	lintua	'bird'
hüllü	hüllüæ	'shelf'
kömpelö	kömpelöæ	'clumsy'
nækö	næköæ	'appearance'

b.			
	yoki	yokea	'river'
	kivi	kiveæ	'stone'
	muuri	muuria	'wall'
	naapuri	naapuria	'neighbor'
	nimi	nimeæ	'name'
	kaappi	kaappia	'chest of drawers'
	kaikki	kaikkea	'all'
	kiirehti	kiirehtiæ	'hurry'
	lehti	lehteæ	'leaf'
	mæki	mækeæ	'hill'
	ovi	ovea	'door'
	posti	postia	'mail'
	tukki	tukkia	'log'
	æiti	æitiæ	'mother'
	englanti	englantia	'England'
	yærvi	yærveæ	'lake'
	koski	koskea	'waterfall'
	reki	rekeæ	'sledge'
	væki	vækeæ	'people'

We might assume that the underlying form of the root is the same as the nominative (which has no suffix). The problem which these data pose is that in some nouns, the partitive appears to be simply the nominative plus the suffix -æ ~ -a (for example *muuri* ~ *muuria*), but for other nouns the final vowel alternates, with [i] in the nominative and [e] in the partitive (e.g. *yoki* ~ *yokea*). It is obvious that the nature of the following vowel does not explain this alternation, since the same surface-quality suffix vowel can appear after either *e* or *i* – compare *yokea, nimeæ* where [e] appears before both [a] and [æ], versus *muuria, kiirehtiæ* where [i] appears before these same vowels. Nor can the preceding consonant be called upon to predict what vowel will appear in the partitive, as shown by pairs such as *tukkia, kaikkea* versus *lehteæ, æitiæ*.

This is an area where there is (potentially) a difference between language-learning pedagogy and a formal linguistic analysis. Faced with the problem of learning the inflectional distinction *muuri* ~ *muuria* versus *yoki* ~ *yokea*, a second-language class on Finnish might simply have the student memorize a list of words like *yoki* ~ *yokea* where the vowel changes in the inflectional paradigm. From the point of view of linguistic analysis this is the wrong way to look at the question, since it implies that this is not a rule-governed property of the language. However, second-language learning is not the same as linguistic analysis: a class in foreign-language instruction has a different goal from a class in analysis, and some students in a language class may receive greater practical benefit from just memorizing a list of words. Thus it is important to distinguish the teaching method where one learns arbitrary lists, and a theoretically based analysis. One simply cannot predict what vowel will appear in the partitive form if one only considers the pronunciation of the nominative. This means: nominative forms are not the same as underlying forms (something that we also know given the previous Russian example). The underlying representation must in some way contain that information which determines whether there will be a vowel alternation in a given word.

In looking for the phonological basis for this vowel alternation, it is important to realize that the alternation in stem-final vowels is not chaotic, for we find precisely two possibilities, either *i* in the nominative paired with *i* in the partitive, or *i* in the nominative paired with *e* in the partitive – never, for example, *i* paired with *u* or *i* paired with *o*. Moreover, only the vowel *i* enters into such a vowel alternation in Finnish, so there are no nouns with *o* in the nominative which is replaced by *u* in the partitive, nor is *u* in the nominative ever replaced by *o* or any other vowel in the partitive. One final fact about the data in (6) suggests exactly how the right underlying representations can explain this alternation: of the eight vowels of Finnish (*i, ü, e, ö, æ, u, o, a*), all of them appear at the end of the word except the vowel *e*. Now, since the stem of the word for 'name,' which appears as *nimi* in the nominative, actually appears on the surface as *nime-* in the partitive, it is not at all unreasonable to assume that the underlying form of the stem is in fact /nime/. It would be a bit bizarre to assume an underlying form such as /nima/, since the vowel [a] never appears in that position in any form of this word: the most natural assumption to make is that the underlying form of a morpheme is actually composed of segments found in some surface manifestation of the morpheme. On the other hand, the stem of the word for 'wall' is pronounced *muuri* in both the nominative and the partitive, and therefore there is no reason to assume that it is underlyingly anything other than /muuri/.

We will then assume that the underlying vowel at the end of the stem is actually reflected by the partitive form, and thus we would assume underlying representations such as /yoke/, /nime/, /kive/, /lehte/, /ove/ and so on, as well as /muuri/, /naapuri/, /kaappi/, /tukki/ and so on. The underlying form of partitive [yoke-a] would thus be /yoke-a/, that is, no rule at all is required to explain the partitive. Instead, a rule is needed to explain the surface form of the nominative [yoki], which derives from /yoke/. A very simple neutralizing rule can explain the surface form of the nominative: underlying word-final *e* is raised to *i*.

> *This is a natural assumption but not an absolute rule, as we see in chapter 9. Underlying forms can contain segments not found in any form of the word. Only when there is strong evidence for departing from this assumption are you justified in setting up underlying forms with such abstract elements.*

(7) *Final vowel raising*
  e → i / __#

This rule is neutralizing since the distinction between /i/ and /e/ is neutralized by applying this rule: an underlying /e/ becomes phonetic [i].

Apart from illustrating how important correct underlying forms are, these two examples have also shown that it is dangerous, and incorrect in these two cases, to assume that the "most basic" form of a word according to morphological criteria is also the underlying form of the word. To reiterate: the underlying form of a morpheme is a hypothesis set forth by the analyst, a claim that by assuming such-and-such an underlying form, plus some simple set of rules (which need to be discovered by the analyst), the observed variation in the shape of morphemes can be explained.

Kerewe.   To better understand the reasoning that leads to correct underlying forms, we investigate other examples. Consider the following data from Kerewe.

(8)

Infinitive	1sg habitual	3sg habitual	Imperative	
kupaamba	mpaamba	apaamba	paamba	'adorn'
kupaaŋga	mpaaŋga	apaaŋga	paaŋga	'line up'
kupima	mpima	apima	pima	'measure'
kupuupa	mpuupa	apuupa	puupa	'be light'
kupekeča	mpekeča	apekeča	pekeča	'make fire with stick'
kupiinda	mpiinda	apiinda	piinda	'be bent'
kuhiiga	mpiiga	ahiiga	hiiga	'hunt'
kuheeka	mpeeka	aheeka	heeka	'carry'
kuhaaŋga	mpaaŋga	ahaaŋga	haaŋga	'create'
kuheeba	mpeeba	aheeba	heeba	'guide'
kuhiima	mpiima	ahiima	hiima	'gasp'
kuhuuha	mpuuha	ahuuha	huuha	'breath into'

In this example we only have direct evidence for the change after m, so it would be possible to restrict our rule to the more specific context "after m." But this would run counter to basic assumptions of science, that we seek the most general explanations possible, not the most restricted ones.

We notice that every infinitive begins with *ku-*, which we surmise is the prefix for the infinitive; the third-singular habitual form has the prefix *a-*, and the first-singular habitual has the prefix *m-*; the imperative involves no prefix. In addition to segmental prefixes, there is a change in the first consonant of the stem in some verbs, in some contexts. The initial consonant of the verb meaning 'guide' alternates between [h] and [p], with [p] appearing in the first-singular habitual after [m] and [h] appearing elsewhere. Since this stem appears in two surface variants, [heeba] and [peeba], two plausible hypotheses are immediately possible: the stem is underlyingly /peeba/, or the stem is underlyingly /heeba/. If we assume that the stem is underlyingly /heeba/, we require a rule to explain the divergence between the predicted form of the first-singular habitual form – we would expect *[mheeba], *[mhiima], etc. – and the actual form of the verb, [mpeeba], [mpiima] and so on. Since in fact we do not see the sequence /mh/ anywhere in the data, we might assume the following neutralizing rule.

(9)   *Postnasal hardening*
      h → p / nasal __

If, on the other hand, we assume that the root is underlyingly /peeba/, we would need a rule which changes /p/ into [h] when not preceded by a nasal – in other words, when preceded by a vowel or by nothing. There is no single property which groups together word-initial position and vowels. Thus, the supposed rule changing /p/ to [h] would have to be a disjunction of two separate environments.

$$(10) \quad p \rightarrow h / \left\{ \begin{matrix} \# \\ V \end{matrix} \right\} \_$$

This suggests that rule (10) is wrong.

More important than the greater complexity of the rule entailed by assuming that the word for 'guide' is underlyingly /peeba/, it is empirically wrong: rule (10) implicitly claims that /p/ should always become [h] word initially or after a vowel, but this is falsified by forms such as *kupaamba, apaamba, paamba* 'adorn' and *kupaaŋga, apaaŋga, paaŋga* 'line up.' If we assume the stems uniformly begin with /p/, then we cannot predict whether the imperative or infinitive has [h] (*kuhaaŋga*) or [p] (*kupaaŋga*). On the other hand, if we assume an underlying contrast between initial /h/ and initial /p/ – i.e. *haaŋga* 'create', *paaŋga* 'arrange' – then we can correctly distinguish those stems which begin with /h/ from those which begin with /p/ when no nasal precedes, as well as correctly neutralizing that distinction just in case the stem is preceded by a nasal (*mpaaŋga* 'I create'; 'I arrange').

English plurals.   A further illustration of how to determine the correct underlying representation comes from English. As the following examples illustrate, the surface form of the plural suffix varies between [s] and [z] (as well as [ɨz], to be discussed later).

(11)	kæps	caps	kæbz	cabs	klæmz	clams
	kæts	cats	kædz	cads	kænz	cans
	kaks	cocks	kagz	cogs	karz	cars
	pruwfs	proofs	huvz	hooves	gəlz	gulls
			fliyz	fleas		
			plæwz	plows		
			pyɾez	purees		

The generalization regarding distribution is straightforward: [s] appears after a voiceless segment, and [z] appears after a voiced one (be it an obstruent, a liquid, nasal or a vowel).

This same alternation can be found in the suffix marking the third singular present-tense form of verbs.

(12)	slæps	slaps	stæbz	stabs	slæmz	slams
	hɪts	hits	haydz	hides	kænz	cans
	powks	pokes	dɪgz	digs	hæŋz	hangs

læfs	laughs	θrayvz	thrives	hiylz	heals
pıθs	piths	beyðz	bathes	hırz	hears
		flayz	flies	viytowz	vetos

If we suppose that the underlying form of the affixes for noun plural and third singular present verbs are /z/, then we would assume the following rule to derive the phonetic variant [s].

(13)   obstruent → voiceless / voiceless __

On the other hand, if we were to assume that these suffixes are underlyingly /s/, we would assume the following rule.

(14)   obstruent → voiced / voiced __

In terms of the simplicity and generality of these two rules, the analyses are comparable. Both formulations require the same number of phonetic specifications to state the rule, and both formulations apply to general and phonetically natural classes. However, the two analyses differ quite significantly in terms of their overall predictions for English. The implicit prediction of the first rule (13) is that there should be no voiced obstruents after voiceless segments in English, since that rule would devoice all such obstruents. This generalization seems to be correct: there are no words like *[yəkd], *[pıfz], *[sdap]. The implicit prediction of the second rule (14) is different: that rule implies that there should be no voiceless segments after any voiced segments. This is manifestly incorrect, as shown by the existence of words such as [hıs] *hiss*, [pæθ] *path*, [dæns] *dance*, [fals] *false*. We prefer a hypothesis which makes the correct prediction about the phonetic structure of the language as a whole, and thus we select the underlying form /z/ and a rule devoicing obstruents after voiceless segments. Looking for such asymmetries plays an important role in determining which of two hypotheses is the correct one.

The alternation *z* ~ *s* is not limited to the two affixes -*z* 'plural' and -*z* '3sg present tense.' The rule of devoicing can also be seen applying to the possessive suffix -*z*.

(15)   *Noun*   *Noun + poss.*
       kæt   kæts   cat
       sləg   sləgz   slug
       klæm   klæmz   clam
       snow   snowz   snow

Moreover, certain auxiliary verbs such as *has* [hæz] and *is* [ıs] undergo a reduction in casual speech, so that they appear simply as [s] or [z], the choice between these two being determined by the devoicing rule which we have motivated.

(16) *Noun + has*	*Reduced*	*Noun + is*	*Reduced*	
jæk hæz iyʔn̩	jæks iyʔn̩	jæk ız iyɒıŋ	jæks iyɒıŋ	Jack
pæt hæz iyʔn̩	pæts iyʔn̩	pæt ız iyɒıŋ	pæts iyɒıŋ	Pat

ǰɛn hæz iyʔn̩	ǰɛnz iyʔn̩	ǰɛn ɪz iyɒɪŋ	ǰɛnz iyɒɪŋ	Jen
bab hæz iyʔn̩	babz iyʔn̩	bab ɪz iyɒɪŋ	babz iyɒɪŋ	Bob
ǰow hæz iyʔn̩	ǰowz iyʔn̩	ǰow ɪz iyɒɪŋ	ǰowz iyɒɪŋ	Joe

The devoicing rule (13) automatically explains the alternation in the surface shape of the consonant here as well.

Jita tone. It is important to look for correlations which may lead to causal explanations, in analyzing data. Consider the following data from Jita, concentrating on the tones of morphemes (H or high tone is marked with acute accent, L or low-toned syllables are unmarked).

(17) a. okuβuma   'to hit'   okusiβa   'to block'
          okuβumira   'to hit for'   okusiβira   'to block for'
          okuβumana   'to hit e.o.'   okusiβana   'to block e.o.'
          okuβumirana   'to hit for e.o.'   okusiβirana   'to block for e.o.'
      b. okulúma   'to bite'   okukúβa   'to fold'
          okulumíra   'to bite for'   okukuβíra   'to fold for'
          okulumána   'to bite e.o.'   okukuβána   'to fold e.o'
          okulumírana   'to bite for e.o.'   okukuβírana   'to fold for e.o'

We can conclude that there is a prefix *oku-* perhaps marking the infinitive, a suffix *-a* appearing at the end of every verb, and two suffixes *-ir-* 'for' and *-an-* 'each other.' There are also root morphemes: *-βum-* 'hit,' *-siβ-* 'block,' as well as *-lúm-* 'bite' and *-kúβ-* 'fold.' We decide that 'bite' and 'fold' underlyingly have H tones in part based on the fact that there actually is an H tone on the vowels of these roots in the simplest verb forms.

In addition, we observe that the suffixes *-ir-* and *-an-* have H tone when they come immediately after these verb roots. The suffixes do not have H tone after the first set of roots: appearance of H on the suffix is correlated with which morpheme immediately precedes the suffix. Since this unpredictable property is correlated with the preceding root morpheme, it must therefore be an aspect of the underlying form of the preceding morpheme.

We thus explain the H tone on these suffix morphemes by positing that [oku-lum-án-a] derives from underlying /oku-lúm-an-a/, by applying a rule of tone shift which shifts a H tone rightward to the following syllable, as long as the syllable is not word-final. Because of the restriction that H does not shift to a final syllable, the underlying H surfaces unchanged in [okulúma].

Now consider the following data.

(18) okumuβúma   'to hit   okumusíβa   'to block
                        him/her'   him/her'
      okumuβúmira   'to hit for   okumusíβira   'to block for
                        him/her'   him/her'
      okučiβúma   'to hit it'   okučisíβa   'to block it'
      okučiβúmira   'to hit   okučisíβira   'to block
                        for it'   for it'

When the L-toned roots of (17a) stand after the object prefixes -*mu*- 'him/her' and -*čɨ*- 'it,' they have an H tone at the beginning of the root. Again, since the presence of the H is correlated unpredictably with the prefixes -*mu*- and -*čɨ*-, we hypothesize that the tones are *part* of the underlying representation of the prefixes – the prefixes are /mú/ and /čɨ́/, and the H tone shifts to the right by the tone shift rule which we have already posited.

4.4 Practice at problem solving

You should now be able to apply this reasoning to data which pose analogous problems; a series of examples are given in this section for practice.

Chamorro vowel alternations. There are alternations in the quality of vowels in initial syllables in some contexts seen in the following data from Chamorro.

(19)

gwíhən	'fish'	i gwíhən	'the fish'
gúmə?	'house'	i gímə?	'the house'
kátta	'letter'	yo? kátta	'a letter (object)'
		i kǽtta	'the letter'
tˢúpa	'cigarettes'	i tˢípa	'the cigarettes'
fino?	'talk'	mi fino?	'lots of talk'
túnu?	'to know'	en tínu?	'you know'
tˢúgo?	'juice'	mi tˢígo?	'lots of juice'
sóŋsuŋ	'village'	i séŋsuŋ	'the village'
húlu?	'up'	sæn hílu?	'upward'
pétˢu	'chest'	i pétˢu	'the chest'
tómu	'knee'	i tému	'the knee'
ótdut	'ant'	mi étdut	'lots of ants'
óksu?	'hill'	gi éksu?	'at the hill'
dáŋkulu	'big one'	i dǽŋkulu	'the big one'
láhi	'male'	i lǽhi	'the male'
lágu	'north'	sæn lǽgu	'toward north'
pulónnun	'trigger fish'	i pulónnun	'the trigger fish'
mundóŋgu	'cow's stomach'	i mundóŋgu	'the cow's stomach'
putamonéda	'wallet'	i putamonéda	'the wallet'

What underlying representations, and what rule or rules, are required to account for these data? When you answer this question, you should consider two hypotheses which differ in particular about what form is taken to be underlying – what are the two most obvious ways of treating these alternations? One of these hypotheses is clearly wrong; the other is the correct hypothesis.

Korean. Now consider the following data from Korean. The first column, the imperative, seems to involve a vowel suffix. One reason to think that there is an imperative suffix is that every imperative ends either in the vowel *a* or in *ə* (the choice between *a* versus *ə* is based on the vowel which precedes that suffix, /a/ or /o/ versus other vowels, and can be ignored here). A second reason comes from comparing the imperative and the plain present forms. Comparing *ana* and *anninta*, or *kama* and *kamninta*, we can see that for each verb, the portions common to both the imperative and the plain present are respectively *an-* and *kam-*. From this we deduce that there must be a suffix, either *-a* or *-ə*, which marks the imperative, and another suffix *-ninta* which marks the plain present.

(20)

Imperative	Plain present	
ana	anninta	'hug'
kama	kamninta	'wind'
sinə	sinninta	'wear shoes'
t'atɨmə	t'atɨmninta	'trim'
nəmə	nəmninta	'overflow'
nama	namninta	'remain'
čʰama	čʰamninta	'endure'
ipə	imninta	'put on'
kupə	kumninta	'bend'
čəpə	čəmninta	'fold'
tatə	tanninta	'close'
putʰə	punninta	'adhere'
čočʰa	čonninta	'follow'
məkə	məŋninta	'eat'
sək'ə	səŋninta	'mix'
tak'a	taŋninta	'polish'
čukə	čuŋninta	'die'
ikə	iŋninta	'ripen'

What is the underlying form of these verb stems, and what phonological rule or rules are required to account for the variations that are seen in the surface shape of the various stems?

Koasati. What is the underlying form of the first-singular possessive prefix in Koasati, and what phonological rule applies in these examples?

(21)

Noun	My N	
apahčá	amapahčá	'shadow'
asikčí	amasikčí	'muscle'
ilkanó	amilkanó	'right side'
ifá	amifá	'dog'
a:pó	ama:pó	'grandmother'
iskí	amiskí	'mother'
pačokkó:ka	ampačokkó:ka	'chair'
towá	antowá	'onion'
kastó	aŋkastó	'flea'
bayá:na	ambayá:na	'stomach'
tá:ta	antá:ta	'father'

čofkoní	añčofkoní	'bone'
kitiłká	aŋkitiłká	'hair bangs'
toní	antoní	'hip'

Kimatuumbi. What phonological rules pertaining to consonants operate in the following examples from Kimatuumbi. What are the underlying forms of the stems of the words for 'rope,' 'palm,' 'tongue,' 'piece of wood,' 'pole' and 'covered'? Ignore tonal changes.

(22)
Singular	Plural	
lugói	ŋgói	'rope'
lugolóká	ŋgolóká	'straight'
lubáu	mbáu	'rib'
lubágalo	mbagálo	'lath'
lujíiŋgyá	ñjíiŋgyá	'entered'
lulaála	ndaála	'pepper'
lulímí	ndími	'tongue'
lulındíúlá	ndındíúlá	'guarded'
lupaláaí	mbaláaí	'bald head'
lupaálá	mbaálá	'wanted'
lutéelá	ndeelá	'piece of wood'
lukíligo	ŋgilígo	'place for initiates'
lukíli	ŋgíli	'palm'
luyímá	ñjíma	'pole'
luyóka	ñjóka	'stomach worm'
luyúsí	ñjúsi	'bee'
luyúwé	ñjúwe	'pumpkin plant'
luwıkílyá	ŋgʷıkílyá	'covered'

A certain degree of uncertainty regarding the exact underlying form of the plural prefix is expected. However, the underlying form of the stem should be clear, and should be the focus of your analysis.

4.5 Underlying forms and sentence-level phonology

In the examples which we have considered so far, we have been comparing morphologically related words, such as a nominative and a genitive, and we have seen that an underlying distinction may be preserved in one word in a particular inflected form (because in that inflected form the conditions for applying the phonological rule are not satisfied), but the difference is neutralized in a related word where the conditions for the rule are present. We now consider two additional cases where underlying distinctions are neutralized depending on context, and the neutralization takes place within one and the same word, depending on where the word appears in a sentence. What this shows is that phonology is not just about variations in pronunciation between words, but also includes variations in the pronunciation of a word in different sentential contexts.

4.5.1 Korean final Cs

The first case is a rule of Korean that nasalizes stops before nasal consonants (a rule that we have seen operating within words in the preceding
section). The first set of examples shows the word for 'rice' when said
alone, or when it is followed by various words which begin with oral consonants and vowels. In these data, the last consonant of the word for 'rice'
is pronounced as [p]. In the second set of examples, the word which follows 'rice' begins with a nasal, and in that case the final consonant of the
word for 'rice' is pronounced as [m].

(23) a.   pa**p**   'rice'

          pa**p** anməkət'a   'didn't eat rice'
          rice   didn't eat

          pa**p** winmoke tuət'a   'put rice on the upper floor'
          rice   on-upper-floor put

          pa**p** saməkət'a   'ate rice at a store'
          rice   ate-at-store

          pa**p** totuki humčʰəkat'a   'a thief stole rice'
          rice   thief (subj) stole

    b.   pa**m** mani məkəla   'eat rice a lot'
          rice   a lot   eat

          pa**m** mək-imyən   'if eats rice'
          rice   eat-if

          pa**m** nəmu masik'e məkət'a   'I enjoyed rice quite a lot'
          rice   very   deliciously   ate

          pa**m** nəkʰo   'add rice'
          rice   add

Compare those examples with the following examples with the word for
'chestnut'.

(24) a.   pa**m**   'chestnut'

          pa**m** anməkət'a   'didn't eat chestnut'
          chestnut   didn't eat

          pa**m** winmoke tuət'a   'put chestnut on the upper floor'
          chestnut   on-upper-floor put

          pa**m** saməkət'a   'ate chestnut at a store'
          chestnut   ate-at-store

          pa**m** totuki humčʰəkat'a   'a thief stole chestnut'
          chestnut   thief (subj)   stole

    b.   pa**m** mani məkəla   'eat chestnut a lot'
          chestnut   a lot   eat

          pa**m** mək-imyən   'if eats chestnut'
          chestnut   eat-if

pam nəmu masik'e məkət'a   'I enjoyed chestnut quite a lot'
chestnut   very   deliciously   ate

pam nəkʰo   'add chestnut'
chestnut   add

In fact the (b) phrases above are actually ambiguous as to whether the word being pronounced means 'chestnut' or 'rice.'

The last consonant of the word for 'chestnut' is always [m], so we would presume that the underlying form of that word is /pam/. Since the word for 'rice' varies between [pap] and [pam], and since we know that the underlying form cannot be /pam/ (this is the underlying form of 'chestnut,' and 'chestnut' cannot have the same underlying form as 'rice' since they do not behave the same), we conclude that the underlying form of the word for 'rice' is /pap/, and that a nasalization rule changes /p/ (in fact, all stops) to nasals before a nasal. Whether a word undergoes that rule depends on what follows the final consonant. One and the same word can be pronounced differently depending on the properties of the phrase in which it appears.

4.5.2 Kimatuumbi tone

In the Korean case which we just considered, it happens that the underlying form of the word is the same as the way the word is pronounced when it is said alone. This situation does not hold in Kimatuumbi, where one has to know how a word is pronounced when it is *not* at the end of an utterance, in order to determine the underlying form of the word. The words in (25) have an H tone (marked with an acute accent) on the second vowel from the beginning of the word when said alone. When another word follows, they seem to lose that H tone.

(25)

kiwíkɪlyo	'cover'	ŋga kiwɪkɪlyo lí	'it isn't a cover'
lubágalo	'lath'	ŋga lubagalo lí	'it isn't a lath'
mikóta	'sugar canes'	ŋga mikota lí	'it isn't sugar canes'
ŋguúŋguni	'bedbug'	ŋga ŋguuŋguni lí	'it isn't a bedbug'
lukólogo	'brewery'	ŋga lukologo lí	'it isn't a brewery'
mabáando	'thighs'	ŋga mabaando lí	'it isn't thighs'
kikóloombe	'shell'	ŋga kikoloombe lí	'it isn't a shell'
lipítanʊʊŋgʊ	'rainbow'	ŋga lipɪtanʊʊŋgʊ lí	'it isn't a rainbow'

In contrast, the words of (26), which also have an H tone on the second vowel from the beginning of the word when the word is said alone, keep their H tone when another word follows.

(26)

lukóŋgobe	'wood'	ŋga lukóŋgobe lí	'it's not wood'
kitʊ́kʊtʊkʊ	'quelea bird'	ŋga kitʊ́kʊtʊkʊ lí	'it's not a quelea'
diíwai	'wine'	ŋga diíwai lí	'it's not wine'
lukóoŋgono	'chicken leg'	ŋga lukóoŋgono lí	'it's not a leg'
lukóoŋgowe	'marble'	ŋga lukóoŋgowe lí	'it's not marble'
matógolo	'waterbucks'	ŋga matógolo lí	'it's not waterbucks'

mivíriiŋgo	'circles'	ŋga mivíriiŋgo lí	'it's not circles'
kiyógoyo	'bird (sp)'	ŋga kiyógoyo lí	'it's not a bird'
kikálaaŋgo	'pan'	ŋga kikálaaŋgo lí	'it's not a pan'

There are no words in Kimatuumbi which are toneless when said by themselves, thus *kitekelyo* said by itself is an unattested kind of word. There is a clear contrast in tonal behavior between the words in (25) where the presence of an H tone on the second vowel depends on whether the word is said alone or is followed by another word, and those in (26) where the second vowel always has an H tone. The solution to this puzzle is that the words in (26) have an underlying H tone on their second vowel, and thus nothing happens to that tone; but the words in (25) have no underlying H, and instead get an H at the end of an utterance by a rule that assigns an H tone to the second vowel of a toneless word which comes at the end of an utterance. Thus in the case of Kimatuumbi tone, the contrast between underlyingly toneless words and words with underlying H is best revealed by looking at the word when it appears *not* by itself: it is the citation form of the word that undergoes the neutralization rule, which is the opposite of the situation we just encountered in Korean.

4.6 Underlying forms and multiple columns in the paradigm

The following data from Samoan illustrate the very important point that it is wrong to think of deriving underlying forms by chopping off affixes from some single column of data. In the first set of examples, our initial task is to deduce the underlying form of each of the verb roots and the affix for the perfective form.

(27)
Simple	*Perfective*	
olo	oloia	'rub'
lafo	lafoia	'cast'
aŋa	aŋaia	'face'
usu	usuia	'get up and go early'
tau	tauia	'reach a destination'
taui	tauia	'repay'
sa:ʔili	sa:ʔilia	'look for'
vaŋai	vaŋaia	'face each other'
paʔi	paʔia	'touch'
naumati	naumatia	'be waterless'
sa:uni	sa:unia	'prepare'
seŋi	seŋia	'be shy'
lele	lelea	'fly'
suʔe	suʔea	'uncover'
taʔe	taʔea	'smash'
tafe	tafea	'flow'
ta:upule	ta:upulea	'confer'
palepale	palepalea	'hold firm'

Examples such as *oloia, aŋaia* and *usuia* suggest that the perfective suffix is *-ia*, and the simple form of the verb reflects the underlying form of the root. Examples such as *seŋi ~ seŋia* or *lele ~ lelea* suggest a phonological rule, since the combination of the presumed stems *ati* and *lele* with the perfective affix *-ia* would result in the incorrect forms *seŋiia, *leleia*. However, this problem can be corrected by positing a phonological rule which deletes a front vowel when it is preceded by a front vowel. In the formalization of the rule, we say that the second front vowel is replaced by zero, which means that it is deleted.

(28)   *Vowel-cluster reduction*
front vowel → Ø / front vowel __

An alternative hypothesis would be that [i] is inserted between a back vowel and the vowel [a], if we were to presume that the perfective suffix is underlyingly /a/.

(29)   Ø → i / back vowel __ a

This would be quite unlikely on grounds of naturalness. It is common across languages for one of two adjacent vowels to be eliminated, and no language has been found with a rule that inserts a vowel between two other vowels. Additional data to be considered below will show that, in addition, this would just be plain wrong. We abandon the idea of inserting the vowel *i* and conclude that the underlying form of the perfective suffix must be *-ia*, hence there must be a rule deleting a front vowel after a front vowel. We would then conclude that the underlying representation of roots is best revealed in the simple verb, rather than the perfective, since the simple form of the verb shows whether the stem ends with /i/, a vowel which may be deleted in the perfective.

A rather different conclusion about arriving at underlying forms would have to be drawn from the following additional Samoan examples.

(30)

Simple	Perfective		Simple	Perfective	
tu:	tu:lia	'stand'	au	aulia	'flow on'
tau	taulia	'cost'	ma:tau	ma:taulia	'observe'
ʔalo	ʔalofia	'avoid'	ili	ilifia	'blow'
oso	osofia	'jump'	ulu	ulufia	'enter'
sao	saofia	'collect'	taŋo	taŋofia	'take hold'
asu	asuŋia	'smoke'	soa	soaŋia	'have a friend'
pole	poleŋia	'be anxious'	fesili	fesiliŋia	'question'
ifo	ifoŋia	'bow down'	ʔote	ʔoteŋia	'scold'
ula	ulaŋia	'mock'	tofu	tofuŋia	'dive'
milo	milosia	'twist'	laʔa	laʔasia	'step'
valu	valusia	'scrape'	taŋi	taŋisia	'cry'
vela	velasia	'be cooked'	motu	motusia	'break'
api	apitia	'be lodged'	mataʔu	mataʔutia	'fear'
eʔe	eʔetia	'be raised'	sau	sautia	'fall'

lava:	lava:tia	'be able'	oʔo	oʔotia	'arrive'
u:	u:tia	'grip'	ufi	ufitia	'cover'
puni	punitia	'be blocked'	tanu	tanumia	'cover up'
siʔo	siʔomia	'be enclosed'	moʔo	moʔomia	'admire'
ŋalo	ŋalomia	'forget'	tao	taomia	'cover'
sopo	sopoʔia	'go across'	fana	fanaʔia	'shoot'

Here, we see that the perfective form of the verb contains a consonant which is not present in the simple form. That consonant can be any one of *l, f, ŋ, s, t, m* or *ʔ*, given these data. An attempt to predict the nature of that consonant by an insertion rule proves fruitless. We could attempt to insert an appropriate consonant on the basis of the preceding vowel: but while *l* appears after *u*, so do *f* ([ulufia]), *ŋ* ([tofuŋia]) and *s* ([valusia]); and while *f* appears after *o*, so do *ŋ* ([ifoŋia]), *m* ([ŋalomia]), and *s* ([milosia]). In short, it is simply impossible to predict from anything in the environment what the consonant of the perfective is going to be, if we start with the simple form as the underlying form: that consonant must be part of the underlying representation of the root. Thus the underlying forms of this second set of roots would be as follows.

(31)

tu:l	'stand'	aul	'flow on'
taul	'cost'	ma:taul	'observe'
ʔalof	'avoid'	ilif	'blow'
osof	'jump'	uluf	'enter'
saof	'collect'	taŋof	'take hold'
asuŋ	'smoke'	soaŋ	'have a friend'
poleŋ	'be anxious'	fesiliŋ	'question'
ifoŋ	'bow down'	ʔoteŋ	'scold'
ulaŋ	'mock'	tofuŋ	'dive'
milos	'twist'	laʔas	'step'
valus	'scrape'	taŋis	'cry'
velas	'be cooked'	motus	'break'
apit	'be lodged'	mataʔut	'fear'
eʔet	'be raised'	saut	'fall'
lava:t	'be able'	oʔot	'arrive'
u:t	'grip'	ufit	'cover'
punit	'be blocked'	tanum	'cover up'
siʔom	'be enclosed'	moʔom	'admire'
ŋalom	'forget'	taom	'cover'
sopoʔ	'go across'	fanaʔ	'shoot'

The postulation of underlying consonants at the end of these roots entails the addition of a phonological rule, in order to account for the surface form of the simple verb where there is no final consonant. Noting that no word ends in a consonant phonetically in these examples, we can postulate the following rule of final consonant deletion.

(32) *Final consonant deletion*
      C → Ø / _ #

The underlying forms of these verbs can be heuristically derived by eliminating the perfective affix -ia from the perfective form. However, notice that we made a different heuristic assumption for the first group of roots, which underlyingly ended in a vowel. The point is that an underlying representation is whatever is required to correctly predict all of the surface variants of a given morpheme: it does not necessarily derive from any one column in a paradigm.

It is also important to understand the difference between saying that the underlying form *is* the simple form, or *is* the perfective form, and saying that we may best *learn* what the underlying form is by looking at the perfective, or simple form, or some other form. The underlying form of the word for 'stand' is /tuːl/. We learn that this is the underlying form by comparing the simple form [tuː] and the perfective [tuːlia] and understanding that the perfective form preserves important information about the underlying form that is lost in the simple form. But the perfective form itself is [tuːlia] – this is not the underlying form.

Palauan.   The language Palauan provides a second clear illustration of the point that one cannot always arrive at the correct underlying representation by looking at any single column in the paradigm. In this language, the underlying form of the word does not actually surface as such in any form of a word. Consider the following examples:

(33) | *Present middle* | *Future innovative* | *Future conservative* | |
|---|---|---|---|
| mədáŋəb | dəŋəbáll | dəŋóbl | 'cover' |
| mətéʔəb | təʔəbáll | təʔíbl | 'pull out' |
| məŋétəm | ŋətəmáll | ŋətóml | 'lick' |
| mətábək | təbəkáll | təbákl | 'patch' |
| məʔárəm | ʔərəmáll | ʔəróml | 'taste' |
| məsésəb | səsəbáll | səsóbl | 'burn' |

The prefix for the present middle is apparently /mə/, the future suffix (found in the future conservative and the future innovative) is -*l*, and the innovative suffix is -*al*. The position of stress can be predicted by a simple rule: the final syllable is stressed if it ends in two consonants, otherwise the second to last (penultimate) syllable is stressed.

The fundamental problem of Palauan is how to predict vowel quality in the root. Notice that the root meaning of the word for 'cover' has three surface realizations: *dáŋəb*, *dəŋəb* and *dəŋób*. Looking at all of the data, we notice that the only full vowel in the word is the stressed vowel, which suggests that unstressed vowels are neutralized to schwa.

(34)   *Unstressed vowel reduction*
unstressed V → ə

Note that this rule has no context: it does not matter what precedes or follows the unstressed vowel.

In order to predict that the stressed first vowel in the word for 'cover' is [a], that choice of vowel must be part of the underlying representation, giving the partial solution /daŋVb/. In contrast, the first vowel of the word for 'pull out' must be specified as [e], since that is the vowel which appears in this word when the first vowel is stressed, giving /teʔVb/. By the same reasoning, the second vowel of the word for 'cover' must be [o], since that is the realization which the vowel has when it is stressed, and the second vowel of the word for 'pull out' must be [i]. Thus, the underlying forms of the stems given above would be the following.

(35) daŋob   'cover'   teʔib   'pull out'
      ŋetom   'lick'   tabak   'patch'
      ʔarom   'taste'   sesob   'burn'

The underlying form of a verb in Palauan is a rather abstract object, something which is never revealed in any single surface form. Rather, it must be deduced by looking at information which is manifested in a number of different morphologically related words derived from a single stem.

English. A similar example can be found in English, as the following examples show. We will ignore other alternations and focus only on vowel alternations. Thus for example, alternations such as the one between *k* and *s* can be ignored. There are many idiolectal differences in the pronunciation of certain words such as *economy*, where some people pronounce the word as [iykánəmiy] and others pronounce it as [əkánəmiy]: only attempt to account for the latter pronunciation.

(36) mánətown   'monotone'   mənátəniy   'monotony'
      téləgræf   'telegraph'   təlégrəfiy   'telegraphy'
      épəgræf   'epigraph'   əpígrəfiy   'epigraphy'
      rélətɪv   'relative'   rəléyšən   'relation'
      əkánəmiy   'economy'   èkənámɪk   'economic'
      díyfɛkt   'defect (noun)' dəféktɪv   'defective'
      déməkræt   'democrat'   dəmákrəsiy   'democracy'
      ítəliy   'Italy'   ətǽlyən   'Italian'
      hámənɪm   'homonym'   həmánəmiy   'homonymy'
      fənétɪks   'phonetics'   fòwnətíšən   'phonetician'
      stətístɪks   'statistics'   stǽtəstíšən   'statistician'
      rəsíprəkḷ   'reciprocal'   rèsəprásətiy   'reciprocity'
      fənáləjiy   'phonology'   fòwnəlájəkḷ   'phonological'
      lájɪk   'logic'   ləjíšn̩   'logician'
      sínənɪm   'synonym'   sənánəmiy   'synonymy'
      ərístəkræt   'aristocrat'   èrəstákrəsiy   'aristocracy'

As in Palauan, there is an alternation between stressed full vowel and unstressed schwa. We assume underlying stems with multiple full vowels, e.g. /manatown/, /tɛlɛgræf/, /ɛpɪgræf/, /dɛmakræt/, /fownalaǰ/, etc. But not every unstressed vowel is reduced: cf. for example *rélətɪv, díyfɛkt, mánətown* where the unstressed vowel is in a closed syllable (followed by one or more consonants within that syllable).

Tonkawa: reaching the analysis step-by-step. Correct assumptions about underlying forms are crucial in understanding the variations found in the verb stem in Tonkawa, as the following examples will illustrate. The first step in accounting for these data is to provide a morphological analysis of the data, to determine what the morphemes are for the progressive, the present, the first-singular object, and the third-plural object, and to set forth hypotheses about the underlying forms of roots.

(37)

picnoʔ	'he cuts'	picnanoʔ	'he is cutting'
wepcenoʔ	'he cuts them'	wepcenanoʔ	'he is cutting them'
kepcenoʔ	'he cuts me'	kepcenanoʔ	'he is cutting me'
notxoʔ	'he hoes'	notxonoʔ	'he is hoeing'
wentoxoʔ	'he hoes them'	wentoxonoʔ	'he is hoeing them'
kentoxoʔ	'he hoes me'	kentoxonoʔ	'he is hoeing me'
netloʔ	'he licks'	netlenoʔ	'he is licking'
wentaloʔ	'he licks them'	wentalenoʔ	'he is licking them'
kentaloʔ	'he licks me'	kentalenoʔ	'he is licking me'
naxcoʔ	'he makes fire'	naxcenoʔ	'he is making fire'
wenxacoʔ	'he makes them fire'	wenxacenoʔ	'he is making them fire'
kenxacoʔ	'he makes me fire'	kenxacenoʔ	'he is making me fire'
yamxoʔ	'he paints a face'	yamxanoʔ	'he is painting a face'
weymaxoʔ	'he paints their face'	weymaxanoʔ	'he is painting their face'
keymaxoʔ	'he paints my face'	keymaxanoʔ	'he is painting my face'
nawloʔ	'he spreads'	nawlenoʔ	'he is spreading'
wenweloʔ	'he spreads them'	wenwelenoʔ	'he is spreading them'
kenweloʔ	'he spreads me'	kenwelenoʔ	'he is spreading me'

It will be noticed that every word in this set ends with *oʔ*, and that all of these verb forms have a third-person subject, which suggests that *-oʔ* is a suffix marking a third-person subject. Comparing the habitual present forms in the first column with the corresponding present progressive form in the second column, it is also obvious that the present progressive is marked by a suffix, *-n-* or *-Vn-*, ordered before the suffix *-oʔ*. Marking of an object on the verb is accomplished by a prefix, *we-* for third-plural object and *ke-* for first-singular object. What remains is the verb stem.

Two problems now remain: determining whether the suffix for the progressive is *-n-*, or whether there is a vowel which is part of the suffix; and, what the underlying form of the verb root is. To resolve the first question, we look just at the forms of the verb with no object:

(38)

picnoʔ	picnanoʔ
notxoʔ	notxonoʔ
netloʔ	netlenoʔ

naxco?   naxceno?
yamxo?   yamxano?
nawlo?   nawleno?

We might think that the vowel before -*n*- is part of the progressive suffix, but if it were part of that suffix, it should have a constant underlying form and all surface variants of that vowel should be derived by some simple rule(s). It is obvious from these examples that the vowel which appears before *n* does not have a single phonetic realization since in these examples it ranges over *a, o* and *e*, and that there is no reasonable way to predict (e.g. from surrounding consonants or vowels) what vowel will appear before *n*. Since that information is unpredictable and is governed by which root appears before the suffix, the vowel must actually be part of the underlying form of the verb stem. Thus, we arrive at the following partial answer to the question about the underlying forms of the verb roots:

(39) /picna/   'cut'
      /notxo/   'hoe'
      /netle/   'lick'
      /naxce/   'make a fire'
      /yamxa/   'paint a face'
      /nawle/   'spread'

The progressive form of the verb can be derived straightforwardly by adding the two affixes -*n*- and -*o*?. The habitual present involves the application of a further phonological process. Based on our hypotheses regarding the underlying forms of the verb stems, we predict the following underlying forms for the habitual forms.

(40) *Predicted form*   *Actual surface form*
      picnao?   picno?   'cut'
      notxoo?   notxo?   'hoe'
      netleo?   netlo?   'lick'
      naxceo?   naxco?   'make a fire'
      yamxao?   yamxo?   'paint a face'
      nawleo?   nawlo?   'spread'

The underlying form is whatever is given by the morphological component, so in this case it would be the root plus progressive suffix, followed by the suffix -*o*?. Our initial hypothesis is that the underlying form should be identical to the surface form until we have evidence that phonological rules change the underlying forms in predictable ways. The difference between the predicted form and the actual surface realization of the verb is that the underlying form has a cluster of vowels which is not found in the surface form. The data do not provide any examples of surface vowel clusters, and this fact allows us to state a very simple rule accounting for the surface form: the first of two consecutive vowels is deleted.

(41)   *Vowel cluster reduction*
       V → Ø / _ V

   Now we turn to the alternations in the shape of the stem that arise
between the plain forms of the verb and the verb with an object prefix.
Verbs with the prefix *ke-* behave exactly like verbs with the prefix *we-*.
Disregarding the suffixes *-n-* and *-oʔ*, we arrive at the following surface
variations in the shape of the stem.

(42)   *Stem without prefix*   *Stem with CV prefix*
       picna   pcena   'cut'
       notxo   ntoxo   'hoe'
       netle   ntale   'lick'
       naxce   nxace   'make a fire'
       yamxa   ymaxa   'paint a face'
       nawle   nwele   'spread'

   Notice that in the form which lacks a prefix there is a vowel between the
first two consonants and none between the second and third consonants.
By contrast, in the form with a CV prefix, there is no vowel between the
first two consonants but there is a vowel between the second and third
consonants. One way to solve this problem would be to assume that this
vowel is epenthetic (inserted); the other is to assume that the vowel is
part of the underlying vowel of the stem and is deleted in some phonological context. It is also obvious that just as there is no way to predict
what vowel will appear between the first and second consonants, it is
also impossible to predict what vowel will appear between the second
and third consonants, and therefore the vowel cannot be epenthetic. In
short, the underlying representation must contain unpredictable vowels
after each consonant.

(43)   picena   'cut'
       notoxo   'hoe'
       netale   'lick'
       naxace   'make a fire'
       yamaxa   'paint a face'
       nawele   'spread'

   The underlying forms of prefixed and unprefixed forms would thus be
as follows (illustrating with the progressive form of the verb).

(44)   *Unprefixed*   *Prefixed*
       |picenanoʔ| |kepicenanoʔ| 'cut'
       |notoxonoʔ| |kenotoxonoʔ| 'hoe'
       |netalenoʔ| |kenetalenoʔ| 'lick'
       |naxacenoʔ| |kenaxacenoʔ| 'make a fire'
       |yamaxanoʔ| |keyamaxanoʔ| 'paint a face'
       |nawelenoʔ| |kenawelenoʔ| 'spread'

Compare this with the surface form of the verbs:

(45) *Unprefixed*   *Prefixed*
      picnano?   kepcenano?   'cut'
      notxono?   kentoxono?   'hoe'
      netleno?   kentaleno?   'lick'
      naxceno?   kenxaceno?   'make a fire'
      yamxano?   keymaxano?   'paint a face'
      nawleno?   kenweleno?   'spread'

The relation between the underlying forms in (44) and surface forms in (45) is simple. Each is subject to a rule deleting the second vowel of the word.

(46) V → Ø / # CVC __

Whether the first or second stem vowel is deleted depends on whether a prefix is present.

Apart from illustrating the point that underlying forms of words may not correspond to any single column in a word's paradigm, this discussion of Tonkawa illustrates two important characteristics of a phonological analysis. The first is that one analyzes data by advancing an initial hypothesis, and then refining the hypothesis as it becomes necessary. Thus we began with the hypothesis that the underlying forms were /picna/, /notxo/, /netle/ and so on, and were able to acount for a certain amount of data based on that hypothesis, but later modified our hypothesis about underlying forms to be /picena/, /notoxo/, /netale/ and so on. In other words, although our first hypothesis turned out to be wrong, it was close to right, and we were able to identify the source of the problem in our hypothesis and correct it.

The second characteristic of our analyis is that we always seek ways to test the predictions of our hypotheses. The hypothesis that the stems are underlying /picna/, /notxo/, /netle/, etc. makes a prediction that if a vowel were ever to appear between the second and third consonants (for example due to a rule of vowel insertion), it would always be a single consistent and predictable vowel (since we are saying that it is not in the underlying form). The fact that a *different* vowel appears in *wepceno?*, *wentoxo?*, *wentalo?* and *wenxaco?* shows that the prediction of this hypothesis is wrong, and this forced us to consider the alternative hypothesis that the underlying form contains a vowel between the second and third consonants: this hypothesis proved to be correct. The most basic form of hypothesis testing that is done in phonology is combining presumed forms of roots and affixes, and mechanically applying the rules which we assume in the analysis. If the wrong form is produced by this test, something is wrong with the hypothesis – either the underlying forms are wrong, or the rules are stated incorrectly (or the rules are being applied in the wrong order, a point we get to in the next chapter).

Summary

Establishing the correct underlying representation for a morpheme is the most important first step in giving a phonological analysis of data. A correct underlying representation unifies surface variants of a morpheme, giving recognition of the basic "sameness" of a morpheme, regardless of variations in pronunciation which arise because phonological rules have applied. The underlying form and the system of rules are thus connected: by making the right choice of underlying form, and given the right system of rules, the rules will correctly operate on just those segments which participate in the alternation. The key to making the right decision about underlying forms is to carefully consider different hypotheses: if a segment in a morpheme has two or more surface realisations, it is often necessary to consider two or more possibilities for what is underlying – is variant [a], [b] or [c] the right choice? The main issue relevant to answering this question is knowing which variant preserves important distinctions and which neutralizes distinctions. The underlying form may not even be seen directly in any one pronunciation of a morpheme: it may be a form inferred from considering a number of specific instantiations of the morpheme.

Exercises

1 Axininca Campa
Provide underlying representations and a phonological rule which will account for the following alternations:

toniro	'palm'	notoniroti	'my palm'
yaarato	'black bee'	noyaaratoti	'my black bee'
kanari	'wild turkey'	noyanariti	'my wild turkey'
kosiri	'white monkey'	noyosiriti	'my white monkey'
pisiro	'small toucan'	nowisiroti	'my small toucan'
porita	'small hen'	noworitati	'my small hen'

2 Kikuyu
What is the underlying form of the infinitive prefix in Kikuyu? Give a rule that explains the nonunderlying pronunciation of the prefix:

ɣoteŋera	'to run'	ɣokuua	'to carry'
ɣokoora	'to root out'	koruɣa	'to cook'
kooria	'to ask'	komɛɲa	'to know'
kohɔta	'to be able'	ɣočina	'to burn'
koɣeera	'to fetch'	kohetoka	'to pass'
koniina	'to finish'	koina	'to dance'
ɣočuuka	'to slander'	ɣokaya	'to cut'
koɣaya	'to divide'		

3 Korean
Give the underlying representations of each of the verb stems found below; state what phonological rule applies to these data. (Note: there is a vowel

harmony rule which explains the variation between final *a* and *ə* in the imperative, which you do not need to be concerned with.)

Imperative	Conjunctive	
ipə	ipk'o	'wear'
kupə	kupk'o	'bend'
kapʰa	kapk'o	'pay back'
čipʰə	čipk'o	'feel the pulse'
tata	tatk'o	'close'
putʰə	putk'o	'adhere'
məkə	məkk'o	'eat'
čukə	čukk'o	'die'
ikə	ikk'o	'ripen'
tak'a	takk'o	'polish'
k'ak'a	k'akk'o	'reduce expenses'
sək'ə	səkk'o	'mix'

4 Hungarian

Explain what phonological process affects consonants in the following data (a vowel harmony rule makes suffix vowels back after back vowels and front after front vowels, which you do not need to account for). State what the underlying forms are for all morphemes.

Noun	In N	From N	To N	
kalap	kalabban	kalapto:l	kalapnak	'hat'
ku:t	ku:dban	ku:tto:l	ku:tnak	'well'
ža:k	ža:gban	ža:kto:l	ža:knak	'sack'
re:s	re:zben	re:stö:l	re:snek	'part'
šro:f	šro:vban	šro:fto:l	šro:fnak	'screw'
laka:š	laka:žban	laka:što:l	laka:šnak	'apartment'
ketretˢ	ketredᶻben	ketretˢtö:l	ketretˢnek	'cage'
test	tezdben	testtö:l	testnek	'body'
rab	rabban	rapto:l	rabnak	'prisoner'
ka:d	ka:dban	ka:tto:l	ka:dnak	'tub'
meleg	melegben	melektö:l	melegnek	'warm'
vi:z	vi:zben	vi:stö:l	vi:znek	'water'
vara:ž	vara:žban	vara:što:l	vara:žnak	'magic'
a:gʸ	a:gʸban	a:kʸto:l	a:gʸnak	'bed'
sem	semben	semtö:l	semnek	'eye'
bün	bünben	büntö:l	bünnek	'crime'
toroñ	toroñban	toroñto:l	toroñnak	'tower'
fal	falban	falto:l	falnak	'wall'
ö:r	ö:rben	ö:rtö:l	ö:rnek	'guard'
sa:y	sa:yban	sa:yto:l	sa:ynak	'mouth'

5 Kuria

Provide appropriate underlying representations and phonological rules which will account for the following data:

Verb	Verb for	
suraaŋga	suraaŋgera	'praise'
taaŋgata	taaŋgatera	'lead'

baamba	baambera	'fit a drum head'
reenda	reendera	'guard'
rema	remera	'cultivate'
hoora	hoorera	'thresh'
roma	romera	'bite'
sooka	sookera	'respect'
tačora	tačorera	'tear'
siika	seekera	'close'
tiga	tegera	'leave behind'
ruga	rogera	'cook'
suka	sokera	'plait'
huuta	hootera	'blow'
riiŋga	reeŋgera	'fold'
siinda	seendera	'win'

6 Farsi

Give the underlying forms for the following nouns, and say what phonological rule is necessary to explain the following data:

Singular	Plural	
zæn	zænan	'woman'
læb	læban	'lip'
hæsud	hæsudan	'envious'
bæradær	bæradæran	'brother'
bozorg	bozorgan	'big'
mæleke	mælekean	'queen'
valede	valedean	'mother'
kæbire	kæbirean	'big'
ahu	ahuan	'gazelle'
hamele	hamelean	'pregnant'
bačče	baččegan	'child'
setare	setaregan	'star'
bænde	bændegan	'slave'
azade	azadegan	'freeborn'
divane	divanegan	'insane'

7 Tibetan

Numbers between 11 and 19 are formed by placing the appropriate digit after the number 10, and multiples of 10 are formed by placing the appropriate multiplier before the number 10. What are the underlying forms of the basic numerals, and what phonological rule is involved in accounting for these data?

ǰu	'10'	ǰig	'1'	ǰugǰig	'11'
ši	'4'	ǰubši	'14'	šibǰu	'40'
gu	'9'	ǰurgu	'19'	gubǰu	'90'
ŋa	'5'	ǰuŋa	'15'	ŋabǰu	'50'

8 Makonde

Explain what phonological rules apply in the following examples (the acute accent in these example marks stress, whose position is predictable):

Repeated imperative	Past	Imperative	
amáŋga	amíle	áma	'move'
tavánga	tavíle	táva	'wrap'
akáŋga	akíle	áka	'hunt'
patánga	patíle	póta	'twist'
tatánga	tatíle	tóta	'sew'
dabáŋga	dabíle	dóba	'get tired'
aváŋga	avíle	óva	'miss'
amáŋga	amíle	óma	'pierce'
tapánga	tapíle	tépa	'bend'
patánga	patíle	péta	'separate'
aváŋga	avíle	éva	'separate'
babáŋga	babíle	béba	'hold like a baby'
utáŋga	utíle	úta	'smoke'
lukáŋga	lukíle	lúka	'plait'
lumáŋga	lumíle	lúma	'bite'
uŋgáŋga	uŋgíle	úŋga	'tie'
iváŋga	ivíle	íva	'steal'
pitáŋga	pitíle	píta	'pass'
imbáŋga	imbíle	ímba	'dig'
limáŋga	limíle	líma	'cultivate'

9 North Saami

Posit appropriate underlying forms and any rules needed to explain the following alternations. The emphasis here should be on correctly identifying the underlying form: the exact nature of the changes seen here is a more advanced problem.

Nominative sg.	Essive	
varit	varihin	'2-year-old reindeer buck'
oahpis	oahpisin	'acquaintance'
čoarvuš	čoarvušin	'antlers, skullcap'
lottaaš	lottaaǰin	'small bird'
čuoivvat	čuoivvagin	'yellow brown reindeer'
ahhkut	ahhkubin	'grandchild of woman'
suohkat	suohkaðin	'thick'
heeǰoš	heeǰoǰin	'poor guy'
aaǰǰut	aaǰǰubin	'grandchild of man'
bissobeahtˢet	bissobeahtˢehin	'butt of gun'
čeahtˢit	čeahtˢibin	'children of elder brother of man'
yaaʔmin	yaaʔmimin	'death'
čuoivat	čuoivagin	'yellow-grey reindeer'
laageš	laageǰin	'mountain birch'
gahpir	gahpirin	'cap'
gaauhtˢis	gaauhtˢisin	'8 people'
aaslat	aaslagin	[man's name]
baðoošgaattˢet	baðoošgaattˢebin	'bird type'
ahhkit	ahhkiðin	'boring'
bahaanaalat	bahaanaalagin	'badly behaved'
beštor	beštorin	'bird type'
heevemeahhtun	heevemeahhtunin	'inappropriate'

beejot	beejohin	'white reindeer'
bissomeahtun	bissomeahtumin	'unstable'
laðas	laðasin	'something jointed'
heaiyusmielat	heaiyusmielagin	'unhappy'
heaŋkkan	heaŋkkanin	'hanger'
yaman	yamanin	'something that makes noise'

(Note: You may find it useful to return to this example after reading chapter 6, and consider the formalization of this process using distinctive features.)

Further reading

Inkelas 1994; Kaisse and Shaw 1985; Kenstowicz and Kisseberth 1977; Stanley 1967.

5 Interacting processes

PREVIEW

KEY TERMS
interaction
ordering

In this chapter, you will broaden your understanding of how phonological systems work by

◆ looking at more complex patterns of phonological alternation

◆ seeing how complex surface patterns of alternations result from the interaction of different but related phonological rules

◆ understanding the effect of different rule orderings on how an underlying form is changed into a surface form

Phonological systems are not made up of isolated and unrelated phonological rules: there are usually significant interactions between phonological processes. This chapter concentrates on two related topics. First, the fact that a seemingly complex set of alternations can often be given a simpler explanation if you separate the effect of different rules which often happen to apply in the same form. Second, applying rules in different orders can have a significant effect on the way that a given underlying form is mapped onto a surface form.

5.1 Separating the effects of different rules

Very often, when you analyze phonological alternations, insights into the nature of these alternations are revealed once you realize that a word may be subject to more than one rule, each of which may affect the same segment. You should not think of a phonology as being just a collection of direct statements of the relation between underlying segments and their surface realization. Such a description is likely to be confusing and complex, and will miss a number of important generalizations. Look for ways to decompose a problem into separate, smaller parts, stated in terms of simple and general rules. The different effects which these rules can have on a segment may accumulate, to give a seemingly complex pattern of phonetic change.

5.1.1 Votic: palatalization and raising/fronting
The following example from Votic (Russia) illustrates one way in which the account of phonological alternations can be made tractable by analyzing the alternations in terms of the interaction between independent phonological processes. In these examples, [ɫ] represents a velarized *l*.

(1) a.   *Nominative*   *Partitive*
          vərkko   vərkkoa   'net'
          čako   čakoa   'cuckoo'
          lintu   lintua   'bird'
          saatu   saatua   'garden'
          yałka   yałkaa   'foot'
          bočka   bočkaa   'barrel'
          einæ   einææ   'hay'
          vævü   vævüæ   'son-in-law'

     b.   siili   siiliæ   'hedgehog'
          łusti   łustia   'pretty'

     c.   yarvi   yarvəa   'lake'
          mæči   mæčeæ   'hill'
          čivi   čiveæ   'stone'

     d.   kurči   kurkəa   'stork'
          əłči   əłkəa   'straw'
          kahči   kahkəa   'birch'

The first group of examples (1a) shows that the nominative has no suffix, and the partitive has the suffix -*a* or -*œ* (the choice depends on the preceding vowels, determined by a vowel harmony rule according to which a suffix vowel is front if the preceding vowel is front – the rule skips over the vowel [i], but if there are no vowels other than [i] preceding, the harmony rule turns the suffix vowel into a front vowel). The second group of examples (1b) illustrates roots which have /i/ as the underlying final vowel of the root. The nouns in the third group (1c) illustrate a phenomenon of final vowel raising and fronting (which we have previously seen in closely related Finnish), whereby *e* and *ə* become [i] word-finally.

(2)   *Final fronting/raising*
      mid non-round vowel → front high / _ #

The essential difference between the examples of (1b) and (1c) is that the forms in (1b) underlyingly end in the vowel /i/, and those in (1c) end in /e/ or /ə/. In the last set of examples (1d), the noun root underlyingly ends in the sequence /kə/, which can be seen directly in *kurkə-a*. However, the final CV of the root appears as [či] in the nominative *kurči*.

It would be unrevealing to posit a rule changing word-final /kə#/ into [či#] in one step. A problem with such a rule is that the change of a velar to a palatal conditioned by following word-final schwa is not a process found in other languages, and depends on a very specific conjunction of facts, that is, not just schwa, but word-final schwa. You may not know at this point that such a rule is not found in other languages – part of learning about phonology is learning what processes do exist in languages, something you will have a better basis for judging by the end of this book. What you can see right now is that such a rule treats it as a coincidence that the underlying final schwa actually becomes [i] on the surface by an independently necessary rule, so that much of the supposed rule applying to /kə#/ is not actually specific to /kə#/.

This alternation makes more sense once it is decomposed into the two constituent rules which govern it, namely final raising (independently motivated by the data in (c)). Applying this rule alone to final /kə/ would result in the sequence [ki]. However, [ki] is not an allowed CV sequence in this language, and a process of palatalization takes place, in accordance with the following rule:

(3)   *Palatalization*
      k → č / _ i

We can thus account for the change of underlying /kurkə/ and /əɬkə/ to [kurči] and [əɬči] by applying these two rules in a specific order, where the rule of vowel raising applies before palatalization, so that vowel raising is allowed to create new occurrences of the vowel [i], and those derived cases of [i] condition the application of palatalization.

(4)   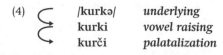   /kurkə/   *underlying*
              kurki   *vowel raising*
              kurči   *palatalization*

5.1.2 Kamba: palatalization and glide formation

There is a phonological process in Kamba (Kenya) whereby the combination of a velar consonant plus the glide *y* fuses into an alveopalatal affricate. This can be seen in (5), which involves the plain and causative forms of verbs. In the examples on the left, the verb is composed of the infinitive prefix /ko-/ (which undergoes a process of glide formation before another vowel, becoming [w]) followed by the verb root (e.g. *-kam-* 'milk'), plus an inflectional suffix *-a*. In the righthand column we can see the causative of the same verb, which is formed by suffixing *-y-* after the verb root before the inflectional marker *-a*.

(5)

	to V	*to Cause to V*	
a.	kokǎmǎ	kokǎmyǎ	'milk'
	kokonà	kokonyà	'hit'
	kolǎàmbà	kolǎàmbyà	'lap'
	kotǎlǎ	kotǎlyǎ	'count'
	kwaambatà	kwaambatyà	'go up'
	kwaàðà	kwaàðyà	'govern'
	kwéětǎ	kwéětyǎ	'answer'
	kwǐǐmbǎ	kwǐǐmbyǎ	'swell'
b.	koβikà	koβičà	'arrive'
	koβálokà	koβáločà	'fall'
	kolikà	količà	'enter'
	kolέèŋgà	kolέèñjà	'aim'
	kwéěŋgǎ	kwéěñjǎ	'clear a field'
	kwaanekà	kwaanečà	'dry'
	kwɔ́ɔkǎ	kwɔ́ɔčǎ	'gather coals'

The examples in (a) illustrate the causative affix following various non-velar consonants of the language. In (b), we see the causative of various roots which end in *k* or *g*, where by analogy to the data in (a) we predict the causatives /koβikyà/, /koβálokyà/, /kolέèngyà/, and so on. Instead of the expected consonant sequences *ky*, *gy*, we find instead that the velar consonant has been replaced by an alveopalatal affricate, due to the following rule:

(6) *Palatalization*
    ky, gy → č, ǰ

Examples of glide formation are seen in (5), where the vowel /o/ becomes [w] before another vowel. This process of glide formation is further illustrated in (7) and (8). In (7), we can see across all of the columns that the prefix for the infinitive is /ko/, and appears phonetically as such when it stands before another consonant. The last three data columns show that the prefixes marking different classes of objects are /mó/ for class 3, /mé/ for class 4, and /ké/ for class 7 (Kamba nouns have a dozen grammatical agreement classes, analogous to gender in some European languages).

(7) | *to V* | *to V it (cl 3)* | *to V them (cl 4)* | *to V it (cl 7)* | |
| --- | --- | --- | --- | --- |
| koðukà | komóðukà | koméðukà | kokéðukà | 'churn' |
| kokaàðà | komókaàðà | komékaàðà | kokékaàðà | 'praise' |
| koliìndà | komóliìndà | koméliìndà | kokéliìndà | 'cover' |
| koménắ | komóménắ | koméménắ | kokéménắ | 'hate' |
| koñuβà | komóñuβà | koméñuβà | kokéñuβà | 'choose' |

When the verb root begins with a vowel, we would predict a sequence of vowels such as **koasya* for 'to lose.' Vowel sequences are avoided in Kamba by the application of the rule of glide formation, according to which any nonlow vowel becomes a glide before another vowel.

> *The stem-initial vowel in these examples becomes long, as a side-effect of the preceding vowel becoming a glide: this is known as* **compensatory lengthening**.

(8) | *to V* | *to V it (cl 3)* | *to V them (cl 4)* | *to V it (cl 7)* | |
| --- | --- | --- | --- | --- |
| kwắắsyắ | komwắắsyắ | komyắắsyắ | kočắắsyắ | 'lose' |
| kwắắkắ | komwắắkắ | komyắắkắ | kočắắkắ | 'build' |
| kwaàsà | komwắàsà | komyắàsà | kočắàsà | 'carve' |
| kốốmbắ | komốốmbắ | komyốốmbắ | kočốốmbắ | 'mold' |
| kookelyà | komóokelyà | komyóokelyà | kočóokelyà | 'lift' |
| kắ́ắ́nắ | komắ́ắ́nắ | komyắ́ắ́nắ | kočắ́ắ́nắ | 'fetch' |
| kuumbekà | komúumbekà | komyúumbekà | kočúumbekà | 'bury' |
| kwéénzắ | komwéénzắ | komyéénzắ | kočéénzắ | 'shave' |
| kwɛɛ̀ndà | komwɛɛ̀ndà | komyɛɛ̀ndà | kočɛɛ̀ndà | 'like' |
| kwɔɔ́nắ | komwɔɔ́nắ | komyɔɔ́nắ | kočɔɔ́nắ | 'see' |
| kwɔɔ́sắ | komwɔɔ́sắ | komyɔɔ́sắ | kočɔɔ́sắ | 'take' |
| kwɔɔ́βắ | komwɔɔ́βắ | komyɔɔ́βắ | kočɔɔ́βắ | 'tie' |

The glide formation rule can be formalized as (9).

(9) *Glide formation*
   e, o → y, w /   V

This rule would be expected to apply to underlying forms such as /ko-una/ 'to fetch' and /ko-omba/ 'to mold,' since those forms have an underlying sequence of a vowel /o/ followed by another vowel. Applying that rule would result in **[kwắ́ắ́nắ] and **[kwốốmbắ], but these are not the correct forms. We can resolve this problem once we observe that the glide [w] never appears between a consonant and the two highest round vowels [u, o] (it can appear before the vowel [ɔ], as seen in [kwɔɔ́nắ] 'to see' from /ko-ɔna/).

It does not help to restrict rule (9) so that it does not apply before /o, u/, since the vowel /e/ does actually undergo glide formation before these vowels (/ko-me-okelya/ becomes [komyóokelyà] 'to lift them' and /ko-mé-únắ/ becomes [komyắ́ắ́nắ] 'to fetch them'). What seems to be a restriction on glide formation is highly specific: the round vowel fails to surface as a glide only if the following vowel is *o* or *u*. Furthermore, the round vowel does not merely fail to become a glide, it actually deletes, so we can't just rewrite (9) so that it doesn't apply before [u, o] since that would give *[koŭná] and *[koómbă]). Two rules are required to account for these vowel-plus-vowel combinations. A very simple solution to this problem is to allow the most general form of the glide formation rule to apply, imposing no restrictions, and derive the intermediate forms *kwŭŭná* and *kwŏŏmbă*. Since we have observed that the surface sequences [Cwo] and [Cwu] (where "C" is "any consonant") is lacking in the language, we may posit the following rule of glide deletion, which explains both why such sequences are lacking and what happened to the expected glide in the intermediate forms.

(10)   *Homorganic glide deletion*
       w → Ø / C _ o,u

The interaction between these processes, that the general glide formation rule first creates a glide, which is then deleted in a restricted subset of forms by (10), is expressed by ordering glide formation before glide deletion.

   Another crucial rule interaction is between glide formation and palatalization. As we have seen, palatalization specifically applies to *ky* and *gy*, which involve glides, and glide formation creates glides from vowels, whose creating can trigger application of palatalization. This is shown in the derivation of [kočăăsyă] from /ko-ké-ăăsyă/.

(11)   /ko-ké-ăăsyă/   *underlying*
       kokyăăsyă   *glide formation*
       kočăăsyă   *palatalization*

Thus glide formation creates phonological structures which are crucially referenced by other phonological rules.

5.1.3 Bukusu: nasal+consonant combinations

The theme which we have been developing in this chapter is that phonological grammars are composed of simpler elements that interact in sometimes complex ways, and that this factoring-out of the fundamental processes is an essential part of phonological analysis. In the examples which we have considered above, such as vowel raising/fronting and velar palatalization in Votic, or syncope and vowel raising in Tagalog, or glide formation and palatalization in Kamba, the phonological processes have been sufficiently different that it would be very difficult to subsume these processes under one rule. Often, a language may have a set of phonological changes which are very similar in nature, or which apply in very similar or even identical environments, and the question arises whether the alternations in question reflect a single phonological rule. Or, do the alternations reflect the operation of more than one independent rule, with only accidental partial similarity? Such a situation arises in Bukusu (Kenya), where a number of phonological changes affect the combination of a nasal plus a consonant. Here, we are faced with a set of similar phonological changes – changes in consonants which are preceded by nasals – and the question is should these processes be combined into one rule?

Place assimilation and voicing. In the first set of examples in (12), a voicing rule makes all underlyingly voiceless consonants voiced when preceded by a nasal, in this case the prefix for the first-singular present-tense subject which is /n/. The underlying consonant at the beginning of the root is revealed directly when the root is preceded by the third-plural prefix *βa-*, or when there is no prefix as in the imperative.

(12)

Imperative	3pl pres.	1sg pres	
ča	βača	ñǰa	'go'
čexa	βačexa	ñǰexa	'laugh'
čučuuŋga	βačučuuŋga	ñǰučuuŋga	'sieve'
talaanda	βatalaanda	ndalaanda	'go around'
teexa	βateexa	ndeexa	'cook'
tiira	βatiira	ndiira	'get ahold of'
piima	βapiima	mbiima	'weigh'
pakala	βapakala	mbakala	'writhe in pain'
ketulula	βaketulula	ŋgetulula	'pour out'
kona	βakona	ŋgona	'pass the night'
kula	βakula	ŋgula	'buy'
kwa	βakwa	ŋgwa	'fall'

We can state this voicing rule as follows.

(13) *Postnasal voicing*
     voiceless → voiced / nasal __

You will also note that a nasal consonant always agrees in place of articulation with the following consonant, a process which we will notate informally as follows (where "αplace. . . .αplace" means "the same place of articulation": this will be discussed in more detail in later chapters).

(14) *Nasal place assimilation*

$$\text{nasal} \rightarrow \alpha\text{place} \underline{\quad} \begin{bmatrix} C \\ \alpha\text{place} \end{bmatrix}$$

The data considered so far have not given clear evidence as to what the underlying place of articulation of the first-singular subject prefix is, since that nasal always assimilates to the following consonant. To determine that the prefix is indeed /n/, we turn to the form of stems which underlyingly begin with a vowel, where there is no assimilation. In the imperative, where no prefix precedes the stem, the glide [y] is inserted before the initial vowel. (The data in (17) include examples of underlying initial /y/, which is generally retained.) When the third-plural prefix /βa/ precedes the stem, the resulting vowel sequence is simplified to a single nonhigh vowel. No rules apply to the first-singular prefix, which we can see surfaces as [n] before all vowels.

(15) *Imperative*   *3pl pres.*   *1sg pres*
      yiixala   βeexala   niixala   'sit'
      yaasama   βaasama   naasama   'gape'
      yoola   βoola   noola   'arrive'
      yeekesya   βeekesya   neekesya   'show'

One question that we ought to consider is the ordering of the rules of voicing and place assimilation. In this case, the ordering of the rules does not matter: whether you apply voicing first and assimilation second, or assimilation first and voicing second, the result is the same.

(16)   /n-kwa/   /n-kwa/
      voicing   ngwa   assimilation   ŋkwa
      assimilation   ŋgwa   voicing   ŋgwa

The reason why the ordering does not matter is that the voicing rule does not refer to the place of articulation of the nasal, and the assimilation rule does not refer to the voicing of the following consonant.

Postnasal hardening.   There is another process of consonant hardening which turns the voiced continuants into appropriate noncontinuants after a nasal: *l* and *r* become *d*, *β* becomes *b*, and *y* becomes *ǰ*.

(17) *Imperative*   *3pl pres.*   *1sg pres*
      lola   βalola   ndola   'look'
      lasa   βalasa   ndasa   'shoot at'
      leβa   βaleβa   ndeβa   'push'
      lwaala   βalwaala   ndwaala   'be sick'
      ra   βara   nda   'put'
      rara   βarara   ndara   'be stung'
      roβa   βaroβa   ndoβa   'ripen'
      rusya   βarusya   ndusya   'vomit'
      rya   βarya   ndya   'fear'
      βakala   βaβakala   mbakala   'spread'
      βala   βaβala   mbala   'count'
      βasa   βaβasa   mbasa   'forge'
      βoola   βaβoola   mboola   'tell'
      yama   βayama   ñǰama   'scout'
      yaaya   βayaaya   ñǰaaya   'scramble with'
      yoola   βayoola   ñǰoola   'scoop'
      yuula   βayuula   ñǰuula   'snatch'

These data can be accounted for by the following rule:

(18) *Postnasal hardening*
      voiced continuant → noncontinuant / nasal __

This statement of the rule illustrates a simplification often made in the way that rules are stated: they are typically written to specify the bare essentials of the change, leaving the exact phonetic consequences of the rule to be filled in by general principles. Consider first the fact that /β/ becomes [b]: this change is accurately described just by the statement that voiced continuants become stops after nasals, since the only difference between [β] and [b] is that [β] is a continuant. However, [r] and [d] differ in two respects: first, [r] is a continuant, and second, [r] is a sonorant whereas [d] is an obstruent. The question is, what would it mean for /r/ to change into a stop which was still a sonorant (as is implied by the rule statement (18))? Sonorant stops are not common in the languages of the world, and are generally restricted to nasals. In analyzing the change of /r/ to [d] as nothing more than a change from continuant to stop, we take advantage of the fact that some changes in phonetic value are automatic side effects of general principles of possible language sounds, and need not be stated in the rule itself. In the case of the change of /r/ to [d], the subsidiary change is from sonorant to obstruent status, being brought about by the lack of oral sonorant stops in languages.

> *The reason is the conflict between the aerodynamic requirements of sonorants and the effect of oral stops on airflow: sonorants require unimpeded airflow, but oral stops have no airflow.*

Analogous reasoning is seen in the change of /l/ to [d] after a nasal. The only other difference from the change of /r/ to [d] is that the resulting sound becomes nonlateral. What would be the result if /l/ were to simply change to being a stop? We expect a change to obstruent status, but what is a lateral obstruent? There actually is such a segment in some languages: a voiced lateral affricate [dˡ] does exist in Tlingit and Navaho. But such a segment is very rare, and in particular does not exist in Bukusu. Given the knowledge that the segment [dˡ] does not exist in Bukusu, you can preclude [dˡ] as being the actual output of a rule which makes /l/ be a stop.

This same approach explains why /y/ becomes [j]. As with *r* and *l*, we expect a change of /y/ to being an obstruent. There does exist an obstruent stop corresponding to /y/ found in languages, namely [ɟ]. As with the immediately preceding case of /l/ becoming [d], we note that there is no segment [ɟ] in Bukusu. We will discover, as we investigate phonological patterns in various languages, that it is not unusual to encounter such effects, where certain classes of segments that are the output of phonological rules are subject to minor readjustments, to bring the result of the rule into conformity with general properties of segments in the language. When the results of a rule are subject to such adjustments, to bring the output into conformity with the phonemic inventory of the language, the rule is said to be **structure preserving**

The independence of voicing and hardening.   You might want to state these two processes, rules (13) and (18), as a single rule which both voices voiceless stops and makes voiced continuants into stops after a nasal, since in both cases, the consonant that appears after the nasal is a voiced stop. Rather than try to accomplish all of this with a single rule, we will assume that there are two separate rules, one which accounts for voicing and the other which turns continuants into stops. This way, each rule will perform a single phonetic change in one unified context: the question of just how much a single rule can actually do is discussed in more detail in later chapters.

Postnasal l-deletion.   A third process affecting sequences of nasal plus consonant can be seen in the following data.

(19)		*Imperative*	*3pl pres.*	*1sg pres*	
	a.	tima	βatima	ndima	'run'
		taaña	βataaña	ndaaña	'hack'
		tiiŋa	βatiiŋa	ndiiŋa	'filter'
		rema	βarema	ndema	'chop'
		riina	βariina	ndiina	'run away'
		ruma	βaruma	nduma	'send'
	b.	laanda	βalaanda	naanda	'go around'
		laaŋgwa	βalaaŋgwa	naaŋgwa	'be named'
		liinda	βaliinda	niinda	'wait'
		loma	βaloma	noma	'say'
		loondelela	βaloondelela	noondelela	'follow'
		luma	βaluma	numa	'bite'

The examples in (a) show the effect of rules of voicing and consonant hardening, applying as expected to /t/ and /r/. However, the examples in (b) show the deletion of underlying /l/ after a nasal. These examples contrast with the first set of examples in (17), where the root also begins with underlying /l/: the difference between the two sets of verbs is that in the second set, where /l/ deletes, the following consonant is a nasal, whereas in the first set where /l/ does not delete, the next consonant is not a nasal.

The significance of the examples in (19a) is that although underlying /t/, /l/ and /r/ all become [d] after a nasal, the deletion of an underlying consonant in the environment N_VN only affects underlying /l/. Since the voicing and hardening rules would neutralize the distinction between the three consonants after a nasal but in fact /l/ acts differently from /t/ and /r/ in the context N_VN, we can deduce that there must be a rule deleting /l/ – but not /t/ or /r/ – in this context.

(20)   *l-deletion*
  l → Ø / nasal _ V nasal

Furthermore, this rule clearly must apply before the hardening rule changes /l/ into [d] after a nasal, since otherwise there would be no way to restrict this rule to applying only to underlying /l/. Once the hardening rule (18) applies, underlying /n-liinda/ would become *n-diinda*, but /n-riina/ would also become *n-diina*. Once that has happened, there would be no way to predict the actual pronunciations [niinda] and [ndiina].

On the other hand, if you were to apply the *l*-deletion rule first, the rule could apply in the case of /n-liinda/ to give [niinda], but would not apply to /n-riina/ because that form does not have an *l*: thus by crucially ordering the rules so that *l*-deletion comes first, the distinction between /l/, which deletes, and /r/, which does not delete, is preserved.

Nasal degemination.   Another phonological process applies to consonants after nasal consonants. When the root begins with a nasal consonant, the expected sequence of nasal consonants simplifies to a single consonant.

(21)

Imperative	3pl pres.	1sg pres	
mala	βamala	mala	'finish'
manya	βamanya	manya	'know'
meela	βameela	meela	'get drunk'
ŋoola	βaŋoola	ŋoola	'see into the spirit world'
ña	βaña	ña	'defecate'
ñaaña	βañaaña	ñaaña	'chew'
ñwa	βañwa	ñwa	'drink'

Thus, in the case of *mala* 'I finish,' the underlying form would be /n-mala/ which would undergo the place assimilation rule (14), resulting in **mmala*. According to the data we have available to us, there are no sequences of identical consonants in the language, so it is reasonable to posit the following rule.

(22)   *Degemination*
$C_iC_i \rightarrow C_i$

The information notation "C_iC_i" means "two consonants with the same value."

Nasal deletion.   The final process which applies to sequences of nasal plus consonant is one deleting a nasal before a voiceless fricative.

(23)

Imperative	3pl pres.	1sg pres	
fuma	βafuma	fuma	'spread'
fuundixa	βafuundixa	fuundixa	'knot'
fwa	βafwa	fwa	'die'
xala	βaxala	xala	'cut'
xalaaŋga	βaxalaaŋga	xalaaŋga	'fry'
xweesa	βaxweesa	xweesa	'pull'
seesa	βaseesa	seesa	'winnow'
siimbwa	βasiimbwa	siimbwa	'have indigestion'
somya	βasomya	somya	'teach'
sukuwa	βasukuwa	sukuwa	'rub legs'
sya	βasya	sya	'grind'

The predicted underlying form of *fuma* 'I spread' is /n-fuma/, which contains a sequence of nasal plus fricative. However, our data indicate that this sequence does not appear anywhere in the language, so we may presume that such sequences are eliminated by the following rule of nasal deletion.

(24)   *Nasal deletion*
       nasal → Ø / __ voiceless continuant

Summary.   We have found in Bukusu that there are a number of phonological processes which affect N+C clusters, by voicing, hardening, or deleting the second consonant, or deleting the nasal before a nasal or a voiceless fricative.

(25)   *Postnasal voicing* (13)   voiceless → voiced / nasal __

       Nasal place assimilation (14)   nasal → αplace / __ $\begin{bmatrix} C \\ \alpha\text{place} \end{bmatrix}$

       l-deletion (20)   l → Ø / nasal __ V nasal
       Postnasal hardening (18)   voiced continuant → stop / nasal __
       Degemination (22) $C_i C_i → C_i$
       Nasal deletion (24)   nasal → Ø / __ voiceless continuant

Despite some similarity in these processes, in that they apply in the same general environment, there is no reasonable way to state these processes as one single rule.

In addition to showing how a complex system of phonological alternations decomposes into simpler, independent, and partially intersecting rules, the preceding analyses reveal an important component of phonological analysis, which is observing regularities in data, such as the fact that Bukusu lacks any consonant sequences composed of a nasal plus a fricative on the surface.

This raises the question how we are to determine that such observations about data are empirically valid: how do we know that the data which we see are representative of the whole language? The confidence with which hypotheses can be made is a function of size of the database available for testing the hypothesis. If a corpus contains only one or two examples, it is very hard to give any level of confidence to the general correctness of any observations made from such a small corpus; on the other hand, if the available corpus contains tens of thousands of datapoints, a much higher level of confidence can be assigned to inferences about the language (provided that the datapoints are taken from various areas of the language: ten thousand examples of verbs in the past tense will tell you little about what will be seen in plural nouns). Even so, a hypothesis supported by tens of thousands of observations may be falsified by the next observation.

To give you an idea of the scale of research needed to become fully confident about a hypothesis regarding a language, consider this example from my own work in Kerewe. After working for three years on Kerewe, I only observed [b] after [m], and, given the tens of thousands of available examples, concluded that [b] only appears after a nasal. Three more years of research turned up four words with [b] not preceded by [m]. The initial hypothesis was falsified: but it was very unlikely that the hypothesis would be falsified.

5.1.4 Kimatuumbi

The following data from Kimatuumbi illustrate the different surface realizations of the noun-class prefixes (nouns are assigned lexically or syntactically to different classes, conventionally numbered between 1 and 21). What phonological rule applies in these examples?

(26) | *Class* | *C-initial noun* | | *V-initial noun* | |
       | --- | --- | --- | --- | --- |
       | 4 | mi-kaáte | 'loaves' | my-oótó | 'fires' |
       | 5 | li-kuŋuúnda | 'filtered beer' | ly-oowá | 'beehive' |

7	ki-kálaaŋgo	'frying pan'	ky-uúlá	'frog'
8	i-kálaaŋgo	'frying pans'	y-uúlá	'frogs'
14	u-tópe	'mud'	w-ımbı	'beer'
11	lu-toóndwa	'star'	lw-aaté	'banana hand'
13	tu-tóopé	'little handles'	tw-aána	'little children'
15	ku-suúle	'to school'	kw-iisíwá	'to the islands'
16	mu-kikú	'in the navel'	mw-iikú	'in the navels'

The examples in (27) illustrate one of the results of an optional rule deleting the vowel *u* after *m*, hence in these words, the prefix /mu/ can be pronounced in two ways, one with *u* and one without *u*. There is an independent rule in the language which assimilates a nasal to the place of articulation of the following consonant (we have seen that rule in previous Kimatuumbi data in chapters 3 and 4). What other phonological process is illustrated by the following data? (An alternative transcription of this form would be *ŋŋwesa*: the point of writing this as [ŋʷ] is to make clear that there is a change in the nature of the initial segment, and not the addition of another segment.)

(27) *Unreduced form*   *Reduced form*
    mu-wesa . . .   ŋ-ŋʷesa   'you (pl) can'
    mu-wíkıliile   ŋ-ŋʷíkıliile   'you (pl) covered'
    mu-yíkıtiile   ñ-ñíkıtiile   'you (pl) agreed'
    mu-yóyʊʊtite   ñ-ñóyʊʊtite   'you (pl) whispered'
    mu-wuúngo   ŋ-ŋʷuúngo   'in the civet'
    mu-yıíga   ñ-ñıíga   'in the body'

(This rule only applies between nasals and glides in separate morphemes.)

The examples in (28) illustrate the point that nouns which are in class 7 in the singular (which is marked with the prefix *ki-*) have their plural in class 8 (with the prefix *i-*). The plural locative form gives further illustration of a phonological process which has previously been motivated for the language, in this section.

(28) *Singular* (cl 7)   *Plural* (cl 8)   *Plural locative*
    ki-báo   i-báo   mwii-báo   'stool'
    ki-bıgá   i-bıgá   mwii-bıgá   'pot'
    ki-bíliítu   i-bíliítu   mwii-bíliítu   'box of matches'
    ki-bógoyó   i-bógoyó   mwii-bógoyó   'toothless person'

How do you explain the following examples of nouns, which also have singulars in class 7 and plurals in class 8, given that the class prefixes in these examples are underlyingly /ki-/ and /i/-?

(29) *Singular* (cl 7)   *Plural* (cl 8)   *Plural locative*
    kyáai   yáai   muyáai ~ ññáai   'soup pot'
    kyaáka   yaáka   muyaáka ~ ññaáka   'bush'

| kyɪɪkí | yɪɪkí | muyɪɪkí ~ ññɪɪkí | 'stump' |
| kyuúbá | yuúbá | muyuúbá ~ ññuúbá | 'chest' |

5.2 Different effects of rule ordering

Besides showing how greater generality can often be achieved by splitting a process into smaller pieces, these examples have illustrated that the application of one rule can bring into existence new environments where the second rule can apply, an environment which did not exist in the underlying form. What we observed happening in these cases was that both of the rules applied. Not all interactions between phonological processes have this characteristic – sometimes applying one rule presents a second rule from applying – and in this section we consider some of the effects of different rule orderings.

5.2.1 Lamba: harmony and palatalization

The following data illustrate the interaction between a rule of vowel harmony and a palatalization rule in the language Lamba (Zambia):

(30)

Plain	Passive	Neuter	Applied	Reciprocal	
čita	čitwa	čitika	čitila	čitana	'do'
tula	tulwa	tulika	tulila	tulana	'dig'
četa	četwa	četeka	četela	četana	'spy'
soŋka	soŋkwa	soŋkeka	soŋkela	soŋkana	'pay tax'
pata	patwa	patika	patila	patana	'scold'
fisa	fiswa	fišika	fišila	fisana	'hide'
česa	česwa	česeka	česela	česana	'cut'
kosa	koswa	koseka	kosela	kosana	'be strong'
lasa	laswa	lašika	lašila	lasana	'wound'
masa	maswa	mašika	mašila	masana	'plaster'
šika	šikwa	šičika	šičila	šikana	'bury'
seka	sekwa	sekeka	sekela	sekana	'laugh at'
poka	pokwa	pokeka	pokela	pokana	'receive'
kaka	kakwa	kačika	kačila	kakana	'tie'
fuka	fukwa	fučika	fučila	fukana	'creep'

In order to see what these data show, we must first understand the morphological structure of these words, a step which leads us to realize that the pronunciation of certain morphemes changes, depending on their phonetic context. Verbs in Lamba are composed of a root of the form CV(C)C, an optional derivational affix marking passive, neuter, applied or reciprocal, and a word-final suffix -a which marks the form as being a verb. The underlying forms of the passive and reciprocal suffixes are clearly -w- and -an-, since they exhibit no phonetic variations. The neuter and applied suffixes appear phonetically as -ik- and -ek-, -il- and -el-. The choice of vowel in the suffix is determined by the vowel which precedes the suffix: if the verb root contains the vowel i, u or a the suffix has the vowel i, and if the root contains the vowel *e* or *o* the suffix has the vowel *e*. The group of vowels *i, u, a* is not a natural phonetic class, so it is implausible that the suffixes are underlyingly *-el-* and *-ek-* with *-il-* and *-ik-* being derived by a rule. The class of vowels *e, o* is the phonetic class of mid vowels; it is thus evident that this language has a vowel harmony rule which assimilates underlying high vowels (in the suffixes /il/ and /ik/) to mid vowels when they are preceded by mid vowels.

(31)   *Height harmony*
    i → e / mid vowel __

There is an alternation in the realization of certain root-final consonants. As shown in examples such as *kaka* ~ *kačika* and *lasa* ~ *lašika*, the velar consonants and the alveolar continuant *s* become alveopalatals when they are followed by the vowel *i*, by a process of palatalization.

(32)   *Palatalization*
    k, s → č, š / __ i

The interaction between these processes is seen in words which could in principle undergo both of these processes: roots with the vowel *e* or *o*, and the final consonant *k* or *s*. The example *sekeka* 'laugh at' from /sek-ik-a/ shows how these processes interact. Suppose, first, that palatalization were to apply before vowel harmony. Since the underlying representation has the sequence /ki/ which is required by palatalization, that rule would apply. Subsequently, vowel harmony would assimilate /i/ to [e] after /e/, giving the wrong surface result. This is illustrated below in a derivation which spells out the results of applying first palatalization, then height harmony.

(33)   /sek-ik-a/   *underlying*
    sečika   *palatalization*
    *sečeka   *height harmony*

Thus, applying the rules in this order gives the wrong results: this order cannot be correct.

    On the other hand, if we apply the processes in the other order, with height harmony applying before palatalization, then the correct form is generated.

(34)   /sek-ik-a/   *underlying*
    sekeka   *height harmony*
    (not applicable)   *palatalization*

5.2.2 Voicing and epenthesis
Lithuanian.   Another example which illustrates how an earlier rule can change a form in such a way that a later rule can no longer apply is

found in Lithuanian. There is a process of voicing assimilation in Lithuanian whereby obstruents agree in voicing with an immediately following obstruent. This rule applies in the following examples to the verbal prefixes /at/ and /ap/.

(35) a.   /at/   at-eiti   'to arrive'
                        at-imti   'to take away'
                        at-nešti   'to bring'
                        at-leisti   'to forgive'
                        at-likti   'to complete'
                        at-ko:pti   'to rise'
                        at-praši:ti   'to ask'
                        at-kurti   'to reestablish'
            /ap/   ap-eiti   'to circumvent'
                        ap-ieško:ti   'to search everywhere'
                        ap-akti   'to become blind'
                        ap-mo:ki:ti   'to train'
                        ap-temdi:ti   'to obscure'
                        ap-šaukti   'to proclaim'

      b.   /at/   ad-bekti   'to run up'
                        ad-gauti   'to get back'
                        ad-bukti   'to become blunt'
                        ad-gimti   'to be born again'
            /ap/   ab-gauti   'to deceive'
                        ab-žʸureti   'to have a look at'
                        ab-želti   'to become overgrown'
                        ab-dauži:ti   'to damage'
                        ab-draski:ti   'to tear'

We would assume that the underlying forms of the prefixes are /at/ and /ap/, and that there is a rule which voices obstruents before voiced obstruents.

(36)   *Voicing assimilation*
       obstruent → voiced / __ voiced obstruent

The alternative hypothesis would be that the prefixes are underlyingly /ad/ and /ab/. However, there is no natural context for describing the process of devoicing. Although devoicing of voiced obstruents before voiceless obstruents is quite natural, assuming that the prefixes have underlying voiced obstruents would also require the consonant to be devoiced before vowels and sonorant consonants, in order to account for the supposed derivations /ad-eiti/ → [ateiti], /ab-eiti/ → [apeiti], /ad-nešti/ → [atnešti] and /ab-mo:ki:ti/ → [apmo:ki:ti]. But there is clearly no constraint against voiced obstruents before vowels and sonorants in this language (in fact, no language has ever been attested with a rule of consonant devoicing where the conditioning environment is a following vowel). On the basis of this reasoning, we conclude that the prefixes have underlying voiceless consonants.

When the initial consonant of the root is an alveolar stop, the vowel [i] appears after the prefix /at/, and similarly when the initial consonant is a bilabial stop, [i] is inserted after the consonant of /ap/.

(37) ati-duoti   'to give back'
      ati-dari:ti   'to open'
      ati-deti   'to delay'
      ati-teisti   'to adjudicate'
      api-berti   'to strew all over'
      api-begti   'to run around'
      api-puti   'to grow rotten'

Given just the voicing assimilation rule, you would expect forms such as *[adduoti], *[abberti] by analogy to [adbekti] and [abdauži:ti]. Lithuanian does not allow sequences of identical consonants, so to prevent such a result, an epenthetic vowel is inserted between homorganic obstruent stops (which is notated in the rule by placing "αplace" under each of the consonants).

(38) *Epenthesis*
      $\emptyset \rightarrow$ i / obstruent stop __obstruent stop
                  [αplace]   [αplace]

The ordering of these rules is important: epenthesis (38) must apply before voicing assimilation, since otherwise the prefix consonant would assimilate the voicing of the root-initial consonant and would then be separated from that consonant by the epenthetic vowel. The result of applying the voicing assimilation rule first would be to create [adduoti], [abberti], and then this would undergo vowel epenthesis to give incorrect *[adiduoti], *[abiberti]. If, on the other hand, epenthesis is the first rule applied, then underlying /at-duoti/ becomes [atiduoti] and /ap-berti/ becomes [apiberti]. Epenthesis eliminates the underlying cluster of obstruents, preventing the voicing rule from applying.

Armenian. Interestingly, a similar pair of rules exists in the New Julfa (Iran) dialect of Armenian, but they apply in the opposite order. If rules apply in a particular order, you would expect to find languages with essentially the same rules A and B where A precedes B in one language and B precedes A in another: this is what we find in comparing Armenian and Lithuanian.

The first-singular future prefix is underlyingly k-, as shown in (39a), where the prefix is added to a vowel-initial stem. That /k/ assimilates voicing and aspiration from an obstruent which immediately follows it underlyingly (but not across a vowel). In addition, initial consonant clusters are broken up by an epenthetic schwa. As the data in (39b) show, the prefix consonant first assimilates to the initial consonant of the root, and then is separated from that consonant by schwa.

(39) a.   k-ertʰam   'I will go'
            k-asiem   'I will say'
            k-aniem   'I will do'
            k-akaniem   'I will watch
            k-oxniem   'I will bless'
            k-urriem   'I will swell'

      b.   kə-tam   'I will give'
            kə-kienam   'I will exist'
            gə-bəzzam   'I will buzz'
            gə-lam   'I will cry'
            gə-zəram   'I will bray'
            kʰə-tʰuoyniem   'I will allow'
            kʰə-čʰapʰiem   'I will measure'
            gʰə-bʰieřiem   'I will carry'
            gʰə-gʰuom   'I will come'
            gʰə-dᶻʰieviem   'I will form'

The difference between this dialect of Armenian and Lithuanian is that vowel epenthesis applies before consonant assimilation in Lithuanian but after that rule in Armenian, so that in Armenian both epenthesis and assimilation can apply to a given word, whereas in Lithuanian applying epenthesis to a word means that assimilation can no longer apply.

5.2.3 Lomongo: B-deletion and resolution of vowel hiatus

Sometimes, what needs to be remarked about the interaction between processes is the failure of one rule to apply to the output of another rule. This is illustrated in (40), (41) and (46) with examples from Lomongo (Congo). The first four examples demonstrate the shape of the various subject prefixes when they stand before a consonant

(40)

Imp	1sg	2sg	3sg	1pl	2pl	3pl	
saŋga	nsaŋga	osaŋga	asaŋga	tosaŋga	losaŋga	basaŋga	'say'
kamba	ŋkamba	okamba	akamba	tokamba	lokamba	bakamba	'work'
mɛla	mmɛla	ɔmɛla	amɛla	tɔmɛla	lɔmɛla	bamɛla	'drink'
ǰila	nǰila	oǰila	aǰila	toǰila	loǰila	baǰila	'wait'

The underlying forms of the subject prefixes are /N/ (which stands for a nasal consonant, whose exact place of articulation cannot be determined), /o/, /a/, /to/, /lo/ and /ba/. There is a vowel harmony process assimilating the closed vowel /o/ to the open vowel [ɔ] when the following syllable contains either of the open vowels [ɛ] or [ɔ], and the prefix for first-singular subject assimilates in place of articulation to the following consonant.

The examples in (41) show how the subject prefixes are realized if the verb root begins with a vowel.

(41)

Imp.	1sg	2sg	3sg	1pl	2pl	3pl	
ɛna	nǰɛna	wɛna	ɛna	tˢwɛna	ǰwɛna	bɛna	'see'
isa	nǰisa	wisa	isa	tˢwisa	ǰwisa	bisa	'hide'
imeǰa	nǰimeǰa	wimeǰa	imeǰa	tˢwimeǰa	ǰwimeǰa	bimeǰa	'consent'
usa	nǰusa	wusa	usa	tˢwusa	ǰwusa	busa	'throw'
ina	nǰina	wina	ina	tˢwina	ǰwina	bina	'hate'

When the first-singular subject prefix stands before the root, it has the shape [nǰ], which we will treat as being the result of insertion of [ǰ] between the prefix and a vowel-initial root. (We might also assume the prefix /nǰ/, which simplifies before a consonant, since such three-consonant sequences, viz. /nǰ-saŋga/, do not exist in the language.)

(42) *Consonant epenthesis*
  Ø → ǰ / n + _ V

The vowel /a/ deletes before another vowel, as shown by the third-singular and third-plural forms /a-ɛna/ → [ɛna] and /ba-ɛna/ → [bɛna].

(43) *Vowel truncation*
  a → Ø / _ V

The prefixes /o/, /to/, and /lo/ undergo a process of glide formation where /o/ becomes [w] before a vowel.

(44) *Glide formation*
  o → w / _ V

In the case of /to/ and /lo/ a further process affricates these consonants before a glide.

(45) *Affrication*
  t, l → tˢ, ǰ / _ w

> Turning /l/ into an affricate seems strange from a functional perspective, but is explained by the fact that l was originally /d/, so this rule comes historically from the more natural change /t, d/ → [tˢ, dᶻ]/_i.

This affrication process must apply after glide formation, since it applies to a sequence of consonant plus glide that is created by the application of glide formation from an underlying consonant-plus-vowel sequence.

The final set of examples illustrates verb roots which underlyingly begin with the consonant /b/. As these data show, when underlying /b/ is preceded by a vowel, it is deleted.

(46)

Imp	1sg	2sg	3sg	1pl	2pl	3pl	
bina	mbina	oina	aina	toina	loina	baina	'dance'
bota	mbota	oota	aota	toota	loota	baota	'beget'

Thus, surface [oina] derives from /obina/ and [baina] derives from /babina/, via the following rule.

(47)   *Labial elision*

    b → Ø / V _ V

In this case, even though deletion of /b/ creates new sequences of *o*+V and *a*+V which could in principle undergo the rules of *a*-deletion and glide formation, those rules do not in fact apply. In other words, in this case the grammar must contain some kind of explicit statement regarding the interaction of these processes, such as an explicit ordering of the rules, which guarantees that the output of *b*-deletion does not undergo glide formation or *a*-deletion. By ordering the *b*-deletion rule so that it applies after the glide formation and vowel truncation rules, we explain why those two rules fail to apply, just in case the consonant *b* is deleted intervocalically. The ordering where *b*-deletion precedes vowel truncation and glide formation, illustrated in (48b), results in ungrammatical forms, which shows that that ordering of the rules is incorrect. ("NA" means that the rule cannot apply, because the conditions called for in the rule are not satisfied in the string.)

(48)   a.   /o-bina/   /a-bina/   *underlying*
              NA   NA   *glide formation*
              NA   NA   *vowel truncation*
              oina   aina   *b-deletion*

     b.   /o-bina/   /a-bina/   *underlying*
              oina   aina   *b-deletion*
              wina   NA   *glide formation*
              NA   ina   *vowel truncation*
              *[wina]   *[ina]

Lomongo thus provides an example of the failure of rules – especially vowel truncation and glide formation – to apply to the output of a specific rule – *b*-deletion – which we explain by ordering *b*-deletion after the vowel rules.

5.2.4 Examples for discussion

Karok.   These data from Karok (California) illustrate three interacting phonological processes. Comment on the underlying forms of the following words, state what phonological rules are motivated, and discuss the order in which these processes apply.

(49)   *Imperative*   *1sg*   *3sg*
    pasip   nipasip   ʔupasip   'shoot'
    si:tva   niši:tva   ʔusi:tva   'steal'
    kifnuk   nikifnuk   ʔukifnuk   'stoop'
    suprih   nišuprih   ʔusuprih   'measure'
    ʔifik   niʔifik   ʔuʔifik   'pick up'
    ʔi:ftih   niʔi:ftih   ʔuʔi:ftih   'growing'
    ʔaktuv   niʔaktuv   ʔuʔaktuv   'pluck at'

ʔakrap	niʔakrap	ʔuʔakrap	'slap'
ʔarip	niʔarip	ʔuʔarip	'cut a strip'
ʔaxyar	nixyar	ʔuxyar	'fill'
ʔiškak	niškak	ʔuskak	'jump'
ʔimniš	nimniš	ʔumniš	'cook'
ʔikšah	nikšah	ʔuksah	'laugh'
ʔišriv	nišriv	ʔusriv	'shoot at a target'

Shona. Often, a seemingly complex problem can be significantly simplified by breaking the problem up into a few interacting processes. If you look at the phonetic realizations of the passive suffix in Shona (Zimbabwe), you see that there are seven different manifestations of this suffix. However, this considerable range of variation can be explained in terms of a much smaller set of very general phonological rules, whose interaction results in many surface realizations of the suffix.

(50)

Active	Passive		Active	Passive	
ɓika	ɓikwa	'cook'	diba	dibɣa	'dip'
pfugama	pfugamŋa	'kneel'	pepa	pepxa	'nurse'
ɓuɗa	ɓuɗɣwa	'go out'	ruma	rumŋa	'bite'
rova	rovɣa	'stay away'	ma̰ña	ma̰ññwa	'run'
suŋga	suŋgwa	'tie'	kwaša	kwašxwa	'hunt'
teŋga	teŋgwa	'buy'	fuŋga	fuŋgwa	'think'
tamba	tambɣa	'play'	bʸunza	bʸunzɣwa	'ask'
imba	imbɣa	'sing'	gara	garɣwa	'stay'
setsa	setsxwa	'amuse'	reɗza	reɗzɣwa	'lengthen'
tapa	tapxa	'capture'	βeza	βezɣwa	'carve'
rega	regwa	'leave'	ibʸa	ibʸɣa	'ripen'
šuža	šužɣwa	'store grain'	taṣa	taṣxwa	'ride'
peta	petxwa	'fold'	dana	danŋwa	'call'
ona	onŋwa	'see'	ɪta	ɪtxwa	'do'
doka	dokwa	'set'	seka	sekwa	'laugh'
fesa	fesxwa	'prick'	rasa	rasxwa	'throw away'
ra̰na	ra̰nŋwa	'kick'	pema̰	pema̰ŋa	'beg food'
goča	gočxwa	'roast'	ṣika	ṣikwa	'arrive'
dzidza	dzidzɣwa	'learn'	fuka	fukwa	'cover'
famba	fambɣa	'walk'	nandza	nandzɣwa	'lick'
gada	gadɣwa	'mount'	ɓata	ɓatxwa	'hold'
tuma	tumŋa	'send'	tora	torɣwa	'take'
oŋa	oŋwa	'growl'	rima	rimŋa	'plow'
sefa	sefxa	'sieve'	kweza̰	kweza̰ɣwa	'attract'
ǰuǰa	ǰuǰɣwa	'leak'	guruva	guruvɣa	'deceive'
maŋga	maŋgwa	'arrest'	miña	miññwa	'swallow'

The precise rules which you postulate will depend on what you assume to be the underlying form of the passive suffix, since there are two plausible underlying forms for the suffix, based on the data above. The phonological alternations seen in the following examples are relevant to deciding what the underlying form of the passive suffix is (and therefore exactly how these phonological alternations are to be analyzed). These inflected forms involve a prefix marking the subject, followed by one of various tense markers such as -ča-, -no-, and -a-, or no marker, finally followed by the verb stem.

(51) *Subjunctive*   *Future*
      urime   'that you (sg) plow'   učarima   'you (sg) will plow'
      murime   'that you (pl) plow'   mučarima   'you (pl) will plow'
      turime   'that they (tiny) plow'   tučarima   'they (tiny) will plow'
      kunatˢe   'that there be nice'   kučanatˢa 'there will be nice'

      Habitual   *Recent past*
      unorima   'you (sg) plow'   warima   'you (sg) plowed'
      munorima   'you (pl) plow'   mŋarima   'you (pl) plowed'
      tunorima   'they (tiny) plow'   txwarima   'they (tiny) plowed'
      kunonatˢa 'there is nice'   kwanatˢa   'there was nice'

A further fact which is relevant to deciding on the correct analysis is that [ɣ], [x] do not appear after vowels or at the beginning of a word.

Klamath. The data in (52)–(56) from Klamath (Oregon) illustrate two processes. The first deaspirates and deglottalizes consonants before obstruents, before glottalized and voiceless resonants, as well as in word-final positions. The examples in (52) illustrate plain voiceless obstruents, which do not undergo any phonetic alternations. The data below involve a range of inflectionally and derivationally related word forms: the common root is underlined (the last form in this set also illustrates an alternation between *i* and *y'*, which is not crucial).

(52) la:<u>p</u>-a   'two (obj.)'   <u>la:p</u>   'two'
      sk^h<u>ot</u>-a   'puts on a blanket'   sk^h<u>ot</u>-pli   'puts on a blanket
                                                                           again'

      q'<u>la:č</u>-aksi   'Blueberry Place'   q'<u>la:č</u>   'blueberry (sp)'
      <u>poq</u>-a   'bakes camas'   <u>poq</u>-s   'camas root'
      <u>laqi</u>   'is rich'   <u>laqy'</u>-a:ka   'little chief'

The data in (53) provide examples of underlyingly glottalized obstruents, which become plain voiceless consonants unless they are followed by a vowel or plain sonorant.

(53) <u>p'ak'</u>-a   'smashes'   <u>p'ak</u>-ska   'chips off (intr)'
      <u>ʔe:t'</u>-a   'distributes'   se-<u>ʔe:t</u>-s   'Saturday'
      poq-<u>poq'</u>-a   'becomes dusty'   <u>po:q</u>-tki   'becomes dusty'
      <u>čʰa:k'</u>-a   'melts (intr)'   <u>čʰa:k</u>-tki   'melts (as butter)'
      ʔi-<u>čʰi:č'</u>-a   'makes shavings'   k-<u>čʰič</u>-ta   'scrapes ones foot on'
      <u>čʰlo:q'</u>-a   'is smooth'   <u>čʰlo:q</u>-tki   'becomes slick'

qit'-lqa   'pours down'   qit-qʰa   'pours out'
-lo:p'-a   'eats soup'   -lo:p-s   'soup'

Data in (53) show that aspirated consonants deaspirate in this same context.

(54)   ličʰ-lič-l'i   'strong'   li:č-tki   'becomes strong'
      ponw-o:tʰ-a   'while drinking'   ponw-o:t-s   'something to drink with'
      so:čʰ-a   'kindles a fire'   so:č-ti:la   'lights a fire under'
      si:yo:tʰ-a   'trades (pl) obj with each other'   si:yo:t-pli   'trade back (pl obj)'
      n'iqʰ-o:wa   'keeps putting a hand in water'   n'iq-tpa   'reaches and touches'

The second process, syncope, deletes a short vowel from the first sylla-ble of a stem when preceded by a CV prefix and followed by CV.

(55)
laqi:ta   'suspects s.o.'   sa-lqita   'suspects e.o.'
mačʰa:t-ka   'listens'   sna-mčʰa:t-i:la   'causes to hear'
meč'a   'moves camp'   me-mč'a   'moves (distributive)'
saqo:tka   'ask for s.t.'   sa-sqo:tqa   'ask for s.t. (distributive)'
sičaqʰwa   'wash hands'   hi-sčaq-tʰa   'are angry with e.o'
som   'mouth'   so-sm'-a:k   'little mouths (distributive)'

What do these examples show about the interaction of these two processes?

(56)
q'oč'a   'bends'   yo-qč'a   'bends with the feet'
qʰew'a   'breaks'   če-qw'a   'sit on and break'
tʰew'a   'surface cracks'   ye-tw'a   'steps on and cracks surface'
s-č'iq'a   'squash with a pointed instrument'   yi-čq'a   'squash by pressure with the feet'
w-k'al'a   'cuts with a long instrument'   kin-kl'a   'makes a mark with pointer'
w-p'eq'a   'hits in the face with a long instrument'   hom-pq'a   'flies in the face'

Summary

Systems of phonological alternations in most languages involve a number of rules. This interaction means that you must discern the effects of individual rules, rather than subsume all alternations under one complex do-everything rule. A rule changes a given set of segments in a uniform manner, in a specified environment. So even when a language like Bukusu has a number of rules pertaining to sequences of nasal plus consonant – rules which have in common a single context

NC – there may be quite a number of specific rules that apply in that context. Besides identifying what rules exist in a language, you must also determine what the proper ordering of those rules is. The correct order of a pair of rules can be determined by applying the rules very literal-mindedly in both of the logically possible orders.

Exercises

1 Kerewe

What two tone rules are motivated by the following data? Explain what order the rules apply in.

to V	to V e.o	to V for	to V for e.o.	
kubala	kubalana	kubalila	kubalilana	'count'
kugaya	kugayana	kugayila	kugayilana	'despise'
kugula	kugulana	kugulila	kugulilana	'buy'
kubála	kubálána	kubálíla	kubálílana	'kick'
kulúma	kulúmána	kulúmíla	kulúmílana	'bite'
kusúna	kusúnána	kusúníla	kusúnílana	'pinch'
kurába	kulábána	kulábíla	kulábílana	'pass'

to V us	to V it	to V for us	to V it for us	
kutúbála	kukíbála	kutúbálila	kukítúbalila	'count'
kutúgáya	kukígáya	kutúgáyila	kukítúgayila	'despise'
kutúgúla	kukígúla	kutúgúlila	kukítúgulila	'buy'
kutúbála	kukíbála	kutúbálila	kukítúbalila	'kick'
kutúlúma	kukílúma	kutúlúmila	kukítúlumila	'bite'
kutúsúna	kukísúna	kutúsúnila	kukítúsunila	'pinch'
kutúlába	kukílába	kutúlábila	kukítúlabila	'pass'

2 Polish

What phonological rules are motivated by the following examples, and what order do those rules apply in?

Singular	Plural		Singular	Plural	
klup	klubi	'club'	trup	trupi	'corpse'
dom	domi	'house'	snop	snopi	'sheaf'
žwup	žwobi	'crib'	trut	trudi	'labor'
dzvon	dzvoni	'bell'	kot	koti	'cat'
lut	lodi	'ice'	grus	gruzi	'rubble'
nos	nosi	'nose'	vus	vozi	'cart'
wuk	wugi	'lye'	wuk	wuki	'bow'
sok	soki	'juice'	ruk	rogi	'horn'
bur	bori	'forest'	vuw	vowi	'ox'
sul	soli	'salt'	buy	boyi	'fight'
šum	šumi	'noise'	žur	žuri	'soup'

3 Ancient Greek

Discuss the phonological rules and underlying representations which are necessary to account for the following nouns; comment on the ordering of these phonological processes.

Nom sg	Gen sg	Dat sg	Dat pl	
hals	halos	hali	halsi	'salt'
oys	oyos	oyi	oysi	'sheep'
sus	suos	sui	susi	'sow'
klo:ps	klo:pos	klo:pi	klo:psi	'thief'
pʰle:ps	pʰle:bos	pʰle:bi	pʰle:psi	'vein'
kate:lips	kate:lipʰos	kate:lipʰi	kate:lipsi	'upper story'
pʰulaks	pʰulakos	pʰulaki	pʰulaksi	'guard'
ayks	aygos	aygi	ayksi	'goat'
salpiŋks	salpiŋgos	salpiŋgi	salpiŋksi	'trumpet'
ɔnuks	ɔnukʰos	ɔnukʰi	ɔnuksi	'nail'
tʰe:s	tʰe:tos	tʰe:ti	tʰe:si	'serf'
kʰaris	kʰaritos	kʰariti	kʰarisi	'grace'
elpis	elpidos	elpidi	elpisi	'hope'
korus	korutʰos	korutʰi	korusi	'helmet'
ri:s	ri:nos	ri:ni	ri:si	'nose'
delpʰi:s	delpʰi:nos	delpʰi:ni	delpʰi:si	'porpoise'

4 Shona

Acute accent indicates H tone and unaccented vowels have L tone. Given the two sets of data immediately below, what tone rule do the following data motivate? There are alternations in the form of adjectives, e.g. *kurefú, karefú, marefú* all meaning 'long.' Adjectives have an agreement prefix, hence *ku-refú* marks the form of the adjective in one grammatical class, and so on. In some cases, the agreement is realized purely as a change in the initial consonant of the adjective, i.e. *gúrú ~ kúrú ~ húrú,* which need not be explained.

bveni	'baboon'	bveni pfúpi	'short baboon'
táfura	'table'	táfura húrú	'big table'
šoko	'word'	šoko bvúpi	'short word'
ɓadzá	'hoe'	ɓadzá gúrú	'big hoe'
zigómaná	'boy (augmentative)'	zigómaná gúrú	'big boy (augmentative)'
imbá	'house'	imbá čéna	'clean house'
mhará	'gazelle'	mhará čéna	'clean gazelle'
marí	'money'	marí čéna	'clean money'
ɓáŋgá	'knife'	ɓáŋga gúrú	'big knife'
ɗémó	'axe'	ɗémo bvúpi	'short axe'
nhúmé	'messenger'	nhúme pfúpi	'short messenger'
jírá	'cloth'	jíra jéna	'clean cloth'
hárí	'pot'	hári húrú	'big pot'
mbúndúdzí	'worms'	mbúndúdzi húrú	'big worms'
fúma	'wealth'	fúma čéna	'clean wealth'
nyíka	'country'	nyíka húrú	'big country'
hákáta	'bones'	hákáta pfúpi	'short bones'
jékéra	'pumpkin'	jékéra gúrú	'big pumpkin'

These data provide further illustration of the operation of this tone rule, which will help you to state the conditions on the rule correctly.

guɗo	'baboon'	guɗo rákafá	'the baboon died'
ɓaɗzá	'hoe'	ɓaɗzá rákawá	'the hoe fell'
nuŋgú	'porcupine'	nuŋgú yákafá	'the porcupine died'
ɓáŋgá	'knife'	ɓáŋga rákawá	'the knife fell'
nhúmé	'messenger'	nhúme yákafá	'the messenger died'
búku	'book'	búku rákawá	'the book died'
mapfeni	'baboons'	mapfeni makúrú	'big baboons'
mapadzá	'hoes'	mapadzá makúrú	'big hoes'
mapáŋgá	'knives'	mapáŋgá makúrú	'big knives'
nhúmé	'messenger'	nhúmé ndefú	'short messenger'
matémó	'axes'	matémó mapfúpi	'short axes'
mabúku	'books'	mabúku mažínjí	'many books'
čitóro	'store'	čitóro čikúrú	'big store'

In the examples below, a second tone rule applies.

guɗo	'baboon'	guɗo refú	'tall baboon'
búku	'book'	búku refú	'long book'
ɓadzá	'hoe'	badzá refú	'long hoe'
nuŋgú	'porcupine'	nuŋgú ndefú	'long porcupine'
mašoko	'words'	mašoko marefú	'long words'
kunyíka	'to the land'	kunyíka kurefú	'to the long land'
mapadzá	'hoes'	mapadzá márefú	'long hoes'
kamhará	'gazelle (dim)'	kamhará kárefú	'long gazelle (dim)'
tunuŋgú	'porcupines (dim)'	tunungú túrefú	'long porcupines (dim)'

guɗo	'baboon'	guɗo gobvú	'thick baboon'
búku	'book'	búku gobvú	'thick book'
ɓadzá	'hoe'	ɓadzá gobvú	'thick hoe'
makuɗo	'baboons'	makuɗo makobvú	'thick baboons'
mapadzá	'hoes'	mapadzá mákobvú	'thick hoes'
tsamba	'letter'	tsamba nhete	'thin letter'
búku	'book'	búku ɗete	'thin book'
ɓadzá	'hoe'	ɓadzá ɗéte	'thin hoe'
imbá	'house'	imbá nhéte	'thin house'

What do the following examples show about these tone rules?

ɓáŋgá	'knife'	ɓáŋgá ɗéte	'thin knife'
ɗémó	'axe'	démó ɗéte	'thin axe'
murúmé	'person'	murúmé mútete	'thin person'
ɓahúní	'firewood (dim)'	kahúní kárefú	'long firewood'
mačírá	'clothes'	mačírá márefú	'long clothes'
hárí	'pot'	hárí nhéte	'thin pot'

5 Catalan

Give phonological rules which account for the following data, and indicate what ordering is necessary between these rules. For each adjective stem, state what the underlying form of the root is. Pay attention to the difference between surface [b, d, g] and [β, ð, γ], in terms of predictability.

Masc sg	Fem sg		Masc sg	Fem sg	
əkelʸ	əkelʸə	'that'	mal	malə	'bad'
siβil	siβilə	'civil'	əskerp	əskerpə	'shy'
šop	šopə	'drenched'	sɛk	sɛkə	'dry'
əspɛs	əspɛsə	'thick'	gros	grosə	'large'
baš	bašə	'short'	koš	košə	'lame'
tot	totə	'all'	brut	brutə	'dirty'
pɔk	pɔkə	'little'	prəsis	prəsizə	'precise'
frənses	frənsezə	'French'	gris	grizə	'grey'
kəzat	kəzaðə	'married'	bwit	bwiðə	'empty'
rɔč	rɔžə	'red'	boč	božə	'crazy'
orp	orβə	'blind'	lʸark	lʸarɣə	'long'
sek	seɣə	'blind'	fəšuk	fəšuɣə	'heavy'
grok	groɣə	'yellow'	puruk	puruɣə	'fearful'
kandit	kandiðə	'candid'	frɛt	frɛðə	'cold'
səɣu	səɣurə	'sure'	du	durə	'hard'
sərəðo	sərəðorə	'reaper'	kla	klarə	'clear'
nu	nuə	'nude'	kru	kruə	'raw'
floñǰu	floñǰə	'soft'	dropu	dropə	'lazy'
əgzaktə	əgzaktə	'exact'	əlβi	əlβinə	'albino'
sa	sanə	'healthy'	pla	planə	'level'
bo	bonə	'good'	sərɛ	sərɛnə	'calm'
suβlim	suβlimə	'sublime'	al	altə	'tall'
fɔr	fɔrtə	'strong'	kur	kurtə	'short'
sor	sorðə	'deaf'	bɛr	bɛrðə	'green'
san	santə	'saint'	kələn	kələntə	'hot'
prufun	prufundə	'deep'	fəkun	fəkundə	'fertile'
dəsen	dəsentə	'decent'	dulen	dulentə	'bad'
əstuðian	əstuðiantə	'student'	blaŋ	blaŋkə	'white'

6 Finnish

Propose rules which will account for the following alternations. It would be best not to write a lot of rules which go directly from underlying forms to surface forms in one step; instead, propose a sequence of rules whose combined effect brings about the change in the underlying form. Pay attention to what consonants actually exist in the language.

Genitive sg	Nom sg	Nom pl	Ablative sg	Essive sg	
kanadan	kanada	kanadat	kanadalta	kanadana	'Canada'
kiryan	kirya	kiryat	kiryalta	kiryana	'book'
aamun	aamu	aamut	aamulta	aamuna	'morning'
talon	talo	talot	talolta	talona	'house'
koiran	koira	koirat	koiralta	koirana	'dog'
hüvæn	hüvæ	hüvæt	hüvæltæ	hüvænæ	'good'
kuvan	kuva	kuvat	kuvalta	kuvana	'picture'
lain	laki	lait	lailta	lakina	'roof'
nælæn	nælkæ	nælæt	nælæltæ	nælkænæ	'hunger'
yalan	yalka	yalat	yalalta	yalkana	'leg'
leuan	leuka	leuat	leualta	leukana	'chin'

paran	parka	parat	paralta	parkana	'poor'
reiæn	reikæ	reiæt	reiæltæ	reikænæ	'hole'
nahan	nahka	nahat	nahalta	nahkana	'hide'
vihon	vihko	vihot	viholta	vihkona	'notebook'
laihan	laiha	laihat	laihalta	laihana	'lean'
avun	apu	avut	avulta	apuna	'help'
halvan	halpa	halvat	halvalta	halpana	'cheap'
orvon	orpo	orvot	orvolta	orpona	'orphan'
leivæn	leipæ	leivæt	leivæltæ	leipænæ	'bread'
pæivæn	pæivæ	pæivæt	pæivæltæ	pæivænæ	'day'
kilvan	kilpa	kilvat	kilvalta	kilpana	'competition'
külvün	külpü	külvüt	külvültæ	külpünæ	'bath'
tavan	tapa	tavat	tavalta	tapana	'manner'
korvan	korva	korvat	korvalta	korvana	'ear'
æidin	æiti	æidit	æidiltæ	æitinæ	'mother'
kodin	koti	kodit	kodilta	kotina	'home'
muodon	muoto	muodot	muodolta	muotona	'form'
tædin	tæti	tædit	tædiltæ	tætinæ	'aunt'
kadun	katu	kadut	kadulta	katuna	'street'
maidon	maito	maidot	maidolta	maitona	'milk'
pöüdæn	pöütæ	pöüdæt	pöüdæltæ	pöütænæ	'table'
tehdün	tehtü	tehdüt	tehdültæ	tehtünæ	'made'
læmmön	læmpö	læmmöt	læmmöltæ	læmpönæ	'warmth'
laŋŋan	laŋka	laŋŋat	laŋŋalta	laŋkana	'thread'
sæŋŋün	sæŋkü	sæŋŋüt	sæŋŋültæ	sæŋkünæ	'bed'
hinnan	hinta	hinnat	hinnalta	hintana	'price'
linnun	lintu	linnut	linnulta	lintuna	'bird'
opinnon	opinto	opinnot	opinnolta	opintona	'study'
rannan	ranta	rannat	rannalta	rantana	'shore'
luonnon	luonto	luonnot	luonnolta	luontona	'nature'
punnan	punta	punnat	punnalta	puntana	'pound'
tunnin	tunti	tunnit	tunnilta	tuntina	'hour'
kunnon	kunto	kunnot	kunnolta	kuntona	'condition'
kannun	kannu	kannut	kannulta	kannuna	'can'
linnan	linna	linnat	linnalta	linnana	'castle'
tumman	tumma	tummat	tummalta	tummana	'dark'
auriŋŋon	auriŋko	auriŋŋot	auriŋŋolta	auriŋkona	'sun'
reŋŋin	reŋki	reŋŋit	reŋŋiltæ	reŋkinæ	'farm hand'
vaŋŋin	vaŋki	vaŋŋit	vaŋŋilta	vaŋkina	'prisoner'
kellon	kello	kellot	kellolta	kellona	'watch'
kellan	kelta	kellat	kellalta	keltana	'yellow'
sillan	silta	sillat	sillalta	siltana	'bridge'
kullan	kulta	kullat	kullalta	kultana	'gold'
virran	virta	virrat	virralta	virtana	'stream'
parran	parta	parrat	parralta	partana	'beard'

7 Korean

Provide rules which will account for the alternations in the stem-final consonant in the following examples. State what underlying representation you are
assuming for each noun.

'rice'	'forest'	'chestnut'	
pamman	summan	pamman	only N
pammaŋkʰɨm	summaŋkʰɨm	pammaŋkʰɨm	as much as N
pamnarɨm	sumnarɨm	pamnarɨm	depending on N
pap	sup	pam	N
papt'ero	supt'ero	pamtero	like N
papk'wa	supk'wa	pamkwa	with N
papp'ota	supp'ota	pampota	more than N
papk'ači	supk'ači	pamk'ači	until N
papi	supʰi	pami	N (nominative)
papɨn	supʰɨn	pamɨn	N (topic)
pape	supʰe	pame	to N
papita	supʰita	pamita	it is N
papɨro	supʰɨro	pamɨro	using N

'field'	'sickle'	'day'	
pamman	namman	namman	only N
pammaŋkʰɨm	nammaŋkʰɨm	nammaŋkʰɨm	as much as N
pannarɨm	nannarɨm	nannarɨm	depending on N
pat	nat	nat	N
patt'ero	natt'ero	natt'ero	like N
pakk'wa	nakk'wa	nakk'wa	with N
papp'ota	napp'ota	napp'ota	more than N
pakk'ači	nakk'ači	nakk'ači	until N
pačʰi	nasi	nači	N (nominative)
patʰɨn	nasɨn	načɨn	N (topic)
patʰe	nase	นače	to N
pačʰita	nasita	načita	it is N
patʰɨro	nasɨro	načɨro	using N

'face'	'half'		
namman	pamman		only N
nammaŋkʰɨm	pammaŋkʰɨm		as much as N
nannarɨm	pannarɨm		depending on N
nat	pan		N
natt'ero	pantero		like N
nakk'wa	paŋkwa		with N
napp'ota	pampota		more than N
nakk'ači	paŋk'ači		until N
načʰi	pani		N (nominative)
načʰɨn	panɨn		N (topic)
načʰe	pane		to N
načʰita	panita		it is N
načʰɨro	panɨro		using N

Further reading

Anderson 1974; Chomsky 1967; Goldsmith 1993; Kiparsky 1968; Koutsoudas, Sanders and Noll 1974.

6 Feature theory

KEY TERMS

observation
predictions
features
natural classes

This chapter explores the theory for representing language sounds as symbolic units. You will:

- see that sounds are defined in terms of a fixed set of universal features

- learn the phonetic definitions of features, and how to assign feature values to segments based on phonetic properties

- understand how phonological rules are formalized in terms of those features

- see how these features makes predictions about possible sounds and rules in human language

The discussion of sound systems has, up to this point, been conducted without attention to what sounds as cognitive units are made of. We have treated them as letters, labeled by traditional articulatory descriptions. It is time now to raise a fundamental question: are segments analyzed into "parts" that define them, or are they truly atomic – units which are not further divisible or analyzable?

6.1 Scientific questions about speech sounds

One of the scientific questions that can be asked about language is: *what is a possible speech sound?* Humans can produce many more sounds than those systematically used in language. One limitation on language regards modality – language sounds are produced exclusively within the mouth and nasal passages, in the area between the lips and larynx. No language employs hand-clapping, finger-snapping, or vibrations of air between the hand and cheek caused by release of air from the mouth when obstructed by the palm of the hand (though such a sound can communicate an attitude). Even staying within the vocal tract, languages also do not, for example, use whistles or inhalation to form speech sounds, nor is a labiolingual trill (a.k.a. "the raspberry") a speech sound in any language. It is important to understand that even though these various odd sounds are not language sounds, they may still be used in communication. The "raspberry" in American culture communicates a contemptuous attitude; in parts of coastal East Africa and Scandinavia, inhaling with the tongue in the position for schwa expresses agreement. Such noises lie outside of language, and we never find plurality indicated with these sounds, nor are they surrounded by other sounds to form the word *dog*. General communication has no systematic limitations short of anatomical ones, but in language, only a restricted range of sounds are used.

The issue of possible speech sounds is complicated by manual languages such as American Sign Language. ASL is technically not a counterexample to a claim about modality framed in terms of "speech sounds." But it is arbitrary to declare manual language to be outside of the theory of language, and facts from such languages are relevant in principle. Unfortunately, knowledge of the signed languages of the world is very restricted, especially in phonology. Signed languages clearly have syntax: what isn't clear is what they have by way of phonologies. Researchers have only just begun to scratch the surface of sign language phonologies, so unfortunately we can say nothing more about them here.

The central question then must be posed: what is the basis for defining possible speech sounds?

6.1.1 Possible differences in sounds

One way to approach the question is to collect samples of the sounds of all of the languages in the world. This search (which has never been conducted) would reveal massive repetition, and would probably reveal that the segment [m] in English is exactly the same as the segment [m] in French, German, Tübatulabal, Arabic, Swahili, Chinese and innumerable other languages. It would also reveal differences, some of them perhaps a bit surprising. Given the richness of our transcriptional resources for notating phonetic differences between segments, you might expect that if a collection of languages had the same vowels transcribed as [i] and [ɪ], then these vowels should sound the same. This is not so.

Varieties of phonetic [i] vs. [ɪ]. Many languages have this pair of vowels; for example, Kimatuumbi has [i] and [ɪ]. But the actual pronunciation of [i] vs. [ɪ] differs between English and Kimatuumbi. Kimatuumbi [i] is higher than in English, and Kimatuumbi [ɪ] is a bit lower than English [ɪ] – to some people it almost sounds like [e] (but is clearly different from [e], even the "pure" [e] found in Spanish). This might force us to introduce new symbols, so that we can accurately represent these distinctions. (This is done in publications on Kimatuumbi, where the difference is notated as "extreme" i̧, u̧ versus "regular" i, u.) Before we embark on a program of adding new symbols, we should be sure that we know how many symbols to add. It turns out that the pronunciation of [i] and [ɪ] differs in many languages: these vowels exist in English, Kamba, Elomwe, Kimatuumbi, Bari, Kipsigis, Didinga and Sesotho, and their actual pronunciation differs in each language.

You do not have to go very far into exotic languages to find this phonetic difference, for the difference between English [i] and German [i] is also very noticeable, and is something that a language learner must master to develop a good German or English accent. Although the differences may be difficult for the untrained ear to perceive at first, they are consistent, physically measurable, and reproducible by speakers. If written symbols are to represent phonetic differences between languages, a totally accurate transcription should represent these differences. To represent just this range of vowel differences involving [i] and [ɪ], over a dozen new symbols would need to be introduced.

Other variants of sounds. Similar variation exists with other phonetic categories. The retroflex consonants of Telugu, Hindi and Ekoti are all pronounced differently. Hindi has what might be called "mild" retroflexion, where the tip of the tongue is placed just behind the alveolar ridge, while in Telugu, the tip of the tongue is further back and contact is made between the palate and the underside of the tongue (sublaminal); in Ekoti, the tongue is placed further forward, but is also sublaminal. Finnish, Norwegian, and English contrast the vowels [a] and [æ], but in each of these languages the vowels are pronounced in a slightly different way. The voiced velar fricative [ɣ] found in Arabic, Spanish and the Kurdish language Hawrami are all phonetically different in subtle but audible ways.

The important details of speech. We will not expand our transcription tools to include as many symbols as needed to capture the myriad of fine distinctions between similar sounds of languages. Fine-tuning transcription is tangential to the goals of phonology, and perfect accuracy is impossible.

Transcriptions actually record a trained analyst's perception of a sound, and are not derived by physical analysis of speech waveforms. Transcriptions include possible perceptual biases from the person describing the language.

Auditory transcriptions are limited in what they accomplish, and cannot be used to achieve exact reproduction of a speech event via symbols. If a speaker produces the English word *putt* [pʌt] 10,000 times, no utterance will be exactly identical to any other utterance. They will be very similar, in ways which might be quantified mathematically, but they would not be exactly the same. Productions of the same word by two speakers of the same language have a greater difference, and supposedly similar utterances in different languages can be much more different. There is no limit to the number of physically different utterances which humans can produce, but there are also only a very small number of discrete transcriptional symbols. The reason for this, as we have emphasized in chapter 1, is that a transcription approximates speech, and omits properties which are unimportant to phonological systems.

Such details are important to phonetics and its interface with phonology, but must be studied quantitatively using acoustic measurements – formant frequencies or segment durations – or articulatorily by measuring the position of the tongue and lips. For the purposes of phonology, these languages have the same vowels, [i] vs. [ɪ]. The differences in pronunciation come from detail rules that are part of the phonetic grammars of the languages.

What is important to phonology is not exactly how sounds are pronounced, but what types of sound differences can be contrastive, i.e. can form the basis for making differences in meaning. Language can contrast tense [i] and lax [ɪ], but cannot further contrast a hyper-tense high vowel (like that found in Kimatuumbi) which we might write as [i⁺] with plain tense [i] as in English, or hyper-lax [ɪ⁻] as in Kimatuumbi with plain lax [ɪ] as found in English. Within a language, you find at most [i] vs. [ɪ]. Languages can have one series of retroflex consonants, and cannot contrast Hindi-style [ʈ] with a Telugu-style phoneme which we might notate as [ʈ⁺]. The phonology simply has "retroflex," and it is up to the phonetic component of a language to say exactly how a retroflex consonant is pronounced.

It is important to emphasize that these phonetic details are not too subtle to hear. The difference between various retroflex consonants is quite audible, and the difference between English and German [i] is appreciable. Children learning German can hear and reproduce German [i] accurately. Speakers can also tell when someone mispronounces a German [i] as an English [i], and bilingual German–English speakers can easily switch between the two phonetic vowels.

What phonological theory wants to know is: *what is a possible phoneme?* How might we answer this? We could look at all languages and publish a list. A monumental difficulty with that is that there are nearly 7,000 languages, but useful information on around only 10 percent of these languages. Worse, this could only say what phonemic contrasts exist at the present: it does not answer the really interesting question, what the *possible* phonemes are, which may have existed in a language spoken 1,000 years ago, or some future language which will be spoken 1,000 years hence. We are not just interested in *observation*, we are interested in *prediction*.

In this connection, consider whether a "bilabial click" is a possible phoneme. We symbolize it as [ʘ] – it is like a kiss, but with the lips flat as for [m], not protruded as for [w]. Virtually all languages have bilabial consonants, and we know of dozens of languages with click consonants (Dahalo, Sesotho, Zulu, Xhosa, Khoekhoe), so the question is whether the combination "bilabial" and "click" can define a phoneme. Such a sound does exist, but only in two closely related languages, !Xoo and Eastern ≠Hoan, members of the Khoisan language family. These languages have under 5,000 speakers combined, and given socio-economic factors where these languages are spoken (Namibia and Botswana), it is likely that the languages will no longer be spoken in 200 years. We are fortunate in this case that we have information of these languages which allows us to say that this *is* a phoneme, but things could have turned out differently. The languages could easily have died out without having been recorded, and then we would wrongly conclude that a bilabial click is not a possible phoneme because it has not been observed. In posing the question of possible phonemes, we must be aware that there can be accidental gaps in the database of observed phonemes.

Predictions versus observations. A list of facts is scientifically uninteresting. A basic goal of science is to have knowledge that goes beyond what has been observed, because we believe that the universe obeys general laws. A list might be helpful in building a theory, but we would not want to stop with a list, because it would give us no explanation why that particular list, as opposed to some other arbitrary list, should constitute the possible phonemes of language. The question "what is a possible phoneme" should thus be answered by reference to a general theory of what speech sounds are made of, just as a theory of "possible atoms" is based on a general theory of what makes up atoms and rules for putting those bits together. Science is not simply the accumulation and sorting of facts, but rather the attempt to discover laws that regulate the universe. Such laws make predictions about things that we have yet to observe: certain things should be found, other things should never be found.

The Law of Gravity predicts that a rock will fall to earth, which says what it will do and by implication what it will not do: it also won't go up or sideways. Physicists have observed that subatomic particles decay into other particles. Particles have an electrical charge – positive, negative or neutral – and there is a physical law that the charge of a particle is preserved when it decays (adding up the charges of the decay products). The particle known as a "kaon" (K) can be positive (K^+), negative (K^-) or neutral (K^0); a kaon can decay into other particles known as "pions" (π) which also can be positive (π^+), negative (π^-) or neutral (π^0). Thus a neutral kaon may become a positive pion and a negative pion ($K^0 \rightarrow \pi^+ + \pi^-$) or it may become one positive, one negative, and one neutral pion ($K^0 \rightarrow \pi^+ + \pi^- + \pi^0$), because in both cases the positives and negatives cancel out and the sum of charges is neutral (0). The Law of Conservation of Charge allows these patterns of decay, and prohibits a neutral kaon from becoming two positive pions ($K^0 \rightarrow \pi^+ + \pi^+$). In the myriad cases of particle decay which have been observed experimentally, none violates this law which predicts what can happen and what cannot.

Analogously, phonological theory seeks to discover the laws for building phonemes, which predict the possible phonemes of languages. We will see that theory, after considering a related question which defines phonology.

6.1.2 Possible rules

Previous chapters have focused on rules, but we haven't paid much attention to how they should be formulated. English has rules defining allowed clusters of two consonants at the beginning of the word. The first set of consonant sequences in (1) is allowed, whereas the second set of sequences is disallowed.

This is not the only rule governing consonant sequences at the beginning of the word in English, so for example the voiceless alveolar fricative [s] can be followed by any nonfricative.

(1) pr pl br bl tr dr kr kl gr gl
     *rp *lp *rb *lb *rt *rd *rk *lk *rg *lg

This restriction is very natural and exists in many languages – but it is not inevitable, and does not reflect any insurmountable problems of physiology or perception. Russian allows many of these clusters, for example [rtut^y] 'mercury' exemplifies the sequence [rt] which is impossible in English.

We could list the allowed and disallowed sequences of phonemes and leave it at that, but this does not explain why these particular sequences are allowed. Why don't we find a language which is like English, except that the specific sequence [lb] is allowed and the sequence [bl] is disallowed? An interesting generalization regarding sequencing has emerged after comparing such rules across languages. Some languages (e.g. Hawaiian) do not allow any clusters of consonants and some (Bella Coola, a Salishan language of British Columbia) allow any combination of two consonants, but *no* language allows initial [lb] without also allowing [bl]. This is a more interesting and suggestive observation, since it indicates that there is something about such sequences that is not accidental in English; but it is still just a random fact from a list of accumulated facts, if we have no basis for characterizing classes of sounds, and view the restrictions as restrictions on letters, as sounds with no structure.

There is a rule in English which requires that all vowels be nasalized when they appear before a nasal consonant, and thus we have a rule something like (2).

(2) ɛ e ι i   ɛ̃ ẽ ĩ ĩ
     a ɔ o ʊ   →   ã ɔ̃ õ ũ   /_ m, n, ŋ
     u ə æ   ũ ə̃ æ̃

If rules just replace one arbitrary list of sounds by another list when they stand in front of a third arbitrary list, we have to ask why these particular sets of symbols operate together. Could we replace the symbol [n] with the symbol [č], or the symbol [õ] with the symbol [ö], and still have a rule in some language? It is not likely to be an accident that these particular symbols are found in the rule: a rule similar to this can be found in quite a number of languages, and we would not expect this particular collection of letters to assemble themselves into a rule in many languages, if these were just random collections of letters.

Were phonological rules stated in terms of randomly assembled symbols, there would be no reason to expect (3a) to have a different status from (3b).

(3)   a.   {p, t, č, k} → {m, n, ñ, ŋ}/ __ {m, n, ñ, ŋ}
      b.   {b, p, d, q} → {d, q, b, p} / __ {s, x, o, ɪ}

Rule (3a) – nasalization of stops before nasals – is quite common, but (3b) is never found in human language. This is not an accident, but rather reflects the fact that the latter process cannot be characterized in terms of a unified phonetic operation applying to a phonetically defined context. The insight which we have implicitly assumed, and make explicit here, is that rules operate not in terms of specific symbols, but in terms of definable classes. The basis for defining those classes is a set of phonetic properties.

As a final illustration of this point, rule (4a) is common in the world's languages but (4b) is completely unattested.

(4)   a.   k, g → č, ǰ / __ i, e
      b.   p, r → i, b / __ o, n

The first rule refers to phonetically definable classes of segments (velar stops, alveopalatal affricates, front vowels), and the nature of the change is definable in terms of a phonetic difference (velars change place of articulation and become alveopalatals). The second rule cannot be characterized by phonetic properties: the sets {p, r}, {i, b}, and {o, n} are not defined by some phonetic property, and the change of [p] to [i] and [r] to [b] has no coherent phonetic characterization.

The lack of rules like (4b) is not just an isolated limitation of knowledge – it's not simply that we haven't found the specific rules (4b) but we have found (4a) – but rather these kinds of rules represent large, systematic classes. (3b) and (4b) represent a general kind of rule, where classes of segments are defined arbitrarily. Consider the constraint on clusters of two consonants in English. In terms of phonetic classes, this reduces to the simple rule that the first consonant must be a stop and the second consonant must be a liquid. The second rule changes vowels into nasalized vowels before nasal consonants. The basis for defining these classes will be considered now.

6.2 Distinctive feature theory

Just saying that rules are defined in terms of phonetic properties is too broad a claim, since it says nothing about the phonetic properties that are relevant. Consider a hypothetical rule, stated in terms of phonetic properties:

all vowels change place of articulation so that the original difference in formant frequency between F_1 and F_3 is reduced to half what it originally was, when the vowel appears before a consonant whose duration ranges from 100 to 135 ms.

> *An acoustic description considers just physical sound, but a perceptual description factors in the question of how the ear and brain process sound. The difference between 100 Hz and 125 Hz is acoustically the same as that between 5,100 Hz and 5,125 Hz. The two sets are perceptually very different, the former being perceived as "more separate" and the latter as virtually indistinguishable.*

What renders this rule implausible (no language has one vaguely resembling it) is that it refers to specific numerical durations, and to the difference in frequency between the first and third formant.

The phonetic properties which are the basis of phonological systems are general and somewhat abstract, such as voicing or rounding, and are largely the categories which we have informally been using already: they are not the same, as we will see. The hypothesis of distinctive feature theory is that there is a small set, around two dozen, of phonetically based properties which phonological analysis uses. These properties, the distinctive features, not only define the possible phonemes of human languages, but also define phonological rules. The classical statement of features derives from Chomsky and Halle (1968). We will use an adapted set of these features, which takes into consideration refinements. Each feature can have one of two values, plus and minus, so for each speech sound, the segment either *has* the property (is $[+F_i]$) or *lacks* the property (is $[-F_i]$). In this section, we follow Chomsky and Halle (1968) and present the generally accepted articulatory correlates of the features, that is, what aspects of production the feature relates to. There are also acoustic and perceptual correlates of features, pertaining to what the segment sounds like, which are discussed by Jakobson, Fant and Halle (1952) using a somewhat different system of features.

6.2.1 Phonetic preliminaries

By way of phonetic background to understanding certain features, two phonetic points need to be clarified. First, some features are characterized in terms of the "neutral position," which is a configuration that the vocal tract is assumed to have immediately prior to speaking. The neutral position, approximately that of the vowel [ɛ], defines relative movement of the tongue.

Second, you need to know a bit about how the vocal folds vibrate, since some feature definitions relate to the effect on vocal fold vibration (important because it provides most of the sound energy of speech). The vocal folds vibrate when there is enough air pressure below the glottis (the opening between the vocal folds) to force the vocal folds apart. This opening reduces subglottal pressure, which allows the folds to close, and this allows air pressure to rebuild to the critical level where the vocal folds are blown apart again. The critical factor that causes the folds to open is that the pressure below the vocal folds is higher than the pressure above.

Air flows from the lungs at a roughly constant rate. Whether there is enough drop in pressure for air to force the vocal folds open is thus determined by the positioning and tension of the vocal folds (how hard it is to force them apart), and the pressure above the glottis. The pressure above the glottis depends on how effectively pressure buildup can be relieved, and this is determined by the degree of constriction in the vocal tract. In short, the configuration of the vocal folds, and the degree and location of constriction above the glottis almost exclusively determine whether there will be voicing.

If the pressure above and below the glottis is nearly equal, air stops flowing and voicing is blocked. So if the vocal tract is completely obstructed (as for the production of a voiceless stop like [k]), air flowing through the glottis rapidly equalizes the pressure below and above the glottis, which stops voicing. On the other hand, if the obstruction in the vocal tract is negligible (as it is in the vowel [a]), the pressure differential needed for voicing is easily maintained, since air passing through the glottis is quickly vented from the vocal tract.

A voiced stop such as [g] is possible, even though it involves a total obstruction of the vocal tract analogous to that found in [k], because it takes time for pressure to build up in the oral cavity to the point that voicing ceases. Production of [g] involves ancillary actions to maintain voicing. The pharynx may be widened, which gives the air more room to escape, delaying the buildup of pressure. The larynx may be lowered, which also increases the volume of the oral cavity; the closure for the stop may be weakened slightly, allowing tiny amounts of air to flow through; the velum may be raised somewhat to increase the size of the air cavity, or it may be lowered somewhat to allow small (usually imperceptible) amounts of air to pass through the nose. The duration of the consonant can be reduced – generally, voiced stops are phonetically shorter than corresponding voiceless stops.

Certain sounds such as vowels lack a radical constriction in the vocal tract, so it is quite easy to maintain voicing during such sounds, whereas with other sounds, specifically obstruents, voicing is difficult to maintain. Some accounts of this distinction, especially that of Chomsky and Halle (1968), refer to "spontaneous voicing," which is grounded on the assumption that voicing occurs automatically simply by positioning the vocal folds in what we might call the "default" position. For sounds that involve a significant obstruction of the vocal tract, special actions are required for voicing. The features [sonorant] and [consonantal] directly relate to the obstruction in the vocal tract, which determines whether the vocal folds vibrate spontaneously.

6.2.2 Major class features

One of the most intuitive distinctions which feature theory needs to capture is that between consonants and vowels. There are three features, the so-called major class features, which provide a rough first grouping of sounds into functional types that includes the consonant/vowel distinction.

syllabic (syl): forms a syllable peak (and thus can be stressed).
sonorant (son): sounds produced with a vocal tract configuration in which spontaneous voicing is possible.

consonantal (con): sounds produced with a major obstruction in the oral cavity.

The feature [syllabic] is, unfortunately, simultaneously one of the most important features and one of the hardest to define physically. It corresponds intuitively to the notion "consonant" (where [h], [y], [m], [s], [t] are "consonants") versus "vowel" (such as [a], [i]): indeed the only difference between the vowels [i, u] and the corresponding glides [y, w] is that [i, u] are [+syllabic] and [y, w] are [−syllabic]. The feature [syllabic] goes beyond the intuitive vowel/consonant split. English has syllabic sonorants, such as [r̩], [l̩], [n̩]. The main distinction between the English words (American English pronunciation) *ear* [ɪr̩] and *your* [yr̩] resides in which segments are [+syllabic] versus [−syllabic]. In *ear*, the vowel [ɪ] is [+syllabic] and [r] is [−syllabic], whereas in *your*, [y] is [−syllabic] and [r̩] is [+syllabic]. The words *eel* [il] and the reduced form of *you'll* [yl̩] for many speakers of American English similarly differ in that [i] is the peak of the syllable (is [+syllabic]) in *eel*, but [l̩] is the syllable peak in *you'll*.

Other languages have syllabic sonorants which phonemically contrast with nonsyllabic sonorants, such as Serbo-Croatian which contrasts syllabic [r̩] with nonsyllabic [r] (cf. *groze* 'fear (gen)' versus *groce* 'little throat'). Swahili distinguishes [m̩buni] 'ostrich' and [mbuni] 'coffee plant' in the fact that [m̩buni] is a three-syllable word and [m̩] is the peak (the only segment) of that first syllable, but [mbuni] is a two-syllable word, whose first syllable peak is [u]. Although such segments may be thought of as "consonants" in one intuitive sense of the concept, they have the feature value [+syllabic]. This is a reminder that there is a difference between popular concepts about language and technical terms. "Consonant" is not strictly speaking a technical concept of phonological theory, even though it is a term quite frequently used by phonologists – almost always with the meaning "nonpeak" in the syllable, i.e. a [−syllabic] segment.

The feature [sonorant] captures the distinction between segments such as vowels and liquids where the constriction in the vocal tract is small enough that no special effort is required to maintain voicing, as opposed to sounds such as stops and fricatives which have enough constriction that effort is needed to maintain voicing. In an oral stop, air cannot flow through the vocal tract at all, so oral stops are [−sonorant]. In a fricative, even though there is some airflow, there is so much constriction that pressure builds up, with the result that spontaneous voicing is not possible, thus fricatives are [−sonorant]. In a vowel or glide, the vocal tract is only minimally constricted so air can flow without impedance: vowels and glides are therefore [+sonorant]. A nasal consonant like [n] has a complete obstruction of airflow through the oral cavity, but nevertheless the nasal passages are open which allows free flow of air. Air pressure does not build up during the production of nasals, so nasals are [+sonorant]. In the liquid [l], there is a complete obstruction formed by the tip of the tongue with the alveolar ridge, but nevertheless air flows freely over the sides of the tongue so [l] is [+sonorant].

The definition of [sonorant] could be changed so that glottal configuration is also included, then the laryngeals would be [−sonorant]. There is little compelling evidence to show whether this would be correct; later, we discuss how to go about finding such evidence for revising feature definitions.

The question whether *r* is [+sonorant] or [−sonorant] has no simple answer, since many phonetically different segments are transcribed as *r*; some are [−sonorant] and some are [+sonorant], depending on their phonetic properties. The so-called fricative *r* of Czech (spelled ř) has a considerable constriction, so it is [−sonorant], but English type [ɹ] is a sonorant since there is very little constriction. In other languages there may be more constriction, but it is so brief that it does not allow significant buildup of air pressure (this would be the case with "tapped" *r*'s). Even though spontaneous voicing is impossible for the laryngeal consonants [h, ʔ] because they are formed by positioning the vocal folds so that voicing is precluded, they are [+sonorant] since they have no constriction above the glottis.

The feature [consonantal] is very similar to the feature [sonorant], but specifically addresses the question of whether there is any major constriction in the oral cavity. This feature groups together obstruents, liquids and nasals which are [+consonantal], versus vowels, glides and laryngeals ([h, ʔ]) which are [−consonantal]. Vowels and glides have a minor obstruction in the vocal tract, compared to that formed by a fricative or a stop. Glottal stop is formed with an obstruction at the glottis, but none in the vocal tract, hence it is [−consonantal]. In nasals and liquids, there is an obstruction in the oral cavity, even though the overall constriction of the whole vocal tract is not high enough to prevent spontaneous voicing. Recent research indicates that this feature may not be necessary, since its function is usually covered as well or better by other features.

The most important phonological use of features is that they identify classes of segments in rules. All speech sounds can be analyzed in terms of their values for the set of distinctive features, and the set of segments that have a particular value for some feature (or set of feature values) is a natural class. Thus the segments [a i r̩ m̩] are members of the [+syllabic] class, and [y h ʔ r m s p] are members of the [−syllabic] class; [a r̩ y ʔ r m] are in the [+sonorant] class and [s z p b] are in the [−sonorant] class; [a i w h ʔ] are in the [−consonantal] class and [r̩ m̩ r m s p] are in the [+consonantal] class. Natural classes can be defined in terms of conjunctions of features, such as [+consonantal, −syllabic], which refers to the set of segments which are simultaneously [+consonantal] and [−syllabic]. Accordingly, the three major class features combine to define five maximally differentiated classes, exemplified by the following segment groups.

(5)

	a, i, u	r̩, l̩, m̩	y, w, h, ʔ	r, l, m	s, z, p, b
syllabic	+	+	−	−	−
sonorant	+	+	+	+	−
consonantal	−	+	−	+	+

Further classes are definable by omitting specifications of one or more of these features: for example, the class [−syllabic, −sonorant] includes {y, w, h, ʔ, r, l, m}.

One thing to note is that all [+syllabic] segments, i.e. all syllable peaks, are also [+sonorant]. It is unclear whether there are syllabic obstruents, i.e. [s̩], [k̩]. It has been claimed that such things exist in certain dialects of Berber, but their interpretation remains controversial, since the principles for detection of syllables are controversial. Another gap is the combination [−sonorant, −consonantal], which would be a physical impossibility. A [−sonorant] segment would require a major obstruction in the vocal tract, but the specification [−consonantal] entails that the obstruction could not be in the oral cavity. The only other possibility would be constriction of the nasal passages, and nostrils are not sufficiently constrictable.

6.2.3 Place of articulation

Features to define place of articulation are our next functional set. We begin with the features typically used by vowels, specifically the [+syllabic, −consonantal, +sonorant] segments, and then proceed to consonant features, ending with a discussion of the intersection of these features.

Vowel place features.   The features which define place of articulation for vowels are the following.

high: the body of the tongue is raised from the neutral position.
low: the body of the tongue is lowered from the neutral position.
back: the body of the tongue is retracted from the neutral position.
round: the lips are protruded.
tense: sounds requiring deliberate, accurate, maximally distinct gestures that involve considerable muscular effort.
advanced tongue root: produced by drawing the root of the tongue forward.

The main features are [high], [low], [back], and [round]. Phonologists primarily distinguish just front and back vowels, governed by [back]: front vowels are [−back] since they do not involve retraction of the tongue body, and back vowels are [+back]. Phonetic central vowels are usually treated as phonological back vowels, since typically central vowels are unrounded and back vowels are rounded. Distinctions such as between the mid vowels [ɘ], [ə], [ɤ], [ɜ] and [ʌ], or the high vowels [ɨ], [ʉ], and [ɯ], are usually considered to be phonologically unimportant over-differentiations of language-specific phonetic values of phonologically back unrounded vowels. In lieu of clear examples of a contrast between central and back rounded vowels, or central and back unrounded vowels, we will not at the moment postulate any feature for the front–back dimension: though, section 6.6 considers possible evidence for the phonological relevance of the concept "central vowel."

Two main features are employed to represent vowel height. High vowels are [+high] and [−low], low vowels are [+low] and [−high]. No vowel can be simultaneously [+high] and [+low] since the tongue cannot be raised and lowered simultaneously; mid vowels are [−high,−low]. In addition, any vowel can be produced with lip rounding, using the feature [round]. These features allow us to characterize the following vowel contrasts.

(6)

	i	ü	ɨ	u	e	ö	ʌ	o	æ	œ	ɑ	ɒ
high	+	+	+	+	−	−	−	−	−	−	−	−
low	−	−	−	−	−	−	−	−	+	+	+	+
back	−	−	+	+	−	−	+	+	−	−	+	+
round	−	+	−	+	−	+	−	+	−	+	−	+

Note that [ɑ] is a back low unrounded vowel, in contrast to the symbol [ɒ] for a back low rounded vowel. As noted in chapter 2, IPA uses more vowel symbols than are typical for reporting linguistic data, especially among low vowels which includes [æ a ɐ ɑ ɒ]. Phonological sources typically use <a> to indicate a low nonround, nonfront vowel — IPA [ɑ] — and do not distinguish <a>, <ɑ> or <ɐ>.

Vowels with a laxer, "less deliberate" and lower articulation, such as [ɪ] in English *set* or [ɛ] in English *set* would be specified as [−tense].

(7)

	ɪ	ü	ɪ	ʊ	ɛ	ɜ	ə	ɔ
high	+	+	+	+	−	−	−	−
low	−	−	−	−	−	−	−	−
back	−	−	+	+	−	−	+	+
round	−	+	−	+	−	+	−	+
tense	−	−	−	−	−	−	−	−

One question which has not been resolved is the status of low vowels in terms of this feature. Unlike high and mid vowels, there do not seem to be analogous contrasts in low vowels between tense and lax [æ]. Another important point about this feature is that while [back], [round], [high] and [low] will also play a role in defining consonants, [tense] plays no role in consonantal contrasts.

> Korean has a set of so-called "tense" consonants but these are phonetically "glottal" consonants.

The difference between *i* and *ɪ*, or *e* and *ɛ* has also been considered to be one of vowel height (proposed in alternative models where vowel height is governed by a single scalar vowel height feature, rather than by the binary features [high] and [low]). This vowel contrast has also been described in terms of the features "Advanced Tongue Root" (ATR), especially in the vowel systems of languages of Africa and Siberia. There has been debate over the phonetic difference between [ATR] and [tense]. Typically, [+tense] front vowels are fronter than their lax counterparts, and [+tense] back vowels are backer than their lax counterparts. In comparison, [+ATR] vowels are supposed to be generally fronter than corresponding [−ATR] vowels, so that [+ATR] back vowels are phonetically fronter than their [−ATR] counterparts. However, some articulatory studies have shown that the physical basis for the tense/lax distinction in English is no different from that which ATR is based on. Unfortunately, the clearest examples of the feature [ATR] are found in languages of Africa, where very little phonetic research has been done. Since no language contrasts both [ATR] and [tense] vowels, it is usually supposed that there is a single feature, whose precise phonetic realization varies somewhat from language to language.

Consonant place features. The main features used for defining consonantal place of articulation are the following.

coronal: produced with the blade or tip of the tongue raised from the neutral position.
anterior: produced with an obstruction located at or in front of the alveolar ridge.
strident: produced with greater noisiness.
distributed: produced with a constriction that extends for a considerable distance along the direction of air flow.

Place of articulation in consonants is primarily described with the features [coronal] and [anterior]. Labials, labiodentals, dentals and alveolars are [+anterior] since their primary constriction is at or in front of the alveolar ridge (either at the lips, the teeth, or just back of the teeth) whereas other consonants (including laryngeals) are [−anterior], since they lack this front constriction. The best way to understand this feature is to remember that it is the defining difference between [s] and [š], where [s] is [+anterior] and [š] is [−anterior]. Anything produced where [s] is produced, or in front of that position, is therefore [+anterior]; anything produced where [š] is, or behind [š] is [−anterior].

(8) [+anterior]   [−anterior]
     f ɸ p θ s ʈ t   š č ṣ ṭ ç x k q ʕ h ʔ

Consonants which involve the blade or tip of the tongue are [+coronal], and this covers the dentals, alveolars, alveopalatals and retroflex consonants. Consonants at other places of articulation – labial, velar, uvular and laryngeal – are [−coronal]. Note that this feature does not encompass the body (back) of the tongue, so while velars and uvulars use the tongue, they use the body of the tongue rather than the blade or tip, and therefore are [−coronal]. The division of consonants into classes as defined by [coronal] is illustrated below.

(9) [+coronal]   [−coronal]
     ṭ θ t s š n l r ñ ṭ   p ɸ f k q ʕ

Two other features are important in characterizing the traditional places of articulation. The feature [distributed] is used in coronal sounds to distinguish dental [t̪] from English alveolar [t], or alveopalatal [š] from retroflex [ṣ]: the segments [t̪, š] are [+distributed] and [t, ṭ, ṣ] are [−distributed]. The feature [distributed], as applied to coronal consonants, approximately corresponds to the traditional phonetic notion "apical" ([−distributed]) versus "laminal" ([+distributed]). This feature is not relevant for velar and labial sounds and we will not specify any value of [distributed] for noncoronal segments.

The feature [strident] distinguishes strident [f, s] from nonstrident [ɸ, θ]: otherwise, the consonants [f, ɸ] would have the same feature specifications. Note that the feature [strident] is defined in terms of the aerodynamic property of greater turbulence (which has the acoustic correlate of greater noise), not in terms of the movement of a particular articulator – this defining characteristic is accomplished by different articulatory configurations. In terms of contrastive usage, the feature [strident] only serves to distinguish bilabial and labiodentals, or interdentals and alveolars. A sound is [+strident] only if it has greater noisiness, and "greater" implies a comparison. In the case of [φ] vs. [f], [β] vs. [v], [θ] vs. [s], or [ð] vs. [z] the second sound in the pair is noisier. No specific degree of noisiness has been proposed which would allow you to determine in isolation whether a given sound meets the definition of strident or not. Thus it is impossible to determine whether [š] is [+strident], since there is no contrast between strident and nonstrident alveopalatal sounds. The phoneme [š] is certainly relatively noisy – noisier than [θ] – but then [θ] is noisier than [φ] is.

[Strident] is not strictly necessary for making a distinction between [s] and [θ], since [distributed] also distinguishes these phonemes. Since [strident] is therefore only crucial for distinguishing bilabial and labial fricatives, it seems questionable to postulate a feature with such broad implications solely to account for the contrast between labiodental and bilabial fricatives. Nonetheless, we need a way of representing this contrast. The main problem is that there are very few languages (such as Ewe, Venda and Shona) which have both [f] and [φ], or [v] and [β], and the phonological rules of these languages do not give us evidence as to how this distinction should be made in terms of features. We will therefore only invoke the feature [strident] in connection with the [φ, β] vs. [f, v] contrast.

Using these three features, consonantal places of articulation can be partially distinguished as follows.

(10)	p	ṭ	t	č	ṭ	c, k, q, ʕ, ʔ
anterior	+	+	+	−	−	−
coronal	−	+	+	+	+	−
distributed	+	−	+	−	−	−

Vowel features on consonants. The features [high], [low], [back], and [round] are not reserved exclusively for vowels, and these typical vowel features can play a role in defining consonants as well. As we see in (10), velar, uvular, pharyngeal and glottal places of articulation are not yet distinguished; this is where the features [high], [low] and [back] become important. Velar, uvular and pharyngeal consonants are [+back] since they are produced with a retracted tongue body. The difference between velar and uvular consonants is that with velar consonants the tongue body is raised, whereas with uvular consonants it is not, and thus velars are [+high] where uvulars are [−high]. Pharyngeal consonants are distinguished from uvulars in that pharyngeals are [+low] and uvulars are [−low], indicating that the constriction for pharyngeals is even lower than that for uvulars.

One traditional phonetic place of articulation for consonants is that of "palatal" consonants. The term "palatal" is used in many ways, for

example the postalveolar or alveopalatal (palatoalveolar) consonants [š]
and [č] might be referred to as palatals. This is strictly speaking a mis-
nomer, and the term "palatal" is best used only for the "true palatals,"
transcribed in IPA as [c ç ɟ]. Such consonants are found in Hungarian, and
also in German in words like [iç] 'I' or in Norwegian [çö:per] 'buys'. These
consonants are produced with the body of the tongue raised and fronted,
and therefore they have the feature values [+hi, −back]. The classical feature system presented here provides no way to distinguish such palatals
from palatalized velars ([kʸ]) either phonetically or phonologically.
Palatalized (fronted) velars exist as allophonic variants of velars before
front vowels in English, e.g. [kʸip] 'keep'; they are articulatorily and
acoustically extremely similar to the palatals of Hungarian. Very little
phonological evidence is available regarding the treatment of "palatals"
versus "palatalized velars": it is quite possible that [c] and [kʸ], or [ç] and
[xʸ], are simply different symbols, chosen on the basis of phonological pat-
terning rather than systematic phonetic differences.

With the addition of these features, the traditional places of articulation for consonants can now be fully distinguished.

(11)

	p	ṭ	t	č	ṭ	c, kʸ	k	q	ʕ	ʔ
anterior	+	+	+	−	−	−	−	−	−	−
coronal	−	+	+	+	+	−	−	−	−	−
distributed		+	−	+	−					
hi	−	−	−	−	−	+	+	−	−	−
back	−	−	−	−	−	−	+	+	+	−
low	−	−	−	−	−	−	−	−	+	−

The typical vowel features have an additional function as applied to consonants, namely that they define secondary articulations such as palatalization and rounding. Palatalization involves superimposing the raised
and fronted tongue position of the glide [y] onto the canonical articulation of a consonant, thus the features [+high, −back] are added to the primary features that characterize a consonant (those being the features that
typify [i, y]). So, for example, the essential feature characteristics of a bilabial are [+anterior, −coronal] and they are only incidentally [−hi,−back].
A palatalized bilabial would be [+anterior,−coronal,+hi −back]. Velarized
consonants have the features [+high, +back] analogous to the features
of velar consonants; pharyngealized consonants have the features [+back,
+low]. Consonants may also bear the feature [round]. Applying various
possible secondary articulations to labial consonants results in the following specifications.

(12)

	p	pʸ	pˠ, pᵚ	pʷ	pʷ̈	pˤ	pˤ	pº	pˤ̈
hi	−	+	+	+	+	−	−	−	−
back	−	−	+	+	−	+	+	+	−
low	−	−	−	−	−	+	−	−	−
round	−	−	−	+	+	−	−	+	+

Labialized (p^w), palatalized (p^y), velarized ($p^ɣ$, $p^ɰ$) and pharyngealized ($p^ʕ$) variants are the most common categories of secondary articulation. Uvularized consonants, i.e. p^q, are rare: uvularized clicks are attested in Jun/'hoansi. It is unknown if there is a contrast between rounded consonants differing in secondary height, symbolized above as p^w vs. p^o or $p^ẅ$ vs. $p^ö$. Feature theory allows such a contrast, so eventually we ought to find examples. If, as seems likely after some decades of research, such contrasts do not exist where predicted, there should be a revision of the theory, so that the predictions of the theory better match observations.

This treatment of secondary articulations makes other predictions. One is that there cannot be palatalized uvulars or pharyngeals. This follows from the fact that the features for palatalization ([+high, −back]) conflict with the features for uvulars ([−hi, +back]) and pharyngeals ([−hi, +back, +low]). Since such segments do not appear to exist, this supports the theory: otherwise we expect – in lieu of a principle that prohibits them – that they will be found in some language. Second, in this theory a "pure" palatal consonant (such as Hungarian [ɟ]) is equivalent to a palatalized (i.e. fronted) velar. Again, since no language makes a contrast between a palatal and a palatalized velar, this is a good prediction of the theory (unless such a contrast is uncovered, in which case it becomes a bad prediction of the theory).

6.2.4 Manner of articulation

Other features relate to the manner in which a segment is produced, apart from the location of the segment's constriction. The manner features are:

continuant (cont): the primary constriction is not narrowed so much that airflow through the oral cavity is blocked.
delayed release (del. rel): release of a total constriction is slowed so that a fricative is formed after the stop portion.
nasal (nas): the velum is lowered which allows air to escape through the nose.
lateral (lat): the mid section of the tongue is lowered at the side.

The feature [continuant] groups together vowels, glides, fricatives, and [h] as [+continuant]. Note that [continuant] is a broader group than the traditional notion "fricative" which refers to segments such as [s], [š] or [θ]. The term "fricative" generally refers to nonsonorant continuants, i.e. the class defined by the conjunction of features [+continuant, −sonorant]. Since continuants are defined as sounds where air can flow continuously through the oral cavity, nasals like [m n ŋ] are [−continuant], even though they allow continuous air flow (through the nose).

Affricates such as [č, p^f] are characterized with the feature [+delayed release]. Necessarily, all affricates are [−continuant], since they involve complete constriction followed by a period of partial fricative-like constriction, and therefore they behave essentially as a kind of stop. This feature is in question, since [p^f č k^x] do not act as a unified phonological class; nevertheless, some feature is needed to characterize stops versus affricates. Various alternatives have been proposed, for example that [kˣ] might just be the pronunciation of aspirated [kʰ] since velar [kˣ] and [kʰ] never seem to contrast; perhaps the feature [strident] defines [tˢ] vs. [t]. The proper representation of affricates is a currently unsolved issue in phonology.

The feature [+nasal] is assigned to sounds where air flows through the nasal passages, for example [n] as well as nasalized vowels like [ã]. Liquids and fricatives can be nasalized as well, but the latter especially are quite rare. L-like sounds are characterized with the feature [lateral]. Almost all [+lateral] sounds are coronal, though there are a few reports of velar laterals. Detailed information on the phonetics and phonology of these segments is not available.

Examples of the major manners of articulation are illustrated below, for coronal place of articulation.

(13)

	t	n	tˢ	s	l	ĩ	tˡ = λ
delayed release	−	−	+	−	−	−	+
continuant	−	−	−	+	+	+	+
lateral	−	−	−	−	+	+	+
nasal	−	+	−	−	−	+	−

6.2.5 Laryngeal features

Three features characterize the state of the glottis:

spread glottis (s.g.): the vocal folds are spread far apart.
constricted glottis (c.g.): the vocal folds are tightly constricted.
voice (voi): the vocal folds vibrate.

Voiced sounds are [+voice]. The feature [spread glottis] describes aspirated obstruents ([pʰ], [bʰ]) and breathy sonorants ([m̤], [a̤]); [constricted glottis] describes implosive ([ɓ]), ejective obstruents ([p']), and laryngealized sonorants ([m̰], [a̰]).

How to distinguish implosives from ejectives is not entirely obvious, but the standard answer is that ejectives are [−voice] and implosives are [+voice]. There are two problems with this. One is that implosives do not generally pattern with other [+voiced] consonants in phonological systems, especially in how consonants affect tone (voiced consonants, but typically not implosives, may lower following tones). The second is that Ngiti and Lendu have both voiced and voiceless implosives. The languages lack ejectives, which raises the possibility that voiceless implosives are phonologically [−voice,+c.g.], which is exactly the specification given to ejective consonants. You may wonder how [−voice,+c.g.] can be realized as an ejective in languages like Navajo, Tigre or Lushootseed, and as a voiceless implosive in Ngiti or Lendu. This is possible because feature values give approximate phonetic descriptions, not exact ones. The Korean "fortis" consonants, found in [k'ata] 'peel (noun),' [ak'i] 'musical instrument' or [alt'a] 'be ill' are often described as glottalized, and phonetic studies have shown that they are produced with glottal constrictions: thus they would be described as [−voice,+c.g.]. Nevertheless, they are not ejectives. Similarly, Khoekhoe (Nama) has a contrast between plain clicks ([!àm̄] 'deep') and glottalized ones ([!'ám̄] 'kill'), but the glottalized clicks realize the feature [+c.g.] as a simple constriction of the glottis, not involving an ejective release.

The usual explanation for the difference between ejectives in Navajo and glottalized nonejective consonants in Korean or Khoekhoe is that they have the same phonological specifications, [−voice,+c.g.], but realize the features differently due to language-specific differences in principles of phonetic implementation. This is an area of feature theory where more research is required.

The representations of laryngeal contrasts in consonants are given below.

(14)	p	ɓ	ɠ	p'	pʰ	ɓʱ
voice	−	+	+	−	−	+
c.g.	−	−	+	+	−	−
s.g.	−	−	−	−	+	+

6.2.6 Prosodic features

Finally, in order to account for the existence of length distinctions, and to represent stressed versus unstressed vowels, two other features were proposed:

long: has greater duration.
stress: has greater emphasis, higher amplitude and pitch, longer duration.

These are obvious: long segments are [+long] and stressed vowels are [+stress].

A major lacuna in the Chomsky and Halle (1968) account of features is a lack of features for tone. This is remedied in chapter 10 when we introduce nonlinear representations. For the moment, we can at least assume that tones are governed by a binary feature [±high tone] – this allows only two levels of tone, but we will not concentrate on languages with more than two tone levels.

6.2.7 Summary of feature values

Features combine quite freely, so we cannot give a complete list. By learning some specific feature values and applying your knowledge of the meaning of features, it should be possible to arrive at the feature values of other segments. This is, of course, possible only if you know relevant phonetic details of the sound that you are considering. In order to know the feature values of [ɭ], you need to know that this is the symbol for a retroflex lateral approximant, thus it has the features appropriate for [l], and it also has the features that characterize retroflex consonants, which are [−ant, −dist]. If you do not know the phonetic characteristics of the segment symbolized as [ʕ], it is necessary to first understand its phonetic properties – it is a voiced pharyngeal continuant – before trying to deduce its feature values. In reading descriptions of languages, it is also important to understand that a symbol used in published data on a language is not always used according to a particular standard of phonetic transcription practices at the moment, so read the phonetic descriptions of letters in the grammar carefully!

The standard feature values for the consonants of (American) English are given in (15), to help you understand how the entire set of features is applied to the sound inventory of a language which you are familiar with.

(15)

	p	t	č	k	b	d	ǰ	g	f	v	θ	ð
syl	−	−	−	−	−	−	−	−	−	−	−	−
son	−	−	−	−	−	−	−	−	−	−	−	−
cons	+	+	+	+	+	+	+	+	+	+	+	+
cont	−	−	−	−	−	−	−	−	+	+	+	+
del.rel	−	−	+	−	−	−	+	−	−	−	−	−
lat	−	−	−	−	−	−	−	−	−	−	−	−
nas	−	−	−	−	−	−	−	−	−	−	−	−
voi	−	−	−	−	+	+	+	+	−	+	−	+
c.g.	−	−	−	−	−	−	−	−	−	−	−	−
s.g.	(−	−	−	−)	−	−	−	−	−	−	−	−
ant	+	+	−	−	+	+	−	−	+	+	+	+
cor	−	+	+	−	−	+	+	−	−	−	+	+
distr		−	+			−	+				+	+
hi	−	−	−	+	−	−	−	+	−	−	−	−
lo	−	−	−	−	−	−	−	−	−	−	−	−
back	−	−	−	+	−	−	−	+	−	−	−	−
round	−	−	−	−	−	−	−	−	−	−	−	−

	s	z	š	ž	h	ʔ	m	n	ŋ	r	l	y	w
syl	−	−	−	−	−	−	−	−	−	−	−	−	−
son	−	−	−	−	+	+	+	+	+	+	+	+	+
cons	+	+	+	+	−	−	+	+	+	−	+	−	−
cont	+	+	+	+	+	−	−	−	−	+	+	+	+
del.rel	−	−	−	−	−	−	−	−	−	−	−	−	−
lat	−	−	−	−	−	−	−	−	−	−	+	−	−
nas	−	−	−	−	−	−	+	+	+	−	−	−	−
voi	−	+	−	+	−	−	+	+	+	+	+	+	+
c.g.	−	−	−	−	−	+	−	−	−	−	−	−	−
s.g.	−	−	−	−	+	−	−	−	−	−	−	−	−
ant	+	+	−	−	−	−	+	+	−	−	+	−	−
cor	+	+	+	+	−	−	−	+	−	+	+	−	−
distr	−	−	+	+			−				−	−	
hi	−	−	−	−	−	−	−	−	+	+	−	+	+
lo	−	−	−	−	−	−	−	−	−	−	−	−	−
back	−	−	−	−	−	−	−	−	+	+	−	−	+
round	−	−	−	−	−	−	−	−	−	+	−	−	+

The assignment of [spread glottis] − aspiration − in English stops varies according to context, so the value [−s.g.] is in parenthesis in the chart because both values of this feature are found on the surface, depending on context. The value [−s.g.] represents the underlying value.

Vowel feature summary. Certain feature values are uniform for all vowels: [+syl, −cons, +son, +cont, −del.rel, −ant, −lat, −dist.]. Typically, vowels are also [+voice, −s.g.,−c.g.]. There are languages such as Mazateco and !Xoo where breathy voicing and glottalization are used contrastively, so in these languages [+s.g.] and [+c.g.] are possible specifications. A number of languages have phonetic voiceless vowels, but the phonological status of voiceless vowels is not so clear, thus it may be that there are no phonologically [−voice] vowels. Values of the main features used to distinguish vowels are given in (16). (Recall that we are not certain whether [tense] applies to low vowels.)

> *The type of r used in American English is unusual and could better be transcribed as [ɹʷ] – in fact, pronunciation of r differs between English dialects. Do not assume that the features of r in some other language such as Finnish, Spanish or Chinese are the same as those for English.*

(16)

	i	ü	ɨ	ʉ	e	ö	ʌ	ɔ	æ	œ	ɑ	ɒ
high	+	+	+	+	−	−	−	−	−	−	−	−
low	−	−	−	−	−	−	−	−	+	+	+	+
back	−	−	+	+	−	−	+	+	−	−	+	+
round	−	+	−	+	−	+	−	+	−	+	−	+
tense	+	+	+	+	+	+	+	+				

	ɪ	ü	ɪ̵	ʊ	ɛ	ɔ̈	ə	ɔ
high	+	+	+	+	−	−	−	−
low	−	−	−	−	−	−	−	−
back	−	−	+	+	−	−	+	+
round	−	+	−	+	−	+	−	+
tense	−	−	−	−	−	−	−	−

Nasality, length, breathiness and creaky voice are properties freely available to vowels, so any of these vowels can have ±nasal, ±long, ±s.g. or ±c.g. counterparts.

Consonant feature summary. Primary place of articulation for consonants is summarized in (17), using continuant consonants (voiceless in the first row, voiced in the second: numbers in the third row are keyed to traditional place of articulation terms). Continuant consonants are used here because they exhibit the maximum number of distinctions, for example there are bilabial and labiodental fricatives, but only bilabial stops. All of these consonants are [−syl, +cont, −del.rel, −nas, −lat, −c.g., −tense, −round].

(17)

1:	bilabial	2:	labiodental
3:	(inter-)dental	4:	alveolar
5:	alveopalatal/postalveolar	6:	retroflex
7:	palatal	8:	velar
9:	uvular	10:	pharyngeal
11:	glottal/laryngeal		

	φ β 1	f v 2	θ ð 3	s z 4	š ž 5	ṣ ẓ 6	ç j̦ 7	x γ 8	χ ʁ 9	ħ ʕ 10	h ɦ 11
ant	+	+	+	+	−	−	−	−	−	−	−
cor	−	−	+	+	+	+	−	−	−	−	−
distr			+	−	+	−					
hi	−	−	−	−	−	−	+	+	−	−	−
lo	−	−	−	−	−	−	−	−	−	+	−
back	−	−	−	−	−	−	−	+	+	+	−

Secondary place of articulation is illustrated in (18), here restricted to secondary articulations on [p t]. All of these consonants are [−syl, −son, +cons, −cont, −del.rel, −lat, −nas, −voice, −s.g., −c.g., −tense].

(18)

	p	pʷ	pᵚ	pʸ	pˤ	pʷ̈, pꟴ	t	tʷ	tᵚ	tʸ	tˤ	tʷ̈, tꟴ
ant	+	+	+	+	+	+	+	+	+	+	+	+
cor	−	−	−	−	−	−	+	+	+	+	+	+
distr	−	−	−	−	−	−	−	−	−	−	−	−
hi	−	(+)	+	+	−	+	−	(+)	+	+	−	+
lo	−	−	−	−	+	−	−	−	−	−	+	−
back	−	+	+	−	+	−	−	+	+	−	+	−
round	−	+	−	−	−	+	−	+	−	−	−	+

Round consonants might simply have the specification [+round]. Tongue raising and backing is not necessary in order to achieve rounding, whereas tongue raising and backing is by definition necessary in order to have a velarized consonant.

A final important point must be made. The twenty-one features discussed here – syllabic, sonorant, consonantal, high, low, back, round, tense (advanced tongue root), coronal, anterior, strident, distributed, continuant, delayed release, nasal, lateral, spread glottis, constricted glottis, voice, long, stress – are specific empirical hypotheses. This means that they are subject to change in the face of evidence that a change is required, so they are not immutable. On the other hand, as scientific hypotheses, they must be taken seriously until good evidence is presented that another system of features is better (see section 6.6 and chapter 10 for discussion of such changes). Features should not be invented willy-nilly: using distinctive features is not the same as placing a plus sign in front of a traditional articulatory description, and thus describing sounds as [+mid], [+alveolar] or [+vowel] misconstrues the theoretical claim of distinctive features.

6.3 Features and classes of segments

Besides defining phonemes, features play a role in formalizing rules, since rules are stated in terms of features. Every specification, such as [+nasal] or [−voice], defines a class of segments. The generality of a class is inversely related to how many features are required to specify the class, as illustrated in (19).

(19)

$$
[+\text{syl}] \quad \begin{bmatrix} +\text{syl} \\ -\text{nasal} \end{bmatrix} \quad \begin{bmatrix} +\text{syl} \\ -\text{round} \end{bmatrix} \quad \begin{bmatrix} +\text{syl} \\ +\text{high} \\ -\text{nasal} \end{bmatrix} \quad \begin{bmatrix} +\text{syl} \\ -\text{hi} \\ -\text{lo} \\ -\text{nas} \\ -\text{tense} \end{bmatrix}
$$

ɛ e ɩ ɛ̃ ẽ ĩ ī	ɛ e ɩ i	ɔ o u õ	ɩ i	ə ɛ ɔ
a ɔ o ʊ ã ɔ̃ õ ũ	a ɔ o ʊ	õ ũ u ū	ʊ u	
u ə æ ũ ə̃ æ̃		u ə æ		

The most general class, defined by a single feature, is [+syllabic] which refers to all vowels. The size of that class is determined by the segments in the language: [+syllabic] in Spanish refers to [i e a o u], but in English refers to [i ɩ e ɛ æ a ɔ o u ʊ ə ʌ ɹ]. As you add features to a description, you narrow down the class, making the class less general. The usual principle adopted in phonology is that simpler rules, which use fewer features, are preferable to rules using more features.

One challenge in formalizing rules with features is recognizing the features which characterize classes. Discovering the features which define a class boils down to seeing which values are the same for all segments in the set, then checking that no other segment in the inventory also has that combination of values. The main obstacle is that you have to think of segments in terms of their feature properties, which takes practice to become second nature. As an exercise towards understanding the relation between classes of segments and feature descriptions, we will assume a language with the following segments:

(20) p t k b d g f s x v ɣ w y l m n a e i o u ü

To assist in solving the problems which we will consider, feature matrices of these segments are given below in (21).

(21)

	cons	son	syl	voi	cont	nas	lat	ant	cor	hi	bk	low	rd
p	+	−	−	−	−	−	−	+	−	−	−	−	−
t	+	−	−	−	−	−	−	+	+	−	−	−	−
k	+	−	−	−	−	−	−	−	−	+	+	−	−
b	+	−	−	+	−	−	−	+	−	−	−	−	−
d	+	−	−	+	−	−	−	+	+	−	−	−	−
g	+	−	−	+	−	−	−	−	−	+	+	−	−
f	+	−	−	−	+	−	−	+	−	−	−	−	−
s	+	−	−	−	+	−	−	+	+	−	−	−	−
x	+	−	−	−	+	−	−	−	−	+	+	−	−
v	+	−	−	+	+	−	−	+	−	−	−	−	−
ɣ	+	−	−	+	+	··	−	−	−	+	+	−	−

w	−	+	−	+	+	−	−	−	+	+	−	+
y	−	+	−	+	+	−	−	−	−	+	−	−	−
l	+	+	−	+	+	−	+	+	+	−	−	−	−
m	+	+	−	+	−	+	−	+	−	−	−	−	−
n	+	+	−	+	−	+	−	+	+	−	−	−	−
a	−	+	+	+	+	−	−	−	−	−	+	+	−
e	−	+	+	+	+	−	−	−	−	−	−	−	−
i	−	+	+	+	+	−	−	−	−	+	−	−	−
o	−	+	+	+	+	−	−	−	−	−	+	−	+
u	−	+	+	+	+	−	−	−	−	+	+	−	+
ü	−	+	+	+	+	−	−	−	−	+	−	−	+

Each of the following sets of segments can be defined in terms of some set of distinctive features.

(22) i.   p t k f s x
    ii. p t b d f s v l m n
    iii. w y l m n a e i o u ü
    iv. p k b g f x v γ
    v.   y l m n a e i
    vi. v γ w y a e i o u ü

In the first set, each segment is a voiceless obstruent, and, equally importantly, every voiceless obstruent of the language is included in this first set. This set could be specified as [−sonorant, −voice] or as [−voice], since all voiceless segments in the language are [−sonorant]. Given that both specifications refer to exactly the same segments, there is no question of one solution being wrong in the technical sense (assuming the language has the segments of (20): if the language had [h], these two feature specifications would not describe the segments). However, unless there is a compelling reason to do otherwise, the simplest definition of the set of segments should be given, using only those features which are absolutely necessary. The features which are used to exactly define a set of segments depends very much on what the entire set of segments in the language is. If we were dealing with a language which had, in addition, the segments [p^h t^h k^h] then in specifying the set [p t k f s x], you would have to also mention [−s.g.] in order to achieve a definition of the set which excludes [p^h t^h k^h].

The set (22ii) contains only consonants (i.e. [−syllabic] segments), but it does not contain all of the [−syllabic] segments of the language. Compare the segments making up (22ii) with the full set of consonants:

Whether mention of a feature is required depends on the theory you use. One theory of assimilations requires the assimilating feature to be explicitly mentioned in a rule, even if it could be predicted on the basis of other features.

(23) p t b d f s v   l m n   ← Selected class of segments
    p t k b d g f s x v γ w y l m n   ← Entire set of consonants

This set does not include glides: [consonantal] is the essential property which distinguishes glides (including *h* and *ʔ*, which are lacking here) from regular consonants. Thus, the segments in (ii) are [+consonantal]. But not all

[+consonantal] segments are included in set (ii): the velars are not included, so we need a further restriction. The features typically used to specify velars are [+high, +back], so we can use one of those features. Thus, you can pick out the segments in (ii) as the class of [+consonantal, −high] segments, or the [+consonantal, −back] segments. Rather than refer to [consonantal], you could try to take advantage of the fact that all glides are [+high] and refer to (ii) as the set of [−high] segments, without mentioning [consonantal]. It is true that all segments in the set are [−high], but [−high] itself cannot be the entire description of this set since not all [−high] segments of the language are in the set: the vowels {aeo} is not in set (ii). We conclude that [+consonantal, −high] is the correct one for this class of segments.

This set can also be identified by reference to a single feature: what one feature makes this distinction?

Set (iii) contains a mixture of vowels and consonants: it includes all vowels, plus the nasals, the lateral [l], and the glides. This class is defined by [+sonorant]. Another feature which is constant in this group is [+voice], so you could define the class as [+sonorant, +voice]. But addition of [+voice] contributes nothing, so there is no point to mentioning that feature as well. Set (iv) on the other hand contains only obstruents, but not all obstruents. Of the whole set of obstruents, what is missing from (iv) is the group {tds}, which are [+coronal]. Therefore, we can refer to set (iv) by the combination [−sonorant, −coronal].

The fifth set, {ylmnaei}, includes a mixture of vowels and consonants. Some properties that members of this set have in common are that they are voiced, and they are sonorants. Given the phoneme inventory, all sonorants are voiced, but not all voiced segments are sonorants. Since the voiced obstruents {bdgvγ} are not included in this set, it would be less efficient to concentrate on the feature [+voice], thus we focus on the generalization that the segments are sonorants. Now compare this set to the total set of sonorants.

(24) y l m n a e i
  w y l m n a e i o u ü

We can see that this set of segments is composed of a subset of sonorants, namely the sonorants excluding {w, o, u, ü}. But that set is the set of [+round] segments; therefore, the set is the set of [+sonorant, −round] segments.

The last set also contains a mixture of consonants and vowels: it includes all of the vowel and glides, plus the voiced obstruents {v, γ}. Therefore, the feature [sonorant] cannot be used to pick out this class of segments, since members of the class can have both values for that feature. However, all of the members of this class are voiced. Now compare set (vi) against the set of all voiced segments.

(25) v γ w y a e i o u ü
  b d g v γ w y l m n a e i o u ü

The fundamental difference between [b] and [v], or between [g] and [γ], is that {b, g} are stops while {v, γ} are continuants. This suggests using [+continuant] as one of the defining features for this class. Vowels and glides are all [+continuant], so we have passed the first test, namely that all segments in set (vi) are [+continuant,+voice]. We must also be sure that this is a sufficient specification for the class: are there any [+continuant,+voice] segments in the language which are not included in set (vi)? The segments to worry about in this case would be {l, m, n}, which are [+voice]. We exclude the nasals via [+continuant] and add [−lateral] to exclude *l*.

As a further exercise in understanding how sets of segments are grouped by the features, assume a language with the following segmental inventory.

(26)   p pᶠ t tˢ č c k b bᵛ v β dᶻ ǰ ɟ g m n ŋ f θ s š d ð z ž i ü e ö ə o u a w y

For each group, determine what feature(s) define the particular set of segments.

(27) i.   č c k ǰ ɟ g ŋ š ž i ü e ö ə o u a w y
      ii.   s i š e f z v β a ž o u y ö θ ü ə w ð
      iii. k y g c w i u ü ɟ ŋ
      iv.   k g a ə ŋ

6.4 Possible phonemes and rules – an answer

We now return to the theoretical questions raised at the beginning of this chapter: what is a possible phoneme and what is a possible phonological rule?

6.4.1 Possible phonemes

The theory of features answers the question of possible phonemes, saying that the segments which can be constructed using these features are all and the only possible phonemes. This gives a mathematical upper limit of 2^n segments, given n binary features, so if there are twenty features (a reasonable number), there are 1,048,576 logically possible feature specifications, and this is quite a lot of segments. It also has to be physically possible to realize a segment, so the number of possible segments is smaller than this. Many segments can be imagined which are phonetically uninterpretable, such as one which is [+high,+low]. Such a segment is physically impossible since the tongue cannot be contradictorily raised and lowered at the same time, so the nonexistence of a large class of such segments is independently explained. Similarly, no segment can be [+cons,−hi, −back,−ant,−cor]. A segment which is [+cons] is not a vowel or glide. The feature [−back] tells us that the segment would have a place of articulation in front of the velar position. [−ant] tells us that it must have a place of articulation behind the alveolar ridge, and [−hi] tells us that it cannot be a palatal. Everything about this description suggests the vowel [e], *except* that it is [+consonantal], whereas vowels are [−consonantal]. No major constriction can be formed with the tongue in the position of [e]: hence this combination of features happens to be physically impossible. To be attested in a language, a segment must be both *combinatorially* possible, i.e. it must use the features given by the theory, and *physically* possible.

Although the set of attested phonemes in human languages is quite large, there are significant limitations on what phonemes are possible. Retroflex consonants have the features [−anterior, +coronal, −distributed]. Recall the question whether a language could contrast two kinds of retroflex consonants, such as apical and sublaminal retroflex as found in Hindi versus Telugu. According to this theory of features, such a contrast is impossible, since no feature is available to describe such a difference within a language. Phonetic differences across languages are possible because phonetic interpretation is not subject to the limitations of phonological feature theory. Were we to discover such a contrast, the theory of features would be challenged, because it has no mechanism for expressing such a distinction. Similarly, the differences attested in the phonetics of [u] and [ʊ] across languages are never found within a language. In a single language, the maximal contrast is between two such vowels, governed by the feature tense (or ATR). The fact that such differences exist at the phonetic level between languages, but are never exploited within a single language as a way to distinguish words, is an example of the difference between phonetic and phonological properties.

Thus one of the main goals of distinctive feature theory is providing a predictive framework for saying what contrasts will and will not be found in the phoneme systems of human languages.

6.4.2 Rule formulation and features

The most important function of features is to form the basis for writing rules, which is crucial in understanding what defines a possible phonological rule. A typical rule of vowel nasalization, which nasalizes all vowels before a nasal, can be formulated very simply if stated in features:

(28)   [+syllabic] → [+nasal] / __ [+nasal]

Such a rule is common in the languages of the world. Very uncommon, if it exists at all, is one nasalizing only the lax vowel [ɪ], and only before [m]. Formulated with features, that rule looks as follows:

$$
(29) \quad
\begin{bmatrix} +\text{syl} \\ -\text{ATR} \\ +\text{hi} \\ -\text{round} \end{bmatrix}
\rightarrow [\,+nasal\,] / \_
\begin{bmatrix} +\text{nasal} \\ +\text{ant} \\ -\text{coronal} \end{bmatrix}
$$

This rule require significantly more features than (28), since [ɪ] which undergoes the rule must be distinguished in features from other high vowels such as [i] or [ʊ] which (in this hypothetical case) do not undergo the rule, and [m] which triggers the rule must be distinguished from [n] or [ŋ] which do not.

Simplicity in rule writing. This relation between generality and simplicity on the one hand, and desirability or commonness on the other, has played a very important role in phonology: all things being equal, simpler rules are preferred, both for the intrinsic elegance of simple rules and because they correlate with more general classes of segments. Maximum generality is an essential desideratum of science.

The idea that rules are stated in terms of the simplest, most general classes of phonetically defined segments has an implication for rule formulation. Suppose we encounter a rule where high vowels (but not mid and low vowels) nasalize before nasal stops (n, m, $ŋ$), thus $in \rightarrow \tilde{i}m$, $uŋ \rightarrow \tilde{u}ŋ$, and so on. We could formulate such a rule as follows:

$$(30) \quad \begin{bmatrix} +\text{syl} \\ +\text{hi} \end{bmatrix} \rightarrow [+\text{nasal}]/\underline{\quad} \begin{bmatrix} +\text{nasal} \\ -\text{cont} \end{bmatrix}$$

However, we could equally well formalize the rule as

$$(31) \quad \begin{bmatrix} +\text{syl} \\ +\text{hi} \\ -\text{low} \end{bmatrix} \rightarrow \begin{bmatrix} +\text{syl} \\ +\text{hi} \\ -\text{low} \\ +\text{nasal} \end{bmatrix} /\underline{\quad} \begin{bmatrix} +\text{nasal} \\ -\text{cont} \\ -\text{low} \end{bmatrix}$$

We could freely add [−low] to the specification of the input segment (since no vowel can be [+hi, +low], thus high vowels automatically would pass that condition), and since the same class of vowels is referenced, inclusion of [−low] is empirically harmless. Saying that the vowel becomes [+syl, +hi, −low] is harmless, since the vowel that undergoes the change already made these specifications. At the same time, the additional features in (31) are useless complications, so on the theoretical grounds of simplicity, we formalize the rule as (30). In writing phonological rules, we specify only features which are mandatory. A formulation like

$$(32) \quad [+\text{syl}] \rightarrow [+\text{nasal}]/\underline{\quad} \begin{bmatrix} +\text{nasal} \\ -\text{cont} \end{bmatrix}$$

would mention fewer features, but it would be wrong given the nature of the rule we assume, since the rule should state that only *high* vowels nasalise, but this rule nasalises *all* vowels.

Formalizability. The claim that rules are stated in terms of phonetically defined classes is essentially an axiom of phonological theory.

What are the consequences of such a restriction? Suppose you encounter a language with a phonological rule of the type $\{p, r\} \rightarrow \{i, b\} \,/\, \_\_ \{o, n\}$. Since the segments being changed (p and r) or conditioning the change (o and n) cannot be defined in terms of any combination of features, nor can the changes be expressed via any features, the foundation of phonological theory would be seriously disrupted. Such a rule would refute a fundamental claim of the theory that processes must be describable in terms of these (or similar) features. This is what it means to say that the theory makes a prediction: if that prediction is wrong, the theory itself is wrong.

Much more remains to be said about the notion of "possible rule" in phonology; nevertheless, we can see that distinctive feature theory plays a vital role in delimiting possible rules, especially in terms of characterizing the classes of segments that can function together for a rule. We now turn to a discussion of rule formalism, in the light of distinctive feature theory.

6.5 The formulation of phonological rules

Many aspects of rule theory were introduced in our informal approach to rule-writing, and they carry over in obvious ways to the formal theory that uses features. The general form of a phonological rule is:

$$(33) \quad \begin{bmatrix} \alpha F_i \\ \beta F_j \\ \vdots \end{bmatrix} \rightarrow \begin{bmatrix} \gamma F_k \\ \mu F_l \\ \vdots \end{bmatrix} \Bigg/ \ldots \begin{bmatrix} \theta F_m \\ \delta F_x \\ \vdots \end{bmatrix} - \begin{bmatrix} \kappa F_y \\ \lambda F_l \\ \vdots \end{bmatrix} \ldots$$

$$\text{Focus} \quad\quad \underset{\text{change}}{\text{Stuctural}} \quad\quad \text{Trigger}$$

where F_i, F_j, F_k ... are features and α, β, γ ... are plus or minus values. The matrix to the left of the arrow is the segment changed by the rule; that segment is referred to as the focus or target of the rule. The matrix immediately to the right of the arrow is the structural change, and describes the way in which the target segment is changed. The remainder of the rule constitutes the trigger (also known as the determinant or environment), stating the conditions outside of the target segment which are necessary for application of the rule.

Each element is given as a matrix, which expresses a conjunction of features. The matrices of the target and trigger mean "all segments of the language which have the features $[\alpha F_i]$ as well as $[\beta F_j]$. . ." The matrix of the structural change means that when a target segment undergoes a rule, it receives whatever feature values are specified in that matrix.

There are a few special symbols which enter into rule formulation. One which we have encountered is the word boundary, symbolized as "#". A rule which lengthens a vowel before a word-final sonorant would be written as follows:

(34)   [+syl] → [+long] / _ [+son] #

A rule which devoices a word-initial consonant would be written as:

(35)   [−son] → [−voice] / # _

A word boundary can come between the target and the trigger segments, in which case it means "when the trigger segment is in the next word." Such processes are relatively infrequent, but, for example, there is a rule in Sanskrit which voices a consonant at the end of a word when it is followed by a sonorant in the next word, so /tat#aham/ becomes [tad#aham] 'that I'; voicing does not take place strictly within the word, and thus /pat-a:mi/ 'I fly' does not undergo voicing. This rule is formulated as in (36).

(36)   [−son] → [+voice] / _ # [+son]

   Another symbol is the null, Ø, used in the focus or structural change of a rule. As the focus, it means that the segment described to the right of the arrow is inserted in the stated context; and as the structural change, it means that the specified segment is deleted. Thus a rule that deletes a word-final short high vowel which is preceded by a sonorant would be written as follows:

(37) $\begin{bmatrix} +\text{syl} \\ -\text{hi} \\ -\text{long} \end{bmatrix} \rightarrow \emptyset / [+\text{son}]\_\#$

   There are occasions where it is necessary to restrict a rule to apply only when a sequence occurs in different morphemes, but not within a morpheme. Suppose you find a rule that deletes a consonant after a consonant, but only when the consonants are in separate morphemes: thus the bimorphemic word /tap-ta/ with /p/ at the end of one morpheme and /t/ at the beginning of another becomes [tapa], but the monomorphemic word /tapta/ does not undergo deletion. Analogous to the word boundary, there is also a morpheme boundary symbolized by "+," which can be used in writing rules. Thus the rule deleting the second of two consonants just in case the consonants are in diferent morphemes (hence a morpheme boundary comes between the consonants) is stated as:

(38)   [−syl] → Ø / [−syl] + _

   You may encounter other conventions of formalism. One such notation is the brace notation. Whereas the standard matrix [. . .] refers to a conjunction of properties – segments which are A *and* B *and* C all at once – braces {. . .} express disjunctions, that is, segments which are A *or* B *or* C. One of the most frequent uses of braces is exemplified by a rule found in a number of languages which shortens a long vowel if it is followed by either two consonants or else one consonant plus a word boundary, i.e. followed by a consonant that is followed by an consonant or #. Such a rule can be written as (39).

(39) $[+\text{syl}] \rightarrow [-\text{long}] /\_ [-\text{syl}] \begin{Bmatrix} -\text{syl} \\ \# \end{Bmatrix}$

Most such rules use the notation to encode syllable-related properties, so in this case the generalization can be restated as "shorten a long vowel followed by a syllable-final consonant." Using [.] as the symbol for a syllable boundary, this rule could then be reformulated as:

(40) $[+\text{syl}] \rightarrow [-\text{long}] / \_ [-\text{syl}].$

Although the brace notation has been a part of phonological theory, it has been viewed with considerable skepticism, partly because it is not well motivated for more than a handful of phenomena that may have better explanations (e.g. the syllable), and partly because it is a powerful device that undermines the central claim that rules operate in terms of natural classes (conjunctions of properties).

Some rules need to refer to a variably sized sequence of elements. A typical example is vowel harmony, where one vowel assimilates a feature from another vowel, and ignores any consonants that come between. Suppose we have a rule where a vowel becomes round after a round vowel, ignoring any consonants. We could not just write the rule as (41), since that incorrectly states that only vowels strictly next to round vowels harmonize.

(41) $[+\text{syl}] \rightarrow [+\text{rd}] / [+\text{syl}, +\text{rd}] \_$

We can use the subscript-zero notation, and formalize the rule as in (42).

(42) $[+\text{syl}] \rightarrow [+\text{rd}] / [+\text{syl}, +\text{rnd}] [-\text{syl}]_0 \_$

The expression "$[-\text{syl}]_0$" means "any number of $[-\text{syl}]$ segments," from none to an infinite sequence of them.

A related notation is the parenthesis, which surrounds elements that may be present, but are not required. A rule of the form $X \rightarrow Y / \_ (WZ)Q$ means that X becomes Y before Q or before WZQ, that is, before Q ignoring WZ. The parenthesis notation essentially serves to group elements together. This notation is used most often for certain kinds of stress-assignment rules and advancements in the theory of stress have rendered parenthesis unnecessary in many cases.

One other very useful bit of notation is the feature variable notation. So far, it has actually been impossible to formalize one of the most common phonological rules in languages, the rule which assimilates a nasal in place of articulation to the following consonant, where /mk/ → [ŋk], /np/

→ [mp] and so on. While we can write a rule which makes any nasal become [+ant,+cor] before a [+ant,+cor] consonant – any nasal becomes [n] before /t/ – and we can write a rule to make any nasal [+ant,−cor] before a [+ant,−cor] consonant – nasals become [m] before [p] – we cannot express both changes in one rule.

(43)

a. $[+\text{nas}] \rightarrow \begin{bmatrix} +\text{ant} \\ +\text{cor} \end{bmatrix} / \_\begin{bmatrix} +\text{ant} \\ +\text{cor} \end{bmatrix}$

b. $[+\text{nas}] \rightarrow \begin{bmatrix} +\text{ant} \\ -\text{cor} \end{bmatrix} / \_\begin{bmatrix} +\text{ant} \\ -\text{cor} \end{bmatrix}$

The structural change cannot be "→[+cor]" because when a nasal becomes [m] it becomes [−cor]. For the same reason the change cannot be "→[−cor]" since making a nasal becomes [n] makes it become [+cor]. One solution is the introduction of feature variables, notated with Greek letters α, β, γ, etc. whose meaning is "the same value." Thus a rule which makes a nasal take on whatever values the following consonant has for place of articulation would be written as follows:

(44) $[+\text{nas}] \rightarrow \begin{bmatrix} \alpha\text{ant} \\ \beta\text{cor} \end{bmatrix} / \_\begin{bmatrix} \alpha\text{ant} \\ \beta\text{cor} \end{bmatrix}$

Thus when the following consonant has the value [+cor] the nasal becomes [+cor] and when the following consonant has the value [−cor] the nasal becomes [−cor]. We will return to issues surrounding this notation in the final chapter.

There are a couple of commonly used informal shorthand practices which you need to recognize. Many rules refer to "consonants" versus "vowels," meaning [−syllabic] and [+syllabic] segments, and the shorthand "C" and "V" are often used in place of [−syllabic] and [+syllabic]. Also, related to the feature variable notation, it is sometimes necessary to write rules which refer to the entire set of features. A typical example would be in a rule "insert a vowel which is a copy of the preceding vowel into a word-final cluster." Rather that explicitly listing every feature with an associated variable, such a rule might be written as:

(45) $\emptyset \rightarrow V_i / V_i \, C\_C\#$

meaning "insert a copy of the preceding vowel."

6.6 Changing the theory

The theory of features is an empirical hypothesis, and is subject to revision in the face of appropriate data. It is not handed down by a higher authority, nor is it arbitrarily picked at the whim of the analyst. It is important to give critical thought to how the set of distinctive features can be tested empirically, and revised. One prediction of the theory which we have discussed in section 4.1 is that the two kinds of phonetic retroflex consonants found in Hindi and Telugu cannot contrast within a language. What would happen if a language were discovered which distinguished two degrees of retroflexion? Would we discard features altogether?

This situation has already arisen: the theory presented here evolved from earlier, similar theories. In an earlier theory proposed by Jakobson and Halle, retroflex consonants were described with the feature [flat]. This feature was also used to describe rounding, pharyngealization, and uvularization. While it may seem strange to describe so many different articulatory characteristics with a single feature, the decision was justified by the fact that these articulations share an acoustic consequence, a downward shift or weakening of higher frequencies. The assumption at that point was that no language could minimally contrast retroflexion, rounding, and pharyngealization. If a language has both [ʈ] and [kʷ], the surface differences in the realization of [flat], as retroflexion versus rounding, would be due to language-specific spell-out rules.

The theory would be falsified if you could show that rounding and pharyngealization are independent, and counterexamples were found. Arabic has the vowels [i a u] as well as pharyngealized vowels [iˤ aˤ uˤ], which derive by assimilation from a pharyngealized consonant. If rounding and pharyngealization are both described by the feature [flat], it is impossible to phonologically distinguish [u] and [uˤ]. But this is not at all inappropriate if the goal is to represent phonological contrasts as opposed to phonetic differences, since the difference between [u] and [u̙] is a low-level phonetic one. The relevance of Arabic – whether it falsifies the feature [flat] – depends on what you consider to be the purpose of features.

Another prediction is that since uvular and round consonants are both [+flat], there should be no contrast between round and nonround uvulars, or between round velars and nonround uvulars, within a language. But a number of languages of the Pacific Northwest, including Lushootseed, have the contrast [k kʷ q qʷ]: this is a fact which is undeniably in the domain of phonology. The Dravidian language Badaga is reported to contrast plain and retroflex vowels, where any of the vowels [i e a o u] can be plain, half-retroflex, or fully retroflex. If [flat] indicates both retroflexion and rounding, it would be impossible to contrast [u] and [u~]. Since such languages actually do exist, their discovery forced the abandonment of the feature [flat] in favor of the system now used.

The specific feature [flat] was wrong, not the theory of features itself. Particular features may be incorrect, which will cause us to revise or replace them, but revisions should be undertaken only when strong evidence is presented which forces a revision. Features form the foundation

Badaga's three-way vowel contrast challenges the standard theory as well. Little is known about this language: the contrast was originally reported by Emeneau (1961), and Ladefoged and Maddieson (1996) report that few speakers have a three-way contrast. The problem posed by this contrast has been acknowledged, but so far no studies have explored its nature.

of phonology, and revision to those features may lead to considerable changes in the predictions of the theory. Such changes should be undertaken with caution, taking note of unexpected consequences. If the theory changes frequently, with new features constantly being added, this would rightly be taken as evidence that the underlying theory is wrong.

Suppose we find a language with a contrast between regular and sublingual retroflex consonants. We could accommodate this hypothetical language into the theory by adding a new feature [sublingual], defined as forming an obstruction with the underside of the tongue. This theory makes a new set of predictions: it predicts other contrasts distinguished by sublinguality. We can presumably restrict the feature to the [+coronal] segments on physical grounds. The features which distinguish coronals subclasses are [anterior] and [distributed], which alone can combine to describe four varieties of coronal – which actually exist in a number of Australian languages. With a new feature [sublingual], eight coronal classes can be distinguished: regular and sublingual alveolars, regular and sublingual dentals, regular and sublingual alveopalatals, and regular and sublingual retroflex consonants. Yet no such segments have been found. Such predictions need to be considered, when contemplating a change to the theory.

Similarly, recall the problem of "hyper-tense," "plain tense," "plain lax" and "hyper-lax" high vowels across languages: we noted that no more than two such vowels exist in a language, governed by the feature [tense]. If a language were discovered with three or four such high vowels, we could add a feature "hyper." But this makes the prediction that there could also be four-way contrasts among mid and low vowels. If these implications are not correct, the modification to the theory is not likely to be the correct solution to the problem. In general, addition of new features should be undertaken only when there is compelling evidence for doing so. The limited number of features actually in use is an indication of the caution with which features are added to the theory.

The case for labial.   A classical case in point of a feature which was added in response to significant problems with the existing feature system is the feature [labial]. It is now accepted that feature theory should include this feature:

[labial]: sound produced with the lips

This feature was not part of the set of features proposed in Chomsky and Halle (1968). However, problems were noticed in the theory without [labial].

The argument for adding [labial] is that it makes rules better formalizable. It was noticed that the following types of rules, inter alia, are frequently attested (see Campbell 1974, Anderson 1974).

(46)   a. $b \rightarrow w$ / _ C
       b. $w \rightarrow b$ / [+nasal] _

c. w → v

d. i → u / {p, b, m, w, u, o} __

In the first three rules, the change from bilabial obstruent to rounded glide or rounded glide to labiodental obstruent is a seemingly arbitrary change, when written according to the then-prevailing system of features. There is so little in common between [b] and [w], given these features, that a change of [b] to [r] would be simpler to formulate as in (47b), and yet the change [b] → [r] is unattested.

(47) a. $\begin{bmatrix} +ant \\ -cor \\ +voi \end{bmatrix} \rightarrow \begin{bmatrix} -ant \\ -cons \\ +hi \\ +bk \\ +rd \end{bmatrix} / \_\_ C$ b. $\begin{bmatrix} -cons \\ +hi \\ +rd \end{bmatrix} \rightarrow \begin{bmatrix} +ant \\ -cor \\ -hi \\ -rd \end{bmatrix}$

In the last rule of (46), no expression covers the class {p, b, m, w, u, o}: rather they correspond to the disjunction [+ant, −cor] or [+round].

These rules can be expressed quite simply with the feature [labial].

(48)

a. $\begin{bmatrix} +labial \\ +voi \end{bmatrix} \rightarrow [-cons]/\_\_C$ b. $\begin{bmatrix} +labial \\ -cons \end{bmatrix} \rightarrow [+cons]/[+nasal]\_\_$

c. $\begin{bmatrix} +labial \\ +round \end{bmatrix} \rightarrow \begin{bmatrix} +cons \\ -round \end{bmatrix}$ d. i → [+labial] [+labial] __

Feature redefinition. Even modifying definitions of existing features must be done with caution, and should be based on substantial evidence that existing definitions fail to allow classes or changes to be expressed adequately. One feature which might be redefined is [continuant]. The standard definition states that a segment is [+continuant] if it is produced with air continuously flowing through the *oral cavity*. An alternative definition is that a segment is [+continuant] if air flows continuously through the *vocal tract*. How do we decide which definition is correct? The difference is that under the first definition, nasals are [−continuant] and under the second definition, nasals are [+continuant].

If the first definition is correct, we expect to find a language where {p, t, č, k, m, n, ŋ, b, d, ǰ, g} undergo or trigger a rule, and {f, s, θ, x, v, z, ð, γ} do not: under the "oral cavity" definition, [−continuant] refers to the class of segments {p, t, č, k, m, n, ŋ, b, d, ǰ, g}. On the other hand, if the second hypothesis is correct, we should find a language where {n, m, n, f, s, x, v, x, γ} undergo or trigger a rule, and the remaining consonants {p, t, č, k, b, d, ǰ, g} do not: under the "vocal tract" definition of [continuant], the feature specification [+continuant] would refer to the set {n, m, n, f, s, x, v, x, γ}.

Just as important as knowing what sets of segments can be referred to by one theory or another, you need to consider what groupings of segments *cannot* be expressed in a theory. Under either definition of [continuant], finding a process which refers to {p, t, k, b, d, g} proves nothing, since either theory can refer to this class, either as [−continuant] in the "oral cavity" theory or as [−continuant, −nasal] in the "vocal tract" theory. The additional feature needed in the "vocal tract" theory does complicate the rule, but that does not in itself disprove the theory. If you find a process referring to {n, m, n, f, s, x, v, x, γ}, excluding {p, t, k, b, d, g}, this would definitively argue for the "oral cavity" theory. Such a class can be referred to with the specification [+continuant] in the "oral cavity" theory, but there is no way to refer to that set under the "vocal tract" theory. As it stands, we have not found such clear cases: but, at least we can identify the type of evidence needed to definitively choose between the theories. The implicit claim of feature theory is that it would be impossible for both kinds of rules to exist in human languages. There can only be one definition of any feature, if the theory is to be coherent.

Central vowels.   We will consider another case where the features face a problem with expressing a natural class, relating to the treatment of central versus back vowels. In chapter 3 we saw that Kenyang [k] and [q] are in complementary distribution, with [q] appearing word-finally after the vowels [o], [ɔ] and [a] and [k] appearing elsewhere. Representative examples are reproduced here.

Phonetic descriptions of vowels are not usually based on physiological data such as x-ray studies. Tongue positions are often deduced by matching sound quality with that of a standardly defined vowel: we assume that Kenyang schwa is central because it sounds like schwa, which is defined as being central.

(49)   enɔq   'tree'   enoq   'drum'
       ŋgaq   'knife'   ekaq   'leg'
       mǝk   'dirt'   ndek   'European'
       pɔbrik   'work project'   ayuk   (person's name)

Schwa does not cause lowering of *k* to *q*. In the standard account of vowels, [ǝ] differs from [ɔ] only in rounding, though phonetic tradition claims that these vowels also differ in being back ([ɔ]) versus central ([ǝ]). As previously discussed, this difference is attributed to a low level, phonologically insignificant phonetic factor.

The problem which Kenyang poses is that it is impossible to formulate the rule of k-lowering if schwa is phonologically a mid back unrounded vowel. A simple attempt at formulizing the rule would be:

(50) $\begin{bmatrix} +\text{hi} \\ +\text{back} \end{bmatrix} \rightarrow [-\text{high}] / \begin{bmatrix} +\text{back} \\ +\text{high} \end{bmatrix}$___

If schwa is [+back, −hi, −round] it would satisfy the requirements of the rule so should cause lowering of /k/, but it does not: therefore this formulation cannot be correct. Since schwa differs from [ɔ] in being [−round], we might try to exclude [ə] by requiring the trigger vowel to be [+round].

$$(51) \quad \begin{bmatrix} +\text{hi} \\ +\text{back} \end{bmatrix} \rightarrow [-\text{high}]/ \begin{bmatrix} +\text{back} \\ -\text{high} \\ +\text{round} \end{bmatrix} \_$$

But this formulation is not correct either, since it would prevent the nonround low vowel [ɑ] from triggering uvularization, which in fact it does do.

These data are a problem for the theory that there is only a two-way distinction between front and back vowels, not a three-way distinction between front, central, and back vowels. The uvularization rule of Kenyang can be formulated if we assume an additional feature, [±front], which characterizes front vowels. Under that theory, back vowels would be [+back, −front], front vowels would be [+front, −back], and central vowels would be [−back, −front]. Since we must account for this fact about Kenyang, the theory must be changed. But before adding anything to the theory, it is important to consider all of the consequences of the proposal.

A positive consequence is that it allows us to account for Kenyang. Another possible example of the relevance of central vowels to phonology comes from Norwegian (and Swedish). There are three high, round vowels in Norwegian, whereas the standard feature theory countenances the existence of only two high rounded vowels, one front and one back. Examples in Norwegian spelling are *do* 'outhouse,' *du* 'you sg' and *dy* 'forbear!'. The vowel *o* is phonetically [u], and *u* and *y* are distinct nonback round vowels. In many IPA transcriptions of Norwegian, these are transcribed as [dʉ] 'you sg' and [dy] 'forbear!', implying a contrast between front, central and back round vowels. This is exactly what the standard view of central vowels has claimed should not happen, and it would appear that Norwegian also falsifies the theory.

The matter is not so simple. The vowels spelled *u* versus *y* also differ in lip configuration. The vowel *u* is "in-rounded," with an inward narrowing of the lips, whereas *y* is "out-rounded," with an outward-flanging protrusion of the lips. This lip difference is hidden by the selection of the IPA symbols [ʉ] versus [y]. While it is clear that the standard theory does not handle the contrast, we cannot tell what the correct basis for maintaining the contrast is. We could treat the difference as a front ~ central ~ back distinction and disregard the difference in lip configuration (leaving that to phonetic implementation); or, we could treat the labial distinction as primary and leave the presumed tongue position to phonetic implementation.

Given that the theory of features has also accepted the feature [labial], it is possible that the distinction lies in [labial] versus [round], where the out-rounded vowel <y> is [+round, +labial] and in-rounded <u> is [−round, +labial] – or vice versa. Unfortunately, nothing in the phonological behavior of these vowels gives any clue as to the natural class groupings of the vowels, so the problem of representing these differences in Norwegian remains unresolved. Thus the case for positing a distinct phonological category of central vowel does not receive very strong support from the vowel contrasts of Norwegian.

A negative consequence of adding [front], which would allow the phonological definition of a class of central vowels, is that it defines unattested classes and segments outside of the realm of vowels. The classical features could distinguish just [k] and [kʸ], using [±back]. With the addition of [front], we would have a three-way distinction between k-like consonants which are [+front, −back], [−front, −back] and [−front, +back]. But no evidence at all has emerged for such a contrast in any language. Finally, the addition of the feature [front] defines a natural class [−back] containing front and central vowels, but not back vowels: such a class is not possible in the classical theory, and also seems to be unattested in phonological rules. This may indicate that the feature [front] is the wrong feature – at any rate it indicates that further research is necessary, in order to understand all of the ramifications of various possible changes to the theory.

Thus the evidence for a change to feature theory, made to handle the problematic status of [ə] in Kenyang phonology, would not be sufficiently strong to warrant complete acceptance of the new feature. We will suspend further discussion of this proposal until later, when nonlinear theories of representation are introduced and answers to some of the problems such as the unattested three-way contrast in velars can be considered. The central point is that changes in the theory are not made at will: they are made only after considerable argumentation and evidence that the existing theory is fundamentally inadequate.

Summary

Language sounds can be defined in terms of a small set of universal phonetically based features, which not only define the basic atoms of phonological representations, but also play a central role in the formal expression of rules. An important theme of this chapter is the nature of scientific theories, such as the theory of features, which make predictions both about what can happen and what cannot happen. The fundamental role of feature theory is to make specific predictions about the kinds of segments and rules that we should find in human languages. One of the main concerns of phonological theory is finding the correct set of features that define the sounds and rule systems of all human languages.

Exercises

1. Assume a segmental inventory composed of: [ʕ k t d s z n p f b i u e o a w h]. Indicate what feature or features characterize the following classes of sounds.
   i. ʕ k u o a w
   ii. f p k h
   iii. f p b t s d z n
   iv. ʕ u o w a b d z n i e
   v. i z n e d

2. Given the segments [w y h ʔ i ɛ a o ɔ u m̥ l r m ŋ p t kʸ k q b ð d dʸ g ɣ], describe the following segment classes, being as economical as you can with your use of features.
   i. m̥ l r m ŋ p t kʸ k q b ð d dʸ g ɣ
   ii. w y i ɛ a o ɔ u m̥ l r m ŋ
   iii. w a o ɔ u ŋ k q g ɣ
   iv. w y h i ɛ a o ɔ u l r ð ɣ
   v. y i ɛ a l r ŋ ð b dʸ g ɣ
   vi. y i kʸ dʸ
   vii. i ɛ a o ɔ u m̥

3. Assume a language with the following segmental inventory:

   p t tˢ č c k ɸ f θ s š x b d dᶻ ǰ ɟ m n ŋ l i e o u a ü ö w y

   (In this case, <c> represents a palatal stop, assumed to be featurally identical to a palatalized *k*.) In each of the following groups, one of the segments is not a member of the natural class which the other sounds belong to. Identify that sound, and state what features characterize the remaining class of segments.
   i. t č c š ǰ ɟ i e ü ö y
   ii. t tˢ č θ s š d dᶻ ǰ ɟ n l
   iii. c k x ǰ ɟ ŋ i u ü w y
   iv. k x ŋ o u a w y
   v. p ɸ f b m l o u ü ö w

4. Based on the segmental inventory [p t k b d m n ɣ ɸ f s l a i o u y], characterize the following segments or groups of segments uniquely using the fewest features possible:
   i. ɣ
   ii. i
   iii. n
   iv. b, d
   v. a, o
   vi. o, u

5. State all of the features which are changed in each of the following rules:
   i. p → ʃ
   ii. t → ŋ
   iii. o → w
   iv. k → s
   v. s → t
   vi. a → i

6. Formalize the following rules using distinctive features (segmental inventories to be assumed for each language are given in brackets):

  i.   b, d, g → β, ð, γ / V __   [p t k b d g β ð γ m n ŋ r i u a ə]

  ii.   p, k, q → β, γ, ʁ/ V __   [p t č ṭ k q β r ž γ ʁ m i ī e ẽ æ o u ũ]

  iii. Ø → y / i, e __ o, u, a   [p t k b d n y w i ü e æ o u a]

  iv. t → s / __ i   [p t k h v d s r l m n y i ü e ö a o u]

  v.   s → r / V_V   [p t k b d g s r l m n h w y e i o u a]

7. Review previous solutions to exercises which you have done in the preceding chapters, and state the rules according to the features given here: discuss any problems which you may encounter in reformalizing these rules.

Further reading

Campbell 1974; Chomsky and Halle 1968; Jakobson and Halle 1956; Jakobson, Fant and Halle 1952; Trubetzkoy 1939.

7 Doing an analysis

PREVIEW

KEY TERMS
hypothesis formation and testing

competing hypotheses

This chapter explores a subset of the phonologies of a number of languages. The purpose of this chapter is to make explicit the reasoning typically applied to the task of solving a phonology problem. By studying models of problem solving, you not only better understand the logic of problem solving, you will also gain experience with rules and issues regarding underlying representations encountered in the languages of the world.

Analyzing a system of phonological alternations is not trivial: it requires practice, where you gain experience by solving phonological problems of increasing complexity, experience which facilitates subsequent problem solving. The wider your experience is with actual phonological processes and problem solving, the better able you will be to appreciate what processes are common in the languages of the world, and to understand the dynamics of hypothesis formation, testing and revision. The first analyses given here will be more explicit about the reasoning that goes into solving data sets of this nature, in some cases deliberately going down the wrong analytical path, so that you have the opportunity to recognize the wrong path, and see how to get back on the right path. In practice, many of the calculations that are involved here are done without explicitly thinking about it – once you have suitable experience with problem solving.

7.1 Yawelmani

Our first problem involves alternations in the verb paradigm in the Yawelmani dialect of Yokuts (California).

7.1.1 The data

Three phonological rules will be motivated by the following examples: vowel epenthesis, vowel shortening, and vowel harmony. It is not obvious what the underlying representation of verb roots is, so besides finding the rules we must make decisions about underlying forms.

(1)

Nonfuture	Imperative	Dubitative	Passive aorist	
xathin	xatk'a	xatal	xatit	'eat'
dubhun	dubk'a	dubal	dubut	'lead by hand'
xilhin	xilk'a	xilal	xilit	'tangle'
k'oʔhin	k'oʔk'o	k'oʔol	k'oʔit	'throw'
doshin	dosk'o	do:sol	do:sit	'report'
ṣaphin	ṣapk'a	ṣa:pal	ṣa:pit	'burn'
lanhin	lank'a	la:nal	la:nit	'hear'
mek'hin	mek'k'a	me:k'al	me:k'it	'swallow'
wonhin	wonk'o	wo:nol	wo:nit	'hide'
p'axathin	p'axatk'a	p'axa:tal	p'axa:tit	'mourn'
hiwethin	hiwetk'a	hiwe:tal	hiwe:tit	'walk'
ʔopothin	ʔopotk'o	ʔopo:tol	ʔopo:tit	'arise from bed'
yawalhin	yawalk'a	yawa:lal	yawa:lit	'follow'
paʔiṭhin	paʔiṭk'a	paʔṭal	paʔṭit	'fight'
ʔilikhin	ʔilikk'a	ʔilkal	ʔilkit	'sing'
logiwhin	logiwk'a	logwol	logwit	'pulverize'
ʔugunhun	ʔugunk'a	ʔugnal	ʔugnut	'drink'
lihimhin	lihimk'a	lihmal	lihmit	'run'
ʔayiyhin	ʔayiyk'a	ʔayyal	ʔayyit	'pole a boat'
t'oyixhin	t'oyixk'a	t'oyxol	t'oyxit	'give medicine'
luk'ulhun	luk'ulk'a	luk'lal	luk'lut	'bury'

soːnilhin	soːnilkʼa	sonlol	sonlit	'put on back'
ʔaːmilhin	ʔaːmilkʼa	ʔamlal	ʔamlit	'help'
moːyinhin	moːyinkʼa	moynol	moynit	'become tired'
ṣaːlikʼhin	ṣaːlikʼkʼa	ṣalkʼal	ṣalkʼit	'wake up'

7.1.2 The first step: morphology

First we need a morphological analysis of the data. In a simple case, this involves looking at columns and rows of data, and figuring out which sub-parts of words are consistently present with one meaning, and which other subparts are consistently present with other meanings. This task is more complicated when the surface shape of roots and affixes changes due to phonological rules. We cannot provide a definitive morphological analysis of these data without knowing what the phonological system is, and certainty as to the phonological rules is impossible without knowing the morphological analysis. We break out of this seeming circle by adopting – and constantly revising – a preliminary and less precise analysis of the phonology and morphology. Improvement in the underlying representations should result in better rules, and as we refine the system of rules, the nature of the underlying distinctions hopefully becomes clearer.

In this case, four suffixes are added to roots, *-hin ~ -hun* 'nonfuture,' *-kʼa ~ -kʼo* 'imperative,' *-al ~ -ol* 'dubitative' and *-it ~ -ut* 'passive aorist.' The notation *-hin ~ -hun* indicates that the suffix is pronounced either as *-hin* or as *-hun*. We need to discover when one form versus the other is used, and express that relation in terms of an underlying form and a rule changing the underlying form.

Stem variants. Some stems have only one surface shape: *xat-* 'eat,' *dub-* 'lead by hand,' *xil-* 'tangle,' and *kʼoʔ-* 'throw,' so the most natural assumption would be that these *are* the underlying forms for these particular stems (this assumption may turn out to be wrong, but it is a good starting assumption). Most stems in the data set have two surface manifestations. An important first step in understanding the rules of the language is to identify the alternations in the data, and one way to make the alternations explicit is to list the phonetic variants of each stem.

(2) | dos ~ doːs | 'report' | ṣap ~ ṣaːp | 'burn' |
|---|---|---|---|
| lan ~ laːn | 'hear' | mekʼ ~ meːkʼ | 'swallow' |
| won ~ woːn | 'hide' | pʼaxat ~ pʼaxaːt | 'mourn' |
| hiwet ~ hiweːt | 'walk' | ʔopot ~ ʔopoːt | 'arise from bed' |
| yawal ~ yawaːl | 'follow' | paʔiṭ ~ paʔṭ | 'fight' |
| ʔilik ~ ʔilk | 'sing' | logiw ~ logw | 'pulverize' |
| ʔugun ~ ʔugn | 'drink' | lihim ~ lihm | 'run' |
| ʔayiy ~ ʔayy | 'pole a boat' | tʼoyix ~ tʼoyx | 'give medicine' |
| lukʼul ~ lukʼl | 'bury' | soːnil ~ sonl | 'put on back' |
| ʔaːmil ~ ʔaml | 'help' | moːyin ~ moyn | 'become tired' |
| ṣaːlikʼ ~ ṣalkʼ | 'wake up' | | |

In these cases, decisions must be made regarding the underlying forms.

Suffix variants. We must decide what the underlying form of each suffix is, and they all have two surface variants in terms of their vowel: either a nonrounded vowel, or a rounded vowel. For each suffix, we group the verbs in terms of which variant of the suffix is used with them.

(3) *-hin*   xat, xil, k'oʔ, dos, ṣap, lan, mek', won, p'axat, hiwet, ʔopot, yawal, paʔiṭ, ʔilik, logiw, lihim, ʔayiy, t'oyix, soːnil, ʔaːmil, moːyin, ṣaːlik'

    -hun   dub, ʔugun, luk'ul

    -k'a   xat, dub, xil, ṣap, lan, mek', p'axat, hiwet, yawal, paʔiṭ, ʔilik, logiw, ʔugun, lihim, ʔayiy, t'oyix, luk'ul, soːnil, ʔaːmil, moːyin, ṣaːlik'

    -k'o   k'oʔ, dos, won, ʔopot

    -al   xat, dub, xil, ṣaːp, laːn, meːk', p'axaːt, hiweːt, yawaːl, paʔṭ, ʔilk, ʔugn, lihm, ʔayy, luk'l, ʔaml, ṣalk'

    -ol   k'oʔ, doːs, woːn, ʔopoːt, logw, t'oyx, sonl, moyn

    -it   xat, xil, k'oʔ, doːs, ṣaːp, laːn, meːk', woːn, p'axaːt, hiweːt, ʔopoːt, yawaːl, paʔṭ, ʔilk, logw, lihm, ʔayy, t'oyx, sonl, ʔaml, moyn, ṣalk'

    -ut   dub, ʔugn, luk'l

7.1.3 Identifying phonological regularities

Vowel harmony. Having grouped the examples in this fashion, a phonological regularity can be detected. For the suffix *hin ~ hun*, the vowel *u* appears when the preceding vowel is *u*, and *i* appears in the suffix after any other vowel. The suffix *it ~ ut* obeys this same rule. The suffixes *k'a ~ k'o* and *al ~ ol* have the vowel *o* after *o*. This can be explained by positing a rule of vowel harmony between the suffix vowel and whatever vowel precedes it, where /a/ assimilates to /o/ and /i/ assimilates to /u/.

$$(4)\quad \begin{bmatrix} V \\ \alpha hi \end{bmatrix} \rightarrow [+\text{round}] / \begin{bmatrix} V \\ \alpha hi \\ +\text{round} \end{bmatrix} C_{o\_}$$

The variable notation – αhi. . . . αhi. . . . – expresses the condition that the vowels must have the same value of [hi], i.e. the harmonizing vowel must be [+hi] after a [+hi] round vowel, and [−hi] after a [−hi] round vowel, in order for the harmony rule to apply.

Vowel shortening. The next problem to tackle is the variation in the shape of the stem. A useful next step in trying to analyze that variation is to see whether the variants can be arranged into a small number of groups, organized according to the nature of the difference between the two stem shapes. In looking for such an organization, notice that some stems alternate in terms of having long versus short vowels, and in terms of having versus lacking a second vowel. Accordingly, we organize the data into the following classes of stem alternations (including the class of stems which have no alternation).

(5) *CVC* –   xat, dub, xil, k'oʔ

    CVC ~ CV:C –   dos ~ doːs, ṣap ~ ṣaːp, lan ~ laːn,
                              mek' ~ meːk', won ~ woːn

    CVCVC ~ CVCV:C –   p'axat ~ p'axaːt, hiwet ~ hiweːt,
                                 ʔopot ~ ʔopoːt, yawal ~ yawaːl

    CVCVC ~ CVCC –   paʔiṭ ~ paʔṭ, ʔilik ~ ʔilk, logiw ~ logw,
                               ʔugun ~ ʔugn, lihim ~ lihm, ʔayiy ~ ʔayy,
                               t'oyix ~ t'oyx, luk'ul ~ luk'l

    CV:CVC ~ CVCC –   soːnil ~ sonl, ʔaːmil ~ ʔaml, moːyin ~ moyn,
                               ṣaːlik' ~ ṣalk'

The initial hypothesis is that the invariant CVC stems have the underlying shape CVC. If there is no reason to make the underlying form be different from the surface form, the two forms should be assumed to be identical. Building on that decision, we will now set forth a hypothesis for stems which vary in shape between CVC and CV:C. It is highly unlikely that these stems also have the underlying shape CVC, since that would make it hard to account for stems such as /xat/ which are invariant CVC. We could not predict whether a stem vowel is supposed to have a length alternation or not, and the reasoning that leads to hypothesizing an underlying distinction /xat/ vs. /doːs/ which is contextually neutralized is exactly the same as that which leads to hypothesizing that in Russian (discussed in chapter 4) the word for 'time' is underlyingly /raz/ and 'forest' is /les/.

Given the conclusion that stems like *doːs ~ dos* have an underlying CV:C form, under what circumstance is the underlyingly long vowel of the stem shortened? Taking /doːs/ as a representative, and mechanically combining the assumed underlying stem with what we take to be the underlying form of the suffix, we arrive at the following underlying and surface relations.

(6) *underlying*   doːs-hin   doːs-k'a   doːs-al   doːs-it
    surface   doshin   dosk'o   doːsol   doːsit

The change of /a/ to [o] is due to vowel harmony. There is also a change in vowel length before *k'a* and *hin*, and not before *-al* and *-it*. These suffixes are distinguished by whether they begin with a consonant or a vowel, thus whether combining the stem and suffix would result in the sequence V:CC. Scanning the entire data set reveals an important generalization, that a long vowel is always followed by CV, that is, a long vowel only occurs in an open syllable. The discovery of this generalization allows us to posit the following vowel shortening rule.

(7) V → [-long] / _ CC

This rule is all that is needed to explain both the invariant CVC stems and the alternating CV:C ~ CVC stems. Underingly /do:s-hin/ undergoes (7) and gives the surface form [doshin] – all other forms preserve the underlying length of the vowel. The existence of this rule also explains why we do not find the surface sequence V:CC – a long vowel before a cluster of two consonants – anywhere in the data, as such sequences undergo vowel shortening.

We turn next to the stems with the shape CVCVC ~ CVCV:C such as *p'axat* ~ *p'axa:t*. Since we have already encountered a rule which accounts for alternations in vowel length, we should immediately suspect that this length alternation is the same as the one just accounted for in CV:C ~ CVC stems. When we inspect the contexts where the long-vowel variant occurs, we see that there are long vowels when a vowel-initial suffix is added, and short vowels when a consonant-initial suffix is added. In other words, these stems are virtually the same as /CV:C/ stems, except that they have the underlying shape /CVCV:C/. We initially hypothesized that there was a rule of vowel shortening based on /CV:C/ stems, and that rule nicely handled those data. The way we formulated that rule was quite general, since it only said "shorten a long vowel before two consonants." Such a statement predicts that, if there are other stem shapes such as /CVCV:C/, they too will undergo that rule. We have now discovered that such stems do undergo the shortening rule, providing independent support for that rule.

Epenthesis. This reduces the unsolved part of the problem to two remaining classes of stems. In one of those, there is an alternation between presence versus absence of a vowel, and in the second group there is an alternation in vowel length as well as an alternation in the presence versus lack of a vowel in the second syllable; this should make us suspect that the vowel shortening rule applies to the second of these sets. Concentrating on the contexts where the stem has the shape CV(:)CVC as opposed to the shape CVCC, we notice that CV(:)CVC appears before consonant-initial suffixes and CVCC appears before vowel-initial suffixes. We do not know at this point whether the second vowel is underlyingly part of the stem and is deleted in one context, or whether the vowel is inserted in a different context. Therefore, we will consider both possibilities: consideration of alternative hypotheses is an essential part of problem solving.

First suppose that the vowel is not part of the underlying representation of the stem. In that case, we assume the following representations

(8)	*underlying*	ʔilk-hin	ʔilk-k'a	ʔilk-al	ʔilk-it
	surface	ʔilik-hin	ʔilik-k'a	ʔilk-al	ʔilk-it
	underlying	ṣa:lk'-hin	ṣa:lk'-k'a	ṣa:lk'-al	ṣa:lk'-it
	surface	ṣa:lik'-hin	ṣa:lik'-k'a	ṣalk'-al	ṣalk'-it

Focusing on the hypothesized underlying representations where a vowel might be inserted, we notice that a vowel appears only where the underlying representation has a sequence of three consonants. Looking at all of the data, we notice that there are no surface sequences of three or more consonants, making such an epenthesis approach plausible.

In order for an epenthesis solution to work, the actual quality of the inserted vowel must be completely predictable. If we were to discover that the quality of the second vowel is unpredictable, then it would necessarily be part of the underlying representation since unpredictble information must be in the underlying form. The vowel in the second syllable is always high, and is round when the preceding vowel is high and round. In other words, the vowel in question is a high vowel whose backness and roundness is predictable, given the rule of vowel harmony, and thus the vowel is fully predictable. Given the harmony rule, we can assume that the second vowel is *i*. It is then possible to account for these examples by applying the following rule of epenthesis.

(9)   Ø → V / C _ CC
          [+hi]

Given (9), the underlying form of the CVCiC ~ CVCC stems would be /CVCC/ and the underlying form of the CV:CiC ~ CVCC stems would be /CV:CC/. For stems like /ʔilk/, epenthesis applies to underlying /CVCC+CV(C)/ to give surface [CVCiC+CV(C)]: /ʔilk-hin/ → [ʔilikhin]. The alternant CVCC before VC suffixes ~ [ʔilkal] ~ directly reflects the underlying form.

For /CV:CC/ stems like /ṣa:lk'/, epenthesis will also apply to underlying /CV:CC+CV(C)/, giving the surface form [CV:CiC+CV(C)]: /ṣa:lk-hin/ → [ṣa:likhin]. When a VC suffix is added to such stems, there is no epenthesis, but we do find shortening of the underlyingly long vowel which stands before a consonant cluster: (/ṣa:lkal/ → [ṣalkal]). The rules of vowel harmony, epenthesis and vowel shortening, combined with our analyses of underlying representations, account for all aspects of the data in (1). We conclude that epenthesis is a *possible* account of these alternations.

The preceding analysis has assumed a rule of epenthesis based on underlying representations of the form /CVCC/ and /CV:CC/, but we should explore the competing hypothesis that the vowel found in these stems is not inserted, and is part of the underlying representation. Under that hypothesis, underlying representations of the relevant stems would be the following.

(10)   paʔit, ʔilik, logiw, ʔugun, lihim, ʔayiy, t'oyix, luk'ul
          so:nil, ʔa:mil, mo:yin, ṣa:lik'

Presuming that these are the underlying stems, a rule of vowel deletion is required to explain the discrepancy between surface and underlying forms, which can be seen in (11).

(11) | *underlying* | luk'ul-hun | luk'ul-k'a | luk'ul-al | luk'ul-ut |
       |---|---|---|---|---|
       | *surface* | luk'ul-hun | luk'ul-k'a | luk'l-al | luk'l-ut |
       | *underlying* | so:nil-hin | so:nil-k'a | so:nil-ol | so:nil-it |
       | *surface* | so:nil-hin | so:nil-k'a | sonl-ol | sonl-it |

In forms which involve an alternation between a vowel and Ø, the context for vowel deletion would initially appear to be in an open syllable. This statement would produce too general a rule, since there are many vowels in open syllables, viz. *xatal, k'oʔit, do:sit, p'axathin* and *p'axa:tal* among others. In some of these, deletion of a vowel would lead to a word-initial consonant cluster, i.e. we would predict *xtal, *k'ʔit, *dsit, *p'xathin, and *p'xa:tal, and we see no word-initial clusters of consonants. If we are to have vowel deletion, the rule must be restricted from creating such clusters, so one way to enforce that requirement is to require the target of deletion to be preceded by the sequence VC. Thus, we might hypothesize the following syncope rule, one found in many languages.

(12)   V → Ø / VC _CV

This rule still makes incorrect predictions, since in fact there are vowels in the context VC_CV, as shown by forms such as *p'axa:tal, ʔopo:tit*, which according to (12) should be deleted. Since all such examples involve long vowels, it is a simple matter to restrict the assumed deletion rule to short vowels.

(13)   V   → Ø / VC_CV
       [−long]

With this rule of vowel syncope, the problem of vowel ∼ Ø alternations can also be accounted for. The remaining details of the analysis are exactly the same as they are under the assumption that there is a rule of vowel insertion.

7.1.4 Evaluating alternatives

In terms of simply generating the data, both the syncope and epenthesis analyses work. The question then becomes, is there a reason to chose one of these hypotheses over the other? It is entirely possible that we will not be able to come up with any compelling reasons for selecting one analysis over the other, in which case we must simply accept the fact that there are two equally plausible ways to account for the facts. As far as the simplicity, naturalness and generality of the two analyses is concerned, neither theory is superior to the other. Processes inserting vowels to break up CCC clusters are very common, as are rules of syncope which delete short vowels in the context VC_CV.

We should also consider the factual predictions of the two analyses. The epenthesis analysis predicts that there should be no CCC sequences in the language, and this appears to be correct. On the other hand, the syncope analysis predicts that there should be no short vowels in the context VC_CV, which also appears to be correct. Interestingly, neither account actually makes the prediction of the competing analysis – so, the epenthesis analysis does not preclude the existence of short vowels in the VC_CV context, and the syncope analysis does not preclude the existence of CCC sequences. If it turns out that there *are* CCC sequences in the language, the epenthesis solution will probably have to be rejected; whereas if there *are* VCVCV sequences in the language, the syncope analysis will probably

By sheer counting of symbols, the epenthesis rule might be slightly superior since it only requires reference to five entities and syncope requires reference to seven entities. Such literal symbol counting, practiced in the early era of generative phonology, is misguided.

have to be rejected. This would motivate further research into the language, to determine if one of these analyses makes a bad prediction.

A related issue to consider is the question of "coincidence," in terms of assumed underlying representations. In lieu of a specific rule which restricts the occurrence of phonemes in some environment, we expect phonemes to combine without any constraints. Clearly there must be some constraints on underlying representations in Yawelmani, since, for example, we do not find underlying representations such as /ioate/ with sequences of vowels. In this case, there is no motivation from phonological alternations to suspect that there might be underlying forms such as /ioate/. As far as logical possibilities in underlying forms are concerned for the issue at hand – epenthesis versus deletion – both analyses result in systematic gaps in the logically possible underlying forms. Under the epenthesis analysis, there are apparently no stems of the underlying form /CVCVC/, although there are stems of the form /CVCV:C/. Under the syncope analysis, we notice that all short second-syllable vowels in disyllabic stems are in fact /i/ (surface [u] in some cases, in accordance with vowel harmony).

At this point, it is impossible to give strong arguments in favor of one analysis over another, so we accept this indeterminacy for now. The fundamental point is that each analysis implies a set of predictions about possible and impossible forms in the language, and these predictions need to be tested against the available data. In this case, we have not been able to determine that one theory is clearly superior to the other. The main research problem which we face is that the corpus of data from Yawelmani available to us at this point is restricted, so we cannot know whether generalizations which we extract about the language based on this particular corpus are representative of the language as a whole. Even if we had access to a reference grammar for the language, there is some chance that our empirical generalizations based on the data from that grammar would not hold for the whole language, if the author of the grammar were not aware of all examples.

7.2 Hehe

The following data illustrate phonological processes of Hehe (Tanzania). Each noun is in one of fifteen numbered noun classes, like genders in French or German. The class of a noun is marked by a prefix. The goal is to determine the underlying form of stems and prefixes, and explain the processes at work in these data.

7.2.1 The data
Here are the relevant data from nouns.

(14)   *Class 1*

mutesi	'trapper'	mulagusi	'sorcerer'
mutelesi	'cook'	muñwi	'drinker'
mwiimbi	'singer'	mweendi	'one who likes people'
mwaasi	'builder'	moogofi	'one who is afraid'
moofusi	'one who washes'	muutˢi	'one who comes'

Class 2

vatesi	'trappers'	valagusi	'sorcerers'
vatelesi	'cooks'	vañwi	'drinkers'
viimbi	'singers'	veendi	'ones who like people'
vaasi	'builders'	woogofi	'ones who are afraid'
woofusi	'ones who wash'	wuutˢi	'ones who come'

Class 3

muhoomi	'cow hump'	muhogo	'cassava'
mufuniko	'cover'	muvili	'body'
mwiina	'hole'	mwiigiigi	'shadow'
mweenda	'cloth'	mooto	'fire'
muuñu	'salt'		

Class 4

mihoomi	'cow humps'	mihogo	'cassavas'
mifuniko	'covers'	mivili	'bodies'
miina	'holes'	miigiigi	'shadows'
myeenda	'cloths'	myooto	'fires'
myuuñu	'salts'		

Class 6

mavafi	'hairy caterpillars'	masaasi	'bullets'
maboga	'pumpkins'	mayayi	'legs'
miino	'teeth'	miiho	'eyes'

Class 7

kigidi	'waist'	kingaamba	'sweet potato'
kisogo	'back of head'	čuula	'frog'
čuunga	'wet lowland'	čaanga	'grave'
kifiniko	'tiny cover'	kivili	'tiny body'
kihoomi	'tiny cow hump'	kivafi	'tiny hairy caterpillar'
čooto	'tiny fire'	čeenda	'tiny cloth'
čuuñu	'tiny salt'	kiiho	'tiny eye'
kiina	'tiny hole'	kiigiigi	'tiny shadow'

Class 8

figidi	'waists'	fingaamba	'sweet potatoes'
fisogo	'backs of head'	fyuula	'frogs'
fyuunga	'wet lowlands'	fyaanga	'graves'
fifiniko	'tiny covers'	fivili	'tiny bodies'
fihoomi	'tiny cow humps'	fivafi	'tiny hairy caterpillars'
fyooto	'tiny fires'	fyeenda	'tiny cloths'
fyuuñu	'tiny salts'	fiiho	'tiny eyes'
fiina	'tiny holes'	fiigiigi	'tiny shadows'

Class 11

luteefu	'reed mat'	lupava	'stirring stick'
lutego	'trap'	ludali	'power
luhaanga	'sand'	lwiimbo	'song'

| lweendo | 'loving' | lwaaniko | 'dry stuff' |
| lwiifwi | 'chameleon' | | |

Class 12

kateefu	'small mat'	kakoongo	'small wound'
kafuniko	'small cover'	kangaamba	'small sweet potato'
kaasi	'small builder'	kiimbi	'small singer'
kaanga	'small grave'	kooto	'small file'
kuula	'small frog'	kuunga	'small wet lowland'

Class 13

tuteefu	'small mats'	tukoongo	'small wounds'
tufuniko	'small covers'	tungaamba	'small sweet potatoes'
twaasi	'small builders'	twiimbi	'small singers'
twaanga	'small graves'	tooto	'small files'
tuula	'small frogs'	tuunga	'small wet lowlands'

Class 14

wuvaso	'sleeping place'	wulime	'cultivating'
wugali	'porridge'	wutiitu	'blackness'
weelu	'whiteness'	wuumi	'life'
woogofu	'fear'	wiiyooga	'mushroom'
waangufu	'speed'		

7.2.2 Morphological analysis

As always, a preliminary morphological analysis is the first step in solving this phonology problem. Each noun has some prefix that marks noun class, followed by a stem. We also see, comparing nouns in various classes, that the same stems can appear in different classes, so for example class 3 *mu-hoomi* 'cow hump' is clearly related to class 4 *mi-hoomi* 'cow humps' – singulars and plurals are marked by changes in class; class 11 *lu-teefu* 'reed mat' is clearly related to *ka-teefu* 'small mat' and *tu-teefu* 'small mats.' The class prefixes have a number of phonetic manifestations, so we find *mu-*, *mw-* and *m-* for classes 1 and 3, *va-*, *v-* and *w-* for class 2, *mi-*, *my-* and *m-* for class 4, *ma-* and *m-* for class 6, *ki-* and *č-* for class 7, *fi-* and *fy-* for class 8, *lu-* and *lw-* for class 11, *ka-* and *k-* for class 12, *tu-* and *tw-* for class 13, and *wu-*, *w-* for class 14.

7.2.3 Phonological alternations

Noun stems fall in two groups in terms of phonological processes: those which begin with a consonant, and those beginning with a vowel. Examples of stems which begin with a consonant are *-tesi* (cf. *mu-tesi*, *va-tesi*) and *-lagusi* (cf. *mu-lagusi*, *va-lagusi*); examples of stems which begin with vowels are *-iimbi* (cf. *mw-iimbi*, *v-iimbi*) and *-eendi* (*mw-eendi*, *v-eendi*). The best phonological information about the nature of the prefix is available from its form before a consonant, so our working hypothesis is that the underlying form of the noun prefix is that found before a consonant – it preserves more information.

As we try to understand the phonological changes found with vowel-initial stems, it is helpful to look for a general unity behind these changes.

One important generalization about the language, judging from the data, is that there are no vowel sequences in the language (what may seem to be sequences such as *ii*, *ee* are not sequences, but are the orthographic representation of single long-vowel segments). Given the assumption that the prefixes for classes 1 and 2 are respectively /mu/ and /va/, the expected underlying forms of the words for 'singer' and 'singers' would be /mu-iimbi/ and /va-iimbi/. These differ from the surface forms [mw-iimbi] and [v-iimbi]: in the case of /mu-iimbi/, underlying /u/ has become [w], and in the case of underlying /va-iimbi/, underlying [a] has been deleted. In both cases, the end result is that an underlying cluster of vowels has been eliminated.

Glide formation versus vowel deletion.   Now we should ask, why is a vowel deleted in one case but turned into a glide in another case? The answer lies in the nature of the prefix vowel. The vowel /u/ becomes the glide [w], and the only difference between *u* and *w* is that the former is syllabic (a vowel) where the latter is nonsyllabic. The low vowel /a/, on the other hand, does not have a corresponding glide in this language (or in any language). In other words, a rule of glide formation simply could not apply to /a/ and result in a segment of the language.

To make progress in solving the problem, we need to advance hypotheses and test them against the data. We therefore assume the following rules of glide formation and vowel deletion.

(15)   V → [-syl] / __ V   *glide formation*
        [+hi]

(16)   V → Ø / __ V   *a-deletion*

By ordering (16) after (15), we can make (16) very general, since (15) will have already eliminated other vowel sequences. At this point, we can simply go through the data from top to bottom, seeing whether we are able to account for the examples with no further rules – or, we may find that other rules become necessary.

For nouns in class 1, the examples *mw-iimbi*, *mw-eendi* and *mw-aasi* are straightforward, deriving from /mu-iimbi/, /mu-eendi/ and /mu-aasi/. The forms *m-oogofi*, *m-oofusi* and *m-uuci* presumably derive from /mu-oogofi/ and /mu-oofusi/ and /mu-uuci/. The vowel /u/ has been deleted, which seems to run counter to our hypothesis that high vowels become glides before vowels. It is possible that there is another rule that deletes /u/ before a round vowel.

(17)   u → Ø / __   V   *u-deletion*
                  [+round]

We could also consider letting the glide formation rule apply and then explain the difference /mu-aasi/ → *mw-aasi* vs. /mu-oofusi/ → *m-oofusi* by subjecting derived *mw-oofusi* to a rule deleting *w* before a round vowel.

(18)   w → Ø / _ [+round]   *w-deletion*

Thus we must keep in mind two hypotheses regarding /u+o/ and /u+u/ sequences.

v-rounding.   Now consider class 2. In stems beginning with a vowel, we easily explain *v-iimbi, v-eendi* and *v-aasi* from *va-iimbi, va-eendi* and *va-aasi*, where *a*-deletion applies. Something else seems to be happening in *w-oogofi, w-oofusi,* and *w-uuci* from *va-oogofi, va-oofusi,* and *va-uutˢi*. Application of *a*-deletion would yield *v-oogofi, v-oofusi* and *v-uutˢi*, which differ from the surface forms only in the replacement of *v* by *w*. Since this process takes place before a round vowel, we conjecture that there may be an assimilation rule such as the following.

(19)   v → w / _ [+round]   *v-rounding*

If there is such a rule in the language, it would eliminate any sequences *vu, vo:* and the data contain no such sequences. There is still a problem to address, that *w*-deletion (18) should apply to *woogofi* but it does not – the surface form is not *[oogofi]. Two explanations come to mind. One is that *v*-rounding is ordered after *w*-deletion, so at the stage where *w*-deletion would apply, this word has the shape *voogofi* and not *woogofi* (so *w*-deletion cannot apply). The other is that (18) needs to be revised, so that it only deletes a postconsonantal *w* before a round vowel.

(20)   w → Ø / C _ [+round]

Our decision-making criteria are not stringent enough that we can definitively choose between these solutions, so we will leave this question open for the time being.

Moving to other classes, the nouns in class 3 present no problems. Glide formation applies to this prefix, so /mu-iina/ → [mw-iina], and before a round vowel derived *w* deletes, so /mu-ooto/ → *mw-ooto* which then becomes [m-ooto].

Front vowels and glides.   The nouns in class 4 generally conform to the predictions of our analysis. Note in particular that underlying /mi-uuñu/ and /mi-ooto/ undergo glide formation before a round vowel. Such examples show that it was correct to state the glide formation rule in a more general way, so that all high vowels (and not just /u/) become glides before any vowel (not just nonround vowels).

We cannot yet fully explain what happens with noun stems beginning with the vowel *i*, as in *m-iina, m-iigiigi*. Given /mi-iina/, /mi-iigiigi/, we predict surface *my-iina, *my-iigiigi. This is reminiscent of the problem of /mu-oogofi/ and /mu-uuci/ and we might want to generalize the rule deleting a glide, to include deleting a front glide before a front vowel (analogous to deleting a round glide before a round vowel). What prevents us from doing this is that while *w* deletes before both *u* and *o*, *y* only deletes before *i* and not *e*, as we can see from *my-eenda*. It might be more elegant or symmetrical for round glides to delete before round vowels of any height *and* front glides to delete before front vowels of any height, but the facts say otherwise: a front glide only deletes before a front *high* vowel.

(21) $\begin{bmatrix} +\text{hi} \\ -\text{back} \\ -\text{syl} \end{bmatrix} \rightarrow \emptyset / \_ \begin{bmatrix} +\text{hi} \\ -\text{back} \end{bmatrix}$ *y–deletion*

Checking other classes: discovering a palatalization rule.   The class 6 prefix *ma-* presents no surprises at all: it appears as *ma-* before a consonant, and its vowel deletes before another vowel, as in *m-iino* from *ma-iino*. The class 7 prefix, on the other hand, is more complex. Before a consonant it appears as *ki-*, and it also appears as *k(i)-* before *i*. Before other vowels, it appears as *č*, as in *č-uula, č-aanga, č-ooto,* and *č-eenda*. Again, we continue the procedure of comparing the underlying and predicted surface forms (predicted by mechanically applying the rules which we have already postulated to the underlying forms we have committed ourselves to), to see exactly what governs this discrepancy. From underlying *ki-uula, ki-aanga, ki-ooto* and *ki-eenda* we would expect *ky-uula, ky-aanga, ky-ooto* and *ky-eenda*, given glide formation. The discrepancy lies in the fact that the predicted sequence *ky* has been fused into *č*, a process of palatalization found in many languages. Since *ky* is nowhere found in the data, we can confidently posit the following rule.

(22)   ky → č   *palatalization*

Since /ki/ surfaces as [č] when attached to a vowel-initial noun stem, the question arises as to what has happened in *k-iiho, k-iina* and *k-iigiigi*. The glide formation rule should apply to /ki-iiho/, /ki-iina/ and /ki-iigiigi/ giving *ky-iiho, ky-iina* and *ky-iigiigi*, which we would expect to undergo (22). But there is a rule deleting *y* before *i*. If *y* is deleted by that rule, it could not condition the change of *k* to *č*, so all that is required is the ordering statement that *y*-deletion precedes palatalization (22). Thus /ki-iina/ becomes *ky-iina* by glide formation, and before the palatalization rule can apply, the *y*-deletion rule (21) deletes the glide that is crucial for (22).

Deciding on the form of w-deletion; degemination.   At this point, we can quickly check the examples in classes 8, 11, 12 and 13 and verify that our analysis explains all of these forms as well. The final set of examples are those in class 14, which has the prefix /wu/. This prefix raises a question in terms of our analysis: why do we have the sequence [wu], which is eliminated by a rule elsewhere? One explanation is the statement of the rule itself: if (20) is the correct rule, then this *w* could not delete because it is not preceded by a consonant. The other possibility is that [wu] actually comes from /vu/ by applying *v*-rounding (19), which we assumed applies after *w*-deletion. While both explanations work, the analysis where [wu] is underlying /vu/ has the disadvantage of being rather abstract, in positing an underlying segment in the prefix which never appears as such. This issue was presaged in chapter 4 and is discussed in more detail in chapter 9: for the moment we will simply say that given a choice between a concrete analysis where the underlying form of a morpheme is composed only of segments which actually appear as such in some surface manifestation of the morpheme, and an abstract form with a segment that never appears on the surface, the concrete analysis is preferable to the abstract one, all other things being comparable. On that basis, we decide that the underlying form of the class 14 prefix is /wu/, which means that the proper explanation for failure of *w*-deletion lies in the statement of *w*-deletion itself, as (20).

Still analyzing this class of nouns, we now focus on examples where the prefix precedes a vowel-initial stem, e.g. *w-eelu, w-uumi, w-oogofu, w-iiyooga* and *w-aangufu* from underlying /wu-eelu/, /wu-uumi/, /wu-oogofu/, /wu-iiyooga/ and /wu-aangufu/. Applying glide formation would give the surface forms *ww-eelu, *ww-uumi, *ww-oogofu, *ww-iiyooga* and *ww-aangufu*, which differ from the surface form in a simple way, that they have a geminate *w* where the actual form has only a single *w* (in fact, there do not seem to be any geminate consonants in the language), which allows us to posit the following degemination rule.

(23) $C_iC_i \rightarrow C_i$ *degemination*

7.2.4 Extending the data

Verbs are subject to these same rules, as some additional data will show, and an analysis of verbs will provide additional support for aspects of this analysis. Hehe is a tone language, and while we have not been concerned with accounting for tone (and have not marked tones), in the following data, tones are marked, and can be predicted by rule. In analyzing these data, we want to account for the placement of the high tone (H), which is marked with an acute accent.

(24)	*V*	*V for*	*V for each*	*make V*
	kúkama	kúkamíla	kúkamilána	kúkamyá
	kúsana	kúsaníla	kúsanilána	kúsanyá
	kútova	kútovéla	kútovelána	kútovyá
	kúlava	kúlavíla	kúlavilána	kúlavyá
	kúfwiima	kúfwiimíla	kúfwiimilána	kúfwiimyá
	kúkalaánga	kúkalaangíla	kúkalaangilána	kúkalaangyá
	kúkaláva	kúkalavíla	kúkalavilána	kúkalavyá
	kwéenda	kwéendéla	kwéendelána	kwéendyá
	kwíimba	kwíimbíla	kwíimbilána	kwíimbyá
	kóogópa	kóogopéla	kóogopelána	kóogopyá

be V'd	V us	V them	
kúkamwá	kútukáma	kúvakáma	'milk'
kúsanwá	kútusána	kúvasána	'comb'
kútowá	kútutóva	kúvatóva	'beat'
kúlawá	kútuláva	kúvaláva	'look at'
kúfwiimwá	kútufwiíma	kúvafwiíma	'hunt'
kúkalaangwá	kútukalaánga	kúvakalaánga	'fry'
kúkalawá	—	—	'take bath'
kwéendwá	kútweénda	kúveénda	'love'
kwíimbwá	kútwiímba	kúviímba	'sing'
kóogopwá	kútoogópa	kúwoogópa	'fear'

The morphology. These data indicate that all verbs begin with *kú* or something derivable from /kú/ by the rules already motivated, thus we assume that *kú-* is an inflectional prefix. In addition, all verbs end with the vowel *a*, which is probably a morpheme since it is unlikely that every root would end in exactly the same vowel. The stem of the word for 'milk' is probably *-kam-*. Various grammatical relations are expressed by suffixes standing between the stem and the suffix *-a*, such as *-il-* 'for,' *-an-* 'each other,' *-y-* 'make,' *-w-* passive: the objects 'us' and 'them' are marked by the prefixes *-tu-* and *-va-* between the prefix *kú-* and the verb stem.

Phonological rules. Looking at the last three roots, which are vowel-initial, the prefixes *kú-*, *tu-* and *va-* are subject to the rules motivated on the basis of nouns, where /u/ becomes [w] before a vowel, but deletes after a consonant and before a round vowel (so, /ku-oogopa/ → *kwoogopa* → [koogopa]); the sequence *vo* becomes *wo* (/ku-va-oogopa/ → *kuvoogopa* → [kuwoogopa]). The change of /v/ to *w* is also seen in examples such as *kútowá* and *kúlawá*, coming (apparently) from /ku-tov-w-a/ and /ku-lav-w-a/. The rule of *v*-rounding would derive *kútowwá* and *kúlawwá*, and the actual phonetic forms can be accounted for based on that intermediate form by degemination.

One additional segmental process of vowel harmony is motivated by the above examples. The benefactive suffix retains its underlying high vowel in forms such as *kúkam-íl-a*, *kúsan-íl-a* and *kúfwiim-íl-a*, but that vowel assimilates in height to a preceding mid vowel in examples such as *kútov-él-a*, *kwéend-él-a* and *kóogop-él-a*. This motivates the following vowel harmony rule:

(25)
$$-V \rightarrow [-\text{high}] / \begin{bmatrix} V \\ -\text{high} \\ -\text{low} \end{bmatrix} C_0 \underline{\quad} \textit{vowel harmony}$$

Regarding tone, most examples have an H tone on the second-to-last vowel of the word (this may be the second part of a long vowel in the penultimate syllable, or the only vowel of a short penultimate syllable), which can be accounted for by the following rule.

(26) $V \rightarrow [+H] / \_ C_0 V\#$ *tone assignment*

In some verbs, this H is missing – cf. *kúkama, kúsana, kútova*. Applying this tone assignment rule to these forms would result in outputs such as **kúkáma, *kúsána, *kútóva*, with H tones on adjacent vowels. Since our examples contain no cases of consecutive H-toned vowels, we may assume a rule along the following lines.

(27) $V \rightarrow [-H] / \quad V \quad C_0 \_$
                     $[+H]$

What about the columns with the suffixes -*y*- 'make' and -*w*- 'passive,' which have word-final H, not penult H ? We expect **kúkalaángwa*. But if these two suffixes are underlyingly *i* and *u*, then the underlying form of *kúkalaangwá* would be /kú-kalaang-u-a/. H tone would be assigned to the penultimate vowel under that assumption, giving *kúkalaangúa*. However, we already know that there is a rule of glide formation which would turn *u* and *i* into *w* and *y* before vowels, a rule which has obviously applied in these forms. Since only syllabic elements can bear tones, the tone on the penultimate vowel apparently shifts to the final syllable, where it can be pronounced.

> *Such tone shift, where the tone of a vowel shifts to another vowel when the original vowel deletes or desyllabifies, is common in tone languages and is discussed in the last chapter.*

7.3 Icelandic

Our next example consists of alternations in noun inflection in Modern Icelandic.

7.3.1 The data
The relevant data are in (28). The task is to provide a unique underlying representation for each stem and case suffix, state what phonological rules are required to account for these data, and indicate what order they apply in, when the ordering of rules matters.

(28)

hestür	hattür	heimür	size gröütür	skougür	*nom sg*
hest	hatt	heim	gröüt	skoug	*acc sg*
hesti	hatti	heimi	gröüti	skougi	*dat sg*
hests	hatts	heims	gröüts	skougs	*gen sg*
hestar	hattar	heimar	gröütar	skougar	*nom pl*
hesta	hatta	heima	gröüta	skouga	*acc pl*
hestüm	höttüm	heimüm	gröütüm	skougüm	*dat pl*
'horse'	'hat'	'home'	'porridge'	'forest'	
garður	laiknir	hirðir	himinn	morgünn	*nom sg*
garð	laikni	hirði	himin	morgün	*acc sg*
garði	laikni	hirði	himni	morgni	*dat sg*

garðs	laiknis	hirðis	himins	morgüns	*gen sg*
garðar	laiknar	hirðar	himnar	morgnar	*nom pl*
garða	laikna	hirða	himna	morgna	*acc pl*
görðüm	laiknüm	hirðüm	himnüm	morgnüm	*dat pl*
'garden'	'doctor'	'herd'	'heaven'	'morning'	

stoull	magaull	yököll	θümall	mour	*nom sg*
stoul	magaul	yökül	θümal	mou	*acc sg*
stouli	magauli	yökli	θümli	mou	*dat sg*
stouls	magauls	yököls	θümals	mous	*gen sg*
stoular	magaular	yöklar	θümlar	mouar	*nom pl*
stoula	magaula	yökla	θümla	moua	*acc pl*
stoulüm	magaulüm	yöklüm	θümlüm	mouüm	*dat pl*
'chair'	'flank'	'glacier'	'thumb'	'peat'	

akür	hamar	hver	galdür	byour	*nom sg*
akür	hamar	hver	galdür	byour	*acc sg*
akri	hamri	hver	galdri	byour	*dat sg*
akürs	hamars	hvers	galdurs	byours	*gen sg*
akrar	hamrar	hverar	galdrar	byourar	*nom pl*
akra	hamra	hvera	galdra	byoura	*acc pl*
ökrüm	hömrüm	hverüm	göldrüm	byourüm	*dat pl*
'field'	'hammer'	'geyser'	'magic'	'beer'	

7.3.2 Morphological analysis

It is not immediately clear what are appropriate underlying representations for some case suffixes. It would appear that the nominative singular ending is something like *-ür* or maybe *-ir*, although sometimes you just find lengthening of a stem-final consonant. We start by assuming that the accusative singular has no case suffix, the dative singular is *-i*, the genitive singular is *-s*, the nominative plural is *-ar*, the accusative plural is *-a* and the dative plural is *-üm*, since in almost all stems, that is how these suffixes are actually manifested. It would similarly not be unreasonable to assume that the accusative singular form is a close approximation of the underlying form of the stem.

7.3.3 Phonological alternations

On the basis of these assumptions about underlying forms, we can identify some phonological alternations which need to be explained. First and foremost, we need to explain the consonantal variation in the nominative singular. Second, we need to explain the alternation between [a] and [ö] in examples such as [hatta] ~ [höttüm]. Third, there is a vowel ~ Ø alternation as in [himin] ~ [himna] and [morgün] ~ [morgna]. Fourth, the dative singular form generally appears as [i], but in some cases does not surface. We will try to solve one of these problems, selecting at random, since at this point we have no reason to think that finding a solution to one of these problems is dependent on finding a solution to any other of these problems.

The vowel of the nominative singular. We will begin with the problem of the nominative singular. The first step in taming this problem is to state exactly what the problem is. There are many apparent realizations of this suffix; depending on the noun stem to which it is attached, we find *-ür*, *-ir*, *-r*, *-Ø* , *-l* and *-n*. Constructing this list of surface realizations alone is enough to allow us to make an intelligent initial guess about the underlying form, which is that the nominative singular is *-(V)r*, since half of the variants of this affix actually contain *-r* (of course, this assumption could be wrong, since numerical counts are not arguments for underlying forms, only suggestions, but again we need to start somewhere). The next step is to extract generalizations about the contexts where each variant is used. We would start by listing the presumably underlying stems themselves, noting that we have *-ur* with /hest/, /hatt/, /gröut/, /heim/, /garð/ and /skoug/, *-r* with /mou/, /laikni/ and /hirði/, Ø with /akür/, /hamar/, /hver/ and /galdür/, *-l* with /stoul/, /magaul/ and /yökül/, and *-n* with /himin/ and /morgün/. At this point, generalizations about the underlying form become easier to see: we find [l] after /l/, [n] after /n/, Ø after /r/, [r] after a vowel, and [ür] after any other consonant. We can conclude that the most likely underlying forms for this suffix are /ür/ and /r/.

Having identified the nature of the conditioning environment and armed with two hypotheses about the underlying form, it is time to transform this information into specific rules. Since underlying representations and rules go hand in hand, we need to determine whether one of the assumed underlying representations for the suffix results in more plausible rules. Let us consider the entailments of these underlying forms in terms of the rules that they commit us to.

> You may wonder, why assume that *garðür* illustrates the variant *-ür* and *galdür* does not? We assumed that the accusative singular best reflects the underlying form, and since [ür] is present in the accusative singular *galdür* but not *garð*, [ür] must be part of the stem in *galdür* and not in *garðür*.

(29) **Hypothesis: /ür/**
   No change: hest-ür → hestür, hatt-ür → hattür, skoug-ür → skougür,
      heim-ür → heimür, garð-ür → garðür, gröut-ür → gröutür
   Deletion of a vowel mou-ür → mour, laikni-ür → laiknir,
      hirði-ür → hirðir
   Deletion of a vowel and deletion of r akür-ür → akür, hver-ür → hver,
      byour-ür → byour, galdür-ür → galdür, hamar-ür → hamar
   Deletion of a vowel and assimilation stoul-ür → stoull,
      yökul-ür → yököll, θümal-ür → θümall, himin-ür → himinn,
      magaul-ür → magaull, morgün-ür → morgünn

   Hypothesis: /r/
   Insertion of a vowel hest-r → hestür, hatt-r → hattür,
      skoug-r → skougür, heim-r → heimür, garð-r → garðür,
      gröut-r → gröutür
   No change mou-r → mour, laikni-r → laiknir, hirði-r → hirðir
   Deletion of r akür-r → akür, hver-r → hver, byour-r → byour,
      galdür-r → galdür, hamar-r → hamar
   Assimilation stoul-r → stoull, yökül-r → yököll, θümal-r → θümall,
      himin-r → himinn, magaul-r → magaull, morgün-r → morgünn

We will start with the assumption that the suffix is underlyingly /ür/. Given that, a deletion rule is required to eliminate ü from this suffix when it is preceded by one of /r, l, n/.

$$(30) \quad \begin{bmatrix} +\text{syl} \\ +\text{hi} \\ +\text{rd} \end{bmatrix} \rightarrow \emptyset / V \begin{bmatrix} +\text{cor} \\ +\text{son} \end{bmatrix} - r\#$$

Applying this rule to underlying *himinür, stoulür, hverür* would yield forms such as *himinr, stoulr, hverr*, and these outputs would be subject to other rules.

In addition, given the assumption of underlyingly /ür/, we would require a rule to delete the vowel from the suffix when the preceding stem ends in a vowel. This rule would allow us to account for forms such as *mour, laiknir* and *hirðir*, from assumed *mou-ür, laikni-ür* and *hirði-ür*. Deletion of a vowel after another vowel is not implausible, so we might postulate the following rule.

(31) $V \rightarrow \emptyset \,/\, V\, \_$

However, this is too general, since *u* can be preceded by other vowels – cf. *mour, skougür, magaull*. This particular statement of the rule makes a prediction that certain kinds of phonetic sequences should not occur, and that prediction is wrong.

Our rule went wrong in that it does not distinguish supposed vowel combinations which would be created by concatenation of morphemes (these sequences do undergo reduction) from diphthongs which are contained wholly within a single morpheme (which do not undergo reduction). We could attempt to overcome this shortcoming by specifically requiring that the two vowels be in separate morphemes, as indicated in the following rule.

(32) $V \rightarrow \emptyset \,/\, V + \_$

Even this restriction is insufficient, since it does not explain why the supposed suffix vowel in /laikni-ür/ and /hirði-ür/ deletes, but in the nominative, accusative, and dative plural, the vowels of the suffix *-ar, -a* and *-üm* are not deleted (cf. *laiknar, hirðar, laikna, hirða, laiknüm, hirðüm*): rather, the vowel of the stem deletes. Particularly troublesome for the hypothesis that the nominative singular suffix is /ür/ is the fact that the dative plural suffix *-üm* acts so differently. These problems could be remedied by requiring the vowel which deletes to be *ü*, and by deleting *ü* only before *r*.

(33) $ü \rightarrow \emptyset \,/\, V + \_r$

In lieu of a competing hypothesis, it is difficult to judge the correctness of this rule, but given the very specific information needed in this rule to make it work, you should be suspicious of the rule. The general idea of vowel deletion after a vowel or before a vowel is reasonable, but if you pay attention to which vowel deletes and when it deletes, the vowel deletion approach is not promising.

At this point, we are so thoroughly suspicious of the hypothesis of underlying /ür/ that we have a reason to look for an alternative hypothesis, to see if different assumptions about underlying forms simplify the description. The competing hypothesis that the suffix is /r/ requires an epenthesis rule to insert *ü* before *r* when a consonant precedes.

$$(34) \quad \emptyset \rightarrow \ddot{u}/C\_\_r\# \qquad (=) \qquad \emptyset \rightarrow \begin{bmatrix} +syl \\ +hi \\ +rd \\ -bk \end{bmatrix} /C\_\_\_\begin{bmatrix} -syl \\ +son \end{bmatrix}\#$$

This rule does not apply to /morgün-r/, since we have [morgünn] and not *[morgünür], but that fact does not have to be directly stated in the epenthesis rule. The explanation is straightforward: another rule eliminates underlying /nr#/, giving [nn] instead: rule ordering matters. Given the generality of the epenthesis rule versus the highly specific nature of the *ü*-deletion rule, we reject the *ü*-deletion hypothesis: therefore the underlying form of the nominative singular must be /r/.

Vowel deletion.   Now that we understand that the nominative singular suffix is /r/, and *ü* which appears before it is actually epenthetic, we turn to vowel-plus-vowel sequences. The stems *lakni*, *hirði* and *mou* end in vowels or diphthongs, and when a vowel-initial suffix comes after the stem, a vowel is deleted. Examples are repeated below, this time including in parentheses the underlying vowel which is deleted.

(35)	laikn(i)-i	hirð(i)-i	mou (i)	*dat sg*
	laikn(i)-ar	hirð(i)-ar	mou-ar	*nom pl*
	laikn(i)-a	hirð(i)-a	mou-a	*acc pl*
	laikn(i)-üm	hirð(i)-üm	mou-üm	*dat pl*
	'doctor'	'herd'	'peat'	

The simple generalization is that the vowel *i* deletes before or after another vowel between morphemes (in an example such as [laikni] from /laikni+i/, we cannot tell which *i* is deleted). Thus we may posit the following rule.

> *This can be written* $i \rightarrow \emptyset\%$ _ *+V. The symbol [%] is the mirror-image notation meaning "before or after."*

$$(36) \quad i \rightarrow \emptyset/ \begin{Bmatrix} V+ \_ \\ \_ +V \end{Bmatrix}$$

Sonorant clusters with r.   Two other rules are required which affect C+r sequences. One assimilates /r/ to a preceding /l/ or /n/. The question arises,

Recall the use of
Greek-letter variables
for formulating
assimilation rules,
discussed in chapter
6. This rule states
that /r/ takes on the
same values for
lateral and nasal as
found in the pre-
ceding consonant.

are /l/ and /n/, excluding /r/, a natural class? The consonants /l/ and /n/ have in common the properties of being coronal sonorants, but so does /r/. The consonant /r/ is [−nasal], but so is /l/; /r/ is [−lateral], but so is /n/. Thus, feature theory says that it would be impossible to refer to the class of consonants /l,n/ excluding /r/. But it is not *necessary* to explicitly state the assimilation rule so that it only applies after /l, n/, since /r/ deletes after another /r/ anyhow. In other words, we need the following rule:

(37) $r \rightarrow \emptyset \ / \ r\_\_$

The sonorant-assimilation rule can therefore be stated generally as:

(38) $r \rightarrow \begin{bmatrix} \alpha \text{lateral} \\ \beta \text{nasal} \end{bmatrix} / \begin{bmatrix} +\text{sonorant} \\ +\text{coronal} \\ \alpha \text{lateral} \\ \beta \text{nasal} \end{bmatrix} \_\_$

This rule change /lr/ into [ll], /nr/ into [nn] and vacuously changes /rr/ into [rr]: the independent process of *r*-deletion will still simplify the resulting sequence of *r*'s.

Syncope.   The next problem which we will take on is the vowel ∼ ∅ alternation found for example in [himin] ∼ [himni]. Not all stems participate in this alternation, so we do find the alternation in the stems *akür, galdür, himin, hamar, morgun, yökül* and *θümal* but not *hest, hatt, heim, garð, gröut, skoug, mou, stoul, hver, byour, magaul* (we will consider /laikni/ and /hirði/ later). A simple generalization determines which stems alternate: only single vowels outside the initial syllable are subject to the alternation.

    Now we must ask under what circumstances the vowel deletes. Taking /himin/ as representative, we can list the contexts:

(39)   *CVCVC stem* himin-n (nom sg), himin (acc sg), himin-s (gen sg)

       CVCC stem himn-i (dat sg), himn-ar (nom pl), himn-a (acc pl), himn-üm (dat pl)

In other words, there is no vowel before a vowel-initial suffix.

    Having isolated the context in which a vowel is deleted, we can offer a phonological rule of vowel syncope.

(40) $\begin{matrix} V \\ [-\text{long}] \end{matrix} \rightarrow \emptyset \ / \ VC_0 \_\_ CV$

ü-umlaut.   This now leaves us with the problem of the alternation between [a] and [ö]. In looking for a context where this vowel change happens, we note that it takes place before the dative plural suffix *-üm*, which underlyingly has the front round vowel [ü], and thus the rule involves an assimilation in roundness and backness.

(41) $a \rightarrow ö / \_\_C_0 ü$ $\left(a \rightarrow \begin{bmatrix} -\text{back} \\ +\text{rd} \end{bmatrix} / \_\_\_C_0 \begin{bmatrix} -\text{back} \\ +\text{rd} \end{bmatrix} \right)$

It is evident, given examples such as [hattür] from /hatt-r/, that the vowel [ü] inserted by *ü*-epenthesis does not trigger this rule, which can be explained by ordering the rule of round-harmony (41) before *ü*-insertion (34).

i-deletion. The final fact to be explained is that while the dative singular suffix is *-i*, the dative singular of the stems *akür, hver, byour, galdür* is identical to the stem – the vowel *i* is missing. This can be accounted for by a rule deleting *i* after *r*.

(42) $i \rightarrow \emptyset / r \_ \#$

Reconsidering /akür/. We are nearly finished with our analysis of Icelandic phonology, but one area of data needs further consideration. We assumed the underlying representations of the words for 'field' and 'magic' to be /akür/ and /galdür/, based on the fact that that is how they appear phonetically in the accusative singular, and this form has generally been a good diagnostic of the underlying representation. However, there is a problem with assuming underlying /akür/ and /galdür/, that the rule of rounding assimilation (41) would be expected to apply in these forms, giving incorrect *ökür, *ökürs. This problem can be resolved by modifying our assumption about the underlying form, since we already have a rule which inserts *ü* before *r* – a rule which applies after rounding assimilation (epenthetic *ü* does not trigger rounding). Therefore, we change our assumption about underlying forms to /akr/ and /galdr/. This entails a small change in the way that we formalize the rule of epenthesis, since that rule, as presently stated, only inserts *ü* before *r* which is in word-final position, and yet we also want to be able to insert *ü* before *r* which stands before another consonant, in order to explain /akr-s/ → [akürs].

(43) $\emptyset \rightarrow ü / C \_ r \{C,\#\}$

Commonly, the expression {C,#} indicates syllable structure: the rule prevents Cr at the end of a syllable.

7.4 Modern Hebrew

The next case study comes from a set of alternations in the conjugation of verbs in a certain derivational class in Modern Hebrew.

These data are from a nonstandard dialect that has pharyngeals which were lost in the standard dialect, either being deleted (in the case of ʕ) or changed to x (in the case of ħ).

7.4.1 The data

The goal of this problem is to determine the underlying representations of the verbal prefix and the stems, as well as whatever rules are needed to account for these phonological alternations. In some cases, a related word is provided in order to clarify aspects of the underlying stem. The data to be accounted for are in (44).

(44)

1sg	2sg masc	3sg fem.		Related word	
itparnasti	itparnes	itparnesu	'earn'		
itparsamti	itparsem	itparsemu	'become famous'		
idbalbalti	idbalbel	idbalbelu	'be confused'		
idgalgalti	idgalgel	idgalgelu	'revolve'		
itħamakti	itħamek	itħamku	'turn away'		
itlabašti	itlabeš	itlapšu	'get dressed'		
idbadarti	idbader	idbadru	'make fun'		
idgarašti	idgareš	idgaršu	'divorce'		
itpalalti	itpalel	itpalelu	'pray'		
itxamamti	itxamem	itxamemu	'warm'		
itmotati	itmotet	itmotetu	'quake'		
itʔošašti	itʔošeš	itʔošešu	'recover'		
idbodati	idboded	idbodedu	'seclude oneself'		
istaparti	istaper	istapru	'get a haircut'	sapar	'barber'
istarakti	istarek	istarku	'comb hair'	ma-srek	'comb'
ištaparti	ištaper	ištapru	'improve'	šipur	'improvement'
itˢtalamti	itˢtalem	itˢtalmu	'have photo taken'	tˢalem	'photographer'
izdakanti	izdaken	izdaknu	'age'	zaken	'old'
izdarasti	izdarez	izdarzu	'hurry'	zariz	'alert'
itamamti	itamem	itamemu	'feign innocence'	tamim	'innocent'
idardarti	idarder	idarderu	'decline'	dirdur	'rolling'
itpataħti	itpateaħ	itpatħu	'develop'		
idgalaħti	idgaleaħ	idgalħu	'shave'		
itnatˢaħti	itnatˢeaħ	itnatˢħu	'argue'		
ištagati	ištagea	ištagʕu	'become mad'		
itparati	itparea	itparʕu	'cause disorder'		
itmaleti	itmale	itmalʔu	'become full'		
itpaleti	itpale	itpalʔu	'become surprised'		
itnaseti	itnase	itnasʔu	'feel superior'		

7.4.2 Morphological analysis

Each of these verbs verb has a prefix which is either /it/ or /id/, and the prefix transparently surfaces as one of these two variants in most examples. The first-person-singular form is marked with a suffix -*ti*, the third-singular feminine has the suffix -*u*, and the second-singular masculine has no suffix. The vowel in the second stem syllable is underlyingly the same for all verbs: this fact is not entirely obvious from these data but is made obvious by a more extensive analysis of the morphological structure of words in the language. An analysis of the phonological factors surrounding the second vowel will show that these surface variants can be derived from one particular underlying vowel. Derivationally related words, such as the root underlying *ištaparti* 'improve' and *šipur* 'improvement,' have in common a set of consonants, but their vowels differ (vowel changes are a means of indicating derivational relations in Semitic languages, which we will not be concerned with).

7.4.3 Phonological alternations

Voicing assimilation. As for the choice between an underlying voiced or voiceless consonant in the prefix, scanning the data reveals that a voiced consonant appears before voiced obstruents and a voiceless consonant appears before voiceless obstruents and sonorants. Since sonorants are phonetically voiced, it is clear that there is no natural context for deriving the voiceless consonant [t], so we assume that the prefix is underlyingly /it/. Before a voiced obstruent, a voiceless obstruent becomes voiced.

(45) $[-\text{sonorant}] \rightarrow [+\text{voice}]/ \_ \quad C$

$$\begin{bmatrix} -\text{son} \\ +\text{voi} \end{bmatrix}$$

Alternations in V$_2$. The second vowel of the stem has three phonetic variants: [a] as in *itparnasti*, [e] as in *itparnes*, and Ø as in *idbadru* (cf. *idbader*). Deletion of the second stem vowel only takes place before the suffix -*u*, so we will first attempt to decide when the vowel is deleted. A partial specification of the context for vowel deletion is before C+V, which explains why the first- and second-person-singular masculine forms (with the suffixes -*ti* and -Ø) do not undergo vowel deletion. The next step in determining when a vowel is deleted is to sort the examples into two groups: those with vowel deletion and those with no vowel deletion. In the following examples, the site of vowel deletion (or its lack) is marked with an underscore.

(46) *Vowel deletion*

itħam_ku	itlap_šu	idbad_ru
idgar_šu	istap_ru	istar_ku
ištap_ru	itˢtal_mu	izdak_nu
izdar_zu	itmal_ʔu	itpal_ʔu
itnas_ʔu	itpat_ħu	idgal_ħu
itnatˢ_ħu	ištag_ʕu	itpar_ʕu

No vowel deletion

itparnesu	itparsemu	idbalbelu
idgalgelu	idarderu	itpalelu
itxamemu	itmotetu	itʔošešu
idbodedu	itamemu	

Based on this grouping, we discover a vowel is deleted when it is preceded by just a single consonant; if two consonants precede the vowel, there is no deletion.

However, it is not always the case that a vowel deletes after a single consonant, so our rule cannot simply look for one versus two consonants. There are cases such as *itʔošešu* where there is no vowel deletion, despite the fact that there is only a single consonant before the vowel. Inspecting all of those examples, we discover that the consonants preceding and following the vowel are the same, and in every case where a vowel is deleted, the preceding and following consonants are different. Thus, a vowel deletes only if it is preceded by a single consonant, and that consonant must be different from the consonant that follows the vowel (which is indicated informally as "$C_i \ldots C_j$" in the rule).

(47) $e \rightarrow \emptyset \, / \, V \, C_i \, \_ \, C_j \, V$

At this point, we now clearly recognize this process as a kind of syncope, a phonological rule which we have encountered many times before.

Closed syllable lowering.   Now we turn to the alternation between [a] and [e]. Concentrating on the first set of examples in the dataset, we find [a] before CC (*itparnasti*), and [e] before C# or CV (*itparnes, itparnesu*). Assuming that this distribution is generally valid, we would therefore posit the following rule to derive [a] from /e/.

(48) $e \rightarrow a \, / \, \_ \, CC$

An attempt to derive [e] from underlying /a/ runs into the difficulty that the context "when followed by C# or CV" is not a coherent context, but is just a set of two partially related contexts. This motivates the decision to select underlying /e/.

In four examples, the second stem vowel /e/ appears as [a] before a single consonant, namely the first-person-singular forms *itmotati, idbodati, ištagati* and *itparati*. These examples fall into two distinct subgroups, as shown by looking at their underlying stems, which is revealed in the third-singular feminine forms (*itmotet-u, idboded-u* and *ištagʕu, itparʕu*). In the first two examples the stems underlyingly end in a coronal stop *t* or *d*, and in the second two examples the stems underlyingly end in the voiced pharyngeal ʕ. At the underlying level, the second stem vowel is followed by two consonants (/itmotetti/, /itbodedti/, /ištageʕti/ and /itpareʕti/). Surface [a] is explained on the basis of the underlying consonant cluster – it must simply be assured that the rules simplifying these clusters apply after (48).

In the first two examples (*itmotati* and *idbodati* from /itmotat-ti/ and /idbodad-ti/) combination of the first-singular suffix with the root would (after assimilation of voicing) be expected to result in *itmotatti* and *idbodatti*. In fact, the data provide no examples of geminate consonants, and where geminates might have been created by vowel syncope in *idbodedu*, syncope is blocked. Thus, the language seems to be pursuing a strategy of avoiding the creation of geminate consonants. We can account for this simplification of consonant clusters by the following rule.

(49) $\begin{Bmatrix} t \\ d \end{Bmatrix} \rightarrow \phi / \_ \begin{Bmatrix} t \\ d \end{Bmatrix}$ or $C_iC_i \rightarrow C_i$

This rule also explains *itamem* and *idarder*, where the stem begins with /t/ or /d/. The underlying forms would be /it-tamem/ and /it-darder/: the surface form with a single consonant reflects the application of this consonant-degemination process.

Stems with final pharyngeals and laryngeals. The vowel quality of /šageʕ/ and /pareʕ/ will be left aside temporarily. We thus turn to the stems represented in *itpataħti*, *idgalaħti* and *itnatˤaħti*. What is problematic about these stems is the appearance of [ea] when no suffix is added, viz. *itpateaħ*, *idgaleaħ* and *itnatˤeaħ*. Assuming the underlying forms to be *itpateħ*, *idgaleħ* and *itnatˤeħ* (selecting /e/ as the second vowel, analogous to *itparnes*, *itlabeš* and *idboded*) we would need a rule inserting the vowel [a]. These stems have in common that their final consonant is the pharyngeal [ħ], suggesting a rule along the following lines.

(50) $\emptyset \rightarrow a / e \_ ħ$

Why does this rule only apply in the suffixless second-singular masculine form? When the stem is followed by *-u* (/itpateħu/ → [itpatħu]) the vowel /e/ is deleted by the syncope rule, so there is no vowel before ħ. Syncope does not apply before the suffix *-ti* in /itpateħti/ → [itpataħti] but there is still no epenthetic vowel. The reason is that underlying /e/ changes to [a] by rule (48), before a cluster of consonants. Since that rule changes /e/ to *a* but (50) applies after *e*, prior application of (50) deprives vowel insertion of a chance to apply.

Now returning to the stems *šageʕ* and *pareʕ*, we can see that this same process of vowel insertion applies in these stems in the second-singular masculine. Starting from /ištageʕ/ and /itpareʔ/, vowel epenthesis obviously applies to give intermediate *ištageaʕ* and *itpareaʕ*. This argues that the epenthesis rule should be generalized so that both of the pharyngeal consonants trigger the process.

(51) $\emptyset \rightarrow \underset{[+\text{low}]}{V} / e \_ \underset{[+\text{low}]}{C}$

The forms derived by (51) are close to the actual forms, which lack the consonant ʕ, and with an appropriate consonant deletion rule we can finish the derivation of these forms. To formalize this rule, we need to determine where the consonant ʕ appears in the language: our data indicate that it appears only before a vowel, never before a consonant or at the end of a word (which is to say it never appears at the end of a syllable). Knowing this generalization, we posit the following rule.

(52)   ʕ → Ø / _ {C,#}   (=)   ʕ → Ø / _.

No further rules are needed to account for this set of examples. In *ištagati* and *itparati*, from *ištageʕti* and *itpareʕti*, there is no epenthetic vowel. This is predicted by our analysis, since these verbs must undergo the rule lowering /e/ to [a] before CC, and, as we have just argued, vowel lowering precedes vowel epenthesis (thus preventing epenthesis from applying). In this respect, *ištagati* and *itparati* are parallel to *itpateaħ*, *idgaleaħ*, and *itnatˢeaħ*. The nonparallelism derives from the fact that syllable-final ʕ is deleted, so predicted *ištagaʕti* and *itparaʕti* are realized as *ištagati* and *itparati* thanks to this deletion.

The final set of verb stems typified by the verb *itmaleti* ~ *itmale* ~ *itmalʔu* exibit a glottal stop in some contexts and Ø in other contexts. The two most obvious hypotheses regarding underlying form are that the stem is /male/, or else /maleʔ/. It is difficult to decide between these possibilities, so we will explore both. Suppose, first, that these stems end in glottal stop. In that case, we need a rule deleting glottal stop syllable-finally – a similar rule was required to delete the consonant ʔ. A crucial difference between stems ending in ʔ and stems presumably ending in ʔ is that the stem vowel /e/ does not lower to [a] before *-ti* in the latter set. Thus, deletion of ʔ would have to be governed by a different rule than deletion of ʔ, since ʔ-deletion precedes lowering and ʔ-deletion follows lowering.

An alternative possibility that we want to consider is that these stems really end in a vowel, not a glottal stop. Assuming this, surface [itpaleti] would simply reflect concatenation of the stem /pale/ with the suffix, and no phonological rule would apply. The problem is that we would also need to explain why the rule of syncope does not apply to [itpaleti], since the phonetic context for that rule is found here. The glottal-final hypothesis can explain failure of syncope rather easily, by ordering glottal stop deletion after syncope – when syncope applies, the form is /itpaleʔti/, where the consonant cluster blocks syncope.

Metathesis.   The last point regarding the Hebrew data is the position of *t* in the prefix. The consonant of the prefix actually appears after the first consonant of the stem in the following examples.

(53)   istaparti   'get a haircut'   istarakti   'comb hair'
       ištaparti   'improve'   itˢtalamti   'have photo taken'
       izdakanti   'age'   izdarasti   'hurry'

We would have expected forms such as [itsaparti], [itšaparti], [ittˢalamti] by just prefixing *it-* to the stem. A metathesis rule is therefore needed which moves *t* after the stem-initial consonant. What makes this group of consonants – [s, š, tˢ, z] – a natural class is that they are all and the only strident coronals. We can thus formalize this rule as follows: a coronal stop followed by a coronal strident switch order.

(54) $\begin{bmatrix} +\text{cor} \\ -\text{cont} \end{bmatrix} \begin{bmatrix} +\text{cor} \\ +\text{strid} \end{bmatrix} \rightarrow \begin{bmatrix} +\text{cor} \\ +\text{strid} \end{bmatrix} \begin{bmatrix} +\text{cor} \\ -\text{cont} \end{bmatrix}$

The ordering of this metathesis rule with respect to the voicing assimilation rule is crucial. Given underlying /it-zakanti/, you might attempt to apply metathesis first, which would yield *iztakanti*, where voiceless *t* is placed after stem-initial *z*. The voicing assimilation rule (in a general form, applying between all obstruents) might apply to yield *istakanti. So if metathesis applies before voicing assimilation, we will derive an incorrect result, either *iztakanti if there is no voicing assimilation (assuming that the rule only turns voiceless consonants into voiced ones) or *istakanti if there is voicing assimilation. However, we will derive the correct output if we apply voicing assimilation first: /itzakanti/ becomes *idzakanti*, which surfaces as [izdakanti] by metathesis. With this ordering, we have completed our analysis of Modern Hebrew phonology.

7.5 Japanese

The analysis of phonological alternations found in connection with the conjugation of verbs in Japanese provides our final illustration of the kinds of issues that must be considered in coming up with appropriate rules and underlying representations. In solving this problem, it is particularly important to make the correct assumptions about underlying representations, since the selection of underlying forms goes hand in hand with stating the rules correctly.

7.5.1 The data
The relevant data are given in (55).

(55)

	Present	Negative	Volitional	Past	Inchoative	
	neru	nenai	netai	neta	neyo:	'sleep'
	miru	minai	mitai	mita	miyo:	'see'
	šinu	šinanai	šinitai	šinda	šino:	'die'
	yomu	yomanai	yomitai	yonda	yomo:	'read'
	yobu	yobanai	yobitai	yonda	yobo:	'call'
	katˢu	katanai	kačitai	katta	kato:	'win'
	kasu	kasanai	kašitai	kašita	kaso:	'lend'
	waku	wakanai	wakitai	waita	wako:	'boil'
	tˢugu	tˢuganai	tˢugitai	tˢuida	tˢugo:	'pour'
	karu	karanai	karitai	katta	karo:	'shear'
	kau	kawanai	kaitai	katta	kao:	'buy'

7.5.2 Morphological analysis

We could make an initial guess regarding suffixes, which leads to the following hypotheses: *-u* = "present," *-nai* = "negative," *-tai* = "volitional," *-ta* = "past" and *-yo:* = "inchoative": that analysis seems reasonable given the first two verbs in the data. We might also surmise that the root is whatever the present-tense form is without the present ending, i.e. underlying *ner, mir, šin, yom, yob, kat^s, kas, wak, t^sug, kar* and *ka*. In lieu of the application of a phonological rule, the surface form of a word should simply be whatever we hypothesize the underlying form of the root to be, plus the underlying form of added affixes. Therefore, given our preliminary theory of roots and suffixes in Japanese, we predict the following surface forms, with hyphens inserted between morphemes to make the division of words into roots and suffixes clear: it is important to understand the literal predictions of your analysis, and to compare them with the observed facts.

(56) *Predicted surface forms*

Present	Negative	Volitional	Past	Inchoative
<u>ner-u</u>	ner-nai	ner-tai	ner-ta	ner-yo:
<u>mir-u</u>	mir-nai	mir-tai	mir-ta	mir-yo:
<u>šin-u</u>	šin-nai	šin-tai	šin-ta	šin-yo:
<u>yom-u</u>	yom-nai	yom-tai	yom-ta	yom-yo:
<u>yob-u</u>	yob-nai	yob-tai	yob-ta	yob-yo:
<u>kat^s-u</u>	kat^s-nai	kat^s-tai	kat^s-ta	kat^s-yo:
<u>kas-u</u>	kas-nai	kas-tai	kas-ta	kas-yo:
<u>wak-u</u>	wak-nai	wak-tai	wak-ta	wak-yo:
<u>t^sug-u</u>	t^sug-nai	t^sug-tai	t^sug-ta	t^sug-yo:
<u>kar-u</u>	kar-nai	kar-tai	kar-ta	kar-yo:
<u>ka-u</u>	ka-nai	ka-tai	ka-ta	ka-yo:

The forms which are correct as is are underlined: as we can see, all of the present-tense forms are correct, and none of the others is. It is no surprise that the present-tense forms are correct, since we decided that the underlying form of the root is whatever we find in the present tense minus the vowel *-u*. It is possible, but unlikely, that every other word undergoes some phonological rule.

Changing our hypothesis. Since our first guess about underlying forms is highly suspect, we should consider alternative hypotheses. Quite often, the cause of analytic problems is incorrect underlying forms. One place to consider revising the assumptions about underlying representations would be those of the affixes. It was assumed – largely on the basis of the first two forms *nenai* and *minai* – that the negative suffix is underlyingly *-nai*. However, in most of the examples, this apparent suffix is preceded by the vowel *a* (*šinanai, yomanai, yobanai* and so on), which suggests the alternative possibility that the negative suffix is really *-anai*. Similarly, the decision that the volitional suffix is underlyingly *-tai* was justified based on the fact that it appears as *-tai* in the first two examples; however, the suffix is otherwise always preceded by the vowel *i* (*šinitai, yomitai, yobitai,* and so on), so this vowel might analogously be part of the suffix.

One fact strongly suggests that the initial hypothesis about the underlying forms of suffixes was incorrect. The past-tense suffix, which we also assumed to be -*ta*, behaves very differently from the volitional suffix, and thus we have *šinitai* versus *šinda, yomitai* versus *yonda, kačitai* versus *katta, karitai* versus *katta* (there *are* similarities such as *kašitai* and *kašita* which must also be accounted for). It is quite unlikely that we can account for these very different phonological patterns by reasonable phonological rules if we assume that the volitional and past-tense suffixes differ solely by the presence of final *i*.

It is this realization, that there is a thorough divergence between the past-tense and volitional suffixes in terms of how they act phonologically, that provides the key to identifying the right underlying forms. Given how similar these two suffixes are in surface forms, -(*i*)*tai* vs. -(*i*)*ta*, but how differently they behave phonologically, they must have quite different underlying forms. Since the past-tense suffix rarely has a vowel and the volitional suffix usually does, we modify our hypothesis so that the volitional is /-itai/ and the past tense is /ta/. Because the negative acts very much like the volitional in terms of where it has a vowel, we also adopt the alternative that the negative is /anai/.

These changed assumptions about underlying representations of suffixes yield a significant improvement in the accuracy of our predicted surface forms, as indicated in (57), with correct surface forms underlined.

(57)　*Modified predicted surface forms*

Present	Negative	Volitional	Past	Inchoative
ner-u	ner-anai	ner-itai	ner-ta	ner-yo:
mir-u	mir-anai	mir-itai	mir-ta	mir-yo:
šin-u	šin-anai	šin-itai	šin-ta	šin-yo:
yom-u	yom anai	yom-itai	yom-ta	yom-yo:
yob-u	yob-anai	yob-itai	yob-ta	yob-yo:
kat^s-u	kat^s-anai	kat^s-itai	kat^s-ta	kat^s-yo:
kas-u	kas-anai	kas-itai	kas-ta	kas-yo:
wak-u	wak-anai	wak-itai	wak-ta	wak-yo:
t^{s}ug-u	t^{s}ug-anai	t^{s}ug-itai	t^{s}ug-ta	t^{s}ug-yo:
kar-u	kar-anai	kar-itai	kar-ta	kar-yo:
ka-u	ka-anai	ka-itai	ka-ta	ka-yo:

Implicitly, we know that forms such as predicted *[kat^{s}anai] (for [katanai]) and *[kas-itai] (for [kašitai]) must be explained, either with other changes in underlying forms, or by hypothesizing rules.

We will consider one further significant modification of the underlying representations, inspired by the success that resulted from changing our assumptions about -*itai* and -*anai*, in reducing the degree to which underlying and surface forms differ. The original and dubious decision to treat these suffixes as *tai* and *nai* was influenced by the fact that that is how they appear with the first two verbs. It is also possible that our initial hypothesis about the underlying form of these two verb roots was incorrect. There is good reason to believe that those assumptions were indeed also incorrect. Compare the surface form of the three verbs in our dataset which, by hypothesis, have roots ending in *r*.

(58)

Present	Negative	Volitional	Past	Inchoative	
ner-u	ne-nai	ne-tai	ne-ta	ne-yo:	'sleep'
mir-u	mi-nai	mi-tai	mi-ta	mi-yo:	'see'
kar-u	kar-anai	kar-itai	katt-a	kar-o:	'shear'

Clearly, the supposed roots /ner/ and /mir/ act quite differently from /kar/. The consonant *r* surfaces in most of the surface forms of the verb meaning 'shear,' whereas *r* only appears in verbs 'sleep' and 'see' in the present tense. In other words, there is little reason to believe that the first two roots are really /ner/ and /mir/, rather than /ne/ and /mi:/: in contrast, there seems to be a much stronger basis for saying that the word for 'shear' is underlyingly /kar/. Now suppose we change our assumption about these two verbs, and assume that /ne/ and /mi/ end in vowels.

(59) *Modified predicted surface forms*

Present	Negative	Volitional	Past	Inchoative
ne-u	ne-anai	ne-itai	ne-ta	ne-yo:
mi-u	mi-anai	mi-itai	mi-ta	mi-yo:
šin-u	šin-anai	šin-itai	šin-ta	šin-yo:
yom-u	yom-anai	yom-itai	yom-ta	yom-yo:
yob-u	yob-anai	yob-itai	yob-ta	yob-yo:
kat^s-u	kat^s-anai	kat^s-itai	kat^s-ta	kat^s-yo:
kas-u	kas-anai	kas-itai	kas-ta	kas-yo:
wak-u	wak-anai	wak-itai	wak-ta	wak-yo:
t^{s}ug-u	t^{s}ug-anai	t^{s}ug-itai	t^{s}ug-ta	t^{s}ug-yo:
kar-u	kar-anai	kar-itai	kar-ta	kar-yo:
ka-u	ka-anai	ka-itai	ka-ta	ka-yo:

In terms of being able to predict the surface forms of verbs without phonological rules, this has resulted in a slight improvement of predictive power (sometimes involving a shuffling of correct and incorrect columns, where under the current hypothesis we no longer directly predict the form of the present tense, but we now can generate the past and inchoative forms without requiring any further rules). More important is the fact that we now have a principled basis, in terms of different types of underlying forms, for predicting the different behavior of the verbs which have the present tense *neru, miru* versus *karu*, which are in the first two cases actually vowel-final roots, in contrast to a consonant-final root.

7.5.3 Phonological rules

Since we have made reasonable progress in solving the problem of underlying forms, we will attempt to discover phonological rules which explain remaining differences between underlying and surface forms – though it always remains possible that we will need to change our assumed under-lying forms, as our analysis progresses. The approach to take is to look at forms which are still not completely explained, and construct hypotheses to account for these forms: what new rules are needed to get from the underlying to surface forms. One useful way to approach this is to look for columns or rows of data where similar things seem to be happening. The incorrectly predicted forms are re-listed below, this time excluding the forms which are already explained, with information about the nature of the problem added. If a segment is predicted but does not actually sur-face, that segment is placed in parentheses; if there is a segment which appears in the surface form but which does not appear to be present in the underlying form, the segment is placed in square brackets; segments whose phonetic quality differs from the predicted quality are italicized.

(60)

	Present	Negative	Volitional	Past	Inchoative	
	ne[r]u	ne(a)nai	ne(i)tai			'sleep'
	mi[r]u	mi(a)nai	mi(i)tai			'see'
				šin*ta*	šin(y)oː	'die'
				yom*ta*	yom(y)oː	'read'
				yob*ta*	yob(y)oː	'call'
		katˢanai		katˢta	katˢ(y)oː	'win'
			kasitai	kas[i]ta	kas(y)oː	'lend'
				wakta	wak(y)oː	'boil'
				tˢug*ta*	tˢug(y)oː	'pour'
				karta	kar(y)oː	'shear'
		ka(w)anai		ka[t]ta	ka(y)oː	'buy'

The glide in the inchoative.   In order to explain most of the problems which arise with the inchoative form, we will consider the possibility that there is a rule deleting consonants after consonants, since that is the nature of the problem with the inchoative column. Such a consonant deletion can-not be totally general, i.e. deleting any consonant after any other consonant, since, as is evident in the past tense column, the consonant clusters [tt] and [nd] are possible in the language. Nevertheless, these two clusters are a rather restricted subset of the imaginable two-consonant combinations which can be formed from the consonants of the language, and this is a good indication that there may be some process deleting a consonant after another consonant. Thus we might assume a rule deleting the glide *y* after a consonant.

(61) $\begin{bmatrix} -\text{cons} \\ -\text{back} \end{bmatrix} \rightarrow \emptyset / C\_\_$

The postulation of any such rule immediately makes a prediction about possible surface forms: there should be no sequences of consonant plus glide in the data. Since there are none in the data at hand, our hypothesis has passed an important test. Armed with this rule, we have accounted for

*If you know Japanese,
you may know of
words with y after
a consonant, e.g.
[To:kyo:]. We restrict
ourselves to the
specific dataset given
here, but a restriction
on the rule that the
deleted consonant
must be suffix-initial
solves this problem*

a very large chunk of otherwise problematic examples in (60) – all of the inchoative forms except for *kao:* 'buy,' where the glide deletes but there seems to be no consonant which would condition deletion of the glide.

Vowel deletion. Another area where some success is possible in reconciling underlying and surface forms by focusing on possible segment sequences is with the verbs 'sleep' and 'see.' The difference between the predicted (*neanai, *mianai; *neitai, *miitai) and actual forms (*nenai, minai; netai, mitai*) of the negative and volitional forms is that the actual forms lack the suffix vowel. In the predicted forms, we find a sequence of vowels, whereas in the actual form, only the first of those vowels is found. This raises the question whether we might postulate a rule deleting a vowel after another vowel. In positing such a rule, we want to consider what V-V sequences are found in the data. The sequence [ai] exists in the volitional and negative suffixes, and in past tense *waita*; also [ui] in the past of the word for 'pour'; also the sequences [ao:] and [au] in the verb 'buy.' We do not find sequences of vowels with the front vowels [e] or [i] plus a vowel ([ia], [ii], [ea] and [ei]). Therefore, we posit the following rule of vowel deletion.

(62) $V \rightarrow \emptyset / \begin{bmatrix} +\text{syl} \\ -\text{back} \end{bmatrix}$—

*We will consider
another possibility
later, that the pre-
sent suffix is /ru/, so
rather than insert-
ing it in neru, we
delete it in [yomu].*

This resolves many problematic forms of the word for 'sleep' and 'die', such as the change /ne-itai/ → [netai], but there are still examples that we cannot explain. In the present tense, we find [neru] and [miru], which we presume derives from /ne-u/ and /mi-u/. The vowel deletion rule (62) should apply to these underlying forms, resulting in incorrect *[ne] and *[mi]. We might try to resolve this by assuming that the vowel [u] cannot be deleted by (62) – we would then need to restrict the rule to exclude round vowels from deletion. Alternatively, /u/ fails to be deleted in /ne-u/, perhaps a consonant is inserted thereby eliminating the cluster of vowels.

(63) $\emptyset \rightarrow r / \begin{bmatrix} +\text{syl} \\ -\text{back} \end{bmatrix}$—V

Armed with these new rules, we will have actually accounted for all forms of the verbs 'sleep' and 'see.'

Nasal + consonant. The remaining problems have been reduced to a very small set. A comparison of presumed underlying and surface past forms is given below.

(64)   /šinta/   [šinda]   /yomta/   [yonda]
       /yobta/   [yonda]   /katˢta/   [katta]
       /kasta/   [kašita]   /wakta/   [waita]
       /tˢugta/   [tˢuida]   /karta/   [katta]
       /kata/   [katta]

The problem posed by the past-tense form is that by combining the root with the suffix -*ta*, underlying clusters of consonants would be created, but there are very severe restrictions on what consonant clusters exist in Japanese. The simplest problem is that presented by [šinda] from /šinta/, where /t/ becomes voiced after a nasal. A process of postnasal voicing is rather common in the languages of the world, so we may hypothesize that there is such a process in Japanese.

(65)   C → [+voice] / [+nasal] __

The data further suggest that the rule applies in other examples, since we see that in the past tense [yonda] of the roots /yom/ and /yob/, the final consonant of the root is a nasal on the surface, and /t/ becomes voiced.

We account for the stems /yob/ and /yom/ by noting that the final consonant in these roots becomes [n], which is part of the change from the nonexistent sequences /mt/ and /bt/ to the actually occurring [nd]. Thus, these consonants become [n] before /t/ (and subsequently, /t/ voices after the derived [n]).

$$(66) \quad [-\text{coronal}] \rightarrow \begin{bmatrix} +\text{coronal} \\ +\text{nasal} \end{bmatrix} / \_\_ C$$

Although the data only illustrate nasalization before /t/, (66) is stated as generally as possible, predicting that /k/ or /d/ would nasalize as well.

Watching for contexts where a phenomenon seems to be relevant to more than one form, we also notice that the surface forms [waita] and [tˢuida] differ from their underlying forms /wakta/ and /tˢugta/ by replacing the preconsonantal velar with the vowel [i], suggesting a vocalization rule such as the following.

(67)   C   V
       [+high] → [−back] / __ C

This rule accounts for [waita], and almost accounts for [tˢuida]: but we still need to explain why the suffix consonant is voiced. The underlying representation itself provides a reason for this voicing, since, underlyingly, /t/ is preceded by a voiced consonant in /tˢugta/. We know that /t/ voices in another context, after a nasal, so we could account for voicing in [tˢuida] by restating the rule so that it applies not just after nasals (which are voiced), but after all voiced consonants. By applying the voicing rule which is sensitive to underlying consonant voicing before the velar-vocalization rule, we can explain the opaque surface difference, [waita] versus [tˢuida], as deriving from the voicing of the consonant which precedes it underlyingly. We also want to be sure to apply rule (67) before rule (66), given the way we have formulated these rules. We did not explicitly restrict (66), which changes noncoronals to [n] before a consonant, to applying only to labials. Therefore, the more specific rule (67) must apply first, otherwise velars would also be incorrectly turned into [n] before a consonant.

7.5.4 Taking stock

We should review the analysis to be sure there are no loose ends. We have six rules – *y*-deletion, vowel deletion, *r*-insertion, consonant voicing, velar vocalization, and labial nasalization – which, given our assumptions regarding roots and suffixes, account for most of the forms in the dataset. It is important to recheck the full dataset against our rules, to be certain that our analysis does handle all of the data. A few forms remain which we cannot fully explain.

The forms which we have not yet explained are the following. First, we have not explained the variation in the root-final consonant seen in the verb meaning 'win' (*katˢ-u, kat-anai, kač-itai, kat-ta, kat-o:*). Second, we have not accounted for the variation between *s* and *š* in the verb 'shear,' nor have we explained the presence of the vowel [i] in the past tense of this verb. Finally, in the verb 'buy' we have not explained the presence of [w] in the negative, the appearance of a second [t] in the past-tense form, and we have not explained why in the inchoative form [kao:] the suffix consonant *y* deletes.

Correcting the final consonant.   The first problem to tackle is the variation in the final consonant of the verb 'win'. Looking at the correlation between the phonetic realization of the consonant and the following segment, we see that [tˢ] appears before [u], [č] appears before [i], and [t] appears elsewhere. It was a mistake to assume that the underlying form of this root contains the consonant /tˢ/; instead, we will assume that the underlying consonant is /t/ (so nothing more needs to be said about the surface forms *kat-anai, kat-ta*, and *kat-o:*). Looking more generally at the distribution of [č] and [tˢ] in the data, [č] only appears before [i], and [tˢ] only appears before [u], allowing us to posit the following rules.

(68) $t \rightarrow [+\text{del. rel}] \,/\, \_\, u$

(69) $t \rightarrow \begin{bmatrix} +\text{del.rel} \\ -\text{anterior} \end{bmatrix} /\_\, i$

Moving to the word for 'lend', we find a related problem that /s/ appears as [š] before [i]. This is reminiscent of the process which we assumed turning *t* into *č* before *i*. In fact, we can decompose the process $t \rightarrow č$ into two more basic steps: /t/ becomes an affricate before [i], and *s* and *tˢ* become alveopalatal [š] and [č] before the vowel [i].

***i*-epenthesis**.   All that remains to be explained about the word for 'lend' is why [i] appears in the past tense, i.e. why does /kasta/ become *kasita* (whence [kašita])? This is simple: we see that [st] does not exist in the language, and no assimilations turn it into an existing cluster, so [i] is inserted to separate these two consonants.

(70) $\phi \rightarrow \begin{bmatrix} +\text{syl} \\ +\text{hi} \\ -\text{bk} \end{bmatrix} / \begin{bmatrix} +\text{cont} \\ -\text{son} \end{bmatrix} - \begin{bmatrix} +\text{cor} \\ -\text{cont} \end{bmatrix}$

r-assimilation and final w.   Turning now to the form [katta] 'shear (past)' from /kar-ta/, a simple assimilation is needed to explain this form:

(71) $r \rightarrow C_i \ / \ \_ \ C_i$

The last remaining problems are in the verb 'buy,' where we must explain the extra [t] in [katta], the presence of [w] in [kawanai], and the loss of /y/ in the inchoative form [kao:]. We might explain the form [kawanai] by a rule of *w*-insertion inserting *w* between two occurrences of the vowel [a]; more puzzling is the form [katta], which we presume derives from /ka-ta/. It would be very unusual for a consonant to spontaneously double between vowels. Since there are so many problems associated with this one root, perhaps the problem lies in our assumptions about the underlying form of this root. Perhaps the *w* in [kawanai] is part of the root itself. What would be the benefit of assuming that this root is really /kaw/? First, it explains the presence of *w* in [kawanai]. Second, it provides a basis for the extra [t] in [katta]: /w/ assimilates to following [t]. Such an assimilation is implicit in our analysis, namely rule (71) assimilating /r/ to /t/. We can generalize this rule to applying to both /r/ and /w/, which are oral sonorants. Finally, positing underlying /kaw/ helps to resolve the mystery of why /y/ deletes in the inchoative form [kao:], when otherwise /y/ only deletes when it is preceded by a consonant. If we start with /ka-yo:/ there is no reason for /y/ to delete, but if we start with /kaw-yo:/, /y/ is underlyingly preceded by a consonant /w/, which causes deletion of *y*, and then /w/ itself is deleted.

The cost of this analysis – a small cost – is that we must explain why [w] does not appear more widely in the root, specifically, why do we not find surface [w] in *ka-u*, *ka-itai* and *ka-o:*. The answer lies in the context where [w] appears: [w] only appears before a low vowel, suggesting the following rule.

(72)   V
        $w \rightarrow \phi / \_ [-\text{low}]$

At this point, we have a complete analysis of the data. The rules (in shorthand versions) and underlying forms are recapitulated below.

(73)   *Roots*: /ne/ 'sleep,' /mi/ 'see,' /šin/ 'die,' /yom/ 'read,' /yob/ 'call,'
        /kat/ 'win,' /kas/ 'lend,' /wak/ 'boil,' /tˢug/ 'pour,' /kar/ 'shear,'
        /kaw/ 'buy'

Suffixes: -u 'present,' *-anai* 'negative,' *-itai* 'volitional,' *-ta* 'past,' *-yo:* 'inchoative'

Rules:

$$y \rightarrow \emptyset \,/\, C\_$$ $$V \rightarrow \emptyset \,/\, e, i\ \_$$
$$\emptyset \rightarrow r \,/\, e, i\ \_V$$ $$[\text{-round}]$$
$$b, m \rightarrow n \,/\, \_t$$ $$k, g \rightarrow i \,/\, \_t$$
$$t \rightarrow t^s \,/\, \_u, i$$ $$t^s, s \rightarrow \check{c}, \check{s} \,/\, \_i$$
$$\emptyset \rightarrow i \,/\, s\_t$$ $$r, w \rightarrow t \,/\, \_t$$
$$w \rightarrow \emptyset \,/\, \_V$$ $$t \rightarrow d \,/\, C\ \_$$
$$[\text{-lo}]$$ $$[\text{+voi}]$$

Progress by hypothesis forming and testing. Three important points have emerged as our analysis developed. First, analysis proceeds step-by-step, by forming specific hypotheses which we then check against the data, revising those hypotheses should they prove to be wrong. Second, it is vital to consider more than one hypothesis: if we had only pursued the first hypothesis that the roots /ne/, /mi/, /kar/ and /kaw/ were really underlying /ner/, /mir/, /kar/ and /ka/, we would never have been able to make sense of the data. The most important skill that you can bring to the task of problem-solving is the ability to create and evaluate competing hypotheses intended to explain some fact. Finally, it is particularly important to remember that assumptions about underlying representations go hand-in-hand with the phonological rules which you postulate for a language. When you check your solution, the problem may not be that your rules are wrong, but that your underlying forms are wrong. By continuously reviewing the analysis, and making sure that the rules work and your assumptions about underlying forms are consistent, you should arrive at the stage that no further improvements to the analysis are possible, given the data available to you.

It might occur to you that there are aspects of the underlying representation which could still be questioned. Consider the present-tense form, which we assumed was /u/. An alternative may be considered: the suffix might be /ru/. The presence of underlying /r/ in this suffix is made plausible by the fact that *r* actually appears in the forms *miru, neru*. We assumed that *r* is epenthetic, but perhaps it is part of the present suffix. That would allow us to eliminate the rule of *r*-epenthesis which is needed only to account for [neru] and [miru]. At the same time, we can also simplify the rule of vowel deletion, by removing the restriction that only nonround vowels delete after [e] and [i]: we made that assumption only because /ne-u/ and /mi-u/ apparently did not undergo the process of vowel deletion.

Any change in assumed underlying forms requires a reconsideration of those parts of the analysis relevant to that morpheme. We would then assume the underlying forms /šin-ru/, /yom-ru/, /kat-ru/, and so on, with the root-final consonant being followed by /r/. This /r/ must be deleted: but notice that we already have a rule which, stated in a more general form, would delete this /r/, namely the rule deleting /y/ after a consonant.

(74)   [+sonor] → Ø / C _

If we generalize that rule to apply to any sonorant consonant after a consonant, we eliminate the rule of *r*-insertion, and generalize the rules *y*-deletion and vowel deletion, which results in a better analysis.

Summary   Analyzing a complex set of data into a consistent system of underlying representations and rules requires you to pay attention to details. A solution to a problem requires that you formulate reasoned hypotheses and test them against the data. The most important skill needed to test a hypothesis is that you must apply your rules completely literally. Do what the rule says must be done, and if that does not give you the correct result, you must change your underlying representations, rules, or rule ordering. The ability to conceive of and evaluate multiple hypotheses is one of the most important skills in problem solving.

Exercises
1 Serbo-Croatian

These data from Serbo-Croatian have been simplified in two ways, to make the problem more manageable. Vowel length is omitted, and some stresses are omitted. The language has both underlying stresses whose position cannot be predicted – these are not marked in the transcriptions – and a predictable "mobile" stress which is assigned by rule – these are the stresses indicated here. Your analysis should account for how stress is assigned in those words marked with a rule-governed stress: you should not try to write a rule that predicts *whether* a word has a stress assigned by rule versus an underlying stress. Ignore the stress of words with no stress mark (other parts of the phonology of such words must be accounted for). Past-tense verbs all have the same general past-tense suffix, and the difference between masculine, feminine and neuter past-tense involves the same suffixes as are used to mark gender in adjectives.

Adjectives

Masc	Fem	Neut	Pl	
mlád	mladá	mladó	mladí	'young'
túp	tupá	tupó	tupí	'blunt'
blág	blagá	blagó	blagí	'mild'
grúb	grubá	grubó	grubí	'coarse'
béo	belá	beló	belí	'white'
veseo	vesela	veselo	veseli	'gay'
debéo	debelá	debeló	debelí	'fat'
mío	milá	miló	milí	'dear'
zelén	zelená	zelenó	zelení	'green'
kradén	kradená	kradenó	kradení	'stolen'
dalék	daleká	dalekó	dalekí	'far'
visók	visoká	visokó	visokí	'high'
dubók	duboká	dubokó	dubokí	'deep'

križan	križana	križano	križani	'cross'
sunčan	sunčana	sunčano	sunčani	'sunny'
svečan	svečana	svečano	svečani	'formal'
bogat	bogata	bogato	bogati	'rich'
rapav	rapava	rapavo	rapavi	'rough'
yásan	yasná	yasnó	yasní	'clear'
vážan	važná	važnó	važní	'important'
sítan	sitná	sitnó	sitní	'tiny'
ledan	ledna	ledno	ledni	'frozen'
tának	tanká	tankó	tankí	'slim'
krátak	kratká	kratkó	kratkí	'short'
blízak	bliská	bliskó	bliskí	'close'
úzak	uská	uskó	uskí	'narrow'
dóbar	dobrá	dobró	dobrí	'kind'
óštar	oštrá	oštró	oštrí	'sharp'
bodar	bodra	bodro	bodri	'alert'
ustao	ustala	ustalo	ustali	'tired'
múkao	muklá	mukló	muklí	'hoarse'
óbao	oblá	obló	oblí	'plump'
pódao	podlá	podló	podlí	'base'

Verbs

1sg pres	*Masc past*	*Fem past*	*Neut past*	
tepém	tépao	teplá	tepló	'wander'
skubém	skúbao	skublá	skubló	'tear'
tresém	trésao	treslá	tresló	'shake'
vezém	vézao	vezlá	vezló	'lead'

2 Standard Ukrainian

Standard Ukrainian has palatalized and nonpalatalized consonants, but only nonpalatalized consonants before *e*. Consonants are generally palatalized before *i*, with some apparent exceptions such as *bil[y]* 'ache,' which need not be seen as exceptions, given the right analysis. Give ordered rules to account for the alternations of the following nouns. The alternation between *o* and *e* is limited to suffixes. Also for masculine nouns referring to persons, *ov/ev* is inserted between the root and the case suffix in the locative singular (see words for 'son-in-law,' 'grandfather'). The data are initially ambiguous as to whether or not the alternations between *o* and *i* and between *e* and *i* are to be implemented by the same rule. Consider both possibilities; give an argument for selecting one of these solutions.

Masculine nouns

Nom sg	*Dat pl*	*Dat sg*	*Loc sg*	
zub	zubam	zubov[y]i	zub[y]i	'tooth'
sv[y]it	sv[y]itam	sv[y]itov[y]i	sv[y]it[y]i	'light'
z[y]at[y]	z[y]at[y]am	z[y]atev[y]i	z[y]atev[y]i	'son-in-law'
koš[y]il[y]	košel[y]am	košelev[y]i	košel[y]i	'basket'
zlod[y]iy	zlod[y]iyam	zlod[y]iyev[y]i	zlod[y]iyev[y]i	'thief'
m[y]is[y]at[sy]	m[y]is[y]at[sy]am	m[y]is[y]at[s]ev[y]i	m[y]is[y]at[sy]i	'month'
korovay	korovayam	korovayev[y]i	korovayi	'round loaf'
kam[y]in[y]	kamen[y]am	kamenev[y]i	kamen[y]i	'stone'
m[y]id[y]	m[y]id[y]am	m[y]idev[y]i	m[y]id[y]i	'copper'

xlʸiw	xlʸivam	xlʸivovʸi	xlʸivʸi	'stable'
holub	holubam	holubovʸi	holubʸi	'dove'
sʸin	sʸinam	sʸinovʸi	sʸinovʸi	'son'
lebʸidʸ	lebedʸam	lebedevʸi	lebedʸi	'swan'
susʸid	susʸidam	susʸidovʸi	susʸidovʸi	'neighbor'
čolovʸik	čolovʸikam	čolovʸikovʸi	čolovʸikovʸi	'man'
lʸid	ledam	ledovʸi	ledʸi	'ice'
bilʸ	bolʸam	bolevʸi	bolʸi	'ache'
riw	rovam	rovovʸi	rovʸi	'ditch'
stiw	stolam	stolovʸi	stolʸi	'table'
dʸid	dʸidam	dʸidovʸi	dʸidovʸi	'grandfather'
lʸit	lʸotam	lʸotovʸi	lʸotʸi	'flight'
mist	mostam	mostovʸi	mostʸi	'bridge'
večiɾ	večoram	večorovʸi	večorʸi	'evening'

Neuter nouns

Nom sg	Gen sg	Dat sg	Loc sg	Gen pl	
tʸilo	tʸila	tʸilu	tʸilʸi	tʸiw	'body'
koleso	kolesa	kolesu	kolesʸi	kolʸis	'wheel'
ozero	ozera	ozeru	ozerʸi	ozʸir	'lake'
selo	sela	selu	selʸi	sʸiw	'village'
pole	polʸa	polʸu	polʸi	pilʸ	'field'
slovo	slova	slovu	slovʸi	sliw	'word'
more	morʸa	morʸu	morʸi	mirʸ	'sea'

3 Somali

In the following Somali data, [ɖ] is a voiced retroflex stop and [ɽ] is a voiced retroflex continuant. Account for all phonological alternations in these data. In your discussion of these forms, be sure to make it clear what you assume the underlying representations of relevant morphemes are. Your discussion should also make it clear what motivates your underlying representations and rules. For instance if you could analyze some alternation by assuming underlying X and rule Y, say why (or whether) that choice is preferable to the alternative of assuming underlying P and rule Q.

Singular	Sing. definite	Plural	
daar	daarta	daaro	'house'
gees	geesta	geeso	'side'
laf	lafta	lafo	'bone'
lug	lugta	luɣo	'leg'
naag	naagta	naaɣo	'woman'
tib	tibta	tiβo	'pestle'
sab	sabta	saβo	'outcast'
bad	bada	baðo	'sea'
ǰid	ǰida	ǰiðo	'person'
feeɖ	feeɖa	feeɽo	'rib'
ʕiir	ʕiirta	ʕiiro	'buttermilk'
ʔul	ʔuša	ʔulo	'stick'
bil	biša	bilo	'month'
meel	meeša	meelo	'place'
kaliil	kaliiša	kaliilo	'summer'
nayl	nayša	naylo	'female lamb'

sun	sunta	sumo	'poison'
laan	laanta	laamo	'branch'
sin	sinta	simo	'hip'
dan	danta	dano	'affair'
daan	daanta	daano	'river bank'
saan	saanta	saano	'hide'
nirig	nirigta	nirgo	'baby female camel'
gaβaḍ	gaβaḍa	gabḍo	'girl'
hoɣol	hoɣoša	hoglo	'downpour'
baɣal	baɣaša	baglo	'mule'
waħar	waħarta	waħaro	'female kid'
irbad	irbada	irbaðo	'needle'
kefed	kefeda	kefeðo	'pan'
ǰilin	ǰilinta	ǰilino	'female dwarf'
bohol	bohoša	boholo	'hole'
jirid	jirida	jirdo	'trunk'
ʔaayad	ʔaayada	ʔaayaðo	'miracle'
gaʕan	gaʕanta	gaʕmo	'hand'
ʔinan	ʔinanta	ʔinano	'daughter'

3sg masc past	3sg fem past	1pl past	
suɣay	sugtay	sugnay	'wait'
kaβay	kabtay	kabnay	'fix'
siðay	siday	sidnay	'carry'
dilay	dišay	dillay	'kill'
ganay	gantay	gannay	'aim'
tumay	tuntay	tunnay	'hammer'
argay	aragtay	aragnay	'see'
gudbay	guðubtay	guðubnay	'cross a river'
qoslay	qososay	qosollay	'laugh'
hadlay	haðašay	haðallay	'talk'

4 Latin

Provide a complete account of the following phonological alternations in Latin, including underlying forms for noun stems.

Nominative	Genitive	
arks	arkis	'fortress'
duks	dukis	'leader'
daps	dapis	'feast'
re:ks	re:gis	'king'
falanks	falangis	'phalanx'
filiks	filikis	'fern'
lapis	lapidis	'stone'
li:s	li:tis	'strife'
fraws	frawdis	'deceit'
noks	noktis	'night'
frons	frontis	'brow'
frons	frondis	'leaf'
inku:s	inku:dis	'anvil'
sors	sortis	'lot'

fu:r	fu:ris	'thief'
murmur	murmuris	'murmur'
augur	auguris	'augur'
arbor	arboris	'tree'
pugil	pugilis	'boxer'
sal	salis	'salt'
adeps	adipis	'fat'
apeks	apikis	'top'
pri:nkeps	pri:nkipis	'chief'
ekwes	ekwitis	'horseman'
miles	militis	'soldier'
no:men	no:minis	'name'
karmen	ka:rminis	'song'
lu:men	lu:minis	'light'
wenter	wentris	'belly'
pater	patris	'father'
kada:wer	kada:weris	'corpse'
tu:ber	tu:beris	'swelling'
piper	piperis	'pepper'
karker	karkeris	'prison'

The following 6 nouns and adjectives select a different genitive suffix, *-i:* as opposed to *is*. You cannot predict on phonological grounds what nouns take this suffix, but otherwise these words follow the rules motivated in the language.

die:s	die:i:	'day'
li:ber	li:beri:	'free'
miser	miseri:	'wretched'
ager	agri:	'field'
sinister	sinistri:	'left'
liber	libri:	'book'

What other phonological rule or rules are needed to account for the following data?

as	assis	'whole'
os	ossis	'bone'
far	farris	'spell'
mel	mellis	'honey'
o:s	o:ris	'mouth'
flo:s	flo:ris	'flower'
mu:s	mu:ris	'mouse'
cru:s	cru:ris	'leg'
kinis	kineris	'ash'
pulvis	pulveris	'dust'

5 Turkish
Provide a phonological analysis of the following data from Turkish.

Nom	Poss	Dat	Abl	Nom pl	
oda	odası	odaya	odadan	odalar	'room'
dere	deresi	dereye	dereden	dereler	'river'
ütü	ütüsü	ütüye	ütüden	ütüler	'iron'
balo	balosu	baloya	balodan	balolar	'ball'

arɨ	arɨsɨ	arɨya	arɨdan	arɨlar	'bee'
la:	la:sɨ	la:ya	la:dan	la:lar	'la (note)'
bina:	bina:sɨ	bina:ya	bina:dan	bina:lar	'building'
imla:	imla:sɨ	imla:ya	imla:dan	imla:lar	'spelling'
be:	be:si	be:ye	be:den	be:ler	'B (letter)'
kep	kepi	kepe	kepten	kepler	'cap'
at	atɨ	ata	attan	atlar	'horse'
ek	eki	eke	ekten	ekler	'affix'
ok	oku	oka	oktan	oklar	'arrow'
güč	güǰü	güǰe	güčten	güčler	'power'
ahmet	ahmedi	ahmede	ahmetten	ahmetler	'Ahmed'
kurt	kurdu	kurda	kurttan	kurtlar	'worm'
türk	türkü	türke	türkten	türkler	'Turk'
genč	genči	genče	genčten	genčler	'young'
halk	halkɨ	halka	halktan	halklar	'folk'
üst	üstü	üste	üstten	üstler	'upper plane'
sarp	sarpɨ	sarpa	sarptan	sarplar	'steep'
harp	harbɨ	harba	harptan	harplar	'war'
alt	altɨ	alta	alttan	altlar	'bottom'
renk	rengi	renge	renkten	renkler	'color'
his	hissi	hisse	histen	hisler	'feeling'
hür	hürrü	hürre	hürden	hürler	'free'
mahal	mahallɨ	mahalla	mahaldan	mahallar	'place'
hak	hakkɨ	hakka	haktan	haklar	'right'
zam	zammɨ	zamma	zamdan	zamlar	'inflation'
af	affɨ	affa	aftan	aflar	'excuse'
arap	arabɨ	araba	araptan	araplar	'Arab'
koyun	koyunu	koyuna	koyundan	koyunlar	'sheep'
pilot	pilotu	pilota	pilottan	pilotlar	'pilot'
kitap	kitabɨ	kitaba	kitaptan	kitaplar	'book'
domuz	domuzu	domuza	domuzdan	domuzlar	'pig'
davul	davulu	davula	davuldan	davullar	'drum'
bayɨr	bayɨrɨ	bayɨra	bayɨrdan	bayɨrlar	'slope'
somun	somunu	somuna	somundan	somunlar	'loaf'
fikir	fikri	fikre	fikirden	fikirler	'idea'
isim	ismi	isme	isimden	isimler	'name'
boyun	boynu	boyna	boyundan	boyunlar	'neck'
čevir	čevri	čevre	čevirden	čevirler	'injustice'
devir	devri	devre	devirden	devirler	'transfer'
koyun	koynu	koyna	koyundan	koyunlar	'bosom'
karɨn	karnɨ	karna	karɨndan	karɨnlar	'thorax'
burun	burnu	burna	burundan	burunlar	'nose'
akɨl	aklɨ	akla	akɨldan	akɨllar	'intelligence'
šehir	šehri	šehre	šehirden	šehirler	'city'
namaz	namazɨ	namaza	namazdan	namazlar	'worship'
zaman	zama:nɨ	zama:na	zamandan	zamanlar	'time'
harap	hara:bɨ	hara:ba	haraptan	haraplar	'ruined'
i:kaz	i:ka:zɨ	i:ka:za	i:kazdan	i:kazlar	'warning'
hayat	haya:tɨ	haya:ta	hayattan	hayatlar	'life'
ispat	ispa:tɨ	ispa:ta	ispattan	ispatlar	'proof'
inek	inei	inee	inekten	inekler	'cow'

mantik	mantɨt	mantia	mantɨktan	mantɨklar	'logic'
ayak	ayaɨ	ayaa	ayaktan	ayaklar	'foot'
čabuk	čabuu	čabua	čabuktan	čabʊklar	'quick'
dakik	dakii	dakie	dakikten	dakikler	'punctual'
merak	mera:kɨ	mera:ka	meraktan	meraklar	'curiosity'
tebrik	tebri:ki	tebri:ke	tebrikten	tebrikler	'greetings'
hukuk	huku:ku	huku:ka	hukuktan	hukuklar	'law'

6 Kera

Propose rules to account for the following alternations. It will prove useful to think about Kera vowels in terms of high versus nonhigh vowels. Also, in this language it would be convenient to assume that [h] and [ʔ] are specified as [+low]. Pay attention to both verbs like *bɨlan* 'want me,' *balnan* 'wanted me' and *balla* 'you must want!', i.e. there are present, past, and imperative forms involved, certain tenses being marked by suffixes. Finally, pay attention to what might look like a coincidence in the distribution of vowels in the underlying forms of verb roots: there are no coincidences.

haman	'eat me'		se:nen	'my brother'
hamam	'eat you (masc)'		se:nem	'your (masc) brother'
hɨmi	'eat you (fem)'		si:ni	'your (fem) brother'
hɨmu	'eat him'		si:nu	'his brother'
hama	'eat her'		se:na	'her brother'
hamaŋ	'eat you (pl)'		se:neŋ	'your (pl) brother'
kolon	'change me'		gi:din	'my belly'
kolom	'change you (masc)'		gi:dim	'your (masc) belly'
kuli	'change you (fem)'		gi:di	'your (fem) belly'
kulu	'change him'		gi:du	'his belly'
kola	'change her'		gi:dɨ	'her belly'
koloŋ	'change you (pl)'		gi:diŋ	'your (pl) belly'
ci:rin	'my head'		gunun	'wake me'
ci:rɨm	'your (masc) head'		gunum	'wake you (masc)'
ci:ri	'your (fem) head'		guni	'wake you (fem)'
cu:ru	'his head'		gunu	'wake him'
ci:rɨ	'her head'		gunɨ	'wake her'
ci:rɨŋ	'your (pl) head'		gunuŋ	'wake you (pl)'
bɨlan	'want me'		ŋifan	'meet me'
bɨlam	'want you (masc)'		ŋifam	'meet you (masc)'
bɨli	'want you (fem)'		ŋifi	'meet you (fem)'
bɨlu	'want him'		ŋifu	'meet him'
bɨla	'want her'		ŋifa	'meet her'
bɨlaŋ	'want you (pl)'		ŋifaŋ	'meet you (pl)'
ʔasan	'know me'		ʔapan	'find me'
ʔasam	'know you (masc)'		ʔapam	'find you (masc)'
ʔɨsi	'know you (fem)'		ʔɨpi	'find you (fem)'
ʔɨsu	'know him'		ʔɨpu	'find him'
ʔasa	'know her'		ʔapa	'find her'
ʔasaŋ	'know you (pl)'		ʔapaŋ	'find you (pl)'

haran	'give me back'
haram	'give you (masc) back'
hɨri	'give you (fem) back'
hɨru	'give him back'
hara	'give her back'
haraŋ	'give you (pl) back'

balnan	'wanted me'	ŋafnan	'met me'
balnam	'wanted you (masc)'	ŋafnam	'met you (masc)'
bɨlni	'wanted you (fem)'	ŋɨfni	'met you (fem)'
bɨlnu	'wanted him'	ŋɨfnu	'met him'
balna	'wanted her'	ŋafna	'met her'
balnaŋ	'wanted you (pl)'	ŋafnaŋ	'met you (pl)'
balla	'you must want!'	ŋafla	'you must meet!'

ba	'not'	pa	'again'	bɨpa	'no more'

7 Keley-i

Account for the alternations in the following verbs. The different forms relate to whether the action is in the past or future, and which element in the sentence is emphasized (subject, object, instrument). Roots underlyingly have the shape CVC(C)VC, and certain forms such as the subject focus future require changes in the stem that result in a CVCCVC shape. This may be accomplished by reduplicating the initial CV– for stems whose first vowel is [e] (ʔum-bebhat ← behat) or doubling the middle consonant (ʔum-buŋŋet – buŋet). The contrastive identification imperfective form conditions lengthening of the consonant in the middle of the stem, when the first vowel is not [e] (memayyuʔ ← bayuʔ). These changes are part of the morphology, so do not attempt to write phonological rules to double consonants or reduplicate syllables. Be sure to explicitly state the underlying form of each root and affix. Understanding the status of [s] and [h] in this language is important in solving this problem. It is also important to consider exactly what underlying nasal consonant is present in these various prefixes and infixes – there is evidence in the data which shows that the underlying nature of the nasal explains certain observed differences in phonological behavior.

Subject focus future	Direct object focus past	Instrumental focus past	
ʔumduntuk	dinuntuk	ʔinduntuk	'punch'
ʔumbayyuʔ	binayuʔ	ʔimbayuʔ	'pound rice'
ʔumdillag	dinilag	ʔindilag	'light lamp'
ʔumgubbat	ginubat	ʔiŋgubat	'fight'
ʔumhullat	hinulat	ʔinhulat	'cover'
ʔumbuŋŋet	binuŋet	ʔimbuŋet	'scold'
ʔumgalgal	ginalgal	ʔiŋgalgal	'chew'
ʔumʔagtuʔ	ʔinagtuʔ	ʔinʔagtuʔ	'carry on head'
ʔumʔehneŋ	ʔinehneŋ	ʔinʔehneŋ	'stand'
ʔumbebhat	binhat	ʔimbehat	'cut rattan'
ʔumdedʔek	dinʔek	ʔindeʔek	'accuse'
ʔumtuggun	sinugun	ʔintugun	'advise'
ʔumtetpen	simpen	ʔintepen	'measure'
ʔumpeptut	pintut	ʔimpetut	'dam'

ʔumhehpuŋ	himpuŋ	ʔinhepuŋ	'break a stick'
ʔumtetkuk	siŋkuk	ʔintekuk	'shout'
ʔumkekbet	kimbet	ʔiŋkebet	'scratch'
ʔumbebdad	bindad	ʔimbedad	'untie'
ʔumdedgeh	diŋgeh	ʔindegeh	'sick'

Instrumental past focus	*Contrastive id. imperfective*	*Contrastive id. perfective*	
ʔinduntuk	menuntuk	nenuntuk	'punch'
ʔimbayuʔ	memayyuʔ	nemayuʔ	'pound rice'
ʔindilag	menillag	nenilag	'light lamp'
ʔiŋgubat	meŋubbat	neŋubat	'fight'
ʔinhulat	menullat	nenulat	'cover'
ʔintanem	menannem	nenanem	'plant'
ʔimpedug	memdug	nemdug	'chase'
ʔimbedad	memdad	nemdad	'untie'
ʔiŋkebet	meŋbet	neŋbet	'scratch'
ʔimbekaʔ	memkaʔ	nemkaʔ	'dig'
ʔintepen	mempen	nempen	'measure'
ʔintebaʔ	membaʔ	nembaʔ	'kill a pig'
ʔintekuk	meŋkuk	neŋkuk	'shout'
ʔindegeh	meŋgeh	neŋgeh	'sick'
ʔinhepaw	mempaw	nempaw	'possess'
ʔinteled	menled	nenled	'sting'
ʔindeʔek	menʔek	nenʔek	'accuse'
ʔinʔebaʔ	meŋbaʔ	neŋbaʔ	'carry on back'
ʔinʔinum	meŋinnum	neŋinum	'drink'
ʔinʔagtuʔ	meŋagtuʔ	neŋagtuʔ	'carry on head'
ʔinʔalaʔ	meŋallaʔ	neŋalaʔ	'get'
ʔinʔawit	meŋawwit	neŋawit	'get'

The following past subject clausal focus forms involve a different prefix, using some of the roots found above. A number of roots require reduplication of the first root syllable.

nandunduntuk	'punch'	nampepedug	'chase'
naŋkekebet	'scratch'	nambebekaʔ	'dig'
nantetekuk	'shout'	nandedeʔek	'accuse'
nanʔeʔebaʔ	'carry on back'	nanʔiʔinum	'drink'
nantanem	'plant'		

8 Kuria

In some (but not all) of the examples below, morphemes boundaries have been been introduced to assist in the analysis. Pronouns are assigned to a grammatical class depending on the noun which they refer to, conventionally given a number (1–20). Tone may be disregarded (however, it is predictable in the infinitive). It is important to pay attention to interaction between processes in this problem.

ogo-táángá	'to begin'	oko-gésa	'to harvest'
oko-róga	'to witch'	oko-réma	'to plow'
oko-hóórá	'to thresh'	ugu-sííká	'to close a door'

| ugu-súraangá | 'to sing praise' | uku-gííngá | 'to shave' |
| ugútúúhá | 'to be blunt' | | |

ogo-kó-bárǎ	'to count you (sg)'	uku-gú-súraánga	'to praise you (sg)'
oko-mó-bárǎ	'to count him'	uku-mú-súraánga	'to praise him'
ogo-tó-bárǎ	'to count us'	ugu-tú-súraánga	'to praise us'
oko-gé-bárǎ	'to count them (4)'	uku-gí-súraánga	'to praise it (4)'
oko-ré-bárǎ	'to count it (5)'	uku-rí-súraánga	'to praise it (5)'
uku-bí-bárǎ	'to count it (8)'	uku-bí-súraánga	'to praise it (8)'
ugu-čí-bárǎ	'to count it (10)'	ugu-č-súraánga	'to praise it (10)'

oko-mó-gó-gesɛ́ra	'to harvest it (3) for him'
uku-mú-gú-siíkya	'to make him close it (3)'
uku-mú-gú-siíndya	'to make him win it (3)'
oko-bá-súraánga	'to praise them'
oko-mó-bá-suráángéra	'to praise them for him'
oko-bá-mú-suráángéra	'to praise him for them'

To V	To make to V	To V for	To make V for	
okoréma	ukurímyá	okorémérǎ	ukurímíryá	'weed'
okoróma	ukurúmyá	okorómúrǎ	ukurúmíryá	'bite'
okohóórá	ukuhúúryá	okohóórúrǎ	ukuhúúríryá	'thresh'
okohéétóká	ukuhíítúkyá	okohéétókerá	ukuhíítúkiryá	'remember'
okogéémbá	ukugíímbyá	okogéémbérá	ukugíímbíryá	'make rain'
ogosóóká	ugusúúkyá	ogosóókérá	ugusúúkíryá	'respect'
ogotégétǎ	ugutígítyǎ	ogotégéterá	ugutígítiryá	'be late'
okorɔ́ga	okorógyá	okorɔ́gérǎ	okorógéryá	'bewitch'
okogɔ́ɔ́gá	okogóógyá	okogɔ́ɔ́gérá	okogóógéryá	'slaughter'
okogɔ́ɔ́tá	okogóótyá	okogɔ́ɔ́térá	okogóótéryá	'hold'
ogosɔ́ka	ogosókyá	ogosɔ́kérǎ	ogosókéryá	'poke'
ogotɛ́rɛ́kǎ	ogotérékyá	ogotɛ́rɛ́kerá	ogotérékeryá	'brew'
okogésa	okogésyá	okogésɛ́rǎ	okogéséryá	'harvest'
ogosɛ́énsá	ogoséénsyá	ogosɛ́énsɛ́rá	ogoséénséryá	'winnow'

To V	To make to V	To V for	To make V for	
ugusííká	ugusííkyá	ogosééékérá	ugusííkíryá	'to close'
ukurúga	ukurúgyá	okorógérǎ	ukurúgíryá	'to cook'
ugusúka	ugusúkyá	ogosókérǎ	ugusúkíryá	'to plait'
ukurííngá	ukurííngyá	okorééngérá	ukurííngíryá	'to fold'
ugusííndá	ugusííndyá	ogosééndérá	ugusííndíryá	'to win'

Imperative	Infinitive	They will V	Then will V for	
remǎ	okoréma	mbareréma	mbareréméra	'cultivate'
barǎ	okobára	mbarebára	mbarebáréra	'count'
atǎ	ogɔɔ́ta	mbarɛɛ́ta	mbarɛɛ́téra	'be split'
ahǎ	okɔɔ́ha	mbarɛɛ́ha	mbarɛɛ́héra	'pick greens'
agǎ	okɔɔ́ga	mbarɛɛ́ga	mbarɛɛ́géra	'weed'
aangá	okɔɔ́nga	mbarɛɛ́nga	mbarɛɛ́ngéra	'refuse'
andeká	okɔɔ́ndékǎ	mbarɛɛ́ndéka	mbarɛɛ́ndékera	'write'

Imperative	3sg subjunctive	3sg subjunctive for	
remǎ	aremě	aremeré	'cultivate'
tɛrɛká	atɛrɛkɛ́	atɛrɛkɛ́rɛ	'brew'

ebǎ	ɛɜbě	ɛɛberɛ́	'forget'
egǎ	ɛɛgě	ɛɛgerɛ́	'learn'
ogǎ	ɔɔgě	ɔɔgerɛ́	'be sharp'
ɛyǎ	ɛɛyě	ɛɛyerɛ́	'sweep'
ɔrɔká	ɔɔrɔké	ɔɔrɔkɛ́rɛ	'come out'

9 Lardil

Account for the phonological alternations seen in the data below.

Bare N	Accusative	Nonfuture	Future	
kentapal	kentapalin	kentapalŋar	kentapaluṛ	'dugong'
keṯar	keṯarin	keṯarŋar	keṯaruṛ	'river'
miyaṛ	miyaṛin	miyaṛŋar	miyaṛuṛ	'spear'
yupur	yupurin	yupurŋar	yupuruṛ	'red rock cod'
taŋur	taŋurin	taŋurŋar	taŋuruṛ	'crab (sp)'
yaraman	yaramanin	yaramanar	yaramankuṛ	'horse'
maan	maanin	maanar	maankuṛ	'spear'
pirŋen	pirŋenin	pirŋenar	pirŋenkuṛ	'woman'
mela	melan	melaŋar	melaṛ	'sea'
ṯawa	ṯawan	ṯawaŋar	ṯawaṛ	'rat'
wanka	wankan	wankaŋar	wankaṛ	'arm'
kuŋka	kuŋkan	kuŋkaŋar	kuŋkaṛ	'groin'
tarŋka	tarŋkan	tarŋkaŋar	tarŋkaṛ	'barracuda'
ŋuka	ŋukun	ŋukuŋar	ŋukuṛ	'water'
ŋuṛa	ŋuṛun	ŋuṛuŋar	ŋuṛuṛ	'forehead'
kaṯa	kaṯun	kaṯuŋar	kaṯuṛ	'child'
muna	munun	munuŋar	munuṛ	'elbow'
ŋawa	ŋawun	ŋawuŋar	ŋawuṛ	'dog'
kenṯe	kenṯin	kenṯiŋar	kenṯiwuṛ	'wife'
tʸimpe	tʸimpin	tʸimpiŋar	tʸimpiwuṛ	'tail'
ɲine	ɲinin	ɲiniŋar	ɲiniwuṛ	'skin'
pape	papin	papiŋar	papiwuṛ	'father's mother'
tʸempe	tʸempen	tʸempeŋar	tʸemper	'mother's father'
wiṯe	wiṯen	wiṯeŋar	wiṯeṛ	'interior'
waŋal	waŋalkin	waŋalkar	waŋalkuṛ	'boomerang'
menʸel	menʸelkin	menʸelkar	menʸelkuṛ	'dogfish (sp)'
makar	makarkin	makarkar	makarkuṛ	'anthill'
yalul	yalulun	yaluluŋar	yaluluṛ	'flame'
mayar	mayaran	mayaraŋar	mayaraṛ	'rainbow'
ṯalkur	ṯalkuran	ṯalkuraŋar	ṯalkuraṛ	'kookaburra'
wiwal	wiwalan	wiwalaŋar	wiwalaṛ	'bush mango'
karikar	karikarin	karikariŋar	karikariwuṛ	'butter-fish'
yiliyil	yiliyilin	yiliyiliŋar	yiliyiliwuṛ	'oyster (sp)'
yukar	yukarpan	yukarpaŋar	yukarpaṛ	'husband'
pulŋar	pulŋarpan	pulŋarpaŋar	pulŋarpaṛ	'huge'
wulun	wulunkan	wulunkaŋar	wulunkaṛ	'fruit (sp)'
wuṯal	wuṯaltʸin	wuṯaltʸiŋar	wuṯaltʸiwuṛ	'meat'
kantukan	kantukantun	kantukantuŋar	kantukantuṛ	'red'
karwakar	karwakarwan	karwakarwaŋar	karwakarwaṛ	'wattle (sp)'
ṯurara	ṯuraraŋin	ṯuraraŋar	ṯuraraŋkuṛ	'shark'
ŋalu	ŋalukin	ŋalukar	ŋalukuṛ	'story'

kurka	kurkaɲin	kurkaɲar	kurkaŋkuɽ	'pandja'
taŋku	taŋkuɲin	taŋkuɲar	taŋkuŋkuɽ	'oyster (sp)'
kurpuɽu	kurpuɽuɲin	kurpuɽuɲar	kurpuɽuŋkuɽ	'lancewood'
putu	putukan	putukaɲar	putukaɽ	'short'
maali	maaliyan	maaliyaɲar	maaliyaɽ	'swamp turtle'
tʸintirpu	tʸintirpuwan	tʸintirpuwaɲar	tʸintirpuwaɽ	'willie wagtail'
pukatʸi	pukatʸiyan	pukatʸiyaɲar	pukatʸiyaɽ	'hawk (sp)'
murkuni	murkuniman	murkunimaɲar	murkunimaɽ	'nullah'
ŋawuɲa	ŋawuɲawun	ŋawuɲawuɲar	ŋawuɲawuɽ	'termite'
tipiti	tipitipin	tipitipiɲar	tipitipiwuɽ	'rock-cod (sp)'
ʈapu	ʈaputʸin	ʈaputʸiɲar	ʈaputʸiwuɽ	'older brother'
muŋkumu	muŋkumuŋkun	muŋkumuŋkuɲar	muŋkumuŋkuɽ	'wooden axe'
tʸumputʸu	tʸumputʸumpun	tʸumputʸumpuɲar	tʸumputʸumpuɽ	'dragonfly'

10 Sakha (Yakut)

Give a phonological analysis of the following case-marking paradigms of nouns in Sakha.

Noun	Plural	Associative	
aɣa	aɣalar	aɣaliin	'father'
paarta	paartalar	paartaliin	'school desk'
tɨa	tɨalar	tɨaliin	'forest'
kinige	kinigeler	kinigeliin	'book'
ǰie	ǰieler	ǰieliin	'house'
iye	iyeler	iyeliin	'mother'
kini	kiniler	kiniliin	'3rd person'
bie	bieler	bieliin	'mare'
oɣo	oɣolor	oɣoluun	'child'
χopto	χoptolor	χoptoluun	'gull'
börö	börölör	börölüün	'wolf'
tial	tiallar	tialliin	'wind'
ial	iallar	ialliin	'neighbor'
kuul	kuullar	kuulluun	'sack'
at	attar	attiin	'horse'
balɨk	balɨktar	balɨktiin	'fish'
iskaap	iskaaptar	iskaaptiin	'cabinet'
oɣus	oɣustar	oɣustuun	'bull'
kus	kustar	kustuun	'duck'
tünnük	tünnükter	tünnüktüün	'window'
sep	septer	septiin	'tool'
et	etter	ettiin	'meat'
örüs	örüster	örüstüün	'river'
tiis	tiister	tiistiin	'tooth'
soroχ	soroχtor	soroχtuun	'some person'
oχ	oχtor	oχtuun	'arrow'
oloppos	oloppostor	oloppostuun	'chair'
ötöχ	ötöχtör	ötöχtüün	'abandoned farm'
ubay	ubaydar	ubaydiin	'elder brother'
saray	saraydar	saraydiin	'barn'
tɨy	tɨydar	tɨydiin	'foal'
atɨir	atɨirdar	atɨirdiin	'stallion'

oyuur	oyuurdar	oyuurduun	'forest'
üčügey	üčügeyder	üčügeydiin	'good person'
ejiiy	ejiiyder	ejiiydiin	'elder sister'
tomtor	tomtordor	tomtorduun	'knob'
moɣotoy	moɣotoydor	moɣotoyduun	'chipmunk'
kötör	kötördör	kötördüün	'bird'
bölköy	bölköydör	bölköydüün	'islet'
χatiŋ	χatiŋnar	χatiŋniin	'birch'
aan	aannar	aanniin	'door'
tiiŋ	tiiŋner	tiiŋniin	'squirrel'
sordoŋ	sordoŋnor	sordoŋnuun	'pike'
olom	olomnor	olomnuun	'ford'
oron	oronnor	oronnuun	'bed'
bödöŋ	bödoŋnor	bödöŋnüün	'strong one'

Noun	Partitive	Comparative	Ablative	
aɣa	aɣata	aɣataaɣar	aɣattan	'father'
paarta	paartata	paartataaɣar	paartattan	'school desk'
tia	tiata	tiataaɣar	tiattan	'forest'
kinige	kinigete	kinigeteeɣer	kinigetten	'book'
jie	jiete	jieteeɣer	jietten	'house'
iye	iyete	iyeteeɣer	iyetten	'mother'
kini	kinite	kiniteeɣer	kinitten	'3rd person'
bie	biete	bieteeɣer	bietten	'mare'
oɣo	oɣoto	oɣotooɣor	oɣotton	'child'
χopto	χoptoto	χoptotooɣor	χoptotton	'gull'
börö	börötö	börötööɣör	böröttön	'wolf'
tial	tialla	tiallaaɣar	tialtan	'wind'
ial	ialla	iallaaɣar	ialtan	'neighbor'
kuul	kuulla	kuullaaɣar	kuultan	'sack'
moχsoɣol	moχsoɣollo	moχsoɣollooɣor	moχsoɣolton	'falcon'
at	atta	attaaɣar	attan	'horse'
balik	balikta	baliktaaɣar	baliktan	'fish'
iskaap	iskaapta	iskaaptaaɣar	iskaaptan	'cabinet'
oɣus	oɣusta	oɣustaaɣar	oɣustan	'bull'
kus	kusta	kustaaɣar	kustan	'duck'
tünnük	tünnükte	tünnükteeɣer	tünnükten	'window'
sep	septe	septeeɣer	septen	'tool'
et	ette	etteeɣer	etten	'meat'
örüs	örüste	örüsteeɣer	örüsten	'river'
tiis	tiiste	tiisteeɣer	tiisten	'tooth'
soroχ	soroχto	soroχtooɣor	soroχton	'some person'
ötöχ	ötöχtö	ötöχtööɣör	ötöχtön	'abandoned farm'
ubay	ubayda	ubaydaaɣar	ubaytan	'elder brother'
saray	sarayda	saraydaaɣar	saraytan	'barn'
tiy	tiyda	tiydaaɣar	tiytan	'foal'
atiir	atiirda	atiirdaaɣar	atiirtan	'stallion'
χirur	χirurda	χirurdaaɣar	χirurtan	'surgeon'
üčügey	üčügeyde	üčügeydeeɣer	üčügeyten	'good person'
tomtor	tomtordo	tomtordooɣor	tomtorton	'knob'
moɣotoy	moɣotoydo	moɣotoydooɣor	moɣotoyton	'chipmunk'

kötör	kötördö	kötördööɣör	kötörtön	'bird'
suorɣan	suorɣanna	suorɣannaaɣar	suorɣantan	'blanket'
χatiŋ	χatiŋna	χatiŋnaaɣar	χatiŋtan	'birch'
aan	aanna	aannaaɣar	aantan	'door'
tiiŋ	tiiŋne	tiiŋneeɣer	tiiŋten	'squirrel'
sordoŋ	sordoŋno	sordoŋnooɣor	sordoŋton	'pike'
olom	olomno	olomnooɣor	olomton	'ford'
bödöŋ	bödöŋnö	bödöŋnööɣör	bödöŋtön	'strong one'

Noun	Dative	Accusative	
aɣa	aɣaɣa	aɣani	'father'
ǰie	ǰieɣe	ǰieni	'house'
iye	iyeɣe	iyeni	'mother'
oɣo	oɣoɣo	oɣonu	'child'
börö	böröɣö	börönü	'wolf'
tɨal	tɨalga	tɨalɨ	'wind'
kuul	kuulga	kuulu	'sack'
at	akka	atɨ	'horse'
balɨk	balɨkka	balɨgɨ	'fish'
iskaap	iskaapka	iskaabɨ	'cabinet'
oɣus	oɣuska	oɣuhu	'bull'
kus	kuska	kuhu	'duck'
sep	sepke	sebi	'tool'
et	ekke	eti	'meat'
tiis	tiiske	tiihi	'tooth'
ot	okko	otu	'grass'
soroχ	soroχχo	soroɣu	'some person'
ötöχ	ötöχχö	ötöɣü	'abandoned farm'
oχ	oχχo	oɣu	'arrow'
saray	sarayga	sarayɨ	'barn'
tɨy	tɨyga	tɨyɨ	'foal'
kötör	kötörgö	kötörü	'bird'

oyuun	oyuuŋŋa	oyuunu	'shaman'
χatiŋ	χatiŋŋa	χatiŋi	'birch'
aan	aaŋŋa	aanɨ	'door'
olom	olomŋo	olomu	'ford'

Noun	OurN		Noun	Our N	
aɣa	aɣabɨt	'father'	iye	iyebit	'mother'
uol	uolbut	'son'	kötör	kötörbüt	'bird'
kɨlaas	kɨlaaspɨt	'classroom'	iskaap	iskaappɨt	'cabinet'
kuorat	kuorappɨt	'town'	tiis	tiispit	'tooth'
ohoχ	ohoχput	'stove'	tünnük	tünnükpüt	'window'
aan	aammɨt	'door'	kapitan	kapitammɨt	'captain'
tiiŋ	tiiŋmit	'squirrel'	oron	orommut	'bed'
kün	kümmüt	'day'			

11 Sadžava Ukrainian

Give a phonological analysis of the following data. Assume that all surface occurrences of kʸ and gʸ in this language are derived by rule. Also assume that stress is located on the proper vowel in the underlying representation:

the rules for shifting stress are too complex to be considered here. Nouns in declension II depalatalize a consonant before the locative suffix, and nouns in declension III depalatalize in the genitive. The variation in the genitive and locative singular suffix in declension I (*-i* or *-a* versus *-u*) is lexically governed: do not write rules which select between these suffixes. Concentrate on establishing the correct underlying representations for the noun stem.

Declension I

Nom sg	Gen sg	Loc sg	
plást	plastá	plasʲkʲí	'layer'
skorúx	skoruxá	skorusʲí	'mountain ash'
ɣʲrʲíx	ɣʲrʲixá	ɣʲrʲisʲí	'sin'
pastúx	pastuxá	pastusʲí	'herdsman'
mʲnʲúx	mʲnʲúxa	mʲnʲʲisʲi	'fish (sp)'
plúɣ	plúɣa	plúzʲi	'plow'
sʲtʲíɣ	stóɣa	stózʲi	'stack'
sák	sáka	sátsʲi	'fishnet'
bék	bəká	bətsʲi	'bull'
lést	ləstá	ləsʲkʲí	'letter'
lést	lésta	lésʲkʲi	'leaf'
pʲlʲít	plóta	plókʲi	'wicker fence'
sʲmʲrʲíd	smróda	smróɣʲi	'stench'
fʲíst	fostá	fosʲkʲí	'tail'
mʲíst	mósta	mósʲkʲi	'bridge'
lʲíd	lǽdu	lədú	'ice'
dʲrʲít	dróta	drókʲi	'thick wire'
mʲíd	mǽdu	mədú	'honey'
vʲíl	volá	volʲí	'ox'
vʲíz	vóza	vózʲi	'cart'
sér	séra	sérʲi	'cottage cheese'
sʲnʲíp	snopá	snopʲí	'sheaf'
ɣréb	ɣrəbá	ɣrəbʲí	'mushroom'
lǽbʲid	lǽbəda	lǽbəgʲi	'swan'
bǽrʲíɣ	bǽrəɣa	bǽrəzʲi	'shore'
pərʲíɣ	pəróɣa	pərózʲi	'dumpling'
porʲíɣ	poróɣa	porózʲi	'threshhold'
bolʲék	bolʲəká	bolʲətsʲí	'abcess'
vórʲíɣ	vóroɣa	vórozʲi	'enemy'
kónək	kónəka	kónətsʲi	'grasshopper'
pótʲik	potóka	potótsʲi	'stream'
tʲík	tóka	tótsʲi	'current'
kʲíl	kolá	kolʲí	'stake'

Declension II

Nom sg	Gen sg	Loc sg	
koválʲ	kovalʲú	kovalé	'blacksmith'
ǰmʲílʲ	ǰmʲilʲé	ǰmʲilé	'bumblebee'
kʲrʲílʲ	kʲrʲilʲé	kʲrʲilé	'rabbit'
učétəlʲ	učétəlʲə	učétələ	'teacher'
grǽbʲinʲ	grǽbənʲə	grǽbənə	'comb'
ólənʲ	ólənʲə	ólənə	'deer'
yačʲmʲínʲ	yačmǽnʲə	yačmǽnə	'barley'

| yásʸinʸ | yásənʸə | yásənə | 'ash tree' |
| zʸékʸ | zʸékʸə | zʸétə | 'son-in-law' |

Declension III

Nom sg	*Gen sg*		
mósʸkʸ	mástə	'fat'	
sʸmʸírʸkʸ	smǽrtə	'death'	
vʸísʸkʸ	vʸístə	'news'	
sʸílʸ	sólə	'salt'	
póšʸisʸkʸ	póšəstə	'epidemic'	
zámʸikʸ	zámətə	'snowstorm'	
skátərʸkʸ	skátərtə	'tablecloth'	
kʸísʸkʸ	kóstə	'bone'	

12 Koromfe

Koromfe has two kinds of vowels, [-ATR] ɩ ʊ ɛ ɔ a and [+ATR] i u e o ʌ.
Provide an analysis of the alternations in the following data, which involve
singular and plural forms of nouns and different tense-inflections for verbs:

Singular	*Plural*		
gɩbrɛ	gɩba	'hatchet'	
hubre	hubʌ	'ditch'	
nɛbrɛ	nɛba	'pea'	
dĩŋgre	dĩŋgʌ	'bush type'	
zoŋgre	zoŋgʌ	'wing'	
lɔ̃ŋgrɛ	lɔ̃ŋga	'shoe'	
hullre	hullʌ	'gutter'	
sɛkrɛ	sɛka	'half'	
tɛfrɛ	tɛfa	'cotton fiber'	
dabɛɛrɛ	dabɛɛya	'camp'	
dɔɔrɛ	dɔɔya	'long'	
gĩgaarɛ	gĩgaaya	'vulture'	
pʊpaarɛ	pʊpaaya	'grass type'	
koire	koyʌ	'bracelet'	
dʊmdɛ	dʊma	'lion'	
hulomde	hulomʌ	'marrow'	
tɛmdɛ	tɛma	'beard'	
logomde	logomʌ	'camel'	
bɩndɛ	bɩna	'heart'	
hɔ̃ndɛ	hɔ̃na	'hoe'	
honde	honʌ	'bean'	
geŋde	geŋʌ	'pebble'	
zɛŋdɛ	zɛŋa	'upper arm'	
bɛllɛ	bɛla	'back'	
yɩllɛ	yɩla	'horn'	
selle	selʌ	'space'	
pallɛ	pala	'stretcher'	
deŋgele	deŋgelʌ	'open area'	
sembele	sembelʌ	'piece'	
dãĩnɛ	dãỹã	'wood'	
hũĩnɛ	hũỹã	'caterpillar'	
kɔ̃ĩnɛ	kɔ̃ỹã	'squirrel'	

kɔ̃ɔ̃nɛ	kɔ̃ɔ̃ỹã	'old'
sɔ̃ɔ̃nɛ	sɔ̃ɔ̃ỹã	'period'
bɛte	bɛra	'male animal'
date	dara	'chest'
gete	gerʌ	'forked stick'
gote	gorʌ	'stream'
bɪte	bɪra	'frog'
dɔte	dɔra	'cloud'

Neutral	*Past*	*Progressive*	
ta	taɛ	taraa	'shoot'
gɔ	gɔɛ	gɔraa	'go back'
kʊ	kɔɛ	kʊraa	'kill'
tu	toe	turʌʌ	'coat'
li	lee	lirʌʌ	'forget'
dɪ	dɛ	dɪraa	'eat'
tā	tãɛ̃	tãnaa	'contradict'
nɛ̃	nɛ̃	nɛ̃naa	'defecate'
saɪ	sayɛ	saɪraa	'separate'
yɛɪ	yɛyɛ	yɛɪraa	'waste'
sɔɪ	sɔyɛ	sɔɪraa	'split'
ỹɛ̃ɪ̃	ỹɛ̃ỹɛ̃	ỹɛ̃ɪ̃naa	'catch'
dɔ̃ɪ̃	dɔ̃ỹɛ̃	dɔ̃ɪ̃naa	'dream'
kendɪ	kendɛ	kendraa	'finish'
kɛ̃sɪ	kɛ̃sɛ	kɛ̃sraa	'surpass'
ketɪ	kete	ketraa	'open'
teŋgɪ	teŋge	teŋgraa	'accompany'
yisi	yise	yisrʌʌ	'suffice'
yɪsɪ	yɪsɛ	yɪsraa	'draw water'
birgi	birge	birgrʌʌ	'blacken'
pasgɪ	pasgɛ	pasgraa	'split'
mɛntī	mɛnte	mɛntraa	'assemble'
gondu	gonde	gondrʌʌ	'depart'
hɔ̃ŋgʊ	hɔ̃ŋgɛ	hɔ̃ŋgraa	'point'
sʊrgʊ	sʊrgɛ	sʊrgraa	'drop'
hɔkʊ	hɔkɛ	hɔkraa	'scratch'
zullu	zulle	zullrʌʌ	'bow'
sɪbʊ	sībɛ	sɪbraa	'die'
zambʊ	zambɛ	zambraa	'deceive'
wufu	wufe	wufrʌʌ	'borrow'
zɪgamsʊ	zɪgamsɛ	zɪgamsraa	'be dirty'
hɛ̃msʊ	hɛ̃msɛ	hɛ̃msraa	'meet'
leli	lele	lellʌʌ	'sing'
pɪlɪ	pɪlɛ	pɪllaa	'trample flat'
tarɪ	tarɛ	tataa	'plaster'
fɛrɪ	fɛrɛ	fɛtaa	'cultivate'
tʊrʊ	tʊrɛ	tʊtaa	'introduce'

Further reading

Kenstowicz and Kisseberth 1979; Zwicky 1973, 1974, 1975; Pullum 1976.

8 Phonological typology and naturalness

PREVIEW

KEY TERMS

typology
crosslinguistic
  comparison
  markedness
functional
  explanation

One of the main goals of many phonologists is explaining why certain phonological patterns are found in many languages, while other patterns are found in few or no languages. This chapter looks at phonological typology – the study of common versus uncommon, natural versus unnatural phonological rules, and looks at some of these commonly occurring phonological properties.

A widely invoked criterion in deciding between analyses of a language is whether the rules of one analysis are more natural, usually judged in terms of whether the rules occur more often across languages. As a prerequisite to explaining *why* some processes are common, uncommon, or even unattested, you need an idea of *what* these common patterns are, and providing this survey information is the domain of typology. While only a very small fraction of the roughly 7,000 languages spoken in the world have been studied in a way that yields useful information for phonological typology, crosslinguistic studies have revealed many recurrent patterns, which form the basis for theorizing about the reason for these patterns.

8.1 Inventories

A comparative, typological approach is often employed in the study of phonological segment inventories. It has been observed that certain kinds of segments occur in very many languages, while others occur in only a few. This observation is embodied in the study of markedness, which is the idea that not all segments or sets of segments have equal status in phonological systems. For example, many languages have the stop consonants [p t k], which are said to be unmarked, but relatively few have the uvular [q], which is said to be marked. Markedness is a comparative concept, so [q] is more marked than [k] but less marked than [ʕ]. Many languages have the voiced approximant [l], but few have the voiceless lateral fricative [ɬ] and even fewer have the voiced lateral fricative [ɮ]. Very many languages have the vowels [i e a o u]; not many have the vowels [ɯ ɜ ʊ ɪ].

Related to frequency of segment types across languages is the concept of implicational relation. An example of an implicational relation is that between oral and nasal vowels. Many languages have only oral vowels (Spanish, German), and many languages have both oral and nasal vowels (French, Portuguese), but no language has only nasal vowels; that is, the existence of nasal vowels implies the existence of oral vowels. All languages have voiced sonorant consonants, and some additionally have voiceless sonorants: no language has only voiceless sonorants. Or, many languages have only a voiceless series of obstruents, others have both voiced and voiceless obstruents; but none have only voiced obstruents.

The method of comparing inventories. Three methodological issues need to be born in mind when conducting such typological studies. First, determining what is more common versus less common requires a good-sized random sample of the languages of the world. However, information on phonological structure is not easily available for many of the languages of the world, and existing documentation tends to favor certain languages (for example the Indo-European languages) over other languages (those of New Guinea).

Second, it is often difficult to determine the true phonetic values of segments in a language which you do not know, so interpreting a symbol in a grammar may result in error. The consonants spelled <p t k> may in fact be ejective [p' t' k'], but <p t k> are used in the spelling system because *p, t, k* are "more basic" segments and the author of a grammar may notate ejectives with "more basic" symbols if no plain nonejective voiceless stops exist in the language. This is the case in many Bantu languages of Southern Africa, such as Gitonga and Zulu, which contrast phonetically voiceless aspirated and ejective stops – there are no plain unaspirated voiceless stops. Therefore, the ejectives are simply written <p t k> because there is no need to distinguish [p] and [p']. This phonetic detail is noted in some grammars, but not in all, and if you do not have experience with the language and do not read a grammar that mentions that <p> is ejective, you might not notice that these languages have no plain voiceless stops.

Third, many typological claims are statistical rather than absolute – they are statements about what happens most often, and therefore encountering a language that does not work that way does not falsify the claim. It is very difficult to refute a claim of the form "X is more common than Y," except if a very detailed numerical study is undertaken.

Typical inventories.   With these caveats, here are some general tendencies of phoneme inventories. In the realm of consonantal place of articulation, and using voiceless consonants to represent all obstruents at that place of articulation, the places represented by [p, t, k] are the most basic, occurring in almost all languages of the world. The next most common place would be alveopalatal; less common are uvulars, dentals, and retroflex coronals; least common are pharyngeals. All languages have a series of simple consonants lacking secondary vocalic articulations. The most common secondary articulation is rounding applied to velars, then palatalization; relatively uncommon is rounding of labial consonants; least common would be distinctive velarization or pharyngealization of consonants. Among consonants with multiple closures, labiovelars like [kp] are the most common; clicks, though rare, seem to be more common than linguolabials.

> *But when a language has only one variety of coronal, that variety may well be phonetically dental or postalveolar.*

In terms of manners of consonant articulation, stops are found in all languages. Most language have at least one fricative (but many Australian languages have no fricatives), and the most common fricative is *s*, followed by *f* and *š*, then *x*, then *θ* and other fricatives. The most common affricates are the alveopalatals, then the other coronal affricates; p^f and k^x are noticeably less frequent. In terms of laryngeal properties of consonants, all languages have voiceless consonants (in many, the voice onset time of stops is relatively long and the voiceless stops could be considered to be phonetically aspirated). Plain voiced consonants are also common, as is a contrast between voiceless unaspirated and voiceless aspirated stops. Ejectives, implosives and breathy-voiced consonants are much less frequent. Among fricatives, voicing distinctions are not unusual, but aspiration, breathy voicing and ejection are quite marked.

Nearly all languages have at least one nasal consonant, but languages with a rich system of place contrasts among obstruents may frequently have a smaller set of contrasts among nasals. Most languages also have at least one of [r] or [l], and typically have the glides [w y]. Modal voicing is the unmarked case for liquids, nasals and glides, with distinctive laryn-gealization or devoicing ~ aspiration being uncommon. Among laryngeal glides, [h] is the most common, then [ʔ], followed by the relatively infre-quent [ɦ].

The optimal vowel system would seem to be [i e a o u], and while the mid vowels [e o] are considered to be more marked than the high vowels [i u] for various reasons having to do with the operation of phonological rules (context-free rules raising mid vowels to high are much more common than context-free rules lowering high vowels to mid), there are fewer lan-guages with just the vowels [i u a] than with the full set [i u e o a]. The com-monness of front rounded and back unrounded vowels is correlated with vowel height, so a number of languages have [ü] and not [ö], but very few have [ö] and not [ü]. Full exploitation of the possibilities for low back and round vowels [æ œ ɑ ɒ] is quite rare, but it is not hard to find languages with [i ü ɨ u]. As noted earlier, oral vowels are more common than nasal vowels, and modal voiced vowels are more common than creaky voiced or breathy vowels.

8.2 Segmental processes

Recurrent patterns are also found in rules themselves. We begin our typo-logical survey of processes with segmental processes and procede to prosodic ones. Put roughly, segmental phonology deals with how the fea-tures of one segment affect the features of another segment, and prosodic processes are those that pertain to the structure of syllables, stress, and the rhythmic structure of words, and phenomena which relate to the position of segments in a phonological string. This division of processes is at this point strictly heuristic, but research has shown that there are important representational differences between segmental, i.e. featural representa-tions and syllabic or rhythmic representations – further questions regard-ing representations are taken up in chapter 10.

8.2.1 Assimilations

The most common phonological process in language is assimilation, where two segments become more alike by having one segment take on values for one or more features from a neighboring segment.

Vowel harmony.   An example of assimilation is vowel harmony, and the archetypical example of vowel harmony is the front–back vowel harmony process of Turkish. In this language, vowels within a word are (generally) all front, or all back, and suffixes alternate according to the frontness of the preceding vowel. The genitive suffix accordingly varies between *in* and *ɨn*, as does the vowel of the plural suffix *lar ~ ler*.

(1)	*Nom sg*	*Gen sg*	*Nom pl*	*Gen pl*	
	ip	ip-in	ip-ler	ip-ler-in	'rope'
	čɨkɨš	čɨkɨš-ɨn	čɨkɨš-lar	čɨkɨš-lar-ɨn	'exit'
	kɨz	kɨz-ɨn	kɨz-lar	kɨz-lar-ɨn	'girl'

ev	ev-in	ev-ler	ev-ler-in	'house'
biber	biber-in	biber-ler	biber-ler-in	'pepper'
sap	sap-ın	sap-lar	sap-lar-ın	'stalk'
adam	adam-ın	adam-lar	adam-lar-ın	'man'

This process can be stated formally as (2).

(2) V → [αback] /   V   C₀ __
                    [αback]

A second kind of vowel harmony found in Turkish is rounding harmony. In Turkish, a rule assimilates any high vowel to the roundness of the preceding vowel. Consider the following data, involving stems which end in round vowels:

(3)	*Nom sg*	*Gen sg*	*Nom pl*	*Gen pl*	
	yüz	yüz-ün	yüz-ler	yüz-ler-in	'face'
	pul	pul-un	pul-lar	pul-lar-ın	'stamp'
	ok	ok-un	ok-lar	ok-lar-ın	'arrow'
	son	son-un	son-lar	son-lar-ın	'end'
	köy	köy-ün	köy-ler	köy-ler-in	'village'

The genitive suffix which has a high vowel becomes rounded when the preceding vowel is round, but the plural suffix which has a nonhigh vowel does not assimilate in roundness. Thus the data in (3) can be accounted for by the following rule.

(4)   V   → [αround] /   V   C₀ __
    [+high]   [αround]

A problem that arises in many vowel harmony systems is that it is difficult if not impossible to be certain what the underlying vowel of the suffix is. For the plural suffix, we can surmise that the underlying vowel is non-round, since it is never phonetically round, so the most probable hypotheses are /a/ or /e/. For the genitive suffix, any of /i, ı, ü, u/ would be plausible, since from any of these vowels, the correct output will result by applying these rules.

It is sometimes assumed that, if all other factors are the same for selecting between competing hypotheses about the underlying form, a less marked (crosslinguistically frequent) segment should be selected over a more marked segment. By that reasoning, you might narrow the choice to /i, u/ since *ı, ü* are significantly more marked that /i, u/. The same reasoning might lead you to specifically conclude that alternating high vowels are /i/, on the assumption that *i* is less marked that *u*: however, that conclusion regarding markedness is not certain. The validity of invoking segmental markedness for chosing underlying forms is a theoretical assumption, and does not have clear empirical support. A further solution to the problem of picking between underlying forms is that [+high] suffix vowels are not specified for backness or roundness, and thus could be represented with the symbol /I/, which is not an actual and pronounceable vowel, but represents a so-called **archiphoneme** having the properties of being a vowel and being high, but being indeterminate for the properties [round] and [back]. There are a number of theoretical issues which surround the possibility of having partially specified segments, which we will not go into here.

Mongolian also has rounding harmony: in this language, only nonhigh vowels undergo the assimilation, and only nonhigh vowels trigger the process.

(5)

Nominative	Instrumental	Accusative	
de:l	de:l-e:r	de:l-i:g	'coat'
gal	gal-a:r	gal-i:g	'fire'
dü:	dü:-ge:r	dü:-g	'younger brother'
nöxör	nöxör-ö:r	nöxör-i:g	'comrade'
doro:	doro:-go:r	doro:-g	'stirrup'

This rule can be forumlated as in (6).

(6) $V \rightarrow [\alpha\text{round}] / V \quad C_0 \_$

$\quad [-\text{hi}] \qquad\qquad \begin{bmatrix} -\text{hi} \\ \alpha\text{rd} \end{bmatrix}$

Typological research has revealed a considerable range of variation in the conditions that can be put on a rounding harmony rule. In Sakha, high vowels assimilate in roundness to round high and nonhigh vowels (cf. *aγa-lïïn* 'father (associative),' *sep-tiin* 'tool (associative)' vs. *oγo-luun* 'child (associative),' *börö-lüün* 'wolf (associative),' *tünnük-tüün* 'window (associative)'), but nonround vowels only assimilate in roundness to a preceding nonhigh vowel (cf. *aγa-lar* 'fathers,' *sep-ter* 'tools,' *tünnük-ter* 'windows,' *kus-tar* 'ducks' vs. *oγo-lor* 'children,' *börö-lör* 'wolves'). As seen in chapter 7, in Yawelmani, vowels assimilate rounding from a preceding vowel of the same height (thus, high vowels assimilate to high vowels, low vowels assimilate to low vowels). As seen in (7), Kirghiz vowels generally assimilate in roundness to any preceding vowel except that a nonhigh vowel does not assimilate to a back high round vowel (though it will assimilate rounding from a front high round vowel).

(7)

Accusative	Dative	
taš-tï	taš-ka	'stone'
iš-ti	iš-ke	'job'
uč-tu	uč-ka	'tip'
konok-tu	konok-ko	'guest'
köz-tü	köz-gö	'eye'
üy-tü	üy-gö	'house'

This survey raises the question whether you might find a language where roundness harmony only takes place between vowels of different heights rather than the same height, as we have seen. Although such examples are not known to exist, we must be cautious about inferring too much from that fact, since the vast majority of languages with rounding harmony are members of the Altaic language family (e.g. Mongolian, Kirghiz, Turkish, Sakha). The existence of these kinds of rounding harmony means that phonological theory must provide the tools to describe them: what we do not know is whether other types of rounding harmony, not found in Altaic, also exist. Nor is it safe, given our limited database on variation within rounding harmony systems, to make very strong pronouncements about what constitutes "common" versus "rare" patterns of rounding harmony.

Another type of vowel harmony is vowel-height harmony. Such harmony exists in Kuria, where the tense mid vowels *e, o* become *i, u* before a high vowel. Consider (8), illustrating variations in noun prefixes (*omo* ~ *umu; eme* ~ *imi; eke* ~ *ege* ~ *iki* ~ *igi; ogo* ~ *ugu*) conditioned by the vowel to the right:

(8)
omoó-nto	'person'	omo-sáácá	'male'
omo-té	'tree'	omo-góóndo	'plowed field'
umu-ríísya	'boy'	umu-múra	'young man'
eme-té	'trees'	imi-sí	'sugar canes'
ege-sáka	'stream'	ege-té	'chair'
egeé-nto	'thing'	igi-túúmbe	'stool'
iki-rúúŋgúuri	'soft porridge'	iki-múúnέ	'deer'
ogo-gábo	'huge basket'	ogo-tábo	'huge book'
ogo-sééndáno	'huge needle'	ogo-géna	'huge stone'
ugu-síri	'huge rope'		

These examples show that tense mid vowels appear before the low vowel *a* and the tense and lax mid vowels *e, ɛ, o, ɔ*, which are [−high], and high vowels appear before high vowels, so based just on the phonetic environment where each variant appears, we cannot decide what the underlying value of the prefix is, [−high] or [+high]. Additional data show that the prefixes must underlyingly contain mid vowels: there are also prefixes which contain invariantly [+high] vowels.

(9)
iri-tɔ́ɔ́kɛ	'banana'	iri-kέέndɔ	'date fruit'
iri-hííndi	'corn cob'	iri-tóro	'buttock'
ibi-góóndo	'small fields'	ibi-gááte	'small breads'
ibi-gúrúbe	'small pigs'	ibi-té	'chairs'
iči-séésé	'dog'	iči-ɲáámwi	'cat'
iči-ɲɔ́ɔ́mbɛ	'cow'	ičii-ŋgúrúbe	'pig'

Thus the alternations in (8) can be described with the rule (10).

(10)   V   → [+hi] / __C₀   V
       [+tense]   [+high]

Another variety of vowel-height harmony is complete height harmony, an example of which is found in Kimatuumbi. This language distinguishes four phonological vowel heights, exemplified by the vowels a, ɛ, ɩ and i. The vowels of the passive suffix -ilw- and the causative suffix -iy- assimilate completely to the height of the preceding nonlow vowel ɛ, ɩ and i.

(11)   ásim-a   'borrow'   ásim-ilw-a   'be borrowed'
        ín-a   'dance'   in-ilw-a   'be danced'
        kún-a   'grate coconut'   kún-ilw-a   'be grated'
        ʊ́ʊg-a   'bathe'   ʊ́ʊg-ɩlw-a   'be bathed'
        twíɩk-a   'lift a load'   twíɩk-ɩlw-a   'be lifted'
        bɔ́ɔl-a   'tear bark off   bɔ́ɔl-ɛlw-a   'be de-barked'
                      a tree'
        kέɛŋgɛɛmb-a   'uproot tubers'   kέɛŋgɛɛmb-ɛlw-a   'be uprooted'
        čáag-a   'grind'   čáag-iy-a   'make grind'
        číinj-a   'slaughter'   číinj-iy-a   'make slaughter'
        ʊ́ʊg-a   'bathe'   ʊ́ʊg-ɩy-a   'make bathe'
        bɔ́ɔl-a   'de-bark'   bɔ́ɔl-ɛy-a   'make de-bark'
        čέɛŋg-a   'build'   čέɛŋg-ɛy-a   'make build'

This process involves the complete assimilation of suffix vowels to the values of [hi] and [tense] (or [ATR]) from the preceding nonlow vowel. Since the low vowel a does not trigger assimilation, the context after a reveals the underlying nature of harmonizing vowels, which we can see are high and tense. The following rule will account for the harmonic alternations in (11).

$$(12) \quad \begin{bmatrix} V \\ -\text{low} \end{bmatrix} \rightarrow \begin{bmatrix} \alpha\text{high} \\ \beta\text{tense} \end{bmatrix} / \begin{bmatrix} -\text{low} \\ \alpha\text{high} \\ \beta\text{tense} \end{bmatrix} C_0 \underline{\quad}$$

Akan exemplifies a type of vowel harmony which is common especially among the languages of Africa, which is assimilation of the feature ATR. In Akan, vowels within the word all agree in their value for [ATR]. In (13a) the prefix vowels are [+ATR] before the [+ATR] vowel of the word for 'eat' and [−ATR] before the [−ATR] vowel of 'be called'; (13b) shows this same harmony affecting other tense-aspect prefixes.

(13) a.   'eat'   'be called'
         1sg   mi-di   mɩ-dɩ
         2sg   wu-di   wʊ-dɩ
         3sg   o-di   ɔ-dɩ
         1pl   ye-di   yɛ-dɩ
         2pl   mu-di   mʊ-dɩ
         3pl   wo-di   wɔ-dɩ

b.   o-be-di   'he will eat'   ɔ-bɛ-dɪ   'he'll be called'
            o-di-i   'he ate'   ɔ-dɪ-ɪ   'he was called'
            o-ko-di   'he goes and eats'   ɔ-kɔ-dɪ   'he goes and is
                                                             called'

Vowel nasalization is also a common assimilatory process affecting vowels, and can be seen in the data of (14) from Gã. These data illlustrate nasalization affecting the plural suffix, which is underlyingly /i/ and assimilates nasality from the immediately preceding vowel.

(14)   mlɛɛbo   mlɛɛbo-i   'liver'
       nãne   nãne-i   'leg'
       čĩĩsi   čĩĩsi-i   'plate'
       akplɔ   akplɔ-i   'spear'
       gbɛ   gbɛ-i   'path'
       mĩ   mĩ-ĩ   'drum'
       sẽ   sẽ-ĩ   'throat'
       tũ   tũ-ĩ   'gun'
       ŋmɔ̃   ŋmɔ̃-ĩ   'farm'
       lemã   lemã-ĩ   'ax'

Another kind of vowel harmony, one affecting multiple features, is sometimes termed "place harmony," an example of which comes from Efik. In Efik, the prefix vowel /ɛ/ (but not /e/) becomes [a] before [a], [ɔ] before [ɔ], [ɛ] before [ɛ], [e] before [e] and [i], and [o] before [o] and [u].

(15)   *3sg*   *3pl*
      e-di   e-di   'come'
      ɛ-bɛri   e-bɛri   'shut'
      a-kaŋ   e-kaŋ   'deny'
      ɔ-bɔ   e-bɔ   'take'
      o-kop   e-kop   'hear'
      o-kut   e-kut   'see'

This process involves assimilation of all features from the following vowel, except the feature [high].

$$(16) \quad \varepsilon \rightarrow \begin{bmatrix} \alpha\text{around} \\ \beta\text{tense} \\ \gamma\text{back} \end{bmatrix} / \_ C_0 \begin{bmatrix} V \\ \alpha\text{round} \\ \beta\text{tense} \\ \gamma\text{back} \end{bmatrix}$$

Finally, complete vowel harmony, where one vowel takes on all features from a neighboring vowel, is found in some languages such as Kolami. This language has a rule of vowel epenthesis which breaks up final consonant clusters and medial clusters of more than two consonants. The inserted vowel harmonizes with the preceding vowel.

(17)

Stem	1sg pres	1sg past	Imperative	
/tum/	tum-atun	tum-tan	tum	'sneeze'
/agul/	agul-atun	agul-tan	agul	'dig'
/dakap/	dakap-atun	dakap-tan	dakap	'push'
/katk/	katk-atun	katak-tan	katak	'strike'
/melg/	melg-atun	meleg-tan	meleg	'shake'
/kink/	kink-atun	kinik-tan	kinik	'break'

Another example of complete vowel harmony is seen in the following examples of the causative prefix of Klamath, whose vowel completely assimilates to the following vowel.

(18) sna-batgal   'gets someone up from bed'
      sne-l'e:ml'ema   'makes someone dizzy'
      sno-bo:stgi   'causes something to turn black'
      sni-nklilk'a   'makes dusty"

Complete harmony is unlikely to ever be completely general – all of these examples are restricted in application to specific contexts, such as epenthetic vowels as in Kolami, or vowels of specific affixal morphemes as in Klamath. Another context where total harmony is common is between vowels separated only by laryngeal glides *h* and *ʔ*, a phenomenon referred to as translaryngeal harmony, as illustrated in Nenets by the alternation in the locative forms *to-hona* 'lake,' *pi-hina* 'street,' *pʸa-hana* 'tree,' *pe-hena* 'stone,' *tu-huna* 'fire.' The consequences of a completely unrestricted vowel harmony would be rather drastic – any word could only have one kind of vowel in it, were such a rule to be totally general.

Consonant assimilations.   One of the most common processes affecting consonants is the assimilation of a nasal to the place of articulation of a following consonant. An example of this process comes from Kimatuumbi, seen in (19), where the plural prefix /ñ/ takes on the place of assimilation of the following consonant.

(19)

Singular	Plural	
lwɪímo	ñímo	'land being weeded'
lwaámbo	ñaámbo	'bead'
lweémbe	ñeémbe	'shaving knife'
lugolóká	ŋgolóká	'straight'
lubáu	mbáu	'rib'
lujíiŋgyá	ñjíiŋgyá	'entered'
lulaála	ndaála	'pepper'
lupaláaí	mbaláaí	'bald head'
lutéelá	ndeelá	'piece of wood'
lučwiíčwi	ñǰwiíčwi	'tomato'
lukíligo	ŋgilígo	'place for initiates'
lukíli	ŋgíli	'palm'

Place assimilation of nasals in Kimatuumbi affects all nasals, so the data in (20a) illustrate assimilation of preconsonantal /n/ resulting from an optional vowel deletion rule, and (20b) illustrates assimilation of /m/.

(20) a. ni-bálaaŋgite   m-bálaaŋgite   'I counted'
          ni-ɟíiŋgiile   ñ-ɟíiŋgiile   'I entered'
          ni-góoñɟite   ŋ-góoñɟite   'I slept'

     b. mu-páalite   m-páalite   'you (pl) wanted'
          mu-téliike   n-téliike   'you (pl) cooked'
          mu-čáawiile   ñ-čáawiile   'you (pl) ground'
          mu-káatite   ŋ-káatite   'you (pl) cut'

Sometimes, a language with place assimilation of nasals will restrict the process to a specific place of articulation. For instance, Chukchi assimilates ŋ to a following consonant, but does not assimilate n or m. Thus the stem *teŋ* 'good' retains underlying ŋ before a vowel, and otherwise assimilates to the following consonant: however, as the last two examples show, n and m do not assimilate to a following consonant.

> Not all preconsonantal nasals condition this voicing process in Kimatuumbi; only nasals which are nonsyllabic in the intermediate representation do. Hence [mp] sequences, such as found in (20), are possible, since the process that deletes the vowel u results in a syllabic nasal in the intermediate representation

(21) teŋ-ɔɬʔ-ɔn   'good'
      tam-waɣərɣ-ən   'good life'
      tam-pera-k   'to look good'
      tan-čotčot   'good pillow'
      tan-ɬəmŋəɬ   'good story'
      tan-rʔarqə   'good breastband'
      nə-mkə-kin   'often'
      ɣa-n-pera-w-ɬen   'decorated'

A common assimilation affecting consonants after nasals is postvocalic voicing, illustrated by Kimatuumbi in (22). The data in (22a) illustrate voicing of an underlyingly voiceless consonant at the beginning of a stem after the prefix ñ. The data in (22b) show voicing of a consonant in a verb after the reduced form of the subject prefix *ni*. In these examples, the vowel /i/ in the prefix optionally deletes, and when it does, it voices an initial stop.

(22) a. *Singular*   *Plural*
          lu-paláaí   m-baláaí   'bald head'
          lu-čwiíčwi   ñ-ɟwiíčwi   'tomato plant'
          lu-téelá   n-deelá   'piece of wood'
          lu-kíligo   ŋ-gilígo   'initiate's place'
          lu-temá.á   n-demá.á   'chopped'
          lu-čapíičá   ñ-ɟapíičá   'clean'

     b. *1sg past*   *Optional pronunciation*
          ni-páalite   m-báalite   'I wanted (recent)'
          ni-téliike   n-déliike   'I cooked (recent)'
          ni-čónite   ñ-ɟónite   'I sewed (recent)'
          ni-kúbiile   ŋ-gúbiile   'I hit on legs (recent)'

Stop consonants frequently nasalize before nasal consonants, and an example of this process is found in Korean. The examples in (23a) are stems with final nasal consonants; those in (23b) have oral consonants, revealed before the infinitive suffix *a* ~ *ə*, and undergo nasalization of that consonant before the past-tense suffix *-nɨnta*.

(23)   *Infinitive*   *Past*
    a. an-a   an-nɨnta   'hug'
           t'atɨm-ə   t'atɨm-nɨnta   'trim'
           nəm-ə   nəm-nɨnta   'overflow'
           čʰam-a   čʰam-nɨnta   'endure'

    b. ip-ə   im-nɨnta   'wear'
           tat-ə   tan-nɨnta   'close'
           putʰ-ə   pun-nɨnta   'adhere'
           čočʰ-a   čon-nɨnta   'follow'
           mək-ə   məŋ-nɨnta   'eat'
           tak'-a   taŋ-nɨnta   'polish'
           ik-ə   iŋ-nɨnta   'ripen'

Kimatuumbi presents the mirror-image process, of postnasal nasalization (this process is only triggered by nasals which are moraic in the intermediate representation). On the left in (24a), the underlying consonant is revealed when a vowel-final noun-class prefix stands before the stem, and on the right a nasal prefix stands before the stem, causing the initial consonant to become nasalized. In (24b), nasalization applies to the example in the second column, which undergoes an optional rule deleting the vowel *u* from the prefix /mu/.

(24) a. a-baánda   'slaves'   m-maánda   'slave'
           a-láalo   'fools'   n-náalo   'fool'
           a-gúndumúyi   'scarers'   ŋ-ŋúndumúyi   'scarer'
           mi-butúka   'cars'   m-mutúka   'car'
           mi-dálaánzi   'bitter oranges'   n-nálaánzi   'bitter orange'
           mi-lipú   'trees (sp.)'   n-nipú   'tree (sp)'
           mi-gúunda   'fields'   ŋ-ŋúunda   'field'

    b. mu-buundíke   m-muundíke   'you should store'
           mu-laabúke   n-naabúke   'you should breakfast'
           mu jiiŋgí   ñ-ñiiŋgí   'you should enter'

Many languages have a process of voicing assimilation, especially in clusters of obstruents which must agree in voicing. Most often, obstruents assimilate regressively to the last obstruent in the cluster. For example, in Sanskrit a stem-final consonant reveals its underlying voicing when the following affix begins with a sonorant, but assimilates in voicing to a following obstruent.

(25) kr̥n̩t̩-mas   bʰind-mas   1pl indicative active
      kr̥n̩t̩-e   bʰind-e   1sg indicative middle
      kr̥n̩t̩-tʰa   bʰint-tʰa   2pl indicative active

krn̩t-te	bʰint-te	3sg indicative middle
krn̩d-dʰve	bʰind-dʰve	2pl indicative middle
'weave'	'bind'	

Other languages with regressive voicing assimilation are Hungarian and Russian.

Progressive voicing harmony is also possible, though less common than regressive voicing. One example of progressive assimilation is found in Norwegian. The (regular) past-tense suffix is *-te*, and shows up as such when attached to a stem ending in a sonorant or voiceless consonant, but after a voiced obstruent, the suffix appears as *-de*.

(26)

smil-e	smil-te	'smile'	svøm-e	svøm-te	'swim'
hør-e	hør-te	'heard'	lon-e	lon-te	'borrow'
les-e	les-te	'read'	spis-e	spis-te	'eat'
reis-e	reis-te	'travel'	çøp-e	çøp-te	'buy'
tenk-e	tenk-te	'think'	behøv-e	behøv-de	'belong'
lev-e	lev-de	'lived'	prøv-e	prøv-de	'try'
bygg-e	byg-de	'build'	hugg-e	hugg-de	'chop'
gnag-e	gnag-de	'gnaw'	krev-e	krev-de	'request'
sag-e	sag-de	'saw'	plag-e	plag-de	'afflict'

Another example of progressive voicing harmony is found in Evenki, where an underlyingly voiced suffix-initial consonant becomes devoiced after a voiceless obstruent: this is illustated below with the accusative case suffix /ba/.

(27)

asi:-ba	'woman'	ɲami:-ba	'female deer'
palatka-ba	'tent'	tolgolki:l-ba	'sleds'
ber-be	'onion'	huna:t-pa	'girl'
det-pe	'tundra'	mit-pe	'1pl inclusive'

Complete assimilation of a consonant to a following consonant is found in Arabic. In the data of (28) from the Syrian dialect, the consonant /l/ of the definite article assimilates completely to a following coronal consonant. Examples in (a) show nonassimilation when the following consonant is non-coronal, and those in (b) provide stems that begin with coronal consonants.

(28)

		Indefinite	*Definite*		*Indefinite*	*Definite*	
	a.	hawa	lhawa	'air'	ba:red	lba:red	'cold'
		ʔadham	lʔadham	'black'	madine	lmadine	'city'
		ʕa:de	lʕa:de	'custom'	ħa:ra	lħa:ra	'quarter'
		waħš	lwaħš	'beast'	yaʔs	lyaʔs	'despair'
		kalb	lkalb	'dog'	xadd	lxadd	'cheek'
		fayy	lfayy	'shadow'	ɣada	lɣada	'lunch'
	b.	sˤaff	sˤsˤaff	'row'	ta:let	tta:let	'third'
		taxt	ttaxt	'bed'	raʔbe	rraʔbe	'neck'
		nəde	nnəde	'dew'	life	llife	'loofah'

difaːʕ	ddifaːʕ	'defense'	smike	ssmike	'thick'
šoːraba	ššoːraba	'soup'	žamil	žžamil	'pretty'
zaki	zzaki	'bright'	tˤaːleb	tˤtˤaːleb	'student'
zˤaːbet	zˤzˤaːbet	'officer'	dˤahuːk	dˤdˤahuːk	'jolly'

Consonants are also often susceptible to assimilation of features from a neighboring vowel, especially place features of a following vowel. One process is palatalization, found in Russian. A consonant followed by a front vowel takes on a palatal secondary articulation from the vowel, as the following data show.

(29)

vkus	'taste'	vkusʸ-en	'tasty'
um	'intellect'	umʸ-en	'clever'
golot /d/	'hunger'	golodʸ-en	'hungry'
stol	'table'	stolʸ-e	'table (loc)'
guba	'lip'	gubʸ-e	'lip (loc)'
mesto	'place'	mestʸ-e	'place (loc)'
glub-ok	'deep'	glubʸ-ina	'depth'
ton-ok	'thin'	tonʸ-ina	'thinness'
vor	'thief'	vorʸ-iska	'thief (pejorative)'
dom	'house'	domʸ-iska	'house (pejorative)'
gorot /d/	'town'	gorodʸ-iska	'town (pejorative)'

> The alveopalatal fricatives š, ž are not phonetically palatalizable in Russian, whereas the alveopalatal affricate is always palatalized

A second kind of palatalization is found in many languages, where typically velar but in some languages also alveolar consonants become alveopalatals: to avoid confusion with the preceding type of palatalization as secondary articulation, this latter process is often referred to as coronalization. This process is found in Russian: it is triggered by some derivational suffixes with front vowels, but not all suffixes.

(30)

druk/g/	'friend'	druž-itʸ	'to be friends with'
muka	'torment'	mučʸ-itʸ	'to torment'
grex	'sin'	greš-itʸ	'to sin'
strok/g/	'strict'	strož-e	'stricter'
dik	'wild'	dičʸ-e	'wilder'
sux	'dry'	suš-e	'stricter'
krut	'steep'	kručʸ-e	'steeper'
gad-ok	'foul'	gaž-e	'fouler'
vɨs-ok	'tall'	vɨš-e	'taller'
niz-ok	'low'	niž-e	'lower'

Another common vowel-to-consonant effect is affrication of coronal obstruents before high vowels. An example of this is found in Japanese, where /t/ becomes [tˢ] before [u] and [č] before [i].

(31)

Negative	Provisional	Infinitive	Volitional	
mat-anai	mat-eba	matˢ-u	mač-itai	'wait'
tat-anai	tat-eba	tatˢ-u	tač-itai	'stand'
kat-anai	kat-eba	katˢ-u	kač-itai	'win'

Outside of the domain of assimilations in place of articulation, the most common segmental interaction between consonants and vowels (or, sometimes, other sonorants) is lenition or weakening. Typical examples of lenition involve either the voicing of voiceless stops, or the voicing and spirantization of stops: the conditioning context is a preceding vowel, sometimes a preceding and following vowel. An example of the spirantization type of lenition is found in Spanish, where the voiced stops /b, d, g/ become voiced spirants [β, ð, γ] after vocoids.

(32)   *N*   *with N*   *there are N's*

burro	kom burro	ay βurros	'donkey'
deðo	kon deðo	ay ðeðos	'finger'
gato	koŋgato	ay γatos	'cat'

This can be seen as assimilation of the value [continuant] from a preceding vocoid.

An example of combined voicing and spirantization is found in Tibetan, where voiceless noncoronal stops become voiced spirants between vowels.

(33)   *Past affirmative*   *Past negative*

čaa-βəree	ma-čaa-βəree	'go'
paa-βəree	ma-βaa-βəree	'light'
pii-βəree	mə-βii-βəree	'renounce'
kuu-βəree	mə-γuu-βəree	'wait'
kə-βəree	mə-γə-βəree	'hide'
qɔɔ-βəree	ma-ʁɔɔ-βəree	'take time out'

In some cases, the result of lenition is a glide, so in Axininca Campa, stem-initial /k, p/ become [y, w] after a vowel.

(34)

yaarato	'black bee'	no-yaaratoti	'my black bee'
kanari	'wild turkey'	no-yanariti	'my wild turkey'
porita	'small hen'	no-woritati	'my small hen'

The converse process, whereby spirants, sonorants, or glides become obstruent stops after consonants, is also found in a number of languages – this process is generally referred to as hardening. In Kimatuumbi, sonorants become voiced stops after a nasal. The data in (35) illustrate this phenomenon with the alternation in stem-initial consonant found between the singular and plural.

(35)

lu-laála	'pepper plant'	n-daála	'pepper plants'
lu-yímá	'pole'	ñ-jíma	'poles'
yúkuta	'to be full'	ñ-jukútá	'full'
wá	'to die'	ŋ-gwaá.á	'dead'
líndɩla	'to guard'	n-dɩndíɩlá	'guarded'

Another context where hardening is common is when the consonant is geminate. One example is found in Fula, where geminate spirants become stops. In (36), plural forms have a medial geminate (this derives by an assimilation to a following *ɗ*, so that [cabbi] derives from /caw-ɗi/ via the intermediate stage *cawwi*).

(36)   *Plural*   *Diminutive singular*
     čabbi   čawel   'stick'
     lebbi   lewel   'month'
     pobbi   powel   'hyena'
     ɲɛbbɛ   ɲewel   'bean'
     leppi   lefel   'ribbon'
     koppi   kofel   'ear'
     čoppi   čofel   'chick'

Geminate hardening also occurs in Luganda. In the data of (37), the singular form of nouns in this particular class is formed by geminating the initial consonant: the underlying consonant is revealed in the plural.

(37)   *Singular*   *Plural*
     ggi   ma-gi   'egg'
     ddaala   ma-daala   'ladder'
     jjuba   ma-yuba   'dove'
     ggʷaanga   ma-waanga   'nation'
     ddaanga   ma-laanga   'lily'

In this language, only sonorants harden to stops.

(38)   *Singular*   *Plural*
     ffumu   ma-fumu   'spear'
     ffuumbe   ma-fuumbe   'civet'
     ssaanja   ma-saanja   'dry plaintain leaf'
     zzike   ma-zike   'chimpanzee'
     zziga   ma-ziga   'tear'
     vviivi   ma-viivi   'knee'

8.2.2 Dissimilation

Less common in the languages of the world are processes of dissimilation, whereby one of two similar consonants changes to become less like the other. An example of such a process is lateral dissimilation found in Sundanese. In this language, the plural is formed by infixing -*ar*- after the initial consonant, as seen in (39a). When another *r* follows within the stem, the *r* of the infix dissimilates to *l*.

(39)   *Singular*   *Plural*
    a.   kusut   k-ar-usut   'messy'
       poho   p-ar-oho   'forget'
       gətol   g-ar-ətol   'diligent'
       ŋoplok   ŋ-ar-oplok   'flop down'
       ŋuliat   ŋ-ar-uliat   'stretch'

| | tuwaŋ | t-ar-uwaŋ | 'eat' |
| | masak | m-ar-asak | 'cook' |

b.	ŋirɨt	ŋ-al-ɨrɨt	'cut'
	nugar	n-al-ugar	'dig up'
	combrek	c-al-ombrek	'cold'
	bocor	b-al-ocor	'leaking'
	biŋhar	b-al-iŋhar	'rich'
	hormat	h-al-ormat	'respect'

A similar process affects the adjectival suffix *-a:lis* in Latin, where /l/ dissimilates to [r] if the preceding stem contains another /l/.

(40) nava:lis   'naval'   episcopa:lis   'episcopal'
      sola:ris   'solar'   milita:ris   'military'
      lupana:ris   'whorish'

Dissimilation of aspiration is attested in other languages such as Manipuri. In (41), the first consonant of the directional suffixes *-tʰok* and *-kʰət* deaspirates if preceded by another aspirate or *h* (and if the immediately preceding segment is a vowel or sonorant, the consonant becomes voiced).

(41) pi-tʰok   'give out'   pi-kʰət   'give upwards'
      cət-tʰok   'go out'   cət-kʰət   'go upwards'
      kʰik-tok   'sprinkle out' kʰik-kət   'sprinkle upwards'
      hut-tok   'bore out'   hut-kət   'bore upwards'
      kʰoy-dok   'trim out'   kʰoy-gət   'trim upwards'
      tʰin-dok   'pierce out'   tʰin-gət   'pierce upwards'

Many Bantu languages such as Kuria have a voicing dissimilation process whereby *k* becomes *g* when the following syllable has a voiceless consonant (excluding *h*). This results in alternations in the form of the infinitive prefix which is underlyingly /oko/, as well as the second-singular object prefix /ko/ and the (diminutive) object prefix /ka/. The data in (42a) motivate the underlying prefix /oko/ and (42b) shows application of dissimilation to the prefix. (42c) shows the object prefixes /ko/ and /ka/ which also dissimilate, and (42d) shows the contrasting prefixes /go/ and /ga/ which have underlyingly voiced consonants, and do not assimilate.

(42) a. | oko-réma | 'to cultivate' | uku-ñáhaaréka | 'to be hurt' |
         | uku-míñooŋgóra | 'to crush' | uku-gíiŋgírá | 'to shave' |
         | oko-gɔ́ɔgá | 'to slaughter' | uku-búna | 'to break' |
         | oko-bɔ́cha | 'to vomit' | oko-hóóra | 'to thresh' |

      b. | ogo-tááŋgá | 'to begin' | ugu-túúhá | 'to be blunt'|
         | ugu-súraaŋgá | 'to sing praise' | ogo-séɛnsá | 'to winnow' |
         | ugu-kyá | 'to dawn' | ogo-kéña | 'to run' |

c. ogo-kó-bárǎ   'to count you sg'
    uku-gú-súraáŋga   'to praise you sg'
    ogo-ká-bárǎ   'to count it'
    oko-gá-súraáŋga   'to praise it'

d. oko-gó-bárǎ 'to count it'   uku-gú-súraáŋga 'to praise it'
    oko-gá-bárǎ 'to count them'   oko-gá-súraáŋga 'to praise them'

The language Chukchi has a number of dissimilatory processes. One of these dissimilates nasality, by changing ŋ to γ before a nasal.

(43)   taraŋ-ək   'build a dwelling'   nə-taraγ-more   'we built a dwelling'
       mətɬəŋ-ən   'five'   mətɬəγ-more   'we five'
       enawrəŋ-ək 'to give as a gift'   enawrəγ-nen   'he gave it'
       petʔiŋ   'cold'   petʔiγ-ŋinqey   'boy with a cold'

A second dissimilation in the language changes the first in a sequence of identical fricatives to a stop.

(44)   meniγ   'cloth'   manek-γəpə   'from cloth'
       ətɬəγ-ən   'father'   ətɬək-γəyiwq-ew   'paternal marking'
       rəγrəγ   'wool'   rəγrək-γəpə   'from wool'
       yeγteɬ-ək   'to live'   γe-yeγtet-ɬin   'he lived'
       ɬəmŋəɬteɬ-ək 'tell stories'   γa-ɬəmŋəɬtet-ɬen   'told stories'
       ŋew-ʔen   'woman'   ŋak-waŋe-γərγ-ən   'woman's sewing'
       iɬγətew-ək   'to wash'   iɬγətek-wʔi   'he washed'

An important feature of this rule is that only homorganic clusters dissimilate. Other combinations, such as *yγ, wɬ,* or *ɬγ* remain unchanged.

(45)   kətəγγat-ək   'blow'   γa-n-pera-w-ɬen 'decorated'
       ʔiw-pipiq-əɬγ-ən 'wolf mouse'

Finally, the glide *y* dissimilates to γ before a coronal consonant.

(46)   wʔey-ək   'grass'   wʔeγ-ti   'grasses'
       ŋin-qey   'boy'   ŋen-qaγ-čəŋ-ən   'big boy'
       čay   'tea'   čaγ-naɬk-ək   'to make tea'
       qey-we   'correct'   qeγ-ɬənanγet   'truth'
       qeyəqey   'nestling'   qaγ-yaʔyaq   'young seagull'

Dissimilation between vowels is also found in languages. One case comes from Woleiaian, where the low back vowel /a/ becomes [e] before the low back vowels /a/ and /ɔ/. This process affects the causative prefix /ga/, seen below.

(47)   ga-repa   'approach it'   ga-beši   'heat it'
       ga-siwe   'make it stand'   ga-sere   'make it hit'

ge-bbaro	'bend it'	ge-makɨ	'give birth to him'
ge-mɔwe	'erase it'	ge-tɔtɔwe	'support it'
ge-wasɨr	'hurt it'	ge-tɔla	'make it bloom'

In Wintu, the vowels /e, o/ become [i, u] before /a/ by a similar kind of dissimilation.

(48)	/lel-a/	→	lila	'to transform'
	/lel-u/	→	lelu	'transform!'
	/lel-it/	→	lelit	'transformed'
	/dek-a/	→	dika	'to climb'
	/dek/	→	dek	'climb!'
	/dek-na:/	→	dekna:	'to step'
	/doy-a:/	→	duya:	'to give'
	/doy-u/	→	doyu	'give!'
	/doy-i/	→	doyi	'gift'

Examples of low vowel dissimilating to nonlow vowels before low vowels are also found in Kera and Southern Russian. Interestingly, most examples of dissimilation between vowels are precisely of this nature: we do not seem to find cases of high vowels dissimilating to nonhigh near other high vowels.

8.2.3 Other segmental processes

There are other segmental processes which do not neatly fit into the category of assimilation or dissimilation. One such example is neutralization, whereby a phonetic contrast is deleted in some context, which consonants are particularly susceptible to. One case is the neutralization of laryngeal contrasts in consonants at the end of the syllable, as exemplified by Korean.

(49)	*Infinitive*	*Conjunctive*	
	ip-ə	ip-k'o	'wear'
	kapʰ-a	kap-k'o	'pay back'
	tat-ə	tat-k'o	'close'
	putʰ-ə	put-k'o	'adhere'
	čočʰ-a	čot-k'o	'follow'
	mək-ə	mək-k'o	'eat'
	tak'-a	tak-k'o	'polish'

Another kind of neutralization is place neutralization, which can be exemplified by Saami. Saami restricts word-final consonants to the set *t*, *n*, *r*, *l*, *s*, *š*, i.e. the voiceless coronal nonaffricates. The data in (50) show that noun stems can end in an array of consonants, as revealed by the essive form of the noun which takes the suffix -(*i*)*n*, but in the nominative, which has no suffix, all places of articulation are neutralized to coronal.

(50)   *Nominative sg*   *Essive*
        oahpis   oahpis-in   'acquaintance'
        čoarvuš   čoarvuš-in   'antlers and skullcap'
        gahpir   gahpir-in   'cap'
        heevemeahhtun   heevemeahhtun-in   'inappropriate'
        varit   varih-in   '2-year-old reindeer buck'
        čuoivvat   čuoivvag-in   'yellow-brown reindeer'
        ahhkut   ahhkub-in   'grandchild of woman'
        lottaaš   lottaaǰ-in   'small bird'
        suohkat   suohkað-in   'thick'
        jaaʔmin   jaaʔmim-in   'death'

It is interesting that Saami also neutralizes laryngeal contrasts finally, so voiced stops become voiceless: it is unknown whether a language may exhibit neutralization of place contrasts without also having neutralization of laryngeal contrasts.

8.3 Prosodically based processes

> *The foot is, roughly, a grouping of two syllables into a rhythmic unit, which is primarily relevant in phonology for the description of stress assignment.*

A second major class of phonological processes can be termed "prosodically motivated processes." Such processes have an effect on the structure of the syllable (or higher prosodic units such as the "foot"), usually by inserting or deleting a consonant, or changing the status of a segment from vowel to consonant or vice versa.

Vowel sequences.   A very common set of prosodic processes is the class of processes which eliminate V+V sequences. Many languages disallow sequences of vowels, and when such sequences would arise by the combination of morphemes, one of the vowels is often changed. One of the most common such changes is glide formation, whereby a high vowel becomes a glide before another vowel. Quite often, this process is accompanied with a lengthening of the surviving vowel, a phenomenon known as compensatory lengthening. For example, in Kimatuumbi, high vowels become glides before other vowels, as shown by the data in (51). The examples on the left show that the noun prefixes have underlying vowels, and those on the right illustrate application of glide formation.

(51)   mi-kaáte   'loaves'   my-oótó   'fires'
        li-kuŋuúnda   'filtered beer'   ly-oowá   'beehive'
        ki-kálaaŋgo   'frying pan'   ky-uúlá   'frog'
        i-kálaaŋgo   'frying pans'   y-uúlá   'frogs'
        lu-toóndwa   'star'   lw-aaté   'banana hand'
        ku-suúle   'to school'   kw-iisíwá   'to the islands'
        mu-kikálaaŋgo   'in the frying   mw-iikálaaŋgo   'in the frying
                         pan'   pans'

Although the stem-initial vowel is long on the surface in these examples, underlyingly the vowel is short, as shown when the stem has no prefix or when the prefix vowel is *a*. Thus, compare *ka-ótó* 'little fire,' *ma-owá* 'beehives,' *ka-úlá* 'little frog,' *até* 'banana hands,' *ipʊkʊ́* 'rats.'

Vowel sequences can also be eliminated by coalescing the two vowels into a single vowel, often one which preserves characteristics of the individual vowel. This happens in Kimatuumbi as well, where the combinations /au/ and /ai/ become [oo] and [ee]. This rule is optional in Kimatuumbi, so the uncoalesced vowel sequence can also be pronounced (thus motivating the underlying representation).

> *In Kimatuumbi, coalescence only applies in a specific grammatical domain, between vowels of prefixes, and thus one does not find this same process affecting the prefix-plus-stem combination found in ka-úlá 'little frog.'*

(52) | | | |
|---|---|---|
| a-i-téliike | ee-téliike | 'he cooked them' |
| pa-ú-kaátité | poó-kaátité | 'when you cut' |
| pa-bá-i-káatité | pa-bée-káatité | 'when they cut them' |
| a-u-káatite | oo-káatite | 'he cut it' |
| ka-u-tʊʊmbúka | koo-tʊʊmbúka | 'when it was falling' |
| pa-i-taábu | pee-taábu | 'where the books are' |
| pa-u-títili | poo-títili | 'where the chicken louse is' |
| ka-u-méyá | kooméyá | 'little white ant' |
| na-u-čaápu | nʊʊ-čaápu | 'with dirt' |

The change of /au/ and /ai/ to [oo] and [ee] can be seen as creating a compromise vowel, one which preserves the height of the initial vowel /a/, and the backness and roundness of the second vowel.

Sometimes, vowel sequences are avoided simply by deleting one of the vowels, with no compensatory lengthening. Thus at the phrasal level in Makonde, word-final /a/ deletes before an initial vowel, cf. *lipeeta engaanga* → *lipeet engaanga* 'the knapsack, cut it!', *likuka engaanga* → *likuk engaanga* 'the trunk, cut it!', *nneemba idanaao* → *nneemb idanaao* 'the boy, bring him!'.

Vowel epenthesis. The converse process of vowel epenthesis is also quite common. One context that often results in epenthesis is when an underlying form has too many consonants in a row, given the syllable structure of the language. Insertion of a vowel then reduces the size of the consonant cluster. An example of such epenthesis is found in Fula. In this language, no more than two consonants are allowed in a row. As the data of (53) show, when the causative suffix /-na/ is added to a stem ending in two consonants, the vowel *i* is inserted, thus avoiding three consecutive consonants.

(53) | *Continuous* | *Causative* | |
|---|---|---|
| hula | hulna | 'laugh' |
| yara | yarna | 'drink' |
| woya | woyna | 'cry' |
| ǰu:la | ǰu:lna | 'be Muslim' |
| wurto | wurtina | 'come out' |
| wuǰǰa | wuǰǰina | 'steal' |
| yotto | yottina | 'arrive' |

Another form of vowel epenthesis is one that eliminates certain kinds of consonants in a particular position. The only consonants at the end of the word in Kotoko are sonorants, so while the past tense of the verbs in (54a) is formed with just the stem, the verbs in (54b) require final epenthetic schwa.

(54)
	Infinitive	Past		Infinitive	Past	
a.	hàm-à	hám	'yawn'	ɗàn-à	ɗàn	'tie'
	skwàl-à	skwál	'want'	vèr-à	vèr	'fly'
	lèhày-à	lèhày	'fear'	làw-à	làw	'fight'
b.	gèɓ-à	gèɓè	'answer'	kàɗ-à	káɗɔ́	'cross'
	làb-à	làbè	'tell'	jàg-à	jàgè	'cook'
	gìč-à	gìčɔ́	'sweep'	ʔèk-à	ʔèkɔ́	'take by force'
	sàp-à	sapɔ́	'chase'	vìt-à	vìtɔ́	'blow on a fire'
	vènàh-à	vènàhè	'vomit'	hès-à	hésɔ́	'spill'
	ɗèv-à	ɗèvè	'put'	bàɣ-à	bàɣè	'split wood'

Another factor motivating epenthesis is a word size, viz. the need to avoid monosyllabic words. One example is seen in the following data from Mohawk, where the first-singular prefix is preceded by the vowel í only when it is attached to a monosyllabic stem.

(55)
k-atirút-haʔ	'I pull it'
k-ataʔkeráhkwaʔ	'I float'
k-kétskw-as	'I raise it'
k-hníːnus	'I buy'
k-tat-s → íktats	'I offer it'
k-yʌ-s → íkyʌs	'I put it'
k-ket-s → íkkets	'I scrape it'

The adaptation of loanwords into Saami from Scandinavian languages (Norwegian or Swedish) illustrates a variant on the Mohawk-type minimal-word motivation for epenthesis. In this case, a vowel is inserted to prevent a monosyllabic stress foot – though interestingly this requirement is determined on the basis of the Norwegian source, whereas in the Saami word stress is (predictably) on the first syllable. Except for a small set of "special" words (pronouns, grammatical words), words in Saami must be at least two syllables long. Thus the appearance of a final epenthetic vowel in the following loanwords is not surprising.

(56)
Saami	Norwegian	
daaigi	deig	'dough'
niibi	kniv	'knife'
vouʔna	vogn	'wagon'
muura	mur	'wall'

In contrast, in the following loanwords there is no epenthetic vowel. The location of stress, which is the key to understanding this problem, is marked on the Norwegian source though stress is not marked in the orthography.

(57) *Saami*   *Norwegian*
      diisdat   tírsdag   'Tuesday'
      kaavrret   kávring   'rusk'
      akaðemihkar   akadémiker   'academic'
      miniistar   miníster   'minister'
      teahter   teáter   'theater'
      tempel   témpel   'temple'
      orgel   órgel   'organ'
      profes'sor   proféssor   'professor'
      plasttar   pláster   'plaster'
      kaahkal   kákkel   'glazed tile'

The above examples are ambiguous in analysis, since the source word is both polysyllabic and has a nonfinal stress. The examples in (58), on the other hand, show epenthesis when the stress-foot in the source word is monosyllabic, even though the overall word is polysyllabic.

(58) hoteella   hotéll   'hotel'
      maratona   maratón   'marathon'
      universiteehta   universitét   'university'
      tabeal'la   tabéll   '(time-)table'
      privaahta   privát   'private'
      kameela   kamél   'camel'
      polaara   polár   'polar'

Onset creation.   Consonants can also be inserted. The main cause of consonant insertion is the avoidance of initial vowels or vowel sequences. In Arabic all syllables begin with a consonant, and if a word has no underlying initial consonant a glottal stop is inserted, thus /al-walad/ → [ʔalwalad] 'the boy.' In the Hare and Bearlake dialects of Slave, words cannot begin with a vowel, so when a vowel-initial root stands at the beginning of a word (including in a compound), the consonant *h* is inserted.

(59) s-ōdee   'my older brother'
      dene-[h]ōdee   'Brother (in church)'
      n-anay   'your (sg) sister-in-law (man speaking)'
      [h]anay   'sister-in-law'
      b-ek'éhdí   'I take care of him/her'
      bebí [h]ek'éhdí   'I take care of the baby'
      ku-edehfe → kúdehfe   'I chased them'
      sah [h]edéhfe   's/he chased the bear'

In Axininca Campa *t* is inserted between vowels – this language does not have a glottal stop phoneme. Thus, /i-N-koma-i/ → [inkomati] 'he will paddle.'

Cluster reduction. Deletion of consonants can be found in languages. The most common factor motivating consonant deletion is the avoidance of certain kinds of consonant clusters – a factor which also can motivate vowel epenthesis. Consonant cluster simplification is found in Korean.

(60)

Imperative	Conjunctive	Indicative	
palp-a	pal-k'o	pal-t'a	'tread on'
ulph-ə	ul-k'o	ul-t'a	'chant'
ilk-ə	il-k'o	il-t'a	'read'
halth-a	hal-k'o	hal-t'a	'taste'
talm-a	tam-k'o	tam-t'a	'resemble'
anc-a	an-k'o	an-t'a	'sit down'

Another cause of cluster simplification is the avoidance of certain specific types of consonant clusters. Shona avoids clusters of the form Cy, although Cw is perfectly acceptable. The deletion of *y* after a consonant affects the form of possessive pronouns in various noun classes. Demonstratives and possessive pronouns are formed with an agreement prefix reflecting the class of the noun, plus a stem, -*no* for 'this' and -*angu* for 'my.' Before the stem -*angu*, a high vowel becomes a glide. Where this would result in a Cy sequence, the glide is deleted.

(61)

'this'	'my'	Class
u-no	w-angu	3
mu-no	mw-angu	18
ku-no	kw-angu	17
ru-no	rw-angu	11
i-no	y-angu	9
ri-no	r-angu	6
či-no	č-angu	7
$ẓ^w$i-no	$ẓ^w$-angu	8
d^zi-no	d^z-angu	10

Since /i-angu/ becomes *yangu*, it is evident that the vowel *i* does become a glide before a vowel rather than uniformly deleting.

Stress lengthening and reduction. Processes lengthening stressed vowels are also rather common. An example of stress-induced vowel lengthening is found in Makonde, where the penultimate syllable is stressed, and the stressed vowel is always lengthened.

> Since Makonde is also a tone language and the accute accent is used to mark H tone, not stress, stress will be indicated with the mark ['] before the stressed syllable.

(62)

kú-'líím-a	'to cultivate'
kú-lí'm-ííl-a	'to cultivate for'
kú-lí'm-áán-a	'to cultivate each other'
kú-lím-á'n-ííl-a	'to cultivate for each other'
kú-lím-án-íl-á-lím-á'n-ííl-a	'to cultivate for each other continuously'

A related process is the reduction of unstressed vowels, as found in English. From alternations like *bərómətɽ* ~ *bèrəmétrɪk, mónəpòwl* ~ *mənópəliy*, we know that unstressed vowels in English are reduced to schwa. Russian also reduces unstressed nonhigh vowels so that /a, o/ become [ə], or [a] in the syllable immediately before the stress.

(63) /gorod-ók/ → [gəradók] 'cities' /górod/ → [górəd] 'city'
      /póda-l/ → [pódəl] 'he gave' /po-dá-t^y/ → [padát^y] 'to give'

Reduction of unstressed vowels can go all the way to deletion, so in Palestinian Arabic, unstressed high vowels in an open sylable are deleted.

(64) *Palestinian Arabic*

3sg masc	3sg fem	1sg	
ḥámal	ḥámalat	ḥamált	'carry'
kátab	kátabat	katábt	'write'
dáras	dárasat	darást	'study'
šírib	šírbat	šríbt	'drink'
nízil	nízlat	nzílt	'descend'
fíhim	fíhmat	fhímt	'understand'

Syllable weight limits. Many languages disallow long vowels in syllables closed by consonants, and the following examples from Yawelmani show that this language enforces such a prohibition against VVC syllables by shortening the underlying long vowel.

(65)

	Nonfuture	Imperative	Dubitative	Passive aorist	
/CVC/	xathin	xatk'a	xatal	xatit	'eat'
	doshin	dosk'o	do:sol	do:sit	'report'
/CVVC/	ṣaphin	ṣapk'a	ṣa:pal	ṣa:pit	'burn'
	wonhin	wonk'o	wo:nol	wo:nit	'hide'

A typical explanation for this pattern is that long vowels contribute extra "weight" to a syllable (often expressed as the mora), and syllable-final consonants also contribute weight. Languages with restrictions such as those found in Yawelmani are subject to limits on the weight of their syllables.

Stress patterns. Stress assignment has been the subject of intensive typological study, and has proven a fruitful area for decomposing phonological parameters. See Hayes (1995) for a survey of different stress systems. One very common stress assignment pattern is the alternating pattern, where every other syllable is assigned a stress. Maranungku exemplifies this pattern, where the main stress is on the first syllable and secondary stresses are on all subsequent odd-numbered syllables.

(66) tíralk 'saliva' mérepèt 'beard'
      yángarmàta 'the Pleaiades' lángkaràteì 'prawn'
      wélepènemànta 'duck (sp)'

A variant of this pattern occurs in Araucanian, where the main stress appears on the second syllable, and secondary stresses appear on every even-numbered syllable following.

(67) wulé   'tomorrow'
      ṭipánto   'year'
      elúmuyù   'give us'
      elúaènew   'he will give me'
      kimúbalùwulày   'he pretended not to know'

The mirror image of the Maranugku pattern is found in Weri, where the last syllable has the main stress and every other syllable preceding has secondary stress.

(68) ŋintíp   'bee'
      kùlipú   'hair of arm'
      ulùamít   'mist'
      àkunètepál   'times'

Finally, Warao places the main stress on the penultimate syllable and has secondary stresses on alternating syllables before.

(69) yiwàranáe   'he finished it'
      yàpurùkitàneháse   'verily to climb'
      enàhoròahàkutái   'the one who caused him to eat'

Another property exhibited by many stress systems is quantity-sensitivity, where stress is assigned based on the weight of a syllable. Palestinian Arabic has such a stress system, where stress is assigned to the final syllable if that syllable is heavy, to the penult if the penult is heavy and the final syllable is light, and to the antepenult otherwise. The typical definition of a heavy syllable is one with either a long vowel or a final consonant; however, it should be noted that in Arabic, final syllables have a special definition for "heavy," which is that a single consonant does not make the syllable heavy, but two consonants do.

(70) radyóo   'radio'   qaréet   'I read'
      katábt   'I wrote'   qára   'he read'
      qárat   'she read'   katábna   'we wrote'
      qaréethum   'I read them'   kátabu   'they wrote'
      kátabat   'she wrote'   ma katabátš   'she didn't write'

8.4 Why do things happen?

Two of the central questions which phonological theory has sought answers to are "why does rule X exist?" and "can rule Y exist?". Very many languages have a process changing velars into alveopalatals (k → č) before front vowels, and a rule voicing voiceless stops after nasals (mp → mb) is also quite common. It is natural to wonder why such rules would occur in many languages, and a number of theoretical explanations have been offered to explain this. It is also important to also ask about imaginable rules: we want to know, for example, if any language has a rule turning a labial into an alveopalatal before a front vowel, one devoicing a voiced stop after a nasal, or one turning {s, m} into {l, k} before {w, š}. Only by contrasting attested with imaginable but unattested phenomena do theories become of scientific interest.

Impossible rules.   There is a clear and justified belief among phonologists that the rule {s, m} → {l, k}/ __{w, š} is "unnatural," and any theory which predicts such a rule would not be a useful theory. We have seen in chapter 6 that it is impossible to formulate such a process given the theory of distinctive features, since the classes of segments defining target and trigger, and the nature of the structural change, cannot be expressed in the theory. The fact that neither this rule nor any of the innumerable other conceivable random pairings of segments into rules has ever been attested in any language gives us a basis for believing that phonological rules should at least be "possible," in the very simple technical sense expressed by feature theory. Whether a rule is possible or impossible must be determined in the context of a specific theory.

Another pair of rules which we might wonder about are those in (71).

(71)   a.   mč → ñč   ŋč → ñč
            ñp → mp   np → mp
            ñk → ŋk   nk → ŋk
            ñt → nt   nč → ñč

       b.   mč → nč (not ñč)   ŋč → ñč
            ñp → ŋp   np → mp
            ñk → ŋk   nk → mk
            ñt → ñt   nč → nč

The pattern of alternation in (a) is quite common, and was exemplified earlier in this chapter as nasal place assimilation. The second pattern of alternation in (b), on the other hand, is not attested in any language. Given the nonexistence of the pattern (b), we may ask "why is this pattern not attested?"

The easy answer to this question is that pattern (b) is not phonetically natural. This begs the question of how we know what is a phonetically natural versus an unnatural pattern, and unfortunately the connection between "actually attested phonological rule" and "phonetically natural" are so closely intertwined that some people may assume that commonly occurring rules are by definition phonetically natural, and unattested rules are unnatural. This is circular: if we are to preclude a pattern such as (b) as phonetically unnatural, there must be an independent metric of phonetic naturalness. Otherwise, we would simply be saying "such-and-such rule is unattested because it is unattested," which is a pointless tautology.

Another answer to the question of why pattern (b) is not attested, but pattern (a) is, would appeal to a formal property of phonological theory. We will temporarily forgo a detailed analysis of how these processes can be formulated – this is taken up in chapter 10 – but in one theory, the so-called linear theory practiced in the 1960s and 1970s, there was also no formal explanation for this difference and the rules in (b) were possible, using feature variable notation. By contrast, the nonlinear theory, introduced in the late 1970s, has a different answer: formalizing such rules is technically impossible. The mechanism for processes where the output has a variable value (i.e. the result can be either [+anterior] or [−anterior]) requires the target segment to take the *same* values for the features, and to take on *all* values within certain feature sets. The alternation in (b) does not have this property (for example, the change of /ñp/ to [ŋp] does not copy the feature [labial]), and therefore according to the nonlinear theory this is an unformalizable rule. The process is (correctly) predicted to be unattested in human language.

Unlikely rules.   Now consider a rule p → č / _{i, e}, which seems hardly different from k → č / _{i, e}, except the latter is common, and the former is apparently not found in any language. Since we don't know of examples, we must wonder why there is such a gap in what is attested. Perhaps if we had the "right theory," every rule that is possible under a theory would actually be attested in some language. In both the linear and nonlinear theories, these are both technically possible rules.

One legitimate strategy is to assume that this is an accidental gap, and hope that further research will eventually turn up such a rule. Given that only a tiny fraction of the world's languages have been suveyed, this is reasonable. There is a bit of danger in assuming that the apparent nonexistence of labial coronalization is an accidental gap, because we don't want to mistakenly ignore the nonexistence of the imaginary rule /s, m/ → [l, k]/_[w, š] as another accidental gap.

The difference between these two kinds of rules lies in an implicit estimation of how big the gap is between prediction and observation. A number of rules would fall under the rubric "labial coronalization," which would be formalizable under standard feature theories:

> *This number has never been calculated, partly because the nature of the theory (hence the characterization "theoretically possible rule") changes rather rapidly, and partly because phonologists aren't usually concerned with combinatorics.*

(72)   p → č / _i   p, b → č, ǰ / _i
       p → č / _i, e, etc.   p, f, b → č, š, ǰ / _i, e, etc.

If the rules /p/ → [č] / _[i], /p/ → [č] / _[i, e] and /p, f, b/ → [č, š, ǰ] / _[i, e] were all attested and only the rule /p, b/ → [č, ǰ] / _[i] were missing, there would be no question that this is an accidental gap. The number of rules which can be formulated in standard theories is large, running in the millions or billions. If we can't find one or some dozen particular rules in the hundred or so languages that we have looked at, this shouldn't cause serious concern because the chances of finding *any* one rule out of the set of theoretically possible rules is fairly low, and this one gap is of no more significance than a failure to toss a million-sided coin a few hundred times and not have the coin land with side number 957,219 land on top.

We should be a bit more concerned when we identify a somewhat large class – hundreds or perhaps even a thousand – of possible rules which are all unattested and which seem follow a discernable pattern (i.e. "alveopalatalization of labials"). Remember though that we are dealing with a million-sided coin and only a few hundred tosses of the coin. The unattested set of rules represents perhaps a tenth of a percent of the logically possible set, and given the small size of the sample of phonological rules actually available to us, the chances of actually finding such a rule are still not very high.

The situation with the rule /s, m/ → [l, k] / _[w, š] is quite different. This rule is a representative of an immense class of imaginable rules formed by arbitrarily combining sounds in lists. If rules are unstructured collections of segments changing randomly in arbitrary contexts, then given a mere 8,192 (=2^{13}) imaginable language sounds, there are around $10^{45,000}$ different ways to arrange those segments into rules of the type {..} → {...} / _{...}, in comparison to around a billion ways with standard rule theory. Almost every rule which is theoretically predicted under the "random segment" theory falls into the class of rules of the type /s, m/ → [l, k] / _[w, š], and yet not a single one of these rules has been attested. Probability theory says that virtually every attested rule should be of this type, given how many of the imaginable arbitrary rules there are. This is why the lack of rules of the type /s, m/ → [l, k] / _[w, š] is significant – it represents the tip of a mammoth iceberg of failed predictions of the "random phoneme" theory of rules.

Another way to cope with this gap is to seek an explanation outside of phonological theory itself. An analog would be the explanation for why arctic mammals have small furry ears and desert mammals have larger naked ears, proportionate to the size of the animal. There is no independent "law of biology" that states that ear size should be directly correlated with average temperature, but this observation makes sense given a little knowledge of the physics of heat radiation and the basic structure of ears. In a nutshell, you lose a lot of body heat from big ears, which is a good thing in the desert and a bad thing in the arctic. Perhaps there is an explanation outside of the domain of phonological theory itself for the lack of labial coronalization in the set of rules attested rules.

What might be the functional explanation for the lack of such a process? We first need to understand what might be a theory-external, functional explanation for the common change k → č/ _{i, e}. In a vast number of languages, there is some degree of fronting of velar consonants to [kʸ] before front vowels. The reason for this is not hard to see: canonical velars have a further back tongue position, and front vowels have a further front tongue position. To produce [ki], with a truly back [k] and a truly front [i], the tongue body would have to move forward a considerable distance, essentially instantaneously. This is impossible, and some compromise is required. The compromise reached in most languages is that the tongue advances in anticipation of the vowel [i] during production of [k], resulting in a palatalized velar, i.e. the output [kʸi], which is virtually the same as [ci], with a "true palatal" stop.

The actual amount of consonantal fronting before front vowels that is found in a language may vary from the barely perceivable to the reasonably evident (as in English) to the blatantly obvious (as in Russian). This relatively small physiological change of tongue-fronting has a disproportionately more profound effect on the actual acoustic output. Essentially, a plain [k] sounds more like a [p] than like [c] ([k] has a lower formant frequency for the consonant release burst), and [c] sounds more like [t] or [č] (in having a higher burst frequency) than like [k], which it is physiologically more similar to. The acoustic similarity of alveopalatals like [č] and palatals like [c] is great enough that it is easy to confuse one for the other. Thus a child learning a language might (mis)interpret a phonetic alternation [k] ~ [c] as the alternation [k] ~ [č].

Explaining why k → č / _ {i, e} *does* exist is a first step in understanding the lack of labial coronalization before front vowels. The next question is whether there are analogous circumstances under which our unattested rule might also come into existence. Since the production of [p] and the production of [i] involve totally different articulators, a bit of tongue advancement for the production of [i] will have a relatively negligible effect on the acoustics of the release burst for the labial, and especially will not produce a sound that is likely to be confused with [č]. The constriction in the palatal region will be more open for /i/ after the release of /p/, because the tongue does not already produce a complete obstruction in that region (a maximally small constriction) as it does with /k/. It is possible to radically advance the tongue towards the [i]-position and make enough of a palatal constriction during the production of a [p] so that a more [č]-like release will result, but this will not happen simply as a response to a small physically motivated change, as it does with /k/. Thus the probability of such a change – p → č – coming about by phonetic mechanisms is very small, and to the extent that phonological rules get their initial impetus from the grammaticalization of phonetic variants, the chances of ever encountering labial coronalization are slim.

Another approach which might be explored focuses on articulatory consequences of velar coronalization versus labial coronalization. Velars and alveolars involve the tongue as their major articulator, as does [č], whereas labials do not involve the tongue at all. We might then conjecture that there is some physiological constraint that prevents switching major articulators, even in phonological rules. But we *can't* just say that labials never become linguals: they typically do in nasal assimilation. In fact, there is a process in the Nguni subgroup of Bantu languages (Zulu, Xhosa, Swati, Ndebele), where at least historically labials become alveopalatals before *w*, which is very close to the unattested process which we have been looking for. By this process, a labial consonant becomes a palatal before the passive suffix *-w-*, as in the following data from Swati.

ive

	kʰándíŋ-w-a	'dry roast'
	-káš-w-a	'chop'
	-kˣéj-w-a	'scrape'
	ì-lúñ-w-a	'bite'
	ú-nwác-w-a	'bury'

...example to any claim that labials cannot switch ... a rather odd rule from a phonetic perspective ... 1978). Rather than just leave it at that, we should ... le could have come into existence. In a number of ... ally those spoken in southern Africa, there is a low-... f velarization and unrounding where sequences of labial consonants ... [w] are pronounced with decreased lip rounding and increased velar constriction, so that underlying /pw/ is pronounced as [pᵚ], with [ᵚ] notating a semi-rounded partial velar constriction. The degree of velar constriction varies from dialect to dialect and language to language, and the degree of phonetic constriction increases as one progresses further south among the Bantu languages of the area, so in Karanga Shona, /pw/ is pronounced with a noticeable obstruent-like velar fricative release and no rounding, as [pˣ]. The place of articulation of the velar release shifts further forward depending on the language and dialect, being realized as [pɕ] in Pedi, or as [pˢ̌] in Sotho, and finally as [č] in Nguni. So what seems like a quite radical change, given just the underlying-to-surface relation /p/ → [č] in Nguni, is actually just the accumulated result of a number of fortuitously combined, less radical steps.

One of the current debates in phonology – a long-standing debate given new vitality by the increased interest in phonetics – is the question of the extent to which phonological theory should explicitly include reference to concepts rooted in phonetics, such as ease of articulation, perceptability, and confusability, and issues pertaining to communicative function. Virtually every imaginable position on this question has been espoused, and it is certain that the formalist/functionalist debate will persist unresolved for decades.

Summary

The distinction between unattested, rare and well-known patterns in phonology has been important in the development of theory. How do we distinguish between actually nonexistent patterns and patterns that we are unaware of? Which unattested patterns should the formal theory preclude? Why are certain patterns found in very many languages? Should the formal theory try to account for frequency of occurrence? These questions will remain vital research topics in phonology for many years.

Further reading
Greenberg 1978; Hale and Reiss 2000; Hume and Johnson 2001; Maddiesson 1984.

9 Abstractness and psychological reality

PREVIEW

KEY TERMS

abstract

absolute neutralization

psychological reality

external evidence

This chapter explores the extent to which underlying and surface forms can be different – what constraints if any are tenable within the formal theory, what the issues are in limiting abstractness, and how to address these questions empirically. The central question raised in this chapter is "what counts as evidence for a phonological analysis?"

A fundamental question in the theory of phonology has been "how abstract is phonology?", specifically, how different can the underlying and phonetic forms of a word be? The essential question is whether grammars use entities that are not directly observed. Related to this is the question of whether a linguistic model requiring elements that cannot be directly observed reflects what the human mind does. The very concept of a mental representation of speech, such as a phonological surface form like [sɔks] *socks* which is not itself an observable physical event, requires abstracting away from many specifics of speech. Without generalizing beyond the directly observable, it would be impossible to make even the most mundane observations about any language. The question is therefore not whether phonology is abstract at all, but rather what degree of abstractness is required.

If underlying representations are fully concrete – if they are the same as surface representations – the underlying forms of English [kʰɔrts] *courts* and [kʰowdz] *codes* would be /kʰɔrt-s/ and /kʰowd-z/. Such an extremely surface-oriented view of phonology would ignore the fact that the words have in common the plural morpheme, whose pronunciation varies according to the environment. By hypothesizing that the underlying form of [kʰɔrts] is /kʰɔrt-z/, we can say that the plural pronounced *s* in [kʰɔrts] and the plural pronounced *z* in [kʰowdz] are one and the same thing. Such abstractness in phonological analysis yields the benefit of explaining the similaries in pronunciation of the various realizations of the plural morpheme.

9.1 Why limit abstractness?

First we must understand what motivates concern over abstractness.

9.1.1 Limiting possible analyses

One reason to limit the divergence between underlying and surface forms is to constrain the theory of phonology, to prevent it from making wrong claims about how languages work. With no constraint on abstractness, every conceivable derivation from underlying to surface form would in principle be allowed by the theory. Just as the theory of phonology seeks to constrain the concept of "possible rule," so that an imaginable rule such as $\{s,p,q,r\} \rightarrow \{m,l,t,v\} / \_ \{s, k, ə, m\}$ (unattested in any human language) can be ruled out on formal grounds, so too might we wish to rule out a derivation from underlying /qöłɨɟʌ/ to surface [gəráž] as too abstract. Since a goal of linguistic theory has been to restrict the class of theoretically possible languages to just the type that is actually observed, limiting abstractness in a well-defined way limits the number of possible languages.

Another reason for concern over abstractness is that it makes a particular claim about human cognition, that the mentally stored units of language can include things that the speaker has not actually heard, but arrives at by inference based on a line of indirect evidence. Since first language acquisition does not proceed by conscious reasoning, it cannot be taken for granted that everyday academic reasoning skills are automatically available to children.

Mental reality and language acquisition. This second consideration, whether abstractness (of some particular degree) is part of human cognitive capacity, is the most important question arising in this debate: this is a fundamental consideration for a theory such as generative grammar that seeks a model of language in the mind. Because the details of specific languages are not built into children at birth but must be induced from the ambient linguistic data aided by whatever language faculty is universally available to all humans (i.e. the theory of grammar), a basic concern regarding the psychological reality of grammatical constructs – for phonology, rules and underlying forms – is whether they can be learned from the primary language data.

The role of a universal grammatical component is to make the job of language acquisition easier, by uncompromisingly removing certain kinds of imaginable descriptions from consideration. Distinctive features are one way of making this job easier, since it limits the ways of analyzing data. Universal constraints on abstractness might similarly help a child trying to arrive at underlying representation for a language, and there have been a number of proposals as to the relationship between the underlying and surface forms. Attractive as it might seem to propose formal constraints on the theory of grammar to prohibit English from having /qȫɬiɟʌ/ be the underlying form of [ɡəráž] *garage*, we will not actually assume that this is a matter for the formal theory of grammar; rather, it is a consequence of how a phonology is learned, thus the question of abstractness is outside the domain of grammatical theory.

Faced with a word pronounced [dɔg], a child learning English has no reason to assume that its underlying form is anything other than /dɔg/. But faced with the word *atom* [ǽɒəm] and the related word *atomic* [ətʰɔ́mɪk], the child needs to arrive at an underlying representation for the root on which these two words are based, such that rules of English phonology can apply to derive the phonetic variants [ǽɒəm] and [ətʰɔ́m-ɪk]: an appropriate representation would be [ǽtɔm]. It is in the face of such a specific motivation for an abstract underlying form that we would assume the underlying form isn't simply the surface form. The solution to the so-called problem of abstractness which will be adopted here is, simply, that abstractness per se is not a problem: what really requires investigation is the kind of evidence that properly motivates a phonological analysis.

Abstractness and phonemic representations. One particular degree of abstractness is widely accepted as self-evident, needing no further justification, namely that underlying representations do not contain allophonic variants of phonemes. It is generally assumed that English [stɔp], [tʰɔp] are underlyingly /stɔp/, /tɔp/, without aspiration, because there is (by assumption) no underlying aspiration in English. Similarly, we know that the underlying form of [hɪɒɪŋ] *hitting* is /hɪtɪŋ/, not only because the flap is an

allophone in English, but also because of the related word [hɪt] *hit* where
the [t] is directly pronounced. Thus, it is commonly assumed that underlying forms are *at least* as abstract as phonemic representations, with all
allophonically predictable features eliminated.

This assumption can lead to problems. What is the medial consonant in
the underlying form of a word like [waɒɹ̩] *water*? Assuming that the flap is
not a phoneme in English (there are no minimal or near-minimal pairs
contrasting [t] or [d] vs. [ɒ]), this forces us to say that it must be something
other than [ɒ]. The word is spelled with *t*, but spelling is not relevant to
underlying representations. Children acquire words without knowing
how to spell, and most languages of the world are unwritten yet underlying representations must be acquired for all human languages. Spelling is
also unreliable, and could lead us to the unjustified conclusion that the
underlying vowels of [tuw] *too, to, two*, [θruw] *through*, [duw] *due* and [druw]
drew are all different.

Since [waɒɹ̩] is not composed of a root plus suffix, we cannot look at
related forms to reveal the underlying consonant (as we can in *wad-er* versus *wait-er*, both [weyɒɹ̩]). Any number of hypotheses could be set forth –
/waɒɹ̩/, /watɹ̩/, /wadɹ̩/, /waðɹ̩/, /waβɹ̩/, /waɣɹ̩/ and so on. Hypotheses like
/waβɹ̩/ and /waɣɹ̩/ can be rejected on the grounds that they are pointlessly
abstract, containing segments which do not occur phonetically in English,
and there is no reason to believe that they exist underlyingly. Nothing is
gained by positing such underlying representations, thus nothing justi-
fies these hypotheses. Two facts argue decisively against hypothetical
/waβɹ̩/, /waɣɹ̩/ and their ilk. First, there is no evidence for a rule in English
effecting the change /ɣ/ → [ɒ] or /β/ → [ɒ] and addition of such a rule,
required to convert the underlying form into the surface form, rules
against such an analysis since there exist analyses which at least do not
force the inclusion of otherwise unmotivated rules. Second, a specific
choice between /waβɹ̩/ and /waɣɹ̩/, or /waʔɹ̩/ and innumerable other possibilities which also lack an underlying flap, is totally arbitrary and leaves
the language analyst – student and child alike – with the unresolvable
puzzle "why *this* underlying form and not some other?", which can only
be resolved by fiat.

The hypothesis /waðɹ̩/ is less abstract since it is composed only of
observed segments of English; it is, however, factually wrong, because it
would be impossible to craft rules for English to turn /ð/ into a flap in this
context (consider *father, bother, weather* which indicate that there cannot
be a rule changing /ð/ into a flap in some context). Only three hypotheses
remain viable: /waɒɹ̩/, /watɹ̩/, and /wadɹ̩/. None of these hypotheses posits
surface nonexistent segments, and given the rules of English – Flapping,
specifically – any of these underlying representations would result in the
correct surface form.

There is no standard answer to the question of the underlying form of
water, but certain arguments can be marshalled to support different positions. We initially rejected the theory that the underlying form might be
/waɒɹ̩/ because it posits what we assumed to be a nonexistent underlying
segment in the language, but we should reconsider that decision, to at

least explain our argument for rejecting an underlying flap. Hypothesizing /waDɹÌ©/ necessitates another phoneme in the inventory of English underlying segments, violating an analytic economy principle which says that you should select a parsimonious underlying inventory for a language. This reflects the basic principle of scientific reasoning that simpler, more economical solutions are better than complicated solutions that posit unnecessary machinery. But no concrete linguistic arguments indicate that elimination of phonemes is an actual goal of phonological acquisition. Economy of the underlying inventory cannot be judged in a theoretical vacuum, and in one contemporary theory, Optimality Theory, it is impossible to state generalizations about underlying representations, so it is impossible to say that English has no underlying flap.

A somewhat stronger argument against allowing an underlying flap is that the surface distribution of [D] is limited. It only appears between vocoids (vowels and glides), and only if the following vowel is unstressed, which is precisely the context where /t, d/ actively are changed into the flap [D] (*hit* [hɪt] ~ *hitting* [hɪDɪŋ]; *hide* [hayd] ~ *hiding* [hayDɪŋ]). We can explain the lack of words in English like *[hiD], *[Duwl], *[æfDɹÌ©] and *[əDǽk], if we assume that the flap [D] is not in the inventory of underlying segments of English, and only derives from /t/ or /d/ by this specific rule. This argument recognizes the importance of capturing major generalizations about language, which is the central concern of linguistics: it says that it would be too much of a coincidence if, in assuming underlying /D/ in *water*, we failed to note that underlying flap only appears in a very few contexts.

This argument is founded on the presumption that distribution of segments in underlying forms cannot be restricted: otherwise we would simply state a restriction on where underlying flaps appear and let the underlying form of [waDɹÌ©] be fully concrete. Some theories do not have conditions on underlying forms (Optimality Theory), others do. Something like conditions on underlying forms seems inevitable, since for example there cannot be any words in English of the form sC_iVC_i, hence *slil, *sneen, *spup, *skuck; yet, it is uncertain what status such conditions have in the theory of grammar.

Still, even if we decide that the underlying form doesn't have a flap, that leaves open the choice between /t/ and /d/, which is purely arbitrary. The choice might be made by appealing to markedness (chapter 8), insofar as [t] is a less marked, i.e. crosslinguistically common, segment than [d]. Whether this reasoning is correct remains to be determined empirically.

9.1.2 A principled limit on abstractness?

In connection with our first neutralization rule, final devoicing in Russian (chapter 4), we explained the alternation [porok] 'threshold (nom sg)' ~ [poroga] 'threshold (gen sg)' by saying that underlyingly the stem ends with /g/. The abstract representation /porog/ for [porok] 'threshold (nom sg)' is justified by the fact that [porok] and [poroga] have the same root morpheme, and /porog/ is one of the two actually occurring pronunciations of the morpheme. In hypothesizing underlying forms of morphemes, we have repeatedly emphasized the utility of considering any and all of the surface realizations of a given morpheme as candidates for being the underlying form. We might even advance a formal principle regarding abstractness (a principle to this effect was proposed in the theory of Natural Generative Phonology, see Vennemann 1974):

(1)   The underlying form of a morpheme must actually be pronounced as such in some surface form containing the morpheme

When you look at a broad range of phonological analyses, it very often turns out that the supposed underlying form of a morpheme is indeed directly observed in some surface form. Nonetheless, such a principle cannot be an absolute condition on the relation between underlying and surface forms, that is, it cannot be a principle in the theory of grammar. Recall from chapter 4 that in Palauan, all unstressed vowels become schwa, and underlying forms of roots may contain two full vowels, for example /daŋob/ 'cover,' /teʔib/ 'pull out,' /ŋetom/ 'lick.' We are justified in concluding that the first vowel in /daŋob/ is /a/ because it is actually pronounced as such in [mə-dáŋəb] when the first root vowel is stressed, and we are justified in concluding that the second vowel is /o/ because that is how it is pronounced in [dəŋóbl]. Although each hypothesized underlying vowel can be pronounced in one surface variant of the root or another, no single surface form actually contains both vowels in their unreduced form: the hypothesized underlying form /daŋob/ is never pronounced as such, thus our analysis of Palauan is a counterexample to the excessively restrictive statement (1). Similar examples come from English (cf. the underlying stem /tɛlɛgræf/ which explains the surface vowel qualities in [tɛ́ləgræf] and [təlɛ́grəf-iy]) and Tonkawa (cf. /picena/ which is justified based on the surface forms *picna-n-oʔ* and *we-pcen-oʔ*). Condition (1) also runs into problems in Yawelmani (chapter 7), which has a rule shortening a long vowel before a cluster of two consonants, and another rule inserting *i* after the first of three consonants. The two rules apply in stems such as /ʔa:ml/, so that epenthesis turns /ʔa:ml-hin/ into [ʔa:mil-him], and shortening turns /ʔa:ml-al/ into [ʔamlal]. The problem for (1) is that /ʔa:ml/ can never be pronounced as such, since either the vowel is shortened, or *i* is inserted.

Rather than abandon the enterprise of doing phonology in these languages out of misguided allegiance to an a priori assumption about the relationship between underlying and surface forms, we might consider a weaker constraint, which allows underlying forms of morphemes to be composed of segments that are actually pronounced in some attestation of the morpheme, but disallows representations that are more abstract.

(2)   The underlying form of a word must contain only segments actually pronounced as such in some related word containing the morpheme

Even this cannot be an absolute requirement. One case that runs afoul of this condition is the case of stem-final voiced stops in Catalan (chapter 5, problem 4). There is a rule devoicing final obstruents, and another rule spirantizing intervocalic voiced stops. These rules result in alternations such as sɛk 'dry (masc)' ~ sɛkə 'dry (fem)' from /sɛk/, versus sek 'blind (masc)' ~ seɣə 'blind (fem)' from /seg/. The underlying voiced stop /g/ is not directly attested in any form of the stem /seg/, and thus runs afoul of constraint (2).

Another counterexample to (2) is Hehe (chapter 7). That language has a rule assigning H tone to a penultimate vowel that is not also immediately preceded by a H. This rule accounts for the position of the second H tone in words like *kú-kam-íl-a* 'to milk for,' *kú-kam-il-án-a* 'to milk for each other,' and the lack of H tone in *kú-kam-a* 'to milk' where the penultimate vowel is preceded by an H-toned vowel. Surface forms such as *kú-kam-y-á* 'to cause to milk' and *kú-kam-w-á* 'to be milked' would seem to be exceptions, but actually they follow the general pattern perfectly, as long as we recognize that the underlying forms are /kú-kam-i-a/ and /kú-kam-u-a/. Given those underlying forms, the H is regularly assigned to the penultimate vowel giving *kú-kam-í-a* and *kú-kam-ú-a*, and then the high vowels become glides before a vowel, causing the H tone to be transferred to the final vowel. The important point about these examples is that the assumed vowels of the causative and passive never surface as vowels: they appear only as glides, since by quirks of Hehe morphology, the morphemes *-i* and *-u* are always followed by a vowel suffix, so they always undergo glide formation.

9.1.3 Case studies in abstract analysis

We will look in depth at two cases of abstract phonological analysis, one from Kimatuumbi and one from Sanskrit, where abstract underlying forms are well motivated; these are contrasted with some proposals for English, which are not well motivated. Our goal is to see that the problem of abstractness is not about the formal phonetic distance between underlying and surface forms, but rather it involves the question of how strong the evidence is for positing an abstract underlying representation.

Abstract *mu* in Kimatuumbi. Kimatuumbi provides an example of an abstract underlying representation, involving an underlying vowel which never surfaces as such. In this language, the noun prefix which marks nouns of lexical class 3 has a number of surface realizations such as [m], [n], [ŋ] and [mw], but the underlying representation of this prefix is /mu/, despite the fact that the prefix never actually has that surface manifestation with the vowel *u*.

We begin with the effect which nasals have on a following consonant. Sequences of nasal plus consonant are subject to a number of rules in Kimatuumbi, and there are two different patterns depending on the nature of the nasal. One such nasal is the prefix /ñ-/, marking nouns and adjectives of grammatical class 9. When this prefix comes before an underlyingly voiced consonant, the nasal assimilates in place of articulation to that consonant, by a general rule that all nasals agree in place of articulation with an immediately following consonant.

(3)   *Adjective* (cl 9)   *Verb*
      m-bomwáaná   bómwaana   'pointlessly destroy'
      ŋ-golóká   góloka   'be straight'
      ñ-ǰilúká   ǰíluka   'fall down'

When added to a stem beginning with a nasal consonant, the nasal deletes.

(4)   *Adjective* (cl 9)   *Verb*
      mamáandwá   mámaandwa   'nail'
      mimíná   mímina   'spill'
      namátá   námata   'be sticky'

The prefix /ñ/ causes a following voiceless consonant to become voiced.

(5)   *Adjective* (cl 9)   *Verb*
      n-dɪníká   tínɪka   'cut'
      n-demá.á   téma   'chop'
      ñ-ǰapíičá   čápiiča   'be clean'

Finally, /ñ/ causes a following glide to become a voiced stop, preserving the place properties of the glide.

(6)   *Adjective* (cl. 9)   *Verb*
      ñ-ǰukútá   yúkuta   'be full'
      ŋ-gwaá.á   wá   'die'
      ŋ-gwɪkílyá   wíkɪlya   'cover'

We know that the prefix is underlyingly /ñ/ because that is how it surfaces before vowel-initial adjectives such as *ñ-epeési* 'light (cl 9),' *ñ-iípi* 'short (cl 9).'

Different effects are triggered by the nasal of the prefix /mu/ which marks second-plural subjects on verbs. This prefix has the underlying form /mu/, and it can surface as such when the following stem begins with a consonant.

(7)   mu-buundíke   'you should store'
      mu-laabúke   'you should breakfast'
      mu-ǰiiŋgí   'you should enter'
      mu-goóñǰe   'you should sleep'

A rule deletes the vowel *u* preceded by *m* when the vowel precedes a consonant, and this rule applies optionally in this prefix. Before a stem beginning with a voiced consonant, deletion of the vowel results in a cluster of a nasal plus a consonant, and *m* causes nasalization of the following consonant (compare the examples in (7) where the vowel is not deleted).

(8)   m-muundíke   'you should store'
      n-naabúke   'you should breakfast'

ñ-ñiiŋgí	'you should enter'
ŋ-ŋoóñje	'you should sleep'

This reveals an important difference between the two sets of postnasal processes. In underlying nasal+C sequences such as /ñ-bomwáaná/ → *m-bomwáaná* 'destroyed (cl 9),' the nasal only assimilates in place of articulation to the following C, but in nasal+consonant sequences derived by deletion of *u*, the prefixal nasal causes nasalization of a following voiced consonant.

Another difference between /ñC/ versus /muC/ is evident when the prefix /mu/ comes before a stem beginning with a nasal consonant. The data in (9) show that when *u* deletes, the resulting cluster of nasals does not undergo nasal deletion. (The reason for this is that /mu/ first becomes a syllabic nasal *m̩*, and nasalization takes place after a syllabic nasal.)

(9)

mu-mímiine	m-mímiine	'you (pl) spilled'
mu-nóolite	n-nóolite	'you (pl) sharpened'
mu-ŋáandite	ŋ-ŋáandite	'you (pl) played'

In comparison, class 9 /ñ-mimíná/ with the prefix /ñ/ surfaces as *mimíná* 'spilled (cl 9),' having undergone degemination.

A third difference between /ñ+C/ versus /mu+C/ emerges with stems that begin with a voiceless consonant. As seen in (10), /mu/ simply assimilates in place of articulation to the following voiceless consonant.

(10)

mu-paánde	m-paánde	'you should plant'
mu-teleké	n-teleké	'you should cook'
mu-čoné	ñ-čoné	'you should sew'
mu-kalaáŋge	ŋ-kalaáŋge	'you should fry'

Remember, though, that /ñ/ causes a following voiceless consonant to become voiced, so /ñ-tɪníká/ → *ndɪníká* 'cut (cl 9).'

Finally, /mu/ causes a following glide to become a nasal at the same place of articulation as the glide.

(11)

mu-wɪkɪlí	ŋ-ŋwɪkɪlí	'you should cover'
mu-yɪkɪtí	ñ-ñɪkɪtí	'you should agree'

Underlying /ñ/, on the other hand, causes a following glide to become a voiced stop, cf. /ñ-wɪkílyá/ → *ŋ-gwɪkílyá* 'covered (cl 9).'

The differences between /ñ/ and /mu/ go beyond just their effects on following consonants: they also have different effects on preceding and following vowels. In the case of /mu/, the preceding vowel lengthens when *u* deletes.

(12)

iwɪkɪlyó mu-toóle	'you should take cover'
iwɪkɪlyóo n-toóle	id.

ñuúmba mu-bomwaáne   'you should destroy the house'
ñuúmbaa m-momwaáne   id.

On the other hand, /ñ/ has no effect on the length of a preceding vowel.

(13)   iwɩkɩlyo m-bwapwáaniká   'broken cover'
       ñumbá m-bomwáaná   'destroyed house'

Finally, /ñ/ surfaces with [ñ] before a vowel and the length of the following vowel is not affected. But /mu/ surfaces as [mw] before a vowel
due to a process of glide formation, and the following vowel is always
lengthened.

(14)   Stem
       /ñ/   /iípi/   ñ-iípi   'short (cl 9)'
                  /epeési/   ñ-epeési   'light (cl 9)'
       /mu/   /ɩɩmba/   mw-ɩímb-e   'you should dig'
                  /eleew/   mw-eeleéw-e   'you should understand'

A number of properties distinguish /mu/ from /ñ/. Apart from the important fact that positing these different underlying representations provides a phonological basis for distinguishing these effects, our choices of
underlying forms are uncontroversial, because the posited forms of the
prefixes are actually directly attested in some surface variant: recall that
the second-plural verbal subject prefix /mu/ can actually be pronounced as
[mu], since deletion of /u/ is optional for this prefix.

Now we are in position to discuss a prefix whose underlying representation can only be inferred indirectly. The prefix for class 3 nouns and
adjectives is underlyingly /mu/, like the second-plural verbal subject prefix. Unlike the verb prefix, the vowel /u/ of the class 3 noun prefix always
deletes, and /mu/ never appears as such on the surface – its underlying
presence can only be inferred indirectly. A strong indication that this prefix is underlyingly /mu/ is the fact that it has exactly the same effect on a
following consonant as the reduced form of the subject prefix *mu* has. It
causes a voiced consonant to become nasalized.

> *Deletion of u is
> obligatory in this
> prefix and optional
> in the subject prefix
> because subject
> prefixes have a
> "looser" bond to the
> following stem than
> lexical class prefixes,
> which are joined with
> the stem to form a
> special phonological
> domain.*

(15)   *Infinitive*   *Adjective* (cl 3)
       búundika   m-muúndiká   'store'
       láabuka   n-naábuká   'breakfast'
       jíiŋgya   ñ-ñíiŋgyá   'enter'
       góoñja   ŋ-ŋoóñjá   'sleep'

It forms a geminate nasal with a following nasal.

(16)   *Infinitive*   *Adjective* (cl 3)
       máta   m-matá.á   'plaster'
       múlika   m-mulíká   'burn'
       námata   n-namátá   'be sticky'

It also does not cause a following voiceless consonant to become voiced.

(17) *Infinitive*   *Adjective* (cl 3)
      páanda   m-paándá   'plant'
      téleka   n-teléká   'cook'
      čóna   ñ-čoná.á   'sew'
      kálaaŋga   ŋ-kaláaŋgá   'fry'

Another reason to believe that this prefix is underlyingly /mu/ is that when it comes before a stem beginning with a vowel, the prefix shows up as [mw] and the following vowel is lengthened.

(18) *Infinitive*   *Adjective* (cl 3)
      álibika   mwaalíbiká   'break'
      épuka   mweepúká   'avoid'
      úmba   mwɪímbá   'dig'
      ótoka   mwootóká   'puncture'

Under the hypothesis that the class 3 prefix is /mu/, we automatically predict that the prefix should have this exact shape before a vowel, just as the uncontroversial prefix /mu/ marking second-plural subject has.

Finally, the data in (19) show that this prefix has the same effect of lengthening the preceding vowel as the second-plural subject prefix has.

(19) mwoógo   'cassava'   mwoogoo m-moú   'rotten cassava'
      mpɪlá   'football'   mpɪláa m-puwáaniká   'broken football'
      nkóta   'sweets'   nkotáa n-nogá.á   'good sweets'
      nkwá   'spear'   nkwáa n-kúlú   'big spear'

The only reasonable assumption is that this prefix is underlyingly /mu/, despite the fact that the vowel *u* never actually appears as such. Direct attestation of a hypothesized underlying segment does provide very clear evidence for the segment in an underlying form, but underlying forms can also be established by indirect means, such as showing that one morpheme behaves in a manner parallel to some other which has a known and uncontroversial underlying form.

Abstract /ai/ and /au/ in Sanskrit. A significantly more abstract representation of the mid vowels [e:, o:] is required for Sanskrit. These surface vowels derive from the diphthongs /ai/, /au/, which are never phonetically manifested in the language. The surface vowels (syllabics) and diphthongs of Sanskrit are in (20).

(20) a i u ṛ ḷ   a: e: i: o: u: ṛ: a:i a:u

Two things to be remarked regarding the inventory are that while the language has diphthongs with a long first element *a:i, a:u*, it has no diphthongs with a short first element. Second, the mid vowels only appear as long, never short. These two facts turn out to be related.

One phonological rule of the language fuses identical vowels into a single long vowel. This process operates at the phrasal level, so examples are quite easy to come by, simply by combining two words in a sentence.

(21) na 'not'+asti 'is'   →   na:sti   'is not'
      na 'not'+a:ste: 'he sits'   →   na:ste: 'he doesn't sit'
      nadi: 'river'+iwa 'like'   →   nadi:wa   'like a river'
      yadi 'if'+i:çwarah 'lord'   →   yadi:çwarah   'if the lord'
      nadi: 'river'+i:çwarah 'lord'   →   nadi:çwarah   'lord river'
      sa:dhu 'well'+uktam 'said'   →   sa:dhu:ktam   'well said'

A second process combines long or short *a* with *i* and *u* (long or short), giving the long mid vowels *e:* and *o:*.

(22) ca 'and'+iha 'here'   →   ce:ha   'and here'
      ca 'and'+uktam 'said'   →   co:ktam   'and said'
      sa: 'she'+uktam 'said'   →   so:ktam   'she said'
      sa: 'she'+i:çwara 'O Lord'   →   se:çwara   'she, O Lord'

These data point to an explanation for the distribution of vowels noted in (20), which is that underlying *ai* and *au* become *e:* and *o:*, and that this is the only source of mid vowels in the language. This explains why the mid vowels are all long, and also explains why there are no diphthongs *ai*, *au*. There is also a rule shortening a long vowel before another vowel at the phrasal level, which is why at the phrasal level /a:/ plus /i/ does not form a long diphthong [a:i].

There is a word-internal context where the short diphthongs *ai* and *au* would be expected to arise by concatenation of morphemes, and where we find surface *e:*, *o:* instead. The imperfective tense involves the prefixation of *a-*.

(23) bhar-at-i   'he bears'   a-bhar-at   'he bore'
      tuñj-at-i   'he urges'   a-tuñj-at   'he urged'
      wardh-at-i   'he grows'   a-wardh-at   'he grew'

If the stem begins with the vowel *a*, the prefix *a-* combines with following *a* to give a long vowel, just as *a+a → a:* at the phrasal level.

(24) aj-at-i   'he drives'   a:j-at   'he drove'
      añc-at-i   'he bends'   a:ñc-at   'he bent'

When the root begins with the vowels *i*, *u*, the resulting sequences *ai*(:), *au*(:) surface as long mid vowels:

(25) il-at-i   'he is quiet'   e:l-at   'he was quiet'
      i:kṣ-at-i   'he sees'   e:kṣ-at   'he saw'

ukṣ-at-i   'he sprinkles'   o:kṣ-at   'he sprinkled'
ubj-at-i   'he forces'   o:bj-at   'he forced'

These alternations exemplify the rule where /ai, au/ → [e:, o:].

We have shown that /a+i, a+u/ surface as [e:, o:], so now we will concentrate on the related conclusion that [e:, o:] derive from underlying /ai, au/. One argument supporting this conclusion is a surface generalization about vowel combinations, that when *a* combines with what would surface as word initial *o:* or *e:*, the result is a long diphthong *a:u, a:i*.

(26)   a.   ca 'and'+o:kṣat 'he sprinkled'   → ca:ukṣat   'and he sprinkled'
           ca 'and'+e:kṣat 'he saw'   → ca:ikṣat   'and he saw'
     b.   ca 'and'+ukṣati 'he sprinkles'   → co:kṣati   'and he sprinkles'
           ca 'and'+i:kṣati 'he sees'   → ce:kṣati   'and he sees'

This fusion process makes sense given the proposal that [e:] and [o:] derive from /ai/ and /au/. The examples in (26b) remind us that initial [e:, o:] in these examples transparently derive from /a+i/, /a+u/, because in these examples /a/ is the imperfective prefix and the root vowels *u, i* can be seen directly in the present tense. Thus the underlying forms of [ca:ukṣat] and [ca:ikṣat] are [ca#a-ukṣat] and [ca#a-ikṣat]. The surface long diphthong derives from the combination of the sequence of *a*'s into one long *a:*.

Other evidence argues for deriving surface [e:, o:] from /ai, au/. There is a general rule where the high vowels /i, u/ surface as the glides [y, w] before another vowel, which applies at the phrasal level in the following examples.

(27)   e:ti 'he comes'+ṛṣi 'seer'   →   e:ty ṛṣi
       yadi 'if'+aham 'I'   →   yady aham
       yadi 'if'+a:ditya:h 'sons of Aditi'   →   yady a:ditya:h
       e:ti 'she comes'+uma: 'Uma'   →   e:ty uma:
       bhawatu 'let it be'+i:çwarah 'Lord'   →   bhawatw i:çwarah
       sadhu 'well'+e:ti 'he comes'   →   sadhw e:ti

The mid vowels [e:, o:] become [ay, aw] before another vowel (an optional rule, most usually applied, deletes the glide in this context, giving a vowel sequence).

(28)   prabho: 'O Master'+e:ti 'he comes'   →   prabhaw e:ti
       wane: 'in the forest'+a:ste: 'he sits'   →   wanay a:ste:
       wane: 'in the forest'+e:ti 'he comes'   →   wanay e:ti
       prabho: 'O Master'+o:kṣat 'he sprinkled' →   prabhaw o:kṣat

This makes perfect sense under the hypothesis that [e:, o:] derive from /ai, au/. Under that hypothesis, /wanai#a:stai/ undergoes glide formation before another vowel (just as /yadi#aham/ does), giving [wanay#a:ste:].

Abstractness in English. Now we will consider an abstract analysis whose legitimacy has been questioned: since the main point being made here is that abstract analyses can be well motivated, it is important to con-sider what is *not* sufficient motivation for an abstract analysis. A classic case of questionable abstractness is the analysis of English [ɔy] proposed in Chomsky and Halle 1968 (*SPE*), that [ɔy] derives from /œ̄/. In *SPE*, English vowels are given a very abstract analysis, with approximately the follow-ing relations between underlying and surface representations of vowels, where /ī ū/ and so forth represent tense vowels in the transcription used there.

(29) /ī/ → [ay]   /ū/ → [aw]
      /ē/ → [iy]   /ō/ → [uw]
      /ǣ/ → [ey]   /ɔ̄/ → [ow]
      /œ̄/ → [ɔy]   /ā/ → [ɔʌ]

The first step in arguing for this representation is to defend the assump-tion that [ay], [aw] [iy], [uw], [ey], [ow] derive from /ī/, /ū/, /ē/, /ō/, /ǣ/ and /ɔ̄/. The claim is motivated by the Trisyllabic Laxing alternation in English which relates the vowels of *divine* ~ *divinity* ([ay] ~ [ɪ]), *profound* ~ *profun-dity* ([aw] ~ [ə]), *serene* ~ *serenity* ([iy] ~ [ɛ]), *verbose* ~ *verbosity* ([ow] ~ [ɔ]) and *sane* ~ *sanity* ([ey] ~ [æ]). These word pairs are assumed to be morphologi-cally related, so both words in the pairs would have a common root: the question is what the underlying vowel of the root is. It is assumed that tense vowels undergo a process known as Vowel Shift, which rotates a tense vowel's height one degree upward – low vowels become mid, mid vowels become high, and high vowels become low. Another process that is relevant is Diphthongization, which inserts a glide after a tense vowel agreeing in backness with that vowel. By those rules (and a few others), /sǣn/ becomes [sēyn], /serēn/ becomes [sərīyn] and /divīn/ becomes [dəvayn]. By the Trisyllabic Laxing rule, when a tense vowel precedes the penultimate syllable of the word the vowel become lax, which prevents the vowel from shifting in height (shifting only affects tense vowels). Accordingly, [dəvayn] and [dəvɪnətiy] share the root /dəvīn/. In [dəvayn], the tense vowel diphthongizes to [dəvīyn], which undergoes Vowel Shift. In /dəvīn-iti/, the vowel /ī/ instead undergoes Trisyllabic laxing, and there-fore surfaces as [ɪ].

In this way, *SPE* reduces the underlying vowel inventory of English to /ī/ /ū/ /ē/ /ō/ /ǣ/ /ā/ /ɔ̄/, plus the diphthong /ɔy/. Having eliminated most of the diphthongs from underlying representations, we are still left with one diphthong. In addition, there is an asymmetry in the inventory, that English has three out of four of the possible low tense vowels, lacking a front round vowel [œ̄]. It is then surmised that this gap in the system of tense vowels, and the remaining diphthong, can both be explained away simultaneously, if [ɔy] derives from underlying /œ̄/. Furthermore, given the system of rules in *SPE*, if there were a underlying vowel /œ̄/, it would automatically become [ɔy].

Briefly, /œ̄/ undergoes diphthongization to become *œ̄y* because *œ̄* is a front vowel and the glide inserted by diphthongization has the same backness as the preceding tense vowel. The vowel *œ̄* is subject to backness readjustment which makes front low vowels [+back] before glides (by the same process, *œy* which derives from /ī/ by Vowel Shift becomes [ay]). Since hypothesized /œ̄/ does not become *[ö], and must remain a low vowel in order to undergo backness adjustment, Vowel Shift must not apply to /œ̄/. This is accomplished by constraining the rule to not affect a vowel whose values of backness and roundness are different.

What constitutes a valid motivation? This analysis of [ɔy] is typical of highly abstract phonological analyses advocated in early generative phonology, where little concern was given to maintaining a close relation between surface and underlying forms. The idea of deriving [ɔy] from /œ̄/ is not totally gratuitous, since it is motivated by a desire to maintain a more symmetrical system of underlying representations. But the goal of producing symmetry in underlying representations cannot be maintained at all costs, and whatever merits there are to a symmetrical, more elegant underlying representation must be balanced against the fact that abstract underlying forms are inherently difficult for a child to learn. Put simply, the decision to analyze English vowels abstractly is justified only by an esoteric philosophical consideration – symmetry – and we have no evidence that this philosophical perspective is shared by the child learning the language. If achieving symmetry in the underlying form isn't a sufficient reason to claim that [ɔy] comes from /œ̄/, what would motivate an abstract analysis?

Abstractness can easily be justified by showing that it helps to account for phonological alternations, as we have seen in Palauan, Tonkawa, Kimatuumbi, Hehe and Sanskrit. No such advantage accrues to an abstract analysis of [ɔy] in English. The only potential alternations involving [ɔy] are a few word pairs of questionable synchronic relatedness such as *joint* ~ *juncture, point* ~ *puncture, ointment* ~ *unctious, boil* ~ *bullion, joy* ~ *jubilant, soil* ~ *sully, choice* ~ *choose, voice* ~ *vociferous, royal* ~ *regal*. This handful of words gives no support to the abstract hypothesis. If underlying /œ̄/ were to undergo laxing, the result should be the phonetically nonexistent vowel [œ], and deriving the mixture of observed vowels [ʌ], [ʊ], [uw], [ow], or [iy] from [œ] would require rather ad hoc rules. The hypothesized underlying vowel system /ī ū ē ō ǣ ɔ̄ œ̄/ runs afoul of an otherwise valid implicational relation in vowel systems across languages, that the presence of a low front rounded vowel (which is one of the more marked vowels in languages) implies the presence of nonlow front round vowels. This typological implicational principle would be violated by this abstract analysis of English, which has no underlying /ü, ö/: in other words, idealizations about underlying forms can conflict.

An important aspect of the argument for [ɔy] as /œ̄/ is the independent motivation for the rules that would derive [ɔy]. The argument for those rules, in particular Vowel Shift, is not ironclad. Its motivation in synchronic English hinges on alternations of the type *divine* ~ *divinity, profound* ~ *profundity*, but these alternations are lexically restricted and totally unproductive in English (unlike the phonological alternations in the form of the plural suffix as well as the somewhat productive voicing alternation in *life ~ lives*). A consequence of the decision to analyze all cases of [ay] as deriving from /ī/ is that many other abstract assumptions had to be made to explain the presence of tense vowels and diphthongs in unexpected positions (such as before the penultimate syllable).

To account for the contrast between *contrite ~ contrition,* where /ī/ becomes lax and *t → š,* versus *right ~ righteous,* where there is no vowel laxing and *t → č,* it was claimed that the underlying form of *right* is /rixt/, and rules are developed whereby /ixC/ → [ayC]. Abstract /x/ is called on to explain the failure of Trisyllabic Laxing in the word *nightingale,* claimed to derive from /nixtVngæl/. To explain the failure of Trisyllabic Laxing in words like *rosary,* it is assumed that the final segment is /y/ and not /i/, viz. /rɔ̄sVry/. Other examples are that the contrast between *veto* (with no flapping and a secondary stress on [o]) vs. *motto* (with flapping and no stress on [o]) was predicted by positing different vowels – /mɔto/ vs. /vētɔ/, even though the vowel qualities are surface identical. Words such as *relevance* are claimed to contain an abstract nonhigh front glide, whose function is to trigger assibilation of /t/ and then delete, so *relevance* would derive from /relevantᵉ/, the symbol /ᵉ/ representing a nonsyllabic nonhigh front vocoid (a segment not attested in any language to date).

It is not enough to just reject these analyses as being too abstract, since that circularly answers the abstractness controversy by fiat. We need to pair that rejection with an alternative analysis that states what we *do* do with these words, and this reanalysis formed a significant component of post-*SPE* research. More importantly, we need to identify the methodological assumptions that resulted in these excessively abstract analyses. One point which emerged from this debate is that a more conservative stance on word-relatedness is called for. A core assumption in phonological analysis is that underlying representations allow related words to be derived from a unified source by rules. The concept "related word" needs to be scrutinized carefully, because liberally assuming that "related words" have common underlying forms can yield very abstract analyses.

Word relatedness.   Consider word pairs such as *happy/glad,* *tall/long,* and *young/old.* Such words are "related," in having similar semantic properties, but they are not morphologically related, and no one would propose deriving *happy* and *glad* from a single underlying root. Nor would anyone propose treating such pairs as *brain/brandy,* *pain/pantry,* *grain/grant* as involving a single underlying root, since there is no semantic relation between members of the pair. Pairs such as *five/punch* are related historically, but the connection is known only to students of the history of English. The words *father* and *paternal* are related semantically and phonologically, but this does not mean that we can derive *father* and *paternal* from a common root in the grammar of English. It may be tempting to posit relations between *choir* and *chorus,* *shield* and *shelter,* or *hole* and *hollow,* but these do not represent word-formation processes of modern English grammar.

The concept of "relatedness" that matters for phonology is in terms of morphological derivation: if two words are related, they must have some morpheme in common. It is uncontroversial that words such as *cook* and *cooked* or *book* and *books* are morphologically related: the words share common roots *cook* and *book*, via highly productive morphological processes which derive plurals of nouns and past-tense forms of verbs. An analysis of word formation which failed to capture this fact would be inadequate. The relation between *tall* and *tallness* or *compute* and *computability* is similarly undeniable. In such cases, the syntactic and semantic relations between the words is transparent and the morphological processes represented are regular and productive.

Some morphological relations are not so clear: *-ment* attaches to some verbs such as *bereavement, achievement, detachment, deployment, payment, placement, allotment*, but it is not fully productive since we don't have **think-ment, *takement, *allowment, *intervenement, *computement, *givement*. There are a number of verb/noun pairs like *explain/explanation, decline/declination, define/definition, impress/impression, confuse/confusion* which involve affixation of *-(Vt)-ion*, but it is not fully productive as shown by the nonexistence of pairs like *contain/*contanation, refine/*refination, stress/*stression, impose/*imposion, abuse/*abusion*. Since it is not totally predictable which *-ion* nouns exist or what their exact form is, these words may just be listed in the lexicon. If they are, there is no reason why the words could not have slightly different underlying forms.

It is thus legitimate to question whether pairs such as *verbose/verbosity, profound/profundity, divine/divinity* represent cases of synchronic derivation from a single root, rather than being phonologically and semantically similar pairs of words, which are nevertheless entered as separate and formally unrelated lexical items. The question of how to judge formal word-relatedness remains controversial to this day, and with it, many issues pertaining to phonological abstractness.

9.2 Independent evidence: historical restructuring

Paul Kiparsky's seminal 1968 paper "How abstract is phonology?" raises the question whether limits on abstractness are possible and desirable. Kiparsky's concern is the postulation of segments which are never realized, where a language is assumed to have an underlying distinction between two segments which are always phonetically merged. A classic example is Hungarian, which has a vowel harmony rule where suffix vowels agree with the preceding vowel in backness, e.g. *ha:z-am* 'my house,' *fül-em* 'my ear,' *vi:z-em* 'my water.' A small number of roots with the front vowels [i: i e:] always have back vowels in suffixes, e.g. *he:j-am* 'my rind,' *nyi:l-am* 'my arrow.' The abstract analysis is that these roots have underlying back vowels [ɨ ɨ: ə:], which later become front vowels. This move makes these roots phonologically regular. The reasoning is that since these front vowels seem to act as though they are back vowels, in terms of the vowel harmony system, maybe they really *are* back vowels at a deeper level.

Kiparsky terms this kind of analysis **absolute neutralization**, to be distinguished from **contextual neutralization**. In contextual neutralization, the distinction between two underlying segments is neutralized in some contexts, but is preserved in others. Final devoicing in Russian is contextual neutralization because in the words /porok/ and /porog/, the distinction between *k* and *g* is neutralized in the nominative singular [porok], but is maintained in genitive [poroka] vs. [poroga]. With absolute neutralization, the distinction is eliminated in all contexts, and thus in Hungarian, /ɨ/ is always neutralized with /i/. Kiparsky argues that while contextual neutralization is common and has demonstrable psychological reality, absolute neutralization is a theoretically constructed fiction.

In arguing against absolute neutralization, Kiparsky faces the challenge that a number of cases of such abstractness had been postulated, so good reasons for rejecting those analyses must be found. Kiparsky focuses on the extent to which the psychological reality of theoretical constructs can be measured – this is an important consideration since linguistic theories are usually intended to be models of the psychological processes underlying linguistic behavior. The problem is that it is impossible to directly test whether linguistic constructs are psychologically valid by any simple or obvious tests. Linguistic properties are highly abstract, and not easily tested in the same way that one can experimentally test the ability to perceive touch or distinguish colors or sounds. Kiparsky argues that one can, in certain circumstances, use the pattern of language change as a theory-external test of grammatical theories. It is argued that historical sound change can provide just such a test.

An abstract phonological distinction cannot be justified on the basis of the fact that two historically distinct sounds merge in the history of a language, so even if it were shown that Hungarian *he:j* 'rind' and *nyi:l* 'my arrow' derived from earlier **hə:j* and **nyɨ:l*, this would not be evidence for an abstract underlying form in modern Hungarian. A child learning the language has no access to this kind of historical information. What Kiparsky points out is that you can inspect a *later* stage of a language to learn about the analysis of a language that was actually given at an earlier stage of the language, and then adduce general principles about grammars based on such independent evidence.

9.2.1 Yiddish final devoicing

The history of Yiddish devoicing is one example of such evidence. In the oldest forms of German, represented by Old High German, there was no restriction against word-final voiced consonants, so Old High German had words like *tag* 'day' ~ *taga* 'days,' *gab* 'he gave' ~ *gābumes* 'we gave,' *sneid* 'he cut' ~ *snīdan* 'to cut,' *hand* 'hand,' *land* 'land.' Between 900 and 1200 in the Middle High German period, a rule of devoicing was added, which resulted in *tac* 'day' ~ *tage* 'days,' *gap* 'he gave' ~ *gāben* 'we gave,' *sneit* 'he cut' ~ *snīden* 'to cut,' *hant* 'hand' ~ *hende* 'hands,' *wec* 'road' ~ *weges* 'roads.'

Around this time, Yiddish began to develop as a language separate from German, and would have shared this devoicing rule. Devoicing of final consonants in Yiddish is attested in manuscripts from the thirteenth century where the word for 'day' is written <tak>, using the letter *kuf* [k] and not *gimel* [g]. In some dialects, such as Central and Western Yiddish, this devoicing persists up to today, where you find *tak* 'day' ~ *tag-n* 'days,' *lant* 'land' ~ *lend-ər* 'lands,' with the stem-final voiced consonants of /tag/ and /land/ undergoing final devoicing in the singular. In some dialects such as the Northeastern dialect of Yiddish, the devoicing rule was lost from the grammar, so that dialect has *tog* 'day' ~ *tog-n* 'days,' where the originally voiced consonant reappears as voiced. This process where an earlier sound change is dropped from the grammar is known as reversal of sound change: consonants revert to their original state found before the sound change applied.

There are mysterious exceptions to restoration of original voiced consonants. One case is the word *gelt* 'money,' which derives historically from *geld* with a voiced consonant. The reason for the different treatments of *gelt* and *tag*, words which both ended with voiced consonants at earlier stages of the language, is the difference in the presence or absence of phonological alternations within the paradigm of a word. In the case of *tag*, the plural form had a suffix -*n*, and so while the singular was subject to devoicing, the plural was not: this word had the paradigmatic alternations [tak] ~ [tagn]. On the basis of these alternations, a child learning the language would have no problem discovering that the underlying form of the stem is /tag/. It is expected that once the final devoicing rule is lost, the underlying form /tag/ resurfaces since there is no longer a devoicing rule.

In the word *gelt*, the situation was different. There was no inflectional ending which followed this particular noun. At the earliest stages of the language, a child learning the language only encounters [geld], and there would be no basis for assuming that the underlying form is anything other than /geld/. When the devoicing rule was added to the grammar, the pronunciation of the word changed to [gelt]. Since this particular consonant was always word-final, the devoicing rule would have always applied to it, so the stem only had the phonetic form [gelt]. Although either /geld/ or /gelt/ as underlying form would yield the surface form [gelt], there is no reason to assume that the surface and underlying forms are different. A priori criteria may support one decision or the other, but what we need to know is, what independent test tells us that our reasoning is correct? The loss of the devoicing rule provides exactly the needed empirical test: it allows us to know what underlying form Yiddish-learning children must have assumed at this earlier stage. Knowing the actual underlying form provides an important insight into the learning strategies that children make during language acquisition.

When the devoicing rule was added, there were no alternations in *gelt* so a child would have no reason to assume that the underlying form of the word is anything other than /gelt/. The child never hears *geld*, and has no reason to think that the underlying form is different from /gelt/. At an even later stage, the rule of final devoicing is dropped from the grammar of certain dialects. This allows the underlying and historically original voiced consonant of *tag* to be pronounced again, since it is no longer subject to devoicing and thanks to the paradigmatic $k \sim g$ alternation the underlying form was established as being /tag/. This rule loss has no effect on *gelt*, since despite being derived historically from a voiced consonant, the final consonant of the stem had been reanalyzed as /t/ – a reanalysis predicted by the presumption that an underlying form is different from the surface form only if there is good reason for assuming so. Because there are no alternations for this word, there was no reason to assume an abstract underlying form.

Another important kind of exception to the reversal of devoicing is seen in the adverb *avek* 'away.' This word was originally *aveg*, with a voiced consonant. This adverb also had no inflected relatives which allowed the underlying voicing of the final consonant to be unambiguously determined, so once the devoicing rule was added to the grammar, it was impossible to determine whether the underlying form was /avek/ or /aveg/. Again, starting from the assumption that underlying forms do not deviate from surface forms without reason, there is no reason to assume that phonetic [avek] derives from anything other than /avek/, since the word is actually pronounced [avek]. The fact that the underlying form is directly revealed as *avek* in the dialects which dropped devoicing supports this decision.

The example also reveals something interesting about what might (but does not) constitute a "reason" for abstractness. The adverb *avek* is historically related to the noun *veg* 'way.' The voicing of the last consonant in the noun stem can be recovered within the paradigm given the earlier alternations *vek* 'way' ~ *vegn* 'ways,' because the singular and plural forms of the noun are clearly related to each other. The evidence from the plural noun had no impact on the child's selection of the underlying form for the adverb, since there is no synchronic connection between the adverb and the noun – no process derives nouns and adverbs from a unified source, so nothing connects the words for 'way' and 'away.' The divergence of *veg* and *avek* in Yiddish points out that you cannot freely assume that any two phonetically and semantically similar words are actually derived from a single underlying form.

9.2.2 Historical evidence and the treatment of absolute neutralization

Kiparsky draws two main conclusions from this and similar cases. First, he points out that in lieu of alternations supporting abstractness, the surface and underlying forms should be assumed to be identical: alternations are central to supporting an abstract underlying form. Second, and more controversially, these examples are used in an argument against the psychological reality of absolute neutralization. The argument is as follows. Cases such as Yiddish show the psychological reality of contextual neutralization, since it can be reversed. However, there is no known case where absolute neutralization has been historically reversed: if absolute neutralization had the psychological reality of contextual neutralization, we would expect to find a reversal of absolute neutralization, and we have not. Therefore, putative cases of absolute neutralization lack psychological reality.

Kiparsky proposes that morphemes which seem to motivate abstract segments are simply lexical exceptions to the rule in question: they fail to undergo or trigger a rule. For the problematic roots of Hungarian where front vowels seem to trigger back harmony, such as *he:j-am* 'my rind,' *nyi:l-am* 'my arrow,' the proposal is that these roots are marked as exceptions to vowel harmony. On the assumption that harmonizing suffixes all contain underlying back vowels, the fact that back vowels appear in suffixes after these roots boils down to the fact that the suffixes have underlying back vowels, and since these roots do not trigger vowel harmony the underlying vowel quality is preserved on the surface.

9.3 Well-motivated abstractness

While it is certainly true that some putative processes of absolute neutralization are not well supported and the abstract property only diacritically marks a root as an exception to one rule, there are internally well-supported cases of absolute neutralization. Two famous cases are Yawelmani discussed by Kisseberth (1969), and Maltese discussed by Brame (1972).

9.3.1 Yawelmani /u:/

Aspects of Yawelmani have been discussed in chapter 7. Two of the most important processes are vowel harmony and vowel shortening. The examples in (30) demonstrate the basics of vowel harmony: a suffix vowel becomes rounded if it is preceded by a round vowel of the same height.

(30) | *Nonfuture* | *Imperative* | *Dubitative* | *Passive aorist* | |
|---|---|---|---|---|
| xat-hin | xat-k'a | xat-al | xat-it | 'eat' |
| dub-hun | dub-k'a | dub-al | dub-ut | 'lead by hand' |
| xil-hin | xil-k'a | xil-al | xil-it | 'tangle' |
| k'oʔ-hin | k'oʔ-k'o | k'oʔ-ol | k'oʔ-it | 'throw' |

Thus the root vowel /o/ has no effect on the suffixes /hin/ and /it/ but causes rounding of /k'a/ and /al/ — and the converse holds of the vowel /u/.

The data in (31) show that long vowels cannot appear before two consonants. These stems have underlying long vowels and, when followed by a consonant-initial affix, the vowel shortens.

(31) | *Nonfuture* | *Imperative* | *Dubitative* | *Passive aorist* | |
|---|---|---|---|---|
| dos-hin | dos-k'o | do:s-ol | do:s-it | 'report' |
| ṣap-hin | ṣap-k'a | ṣa:p-al | ṣa:p-it | 'burn' |
| mek'-hin | mek'-k'a | me:k'-al | me:k'-it | 'swallow' |

Another class of verb roots has the surface pattern CVCV:C – the peculiar fact about these roots is that the first vowel is always a short version of the second vowel.

(32) | *Nonfuture* | *Imperative* | *Dubitative* | *Passive aorist* | |
|---|---|---|---|---|
| p'axat-hin | p'axat-k'a | p'axa:t-al | p'axa:t-it | 'mourn' |
| ʔopot-hin | ʔopot-k'o | ʔopo:t-ol | ʔopo:t-it | 'arise from bed' |
| yawal-hin | yawal-k'a | yawa:l-al | yawa:l-it | 'follow' |

In [wo:ʔuy-hun],
[do:lul-hun], the
second vowel is
epenthetic, so these
roots underlyingly
have the shape
CV:CC, parallel to
[ʔa:mil-hin] ∼
[ʔamlal] 'help.'

There are problematic roots in (33). Although the stem vowel is a mid vowel, a following nonhigh vowel does not harmonize – they seem to be exceptions. Worse, a high vowel *does* harmonize with the root vowel, even though it does not even satisfy a basic phonological requirement for harmony (the vowels must be of the same height).

(33)

	Nonfuture	Imperative	Dubitative	Passive aorist	
	c'om-hun	c'om-k'a	c'o:m-al	c'o:m-ut	'destroy'
	ṣog-hun	ṣog-k'a	ṣo:g-al	ṣo:g-ut	'uncork'
	wo:ʔuy-hun	wo:ʔuy-k'a	woʔy-al	woʔy-ut	'fall asleep'
	do:lul-hun	do:lul-k'a	doll-al	doll-ut	'climb'

A noteworthy property of such roots is that their vowels are always long.

There is another irregularity connected with certain surface mid vowels. The data in (34) illustrate a set of CVCVV(C) roots, where, as we noticed before, the two vowels are otherwise identical. In these verbs, the second long vowel is a nonhigh version of the first vowel.

(34)

	Nonfuture	Imperative	Dubitative	Passive aorist	
	hiwet-hin	hiwet-k'a	hiwe:t-al	hiwe:t-it	'walk'
	ʔile:-hin	ʔile-k'	ʔile-l	ʔile-t	'fan'
	ṣudok'-hun	ṣudok'-k'a	ṣudo:k'-al	ṣudo:k'-ut	'remove'
	t'unoy-hun	t'unoy-k'a	t'uno:y-al	t'uno:y-ut	'scorch'
	c'uyo:-hun	c'uyo-k'	c'uyo-l	c'uyo-t	'urinate'

The surface mid vowels of these stems act irregularly for harmony – they do not trigger harmony in mid vowels, so they do not act like other mid vowels. They also exceptionally trigger harmony in high vowels, as only high vowels otherwise do.

When you consider the vowels of Yawelmani – [i e a o u e: o: a:] – you see that long high vowels are lacking in the language. The preceding mysteries are solved if you assume, for instance, that the underlying stem of the verb 'scorch' is /tunu:y/. As such, the root would obey the canonical restriction on the vowels of a bivocalic stem – they are the same vowel – and you expect /u:/ to trigger harmony on high vowels but not on mid vowels, as is the case. A subsequent rule lowers /u:/ to [o:], merging the distinction between underlying /o:/ and /u:/.

The assumption that /u:/ becomes [o:] and therefore some instances of [o:] derive from /u:/ explains other puzzling alternations. There is a vowel shortening process which applies in certain morphological contexts. One context is the causative, which adds the suffix -a:la and shortens the preceding stem vowel.

(35)

	Nonfuture plain	Nonfuture causative	
	tis-hin	tis-a:la-hin	'come out'
	hoyo:-hin	hoy-o:lo-hin	'have a name'
	mek'-hin	mik'-a:la-hin	'eat'
	c'om-hun	c'um-a:la-hin	'destroy'

We have seen in (33) that the root [c'o:m] has the phonological character-istics of an abstract vowel, so given the surface-irregular pattern of vowel harmony in *c'om-hun, c'om-k'a* we can see that the underlying vowel must be a high vowel. The fact that the vowel actually shows up as a high vowel as a result of the morphologically conditioned shortening rule gives fur-ther support to the hypothesized abstract underlying vowel.

The approach which Kiparsky advocates for absolute neutralization does not work for Yawelmani: these words are not exceptions. Being an exception has a specific meaning, that a given morpheme fails to undergo or trigger a rule which it otherwise would undergo. The fact that vowel harmony does not apply in *c'o:m-al* can be treated as exceptionality. But this root does actually trigger vowel harmony, as shown by *c'o:m-ut*, and such application is problematic since the rule is applying when the for-mal conditions of the rule are not even satisfied on the surface. Marking a root as an exception says that although the root would be expected to undergo a rule, it simply fails to undergo the rule. What we have in Yawelmani is something different – a form is triggering a rule even though it should not. The exceptionality analysis also offers no account of stems such as *c'uyo:-hun*, where the first vowel should have been a copy of the second vowel but instead shows up as a high vowel; nor does the excep-tionality account have any way to explain why the "exceptional" roots show up with high vowels when the root is subject to morphological vowel shortening as in *c'om-hun* ~ *c'um-a:la-hin*.

9.3.2 Maltese /ʕ/

Another well-supported case of absolute neutralization comes from Maltese. We will just outline the basics of the argument: you should read Brame (1972) to understand the full argument. After outlining some basic phonological processes, we consider examples which seem superficially inexplicable, but which can be explained easily if we posit an abstract underlying consonant /ʕ/.

9.3.2.1 Basic Maltese phonology

Stress and apocope. (36) examplifies two central processes of the lan-guage, namely stress assignment and apocope. Disregarding one conso-nant at the end of the word, the generalization is that stress is assigned to the last heavy syllable – one that ends in a (nonfinal) consonant or one with a long vowel.

(36)	séna	'year'	sultáan	'king'
	ʔattúus	'cat'	ħdúura	'greenness'
	ħátaf	'he grabbed'	bézaʔ	'he spat'
	ħátf-et	'she grabbed'	bézʔ-et	'she spat'
	ħtáf-t	'I grabbed'	bzáʔ-t	'I spat'
	ħtáf-na	'we grabbed'	bzáʔ-na	'we spat'

The second group illustrates apocope, which deletes an unstressed vowel followed by CV. The underlying stem of the word for 'grabbed' is /ħataf/, seen in the third-singular masculine form. After stress is assigned in third-singular feminine /ħátaf-et/, (37) gives surface [ħataf-et].

(37)   V   → Ø / __ CV   *Apocope*
        [−stress]

In /ħataf-t/ stress is assigned to the final syllable since that syllable is heavy (only one final consonant is disregarded in making the determination whether a syllable is heavy), and therefore the initial vowel is deleted giving [ħtáft].

Unstressed reduction and harmony.   Two other rules are unstressed-vowel reduction and vowel harmony. By the former process, motivated in (38), unstressed *i* reduces to *e*. The third-singular feminine suffix is underlyingly /-it/, which you can see directly when it is stressed. The underlying form of *kíteb* is /kitib/. When stress falls on the first syllable of this root, the second syllable reduces to *e*, but when stress is final, the second syllable has *i*.

(38)   hátf-et   'she grabbed'   ħatfít-kom   'she grabbed you (pl)'
       béz?-et   'she spat'   bez?-ít-l-ek 'she spat at you'
       kíteb   'he wrote'   ktíb-t   'I wrote'

Thus the following rule is motivated.

(39)   i   → [−hi]   *Unstressed V-reduction*
        [−stress]

By vowel harmony, /i/ becomes [o] when preceded by *o*.

(40)   kórob   'he groaned'   kórb-ot   'she groaned'
       šórob   'he drank'   šórb-ot   'she drank'

Surface *kórb-ot* derives from /korob-it/ by applying stress assignment, the vowel harmony in (41), and apocope.

(41)   i → [+round] /   V C_0 __   *Harmony*
                       [+round]

Epenthesis.   The data in (42) illustrate another rule, which inserts [i] before a word-initial sonorant that is followed by a consonant.

(42)   lá?at   'he hit'   róħos   'it (masc) became cheap'
       lá?t-et   'she hit'   róħs-ot   'it (fem) became cheap'
       il?át-t   'I hit'   irħós-t   'I became cheap'
       il?át-na 'we hit'   irħós-na 'we became cheap'

       márad   'he became sick'   néfaħ   'he blew'
       márd-et   'she became sick'   néfħ-et   'she blew'
       imrád-t   'I became sick'   infáħ-t   'I blew'
       imrád-na 'we became sick'   infáħ-na 'we blew'

Stress assignment and apocope predict /laʔat-na/ → *lʔát-na*: the resulting consonant cluster sonorant plus obstruent sequence is eliminated by the following rule:

(43)　∅ → i / # _ [+sonor] C　　*Epenthesis*

Regressive harmony and precoronal fronting.　These rules apply in the imperfective conjugation, which has a prefix *ni-* '1st person,' *ti-* '2nd person' or *yi-* '3rd person' plus a suffix *-u* 'plural' for plural subjects. The underlying prefix vowel *i* is seen in the following data:

(44)　ní-msaħ　　'I wipe'　　　　tí-msaħ　　'you wipe'
　　　ní šbaħ　　'I resemble'　　tí-šbaħ　　'you resemble'
　　　ní-kteb　　'I write'　　　tí-kteb　　'you write'
　　　ní-tlef　　'I lose'　　　　tí-tlef　　'you lose'

When the first stem vowel is *o*, the prefix vowel harmonizes to *o*:

(45)　nó-bzoʔ　　'I spit'　　　tó-bzoʔ　　'you spit'
　　　nó-krob　　'I groan'　　tó-krob　　'you groan'
　　　nó-ħlom　　'I dream'　　tó-ħlom　　'you dream'
　　　nó-ʔtol　　'I kill'　　　tó-ʔtol　　'you kill'
　　　nó-rbot　　'I tie'　　　tó-rbot　　'you tie'
　　　nó-lʔot　　'I hit'　　　tó-lʔot　　'you hit'

This can be explained by generalizing harmony (41) so that it applies before or after a round vowel. The nature of the stem-initial consonant is important in determining whether there is surface harmony; if the first consonant is a coronal obstruent, there appears to be no harmony.

(46)　ní-drob　　'I wound'　　　　　tí-drob　　'you wound'
　　　ní-tlob　　'I pray'　　　　　tí-tlob　　'you pray'
　　　ní-skot　　'I become silent'　tí-skot　　'you become silent'
　　　ní-zloʔ　　'I slip'　　　　　tí-zloʔ　　'you slip'
　　　ní-šrob　　'I drink'　　　　tí-šrob　　'you drink'

Examples such as *nó-bzoʔ* show that if the coronal obstruent is not immediately after the prefix vowel, harmony applies. The explanation for apparent failure of harmony is simply that there is a rule fronting *o* when a coronal obstruent follows.

(47)　o → [−back] / _ $\begin{bmatrix} + \text{cor} \\ - \text{son} \end{bmatrix}$

Guttural lowering.　Another process lowers /i/ to *a* before the "guttural" consonants ʔ and ħ:

Treating glottal stop as [+low] is controversial since that contradicts the standard definition of [+low], involving tongue lowering. Recent research in feature theory shows the need for a feature that includes laryngeal glides in a class with low vowels and pharyngeal consonants.

(48) ná-ʔsam   'I divide'   tá-ʔsam   'you divide'
      ná-ʔbel   'I agree'   tá-ʔbel   'you agree'
      ná-ħrab   'I flee'   tá-ħrab   'you flee'
      ná-ħleb   'I milk'   tá-ħleb   'you milk'

This motivates the following rule:

(49) $i \rightarrow$ [+low] / _   C   *guttural lowering*
                       [+low]

Metathesis.   (50) and (51) illustrate another process. When the stem has a medial obstruent, the prefix vowel is stressed and the stem vowel deletes before *-u*.

(50) ní-msaħ   'I wipe'   ní-msħ-u   'we wipe'
      nó-bzoʔ   'I spit'   nó-bzʔ-u   'we spit'
      ní-dħol   'I enter'   ní-dħl-u   'we enter'
      ná-ʔsam   'I divide'   ná-ʔsm-u   'we divide'
      ná-ħdem   'I work'   ná-ħdm-u   'we work'

This is as expected: underlying /ni-msaħ-u/ is stressed on the first syllable, and the medial unstressed vowel deletes because it is followed by CV. The example [nóbzʔu] from /ni-bzoʔ-u/ shows that harmony must precede apocope, since otherwise apocope would have deleted the stem vowel which triggers harmony.

When the second stem consonant is a sonorant, in the presence of the suffix *-u* the prefix has no stress, and the stem retains its underlying vowel, which is stressed. Unstressed *i* reduces to [e], so [ní-dneb] derives from /ni-dnib/. The underlying high vowel is revealed with the stem vowel is stressed, as in [nidínbu].

(51) ní-dneb   'I sin'   ni-dínb-u   'we sin'
      ní-tlef   'I lose'   ni-tílf-u   'we lose'
      ní-tlob   'I pray'   ni-tólb-u   'we pray'
      nó-krob   'I groan'   no-kórb-u   'we groan'
      nó-ʔmos   'I kick'   no-ʔóms-u   'we kick'
      ná-ħrab   'I flee'   na-ħárb-u   'we flee'
      ná-ħraʔ   'I burn'   na-ħárʔ-u   'we burn'
      ná-ʔleb   'I overturn'   na-ʔílb-u   'we overturn'

Based solely on stress assignment and apocope, as illustrated in (50), we would predict *nídnbu, *nótlbu. This again would result in an unattested consonant cluster in the syllable onset – a sonorant followed by an obstruent – which is avoided by a process of vocalic metathesis whereby *ní-tlif-u → ni-tílf-u*.

(52)   V C   C V_i C V $\rightarrow$ V C V_i C C V   *Metathesis*
                [+son]

In some stems which undergo (52), the vowel alternates between *i* and *a*:

(53) ní-fraħ   'I rejoice'   ni-fírħ-u   'we rejoice'
      ní-tla?   'I leave'   ni-tíl?-u   'we leave'
      ní-sra?   'I steal'   ni-sír?-u   'we steal'

The underlying stem vowel is /i/ in these cases. When no vowel suffix is added, underlying /ni-friħ/ becomes [ní-fraħ] by Guttural Lowering (49). When -*u* is added, metathesis moves underlying /i/ away from the guttural consonant which triggered lowering, hence the underlying vowel is directly revealed.

Stems with long vowels.   The stems which we have considered previously are of the underlying shape CVCVC. There are also stems with the shape CVVC, illustrated in the perfective aspect in (54):

(54) dáar   'he turned'   sáar   'it (masc) grew ripe'
      dáar-et   'she turned'   sáar-et   'it (fem) grew ripe'
      dáar-u   'they turned' sáar-u   'they grew ripe'
      dór-t   'I turned'   sír-t   'I became ripe'
      dór-na   'we turned'   sír-na   'we became ripe'
      dór-tu   'you turned'   sír-tu   'you became ripe'

These stems exhibit a process of vowel shortening where *aa* becomes *o* or *i* (the choice is lexically determined) before a CC cluster.

(55) aa → i,o / _ CC

When the imperfective prefixes *ni-*, *ti-* are added to stems beginning with a long vowel, stress is assigned to that vowel and the prefix vowel is deleted. In the case of the first-person prefix /ni/, this results in an initial nC cluster, which is repaired by inserting the vowel *i*.

(56) in-dúur   'I turn'   in-síir   'I become ripe'
      t-dúur   'you turn'   t-síir   'you become ripe'
      in-súu?   'I drive'   in-zíid   'I add'
      t-súu?   'you drive'   t-zíid   'you add'

From /ni-duur/, you expect stress to be assigned to the final syllable because of the long vowel. Since the vowel of /ni/ is unstressed and in an open syllable, it should delete, giving *ndúur*. The resulting cluster then undergoes epenthesis.

9.3.2.2 Apparent irregularities.   A number of verbs seem to be irregular, and yet they are systematic in their irregularity: the irregularity is only in terms of the surface form, which can be made perfectly regular by positing an abstract underlying consonant /ʕ/. One set of examples is seen in the data in (57), where the stem contains a surface long vowel. This long vowel is unexpectedly skipped over by stress assignment, unlike verbs with underlying long vowels such as *in-dúur* 'I turn' seen in (54).

(57) ní-sool   'I cough'   ni-sóol-u   'we cough'
      ní-laab   'I play'   ni-láab-u   'we play'
      ní-baat   'I send'   ni-báat-u   'we send'
      nó-ʔood   'I stay'   no-ʔóod-u   'we stay'
      nó-bood   'I hate'   no-bóod-u   'we hate'

The location of stress and the retention of the prefix vowel in *nó-ʔood* is parallel to the retention of the prefix vowel in other tri-consonantal stems in (44)–(48), such as *ní-msaħ* 'I wipe.' If the underlying stem of *ní-sool* had a consonant, i.e. were /sXol/ where X is some consonant yet to be fully identified, the parallelism with *ni-msaħ* and the divergence from *in-dúur* would be explained. The surface long vowel in *nísool* would derive by a compensatory lengthening side effect coming from the deletion of the consonant X in /ní-sXol/.

Another unexpected property of the stems in (57) is that when the plural suffix *-u* is added, the prefix vowel is stressless and unelided in an open syllable, and the stress shifts to the stem, e.g. *ni-sóol-u* 'we cough.' Thus, contrast *ni-sóol-u* with *ní-msħ-u* 'we wipe,' which differ in this respect, and compare *ni-sóol-u* to *ni-šórb-u* 'we drink,' which are closely parallel. Recall that if the medial stem consonant is a sonorant, expected V-CRC-V instead undergoes metathesis of the stem vowel around the medial consonant, so /ni-šrob-u/ becomes *ni-šórb-u* (creating a closed syllable which attracts stress). If we hypothesize that the underlying stem is /sXol/, then the change of /ni-sXol-u/ to *ni-sóXl-u* (phonetic *nisóolu*) would make sense, and would further show that X is a sonorant consonant: ʕ qualifies as a sonorant (it involves minimal constriction in the vocal tract).

Another pecularity is that these long vowels resist shortening before CC:

(58) sóol   'he coughed'   sóolt   'I coughed'   sóolna   'we coughed'
      sóob   'he lamented'   sóobt   'I lamented'   sóobna   'we lamented'
      ʔáad   'he stayed'   ʔáadt   'I stayed'   ʔáadna   'we stayed'
      báad   'he hated'   báadt   'I hated'   báadna   'we hated'

In contrast to examples in (54) such as *dáar* 'he turned,' *dór-t* 'I turned' with vowel shortening before CC, these long vowels do not shorten. Continuing with the hypothesis of an abstract consonant in /soXol/, we explain the preservation of the long vowel in [sóolt] if this form derives from *sXol-t*, where deletion of X (which we suspect is specifically ʕ) lengthens the vowel, and does so after vowel shortening has applied.

There is a further anomaly in a subset of stems with the consonant X in the middle of the root: if the initial stem consonant is a sonorant, epenthetic *i* appears when a consonant-initial suffix is added. Compare (59a) where the first consonant is not a sonorant with (59b) where the first consonant is a sonorant.

(59) a. ʔáad   'he stayed'   ʔáadt   'I stayed'
          báad   'he hated'   báadt   'I hated'
          sóol   'he coughed'   sóolt   'I coughed'

      b. máad   'he chewed'   imáadt   'I chewed'
          náas   'he dozed'   ináast   'I dozed'
          láaʕ   'he licked'   iláaʕt   'I licked'

The verbs in (59b) behave like those in (42), e.g. *láʕat* 'he hit' ~ *ilʕát-t* 'I hit' where the initial sonorant+C cluster undergoes epenthesis of *i*. The forms in (59b) make sense on the basis of the abstract forms *máʕad* ~ *mʕádt*, where the latter form undergoes vowel epenthesis and then the consonant *ʕ* deletes, lengthening the neighboring vowel. Before *ʕ* is deleted, it forms a cluster with the preceding sonorant, which triggers the rule of epenthesis.

Other mysteries are solved by positing this consonant in underlying forms. In (60), the first stem consonant appears to be a coronal obstruent. We have previously seen that when the stem-initial consonant is a coronal, obstruent vowel harmony is undone (*ní-tlob* 'I pray'), so (60) is exceptional on the surface. In addition, the prefix vowel is long, whereas otherwise it has always been short.

(60) nóodos   'I dive'   tóodos   'you dive'
      nóojob   'I please'   tóojob   'you please'
      nóotor   'I stumble'   tóotor   'you stumble'

These forms are unexceptional if we assume that the initial consonant of the stem is not *d, ǰ, t,* but the abstract consonant *ʕ,* thus /ʕdos/, /ʕjob/, /ʕtor/: *ʕ* is not a coronal obstruent, so it does not cause fronting of the prefix vowel.

Other examples provide crucial evidence regarding the nature of this abstract consonant. The data in (61) show a lengthened prefix vowel, which argues that the stems underlyingly have the initial abstract consonant that deletes and causes vowel lengthening: [náalaʔ] comes from /ni-ʕlaʔ/.

(61) náalaʔ   'I close'   táalaʔ   'you close'
      náasar   'I squeeze'   táasar   'you squeeze'
      náaraš   'I tickle'   táaraš   'you tickle'

In addition, the quality of the prefix vowel has changed from /i/ to [aa], even though in these examples the consonant which follows on the surface is a coronal. If the abstract consonant is a pharyngeal, then the vowel change is automatically explained by the Guttural Lowering rule.

We have considered stems where the first and second root consonants are the consonant *ʕ:* now we consider root-final *ʕ.* The data in (62) show examples of verbs whose true underlying imperfective stems are CCV.

(62) ná-ʔra   "I read"   ná-ʔra-w   'we read'
      ní-mla   'I fill'   ní-mla-w   'we fill'

The plural suffix /u/ becomes [w] after final *a*. Although the second consonant is a sonorant, the metathesis rule does not apply in *ná?raw* because no cluster of consonants containing a sonorant in the middle would result.

Now compare verbs with a medial sonorant where the final consonant is hypothesized /ʕ/. The singular columns do not have any striking irregularities which distinguish them from true CVCV stems.

(63) ní-sma   'I hear'   ni-síma-w   'we hear'
      ní-zra   'I sow'   ni-zíra-w   'we sow'
      ní-bla   'I swallow'   ni-bíla-w   'we swallow'
      ná-?la   'I earn'   na-?íla-w   'we earn'

The prefix vowel is unstressed and in an open syllable, which is found only in connection with metathesis: but metathesis is invoked only to avoid clusters with a medial sonorant, which would not exist in hypothetical *[níblau]. This is explained if the stem ends with /ʕ/. Thus /ni-smiʕ-u/ should surface as *nisímʕu*, by analogy to /ni-tlob-u/ → [nitólbu] 'we ask.' The consonant /ʕ/ induces lowering of the vowel *i*, and ʕ itself becomes *a*, giving the surface form.

A final set of examples provides additional motivation for assuming underlying ʕ. Participles are formed by giving the stem the shape CCVVC, selecting either *ii* or *uu*. As the data in (64) show, stems ending in the consonant /ʕ/ realize that consonant as [ħ] after long high vowels.

(64) ?átel   'he killed'   ?tíil   'killing'   ma?túul   'killed'
      ħátaf   'he grabbed'   ħtíif   'grabbing'   maħtúuf   'grabbed'
      fétaħ   'he opened'   ftíiħ   'opening'   miftúuħ   'opening'
      téfa   'he threw'   tfíiħ   'throwing'   mitfúuħ   'thrown'
      bála   'he swallowed' blíiħ   'swallowing'   miblúuħ   'swallowed'
      ?ála   'he earned'   ?líiħ   'earning'   ma?lúuħ   'earned'

These data provide evidence bearing on the underlying status of the abstract consonant, since it actually appears on the surface as a voiceless pharyngeal in (64). Although the forms of the participials [ftíiħ] and [tfíiħ] are analogous, we can tell from the inflected forms [fétaħ] 'he opened' versus [téfa] 'he threw' that the stems must end in different consonants. The most reasonable assumption is that the final consonant in the case of [téfa] is some pharyngeal other than [ħ], which would be [ʕ]. Thus, at least for verb stems ending in /ʕ/, the underlying pharyngeal status of the consonant can be seen directly, even though it is voiceless. Since the abstract consonant can be pinned down rather precisely in this context, we reason that in all other contexts, the abstract consonant must be /ʕ/ as well.

The crucial difference between these examples of abstractness and cases such as putative /ɨ/ and /ə/ in Hungarian, or deriving [ɔy] from /œ/ in English, is that there is strong language-internal evidence for the abstract distinction /uː/ vs. /oː/ in Yawelmani, or for the abstract consonant /ʕ/ in Maltese.

9.4 Grammar-external evidence for abstractness

Yawelmani and Maltese provide well-motivated abstract analyses, based on patterns of alternation in the grammar. We would still like to find grammar-external evidence that abstract analyses can be psychologically valid, analogous to the historical arguments which Kiparsky adduced from the history of Yiddish and other languages in support of the more surface-oriented approach to phonology.

9.4.1 Abstract analysis and historical change: Tera

One such argument for the psychological reality of abstract analysis comes from Tera. Newman 1968 provides a synchronic and diachronic argument for abstract phonology, where similar surface forms have different underlying forms.

The synchronic argument. Data in (65) illustrate a basic alternation. Some nouns ending in [i] in their citation forms lack that vowel in phrase medial contexts:

(65) na **seɗi**   'this is a snake'   na **seɗ** 6a   'this is not
                                                                   a snake'

     na **deβi**   'this is gum'   na **deb** 6a   'this is not
                                                                   gum'

     dala wa **wuɗi**   'Dala pointed'
     dala wa **wuɗ** koro 'Dala pointed at
                           the donkey'

     dala wa **mbuki**   'Dala threw'
     dala wa **mbuk** koro 'Dala threw at
                           the donkey'

Not all words ending in [i] prepausally engage in this alternation, as the data in (66) demonstrate:

(66) na **wuɗi** 'this is milk'   na **wuɗi** 6a 'this is not milk'
     a **saβi**   'this is a stick'   na **saβi** 6a 'this is not a stick'

Given a vowel ~ Ø alternation plus a set of stems which are invariantly *i*-final in (66), we might be led to surmise that the stems in (65) are C-final, and take an epenthetic vowel [i] phrase-finally. This can be ruled out given (67), where the stem ends in a consonant both phrase-medially and phrase-finally.

(67) na **ruf**   'this is a baboon'   na **ruf** 6a   'this is not a baboon'
     tin **zoβ** 'she is a slob'   tin **zoβ** 6a 'she is not a slob'
     na **boŋ**   'this is white'   na **boŋ** 6a   'this is not white'

A completely surface-oriented account where the underlying form must be one of the surface variants is untenable: the nouns in (65) have a variant with the vowel [i], but selecting /i/ for the underlying form fails to distinguish (65) from (66) which always have [i]; and the nouns of (65) also have a variant with no final vowel, but the nouns in (67) *always* lack a final vowel.

Other roots of the variable-final type give evidence that the problematic stems in (65) underlyingly end in schwa. The data in (68) provide monosyllabic words which have the shape *Ci* prepausally and *Cə* phrase medially.

(68)   dala wa ʄi   'Dala received'
       dala wa ʄə sule   'Dala received a shilling'
       dala wa ɗi   'Dala went'
       dala wa ɗə goma   'Dala went to the market'

These words contrast with ones that have invariant [i] in both contexts.

(69)   dala wa ʄi   'Dala paid'
       dala wa ʄi sule   'Dala paid a shilling'
       dala wa vi   'Dala roasted'
       dala wa vi ʄu   'Dala roasted meat'

For the stems in (68), an obvious nonabstract solution is available: the stems end with /ə/, and there is a rule turning schwa into [i] prepausally:

(70)   ə → i / _ ##

This applies in *dala wa ɗi* 'Dala went' from *dala wa ɗə*, but final schwa is unaffected in *dala wa ɗə goma* 'Dala went to the market.' The stems in (69) do not alternate since they end in the vowel /i/. This solution is nonabstract since the underlying form, /ɗə/, is one of the observed surface variants.

There are other stems with final [i] prepausally and [ə] phrase medially.

(71)   na pərsi   'this is a horse'
       na pərsə 6a   'this is not a horse'
       dala wa kədi   'Dala pulled'
       dala wa kədə koro   'Dala pulled a donkey'

These stems either have the shape [CVCCə] phrase-medially, or else [CVZə] where Z is a voiced consonant.

This gives the following groups of stems with an underlying final schwa:

(72)   *Stem shape*   *Medial*   *Prepausal*
       Cə   Cə   Ci
       CVCCə   CVCCə   CVCCi
       CVZə   CVZə   CVZi
       CVCə   CVC   CVCi

For most of these stems, postulating underlying schwa is quite concrete, since schwa actually surfaces in phrase-medial context. However,

in polysyllabic stems such as *deɓi* ~ *deɓ* with a single voiceless consonant before final schwa, the analysis is abstract because schwa is never
phonetically manifested in the morpheme. The decision that the vowel
in question is schwa is based on analogy with a known behavior of
schwa: it becomes [i] prepausally.

Our analysis requires a rule that deletes word-final phrase-medial
schwa providing the stem is polysyllabic and ends only in a single voiceless consonant.

(73)   ə → Ø / V   C   _ # ...
                   [−voice]

More evidence supports abstract schwa in certain words. The examples
in (74a) show that when a vowel -*a* marking definite nouns is suffixed to a
stem such as /pərsə/ which ends in schwa, schwa deletes, whereas underlying /i/ is not deleted. The data in (74b) show the same thing with the
imperative suffix /u/:

(74)   a.   pərsi ← /pərsə/   'horse'   pərs-a   'the horse'
            wudi   'milk'   wudi-a   'the milk'
       b.   vi   'to roast'   vi-u   'roast!'
            ɗi ← /ɗə/   'to go'   ɗ-u   'go!'
            kədi ← /kədə/   'to pull'   kəd-u   'pull!'
            mbuki ← /mbukə/   'to throw'   mbuk-u   'throw!'

This motivates a rule of prevocalic schwa deletion, which provides
another diagnostic that differentiates schwa from /i/.

(75)   ə → Ø / _ V

Although 'throw' only has the surface variants [mbuki] ~ [mbuk], it
behaves exactly like stems such as /kədə/ where schwa is phonetically realized, and acts unlike /vi/, in losing its final vowel before another vowel.
Finally, there is an allomorphic variation in the form of the adjective suffix -*kandi*, which shows up as -*kandi* when the stem ends in a vowel (*saɓir
tada-kandi* 'heavy stick') and as -*ndi* when the stem ends in a consonant
(*saɓir teɓer-ndi* 'straight stick'). The stem of the word for 'long' ends in
abstract schwa, since it alternates between final [i] (*saɓira kəri* 'the stick is
long') and medial Ø (*saɓira kər ɓa* 'the stick is not long'). Furthermore, the
stem selects the postvocalic variant of the adjective suffix (*saɓir kər-kandi*
'long stick'), even though on the surface the stem ends with a consonant
and not a vowel. This anomaly is explained by the hypothesis that the
stem does in fact end in a vowel, namely schwa. Thus multiple lines of
argument establish the presence of an abstract vowel schwa in a number
of words in the synchronic grammar of Tera.

The diachronic argument.   A recent sound change in Tera provides a
grammar-external test of the abstract hypothesis. In one dialect of Tera,

spoken in the town of Zambuk, a rule was added which palatalized *t*, *d* and *ɗ* to *č*, *ǰ* and *ǰ'* before *i*. The dialect of Tera spoken in Wuyo is representative of the rest of Tera, in retaining the original alveolars. Thus we find Wuyo *da*, Zambuk *da* 'one' with no palatalization, but Wuyo *di*, Zambuk *ǰi* 'to get up' where *d* palatalizes. There are synchronic alternations which further motivate this palatalization process in the contemporary grammar of the Zambuk dialect, so where the Wuyo dialect has *xat-a* 'my brother,' *xat-in* 'his brother,' the Zambuk dialect has *xat-a*, *xač-in*. In Wuyo one finds *wuɗi* 'milk' and in Zambuk one finds *wuǰ'i*, deriving from /wuɗi/ – that the final vowel is /i/ and not /ə/ is shown by the phrase medial form *wuɗi*.

While palatalization is active in the Zambuk dialect, it does not affect all surface sequences of alveolar plus [i], in particular it does not affect [i] which derives from schwa. In the Wuyo dialect 'to pull' is *kədi* before pause, *kədə* medially (cf. *dala wa kədə koro* 'Dala pulled a donkey'), and therefore we know that the stem is /kədə/. In the Zambuk dialect, the medial form is also *kədə*, showing that the stem ends in schwa in that dialect, and the prepausal form is *kədi*. Thus palatalization does not apply to the output of final schwa-fronting: the failure of palatalization to apply to this derived [di] sequence provides another diagnostic of the distinction between /i/ and [i] derived from /ə/.

Further confirming our hypothesis about abstract schwa, the stem /wuɗə/ 'to point' which appears in the Wuyo dialect as *wuɗi* prepausally and as *wuɗ* medially (*dala wa wuɗ koro* 'Dala pointed at a donkey') appears as *wuɗi* in the Zambuk dialect, without palatalization, as is regularly the case with the vowel [i] derived from /ə/. The fact that the innovative sound change of palatalization found in the Zambuk dialect is sensitive to the sometimes abstract distinction between underlying versus derived schwas, especially when the schwa never surfaces, supports the claim that abstract underlying forms can be psychologically real.

9.4.2 Abstract reanalysis in Kimatuumbi NC sequences

Other evidence for abstract phonology comes from a historical reanalysis of postnasal consonants in the Bantu language Kimatuumbi. Nouns in Bantu are composed of a prefix plus stem, and the prefix changes between singular and plural. For example, proto-Bantu *mu-ntu* 'person' contains the class 1 prefix *mu-* marking certain singular nouns, and the plural *ba-ntu* 'people' contains the class 2 prefix *ba-*. Different nouns take different noun-class prefixes (following the tradition of historical linguistics, reconstructed forms are marked with an asterisk).

(76)	Proto-Bantu sg	Class	Proto-Bantu pl	Class	
	*mʊ-ntʊ	1	*ba-ntʊ	2	'person'
	*mʊ-gʊnda	3	*mɪ-gʊnda	4	'field'
	*li-tako	5	*ma-tako	6	'buttock'
	*m-paka	9	*dim-paka	10	'cat'
	*lʊ-badu	11	*dim-badu	10	'rib'

A postnasal voicing rule was added in the proto-Rufiji-Ruvuma sub-group of Bantu (a subgroup which includes Kimatuumbi), so that original *mpaka* 'cat' came to be pronounced *mbaka* in this subgroup.

(77) | Proto-Bantu | Kimatuumbi | |
|---|---|---|
| | *mpaka | mbaka | 'cat' |
| | *ŋkaŋga | ŋgaaŋga | 'guinea fowl' |
| | *ntembo | ndeembo | 'elephant' |
| | *muntʊ | muundu | 'person' |
| | *ŋkʊŋgʊnɪ | ŋguuŋguni | 'bedbug' |
| cf. | *mbabada | mbabala | 'bushbuck' |
| | *mbʊdị | mbwi | 'goat' |
| | *mbʊa | mbwa | 'dog' |

Another inconsequential change is that the class 10 prefix, originally *din-*, lost *di*, so the class 10 prefix became completely homophonous with the class 9 prefix.

In the Nkongo dialect of Kimatuumbi, there was a change in the morphological system so that nouns which were originally assigned to classes 9–10 now form their plurals in class 6, with the prefix *ma-*. Earlier *ŋaambo* 'snake ~ snakes' now has the forms *ŋáambo* 'snake' / *ma-ŋáambo* 'snakes.'

Given surface [mbwa] 'dog' (proto-Bantu *m-bʊa*) originally in classes 9–10, the concrete analysis is that the underlying form in proto-Rufiji is /m-bwa/. It was always pronounced as [mbwa], since the root was always preceded by a nasal prefix. The absence of alternations in the phonetic realization of the initial consonant would give reason to think that phonetic [b] derives from underlying /b/. By the same reasoning, we predict that earlier *mpaka* 'cat' is reanalyzed as /b/, once the word came to be pronounced as *mbaka* in all contexts: compare Yiddish *gelt*.

The restructuring of the morphological system of Nkongo Kimatuumbi where the original class pairing 9–10 is reanalyzed as 9–6 allows us to test this prediction, since nouns with their singulars in class 9 no longer have a nasal final prefix in all forms; the plural has the prefix *ma-*. As the following data show, the concrete approach is wrong.

(78) | Proto-Bantu | Kimatuumbi sg | Original pl | Innovative pl | |
|---|---|---|---|---|
| *m-pembe | m-beembe | m-beembe | ma-peembe | 'horn' |
| *ŋ-kʊkʊ | ŋ-guku | ŋ-gʊkʊ | ma-kuku | 'chicken' |
| *m-bʊa | m-bwa | m-bwa | ma-pwa | 'dog' |
| *m-babada | m-babala | m-babala | ma-pabala | 'bushbuck' |
| *m-bʊdi | m-bwi | m-bwi | ma-pwi | 'goat' |
| *m-baŋgo | m-baaŋgo | m-baaŋgo | ma-paaŋgo | 'warthog' |
| *m-bʊtʊka | m-bʊtʊka | m-bʊtʊka | ma-pʊtʊka | 'antelope' |

While the distinction /mp/ ~ /mb/ was neutralized, it was neutralized in favor of a phonetically more abstract consonant /p/ rather than the concrete consonant /b/.

This reanalysis did not affect all nouns which had a singular or plural in classes 9–10; it affected only nouns which originally had both their singulars and plurals in this class, i.e. only those nouns lacking alternation. Nouns with a singular in class 11 and a plural in class 10 preserve the original voicing of the consonant.

(79)	*Proto-Bantu*	*Kimatuumbi sg*	*Kimatuumbi pl*	
	*m-badu	lu-bau	m-bau	'rib'
	*n-godi	lu-goi	ŋ-goi	'rope'
	*n-dɪmi	lu-lɪmi	n-dɪmi	'tongue'
	*ŋ-kʊŋgʊnɪ	lu-kuuŋguni	ŋ-guuŋguni	'bedbug'
	*n-tondʊa	lu-toondwa	n-doondwa	'star'

A word such as 'rib' always had a morphological variant which transparently revealed the underlying consonant, so the contrast between /n-toondwa/ → [ndoondwa] and /n-goi/ → [ŋgoi] was made obvious by the singulars [lu-toondwa] and [lu-goi].

While it is totally expected that there should be a neutralization of *mp and *mb in words like *mbaka, mbwa* – there would have been no evidence to support a distinction between surface [mb] deriving from /mb/ versus [mb] deriving from /mp/ – surprisingly from the viewpoint of concrete phonology, the direction of neutralization where [mb] is reanalyzed as /mp/ is unexpected. One explanation for this surprising reanalysis regards the question of markedness of different consonants. Given a choice between underlying /m+b/ and /m+p/, where either choice would independently result in [mb], one can make a phonetically conservative choice and assume /m+b/, or make a choice which selects a less marked consonant, i.e. /m+p/. In this case, it is evident that the less marked choice is selected where the choice of consonants is empirically arbitrary.

Such examples illustrating phonetically concrete versus abstract reanalyses motivated by considerations such as markedness are not well enough studied that we can explain why language change works one way in some cases, and another way in other cases. In the case of Yiddish *avek* from historically prior *aveg*, there would be no advantage at all in assuming underlying /aveg/, from the perspective of markedness or phonetic conservatism.

9.4.3 Language games and Bedouin Arabic

Language games can also provide evidence for the mental reality of underlying representations. Their relevance is that language game modifications are not always performed on the surface form, so by modifying the phonetic environment in which segments appear in the language, games may cause rules to apply when they would not normally (providing evidence for the reality of the phonological process), or prevent a rule from applying when it normally would (revealing the abstract underlying form). An example of such evidence comes from Bedouin Arabic spoken in Saudi Arabia, discussed by Al-Mozainy 1981. A number of verbs have the underlying form /CaCaC/, but this analysis is abstract in that, for these verbs, the first vowel sequence is never found on the surface, and the root surfaces as [CiCaC].

9.4.3.1 Regular language phonology. We begin by motivating aspects of the phonology of the language, especially underlying representations, using regular language data. Verb stems may have different underlying vowels, but the passive is formed by systematically replacing all underlying vowels with /i/. Underlying /i/ deletes in an open syllable, as shown by the following data:

(80)

3sg masc	3sg fem	1sg	
ħzim	ħizm-at	ħzim-t	'be tied'
ħfir	ħifr-at	ħfir-t	'be dug'
šrib	širb-at	šrib-t	'be drunk'
ʕzim	ʕizm-at	ʕzim-t	'be invited'
lbis	libs-at	lbis-t	'be worn'

Taking underlying /ħizim/ and /ħizim-t/ as examples, the vowel /i/ in the first syllable is in an open syllable, so the rule of high-vowel deletion applies, giving [ħzim] and [hzimt]. In the case of /ħizim-at/, both vowels *i* are in an open syllable: the second *i* deletes, which makes the first syllable closed, so the first vowel does not delete resulting in [ħizmat]. The following rule is motivated by (80).

(81) i → Ø / _ CV   *high-vowel deletion*

Now we consider another class of nonpassive verbs, where the underlying stem shape is CaCiC. In these stems, the second vowel shows up as *i* when there is no vowel after the stem. The first vowel of the stem alternates between [i] and [a], surfacing as [i] when the second vowel appears as [i], otherwise surfacing as [a]. Examples of verbs with this vocalic pattern are seen in (82):

(82)

3sg masc	3sg fem	1sg	
simiʕ	samʕ-at	simiʕ-t	'hear'
libis	labs-at	libis-t	'wear'
širib	šarb-at	širib-t	'drink'
yibis	yabs-at	yibis-t	'become dry'
silim	salm-at	silim-t	'save'
liʕib	laʕb-at	liʕib-t	'play'
ħilim	ħalm-at	ħilim-t	'dream'

In underlying /samiʕ-at/, the vowel /i/ is in an open syllable so it deletes, giving [samʕat]. In /samiʕ/ and /samiʕ-t/, final /i/ does not delete since it is not in an open syllable, and /a/ assimilates to [i] before [i], by the following harmony rule:

(83) a → i / _ C i

Following Semitic transcription practices, pharyngealized coronals are indicated with a dot underneath the consonant.

This creates a surface [i] in an open syllable which does not undergo deletion.

Now we turn to stems with the underlying shape /CaCaC/. In a number of such verbs this representation is uncontroversial since that is how it surfaces.

(84)

3sg masc	3sg fem	1sg	
gaʕad	gʕad-at	gaʕad-t	'sit'
waʕad	wʕad-at	waʕad-t	'promise'
ṭaʕan	ṭʕan-at	ṭaʕan-t	'stab'
saħab	sħab-at	saħab-t	'pull'
ṭaħan	ṭħan-at	ṭaħan-t	'grind'
daxal	dxal-at	daxal-t	'enter'
naxal	nxal-at	naxal-t	'sift'

Examples such as [gʕadat] from /gaʕad-at/ illustrate the application of another rule, one deleting /a/ when followed by CVCV.

(85)   a → Ø / _ CVCV

An important fact about the stems in (84) is that the second consonant is a guttural (x, γ, ħ, h, ʕ or ʔ). There is a dissimilative process in the language turning /a/ into [i] in an open syllable if the next vowel is /a/, providing that the vowel is neither preceded nor followed by a guttural consonant. In the above examples, the consonant in the middle of the stem is a guttural, so neither the first nor the second vowels can undergo the dissimilative raising rule. Now consider the data in (86), where the first consonant is a guttural but the second is not.

(86)

3sg masc	3sg fem	1sg	
ʕazam	ʕzim-at	ʕazam-t	'invite'
ħazam	ħzim-at	ħazam-t	'tie'
hakam	hkim-at	hakam-t	'rule'

This verbal restriction on the consonant next to the target vowel goes beyond what is allowed in the version of the formal theory presented here. How such conditions are to be incorporated into an analysis has been the subject of debate.

Here the first vowel of the stem cannot become [i] because of the preceding consonant, but the second vowel does dissimilate to [i] when followed by /a/, and thus /ʕazam-at/ becomes [ʕzimat] (with deletion of the first vowel by (85)). This rule is separate from the harmony rule that turns /a/ into [i] before [i], because harmony applies irrespective of the flanking consonants, cf. [ħilim] 'he dreamt.'

(87)   a → i / _ C a   (target is not adjacent to a guttural consonant)

In [ʕazam] and [ʕazamt], there is no dissimilation because the first consonant is guttural, which prevents the following /a/ from undergoing dissimilation.

Examples in (88) show the same restriction on dissimilation of the second vowel /a/, which does not become [i] when the last consonant is a guttural.

(88) *3sg masc*   *3sg fem*   *1sg*
    difaʕ   dfaʕ-at   difaʕ-t   'push'
    ṛikaʕ   ṛkaʕ-at   ṛikaʕ-t   'bend'
    xadaʕ   xdaʕ-at   xadaʕ-t   'cheat'

Another consonantal property inhibiting dissimilation is a coronal sonorant. In this case, if the two vowels are separated by any of /n, r, l/, there is no dissimilation. In the examples of (89), the first vowel is prevented from dissimilating because it is preceded by a guttural. In addition, the second stem vowel is prevented from dissimilating because it is separated from suffixal /a/ by a coronal sonorant. Therefore, both underlying stem vowels remain unchanged.

(89) *3sg masc*   *3sg fem*   *1sg*
    ħafar   ħfar-at   ħafar-t   'dig'
    ħamal   ħmal-at   ħamal-t   'carry'
    ɣasal   ɣsal-at   ɣasal-t   'wash'

In the examples of (90), the first vowel is followed by a consonant other than a coronal sonorant, and is neither preceded nor followed by a guttural, so it dissimilates to [i]. The second vowel is followed by a coronal sonorant, so there is no dissimilation in the second syllable.

(90) *3sg masc*   *3sg fem*   *1sg*
    nizal   nzal-at   nizal-t   'get down'
    sikan   skan-at   sikan-t   'occupy'
    kisar   ksar-at   kisar-t   'break'
    difan   dfan-at   difan-t   'bury'
    nital   ntal-at   nital-t   'steal'
    šitar   štar-at   šitar-t   'divide'

In (91) we find verbs with a coronal sonorant as the second consonant. The second vowel /a/ dissimilates before *a*, since the intervening consonant is neither guttural nor a coronal sonorant. The preceding coronal sonorant has no effect on dissimilation, since unlike the effect of gutturals, coronal sonorants only have an effect if they stand after the target vowel.

(91) *3sg masc*   *3sg fem*   *1sg*
    jalas   jlis-at   jalas-t   'sit'
    gaṛaṣ   gṛiṣ-at   gaṛaṣ-t   'sting'
    gaṛaṭ   gṛiṭ-at   gaṛaṭ-t   'throw'
    sarag   srig-at   sarag-t   'steal'
    balas   blis-at   balas-t   'denounce'
    šanag   šnig-at   šanag-t   'hang'
    daras   dris-at   daras-t   'study'

Finally, verbs with no gutturals or coronal sonorants are given in (92).

(92) | 3sg masc | 3sg fem | 1sg | |
|---|---|---|---|
| kitab | ktib-at | kitab-t | 'write' |
| misak | msik-at | misak-t | 'catch' |
| sikat | skit-at | sikat-t | 'stop talking' |
| nitaf | ntif-at | nitaf-t | 'pluck' |
| gisam | gsim-at | gisam-t | 'divide' |
| giðab | gðib-at | giðab-t | 'catch' |
| nikas | nkis-at | nikas-t | 'retain' |

By the deletion rule (85), underlying /katabat/ becomes *ktabat*, which becomes [ktibat] by dissimilation. In /katab-t/, since the first vowel is not followed by CVCV it cannot elide, and it dissimilates to [i] before [a] in the second syllable.

The vowel /a/ in the second syllable of verbs like [kitab] is only mildly abstract, since it does surface as [a] as long as the syllable is not open. The initial /a/, the syllable on the other hand, is fully abstract since there is no context in this verb where the underlying /a/ appears as such in these verbs, and instead the vowel only appears as [i]. However, we know that the initial vowel cannot be /i/, since if it were, that vowel would delete in an open syllable – contrast active [kitab] and [kitabt] from /katab/ and /katab-t/, with the passives [ktib] and [ktibt] from /kitib/ and /kitib-t/.

The occurrence of initial nondeleting [i] in an open syllable is entirely predictable. It appears when neither the first nor second stem consonant is a guttural, and when the second stem consonant is not a coronal sonorant. This nondeleting [a] is thus in complementary distribution with surface [a] (which nonabstractly derives from underlying /a/), which only appears when one of the first two consonants is a guttural or the second consonant is a coronal sonorant.

Hence there is strong language-internal motivation for claiming that the initial vowel of stems such as [kitab] is underlyingly /a/, and is subject to dissimilation to [i] or deletion.

9.4.3.2 Language game evidence. There is a language game used by speakers of Arabic which provides independent evidence for the mental reality of these rules and underlying representations. The rule for the language game is very simple: permute the order of consonants within the root. Now let us consider the various phonetic results of permutation on the verb forms ħazam 'he tied' and ħzim-at 'she tied.' In ħazam, the first vowel does not dissimilate because of the preceding guttural; in ħzimat the second stem vowel dissimilates because it is neither preceded nor followed by a gutural, and it is not followed by a coronal sonorant.

(93) | 'he tied' | 'she tied' | |
|---|---|---|
| ħamaz | ħmizat | ~ |
| zaħam | zħamat | ~ |
| zimaħ | zmaħat | |

In the permuted forms ħamaz and ħmizat, where the second and third consonants have exchanged place, the vocalic pattern remains the same because the transposition has not crucially changed the consonantal environment.

Now consider the forms *zimaħ* ~ *zmaħat*. This pattern of transposition has two effects on the vowel pattern. First, because the first consonant is now not a guttural, the dissimilation rule can apply in the first syllable, demonstrating the reality of the dissimilation rule. Second, because the final consonant is now a guttural, the dissimilation rule cannot apply in the second syllable, demonstrating the reality of the blocking condition on dissimilation. Finally, in the case of *zaħam* ~ *zħamat*, because the medial consonant is a guttural, neither vowel can dissimilate.

A crucial example, in terms of testing the validity of the proposed /CaCaC/ underlying form for surface [CiCaC] stems, is a stem such as /dafaʕ/ 'push,' which surfaces as [difaʕ]. Such a supposed underlying representation is abstract, since the vowel of the first syllable always surfaces as [i] or Ø, cf. *difaʕ* 'he pushed,' *dfaʕat* 'she pushed,' never as *a*. This stem contains a final pharyngeal consonant, and therefore movement of that consonant to first or second position will put the first vowel in contact with a pharyngeal. This should then block dissimilation, and will directly reveal the hypothesized underlying vowel to be [a].

(94) 'he pushed'   'she pushed'
    fidaʕ   fdaʕat   ~
    daʕaf   dʕafat   ~
    ʕadaf   ʕdifat   ~
    ʕafad   ʕfidat

The fact that this vowel actually surfaces as [a] under the circumstances predicted by the abstract hypothesis gives strong support to the claim for an abstract representation of such stems as having the vowel pattern /CaCaC/.

9.5 How abstract *is* phonology?

On the one hand we have argued for abstract analyses of Kimatuumbi, Yawelmani, Maltese and other languages; but we have argued against abstract analyses of English. The reason for this apparently inconsistent view of abstractness is that abstractness per se is not the issue; the proper question to be focusing on is what motivates an analysis. Thus we conclude that the formal theory of grammar imposes no constraints on the relation between underlying and surface forms, though the theory does state what kinds of elements can exist in underlying representations: phonetically interpretable combinations of features, i.e. segments.

This does not mean that highly abstract underlying representations can be gratuitously assumed. Underlying representations require motivation: they must be acquired by children learning the language, and the best assumption to make is that in lieu of evidence to the contrary, underlying and surface forms are identical. The question that needs further investigation is, what constitutes valid "evidence to the contrary"? Phonological alternations in the shape of a morpheme provide very powerful evidence for abstractness. It remains an open question whether other considerations are also valid in constructing an underlying form.

Although we have focused on the relation between underlying and surface forms, the larger question which this debate raises is, what counts as valid evidence for testing a phonological theory. It has proven extremely difficult to resolve questions about the psychological reality of theorized linguistic constructs. Two approaches, both valid, have been taken. One is the "domain-internal" approach, where formal constraints are proposed to the effect that (for example) underlying forms should be a subpart of an actually pronounced word in the language, or underlying forms should only contain segments actually pronounced in the language. We cannot show that these claims are literally "wrong": what we can do is show that such a position renders us incapable of capturing important generalizations about the phonologies of Maltese and Yawelmani, for example.

The other approach, the "domain-external" approach, seeks evidence from outside the domain of synchronic phonological grammars themselves, in an attempt to find independent evidence that answers the question of what is actually in the mind of the speaker. Any number of such approaches can be imagined – neurosurgery, psycholinguistic testing, language games, historical change, the study of language acquisition, and so on. Such evidence is extremely hard to find in the first place: virtually all relevant experimental work is conducted on a tiny handful of commonly spoken languages, which typically do not have internally well-motivated abstractness. Additionally, the experimental methodology must be critically evaluated, which is usually very difficult to do outside of one's own discipline. Finally the evidence must be interpreted against a general theory of, for example, child developmental psychology. The question of how to empirically validate theory-internal hypotheses remains very much an open question in phonology, as it is in all scientific domains.

Exercises

1 Slovak

The focus of this problem is the underlying representation of diphthongs. Discuss the underlying status of diphthongs in Slovak, based on these data. Nouns in Slovak come in three genders, which determines what suffix if any is used in the nominative singular: masculines have no suffix, feminines have -*a*, and neuters have -*o*.

A. There is a process of lengthening which takes place in certain morphological contexts, including the genitive plural and the diminutive.

Nom sg	Gen pl	
lipa	li:p	'linden tree'
muxa	mu:x	'fly'
lopata	lopa:t	'shovel'
sr̥na	sr̥:n	'deer'

žena	žien	'woman'
kazeta	kaziet	'box'
hora	huor	'forest'
sirota	siruot	'orphan'
pæta	piat	'heel'
mæta	miat	'mint'
kopito	kopi:t	'hoof'
bruxo	bru:x	'belly'
blato	bla:t	'mud'
salto	sa:lt	'somersault'
embargo	emba:rg	'embargo'
yabḷko	yabḷ:k	'apple'
koleso	kolies	'wheel'
lono	luon	'lap'
hovædo	hoviad	'beast'
vla:da	vla:ɟ	'government'
blu:za	blu:z	'blouse'
dla:to	dla:t	'chisel'
vi:no	vi:n	'vine'
čiara	čiar	'line'
hniezdo	hniezd	'nest'

noun	*diminutive*	
hrad	hra:dok	'castle'
list	li:stok	'leaf'
xḷp	xḷ:pok	'hair'
kvet	kvietok	'flower'
hovædo	hoviadok	'beast'

B. There is also a shortening rule that applies in certain morphological contexts, including the imperfective of verbs and the comparative of adjectives.

Perfective	*Imperfective*	
odli:sitʸ	odlisovatʸ	'to distinguish'
ku:pitʸ	kupovatʸ	'to buy'
ohla:sitʸ	ohlasovatʸ	'to announce'
predḷ:žitʸ	predḷzovatʸ	'to extend'
oblietatʸ	obletovatʸ	'to fly around'
uviazatʸ	uvæzovatʸ	'to bind'

adjective	*comparative*	
bli:ski	blišši:	'near'
u:ski	ušši:	'narrow'
kra:tki	kratši:	'short'
bieli	belši:	'white'
rietki	retši:	'rare'

C. There is an alternation in the form of case suffixes which is governed by properties of the stem which precedes

Nom sg	*Gen sg*	*Nom pl*	*Dat pl*	*Loc pl*	
mesto	mesta	mesta:	mesta:m	mesta:x	'town'
blato	blata	blata:	blata:m	blata:x	'mud'

hovædo	hovæda	hovæda:	hovæda:m	hovæda:x	'town'
pi:smeno	pi:smena	pi:smena:	pi:smena:m	pi:smena:x	'letter'
za:meno	za:mena	za:mena:	za:mena:m	za:mena:x	'pronoun'
dla:to	dla:ta	dla:ta	dla:tam	dla:tax	'town'
vi:no	vi:na	vi:na	vi:nam	vi:nax	'wine'
hniezdo	hniezda	hniezda	hniezdam	hniezdax	'nest'

D. The rule that explains the alternations in C also explains why a rule motivated by the data in A seems not to have applied.

Nom sg	Gen pl	
za:hrada	za:hrad	'garden'
ni:žina	ni:žin	'hollow'
za:toka	za:tok	'inlet'
pi:smeno	pi:smen	'letter'
za:meno	za:men	'pronoun'
liečivo	liečiv	'drug'

E. Some stems underlyingly end with consonant clusters, and undergo a
process of vowel epenthesis that eliminates certain kinds of consonant
clusters.

Nom sg	Gen pl		
ikra	ikier	'roe'	(cf. also *ikernati*: 'abounding in roe')
ihla	ihiel	'needle'	
dogma	dogiem	'dogma'	
sosna	sosien	'pine tree'	
bedro	bedier	'hip'	
radlo	radiel	'plow'	
hradba	hradieb	'rampart'	
doska	dosiek	'board'	
kri:dlo	kri:del	'wing'	
či:slo	či:sel	'number'	
pa:smo	pa:sem	'zone'	
vla:kno	vla:ken	'fiber'	
pla:tno	pla:ten	'linen'	

Further reading

Chomsky and Halle 1968; Hudson 1974; Hyman 1970; Kiparsky 1968; Sapir 1933.

10 Nonlinear representations

PREVIEW

KEY TERMS

autosegmental phonology

tone stability

floating tone

across-the-board effects

feature geometry

This final chapter introduces an alternative model, the non-linear theory, of how sounds are represented. The purpose of this chapter is to show how troublesome facts can lead to a reconceptualization of a domain which seemed to be understood, leading to an even better understanding of the nature of language sounds. This will also help you to understand how and why theories change.

The theoretical model we have been assuming – known as the linear theory of representation – was quite successful in explaining a number of facts about sound systems. A defining characteristic of the theory is the view that segments are matrices of feature values, where every segment has a specification for each of the two dozen distinctive features. There was, however, one phonological realm which the theory had largely ignored, and that was tone.

10.1 The autosegmental theory of tone: the beginnings of a change

There were a few proposals regarding tone features, but they did not reach the degree of acceptance that those for other features reached. One of the primary problems was how to represent contour tones such as rising and falling.

10.1.1 The problem of contours

One possibility is that contour tones are simply H (high) or L (low) tones with a positive specification for a feature "contour." We could take the pitch at the beginning of a vowel as representing the "basic" tone value, and if the pitch changes from that point (either up or down), then the vowel is [+contour]. This gives us the following representations of H, L, R (rising) and F (falling) tones.

(1)   H = [+H,−contour]   R = [−H,+contour]
      L = [−H,−countour]   F = [+H,+contour]

Such a theory is ultimately inadequate since it ignores tone levels (Mid, Superlow, Superhigh), but we can pursue this theory to see what progress can be made. Perhaps if this theory works, it can be modified to account for other tone levels.

   An essential test of a theory of features is how it accounts for phonological processes. This theory of tone makes predictions: it predicts that R and F will be a natural class because they are [+contour], and it predicts that L and R are a natural class because they are [−H]. As it happens, some relevant typological work had been done on natural tone rules, most notably Hyman and Schuh (1974). Such research has shown that the following are fairly common tonal processes.

(2)   a. H → R / {L,F} __   b. L → F /{H,R} __
      c. H → F / __ {L,R}   d. L → R / __ {H,F}

The problem is that the "[±contour]" theory does not provide any natural way to express all of these processes. The last two processes can be formulated:

(3)   c. [+H] → [+contour] / _ [−H]
     d. [−H] → [+contour] / _ [+H]

However, the first two processes cannot be formalized, since {L,F} or {H,R} are not a definable class using this theory.

This theory also predicts the following rules, which are simply the rules in (3) with the conditioning environment on the left rather than the right:

(4)   *[+H] → [+contour] / [−H] _   (H → F / {L,R} _)
     *[−H] → [+contour] / [+H] _   (L → R / {H,F} _)

Unlike the common rules in (2), such rules are totally nonexistent in the languages of the world. The "[±contour]" theory thus makes a bad prediction, that certain processes should exist when they do not, and in addition the theory provides no way to express certain very natural processes, in particular processes where the conditioning environment is on the left. Finally, even for the two processes which the theory can formalize in (3), there is an unexplained element of arbitrariness – why should an H tone become a falling tone before [−H]? Those processes are formally just as simple to express as the rules in (5), and should therefore be found as commonly as the former set of rules, but in fact this latter set of rules is completely unattested.

(5)   c. [+H] → [+contour] / _ [+H]   (H → F / _ {H,F})
     d. [−H] → [+contour] / _ [−H]   (L → R / _ {L,R})

It is obvious that this theory of tone is wrong, but what is the alternative? There was a long-standing intuition that contour tones were in some sense composite tones, so that a rise was simply a combination of an L followed by an H, and a fall is a combination of an H followed by an L; falling and rising pitch is simply the continuous transition between the higher and lower pitch levels that H and L define. An example of the kind of phonological patterns which were responsible for this intuition is the pattern of tone changes that result from merging vowels between words in Yekhee, illustrated below.

(6)   ídzé élà → ídzélà   'three axes'
     èké élà → èkélà   'three rams'
     údzé òkpá → údzôkpá   'one axe'
     òké òkpá → òkôkpá   'one ram'
     ówà ówà → ówŏwà   'every house'

The combination of H+L results in a falling tone, and L+H results in a rising tone. How can the intuition that fall is H+L and rise is L+H be expressed in the theory?

There is little problem in doing this for contour tones on long vowels, since long vowels can be represented as a sequence of identical vowels, so treating a long rising tone as being a sequence of tones is easy.

(7) ă: = àá = $\begin{bmatrix} +\text{syllabic} \\ +\text{back} \\ -\text{round} \\ -\text{H-tone} \end{bmatrix} \begin{bmatrix} +\text{syllabic} \\ +\text{back} \\ -\text{round} \\ +\text{H-tone} \end{bmatrix}$

The problem is short contour tones.

10.1.2 Autosegmental contours

A resolution of this problem was set forth in Goldsmith (1976), who proposed that tones be given an autonomous representation from the rest of
the segment, so that regular segments would be represented at one level
and tones would be an another level, with the two levels of representation
being synchronized via association lines. This theory, known as autosegmental phonology, thus posited representations such as those in (8).

(8) á =   H   ă =   L H   â =   H L
           | \ /   \ /
           a   a   a

The representation of [á] simply says that at the same time that the rest of
the vocal tract is in the configuration for the vowel [a], the vocal folds
should be vibrating at a high rate as befits an H tone. The representation
for [ă] on the other hand says that during the time that the rest of the
vocal tract is producing the short vowel [a], the larynx should start vibrating slowly (produce an L tone) and change to a higher rate of vibration to
match that specified for an H tone – this produces the smooth increase
in pitch which we hear as a rising tone. The representation of [â] simply
reverses the order of the tonal specifications.

    The view which autosegmental phonology takes of rules is different
from that taken in the classical segmental theory. Rather than viewing the
processes in (2) as being random changes in feature values, autosegmental
theory views these operations as being adjustments in the temporal relations between the segmental tier and the tonal tier. Thus the change in (2a)
where H becomes rising after L and fall can be expressed as (9).

(9) (H) L   H   (H) L   H
        \ | | →   \ \ |
          V   V   V   V

By simply adding an association between the L tone element on the left and
the vowel which stands to the right, we are able to express this tonal change,
without actually changing the intrinsic feature content of the string: we
change only the timing relation between tones and vowels. This is notated as
in (10), where the dashed association line means "insert an association line."

(10)   L   H
       | ·····. |
       V   V

Two other notational conventions are needed to understand the formulation of autosegmental rules. First, the deletion of an association line is indicated by crossing out the line:

(11)   H
       |
       ⊬
       V

Second, an element (tone or vowel) which has no corresponding association on the other tier (vowel or tone) is indicated with the mark ['], thus, V' indicates a toneless vowel and H' indicates an H not linked to a vowel.

One striking advantage of the autosegmental model is that it allows us to express this common tonal process in a very simple way. The theory also allows each of the remaining processes in (2) to be expressed equally simply – in fact, essentially identically, as involving an expansion of the temporal domain of a tone either to the left or to the right.

(12)   H   L   (=(2b))   H L   (=(2c))   L   H (= (2d))
                              | |
       V   V   V V   V   V

The problem of the natural classes formed by contour tones and level tones was particularly vexing for the linear theory. Most striking was the fact that what constitutes a natural class for contour tones depends on the linear order of the target and conditioning tones. If the conditioning tones stand on the left, then the natural classes observed are {L,F} and {H,R}, and if the conditioning tones stand on the right, then the natural groupings are {L,R} and {H,F}. In all other cases, the groupings of elements into natural classes are independent of whether the target is to the right or the left of the trigger. The autosegmental representation of contour tones thus provides a very natural explanation of what is otherwise a quite bizarre quirk in the concept "natural class."

The autosegmental model also provides a principled explanation for the nonexistence of rules such as (4), i.e. the rules $H \rightarrow F / \{L,R\}$ _ and $L \rightarrow R / \{H,F\}$ _. The change of H to F after L would involve not just an adjustment in the temporal organization of an L–H sequence, but would necessitate the insertion of a separate L to the right of the H tone, which would have no connection with the preceding L; the change of H to F after R is even worse in that the change involves insertion of L when H is remotely preceded by a L. Thus, the closest that one could come to formalizing such a rule in the autosegmental approach would be as in (13).

(13)   L (H) H   →   L (H) H L
         \/ | \/   \/
         V   V   V   V

As we will discuss in this chapter, autosegmental theory resulted in a considerable reconceptualization of phonological processes, and allowed the theory of rules to be considerably constrained so that such rules which perform arbitrary actions in arbitrary contexts simply were rendered formally impossible to state.

In addition to the fact that the theory provides a much-needed account of contour tones, quite a number of other arguments can be given for the autosegmental theory of tone. The essential claim of the theory is that there is not a one-to-one relation between the number of tones in an utterance and the number of vowels: a single tone can be associated with multiple vowels, or a single vowel can have multiple tones. Moreover, an operation on one tier, such as the deletion of a vowel, does not entail a corresponding deletion on the other tier. We will look at a number of arguments for the autonomy of tones and the vowels which phonetically bear them in the following sections.

10.1.3 Tone preservation

One very common property exhibited by tones is stability, where the deletion of a vowel does not result in the deletion of the tone born by the vowel. Very commonly, the tone of a deleted vowel is transferred to the neighboring vowel, often resulting in a contour tone. We have seen an example of this phenomenon in Yekhee, where the combination of an L vowel plus H vowel results in a rising-toned vowel, and H+L gives a falling-toned vowel.

(14)   òké òkpá → òkôkpá   'one ram'
       ówà ówà → ówǒwà   'every house'

In the autosegmental theory, deletion of a vowel does not directly affect the tone which was associated with it, and as a result, after deletion of the vowel the tone simply remains on the tonal tier with no association with the segmental tier – such an unassociated tone is referred to as a floating tone.

(15)   L H L   H   LH L   H   H   L H L   H LH   L
       | | | | | | | | | | | | | |
       o ke okp a   →   o ko kp a   o w a o w a   →   o wo w a

One of the principles proposed in this theory is that all vowels must (eventually) bear some tone, and all tones must be born by some vowel – this condition is known as the Well-formedness Condition. Accordingly, the unassociated tones which resulted from the deletion of a vowel would then be associated with the following vowel, resulting in a falling or rising tone.

(16)   LH L   H   H LH   L
       | \| | | \| |
       o k o kp a   o w o w a

The combination of two like-toned vowels, as in the case of èké élà → èkélà 'three rams,' brings out another principle of the theory. By the operation of vowel deletion and reassociation of the floating tone, one would expect the following representation.

(17)
```
L H H L
|  \/  |
e k e l a
```

This would not be distinct from the simple tone melody LHL: (17) says that the vowel *e* should be produced at high pitch at the beginning and at the end, with no other pitches being produced. The Twin Sister Convention was proposed as a constraint on the theory, so that such a phonetically indistinguishable representation is formally disallowed.

(18)   *Twin Sister Convention*
Adjacent identical tones on one vowel are automatically simplified

Another illustration of the autosegmental treatment of tone preservation comes from Lomongo. When vowels are brought together, either directly in the underlying representation or as the result of deleting certain consonants, the vowel sequence is reduced to a single vowel which preserves all of the component tones of the two vowels. This can result not just in the simple contours R and F, but also in the complex three-tone contours fall–rise (FR) and rise–fall (RF).

(19)

H+H → H	bètámbá béfé	→	bètámbéfé	'two trees'
L+L → L	là ìtókò	→	lìtókò	'with the fork'
H+L → F	mpùlú ìné	→	mpùjwînέ	'these birds'
L+H → R	là bɔ́nà	→	lɔ̌nà	'with the baby'
H+F → F	sóngóló ɔ̂tswὲ	→	sóngólɔ̂tswὲ	'may S. enter'
H+R → FR	bàlóngá bǎkáé	→	bàlóngǎ káé	'his blood'
L+F → RF	fàkàlà ɔ̂tswà	→	fàkàlɔ̌ tswà	'F. comes in'
L+R → R	bǎnkò bǎmɔ̌	→	bǎnkǎmɔ̌	'those others'
R+F → RF	ɔ̌mɔ̌ êmbè	→	ɔ̌mě mbè	'may someone else sing'

The derivation of the last example illustrates how the autosegmental theory explains the pattern elegantly. In this case, the first vowel deletes, causing its two tones to become floating. Those tones are associated with the following vowel by the Well-formedness Conditions. This results in two adjacent H tones on one vowel, which by the Twin Sister Convention reduce to one H, giving the phonetic output.

(20)
```
LH LH HL  L            LH LH HL  L
 \/  \/  \/  |      →    \/  \/  \/  |      →
 ɔ  m  ɔ  e mb e         ɔ  m    e mb e


LH  LH HL L            LH  L  H  L L
 \/  \/ \/ |        →    \/  \/ \/ |
 ɔ  m  e mb e            ɔ  m   e mb e
```

The fact that the theory effortlessly handles three-tone contours, when the linear theory struggled to handle even two-tone contours, is clear evidence that autosegmental theory is the better theory.

10.1.4 Across-the-board effects

Another phenomenon which argues for the autosegmental representation of tone is across-the-board tone change. An illustration of such a tonal effect can be found in Shona. The examples in (21) show that if a noun begins with some number of H tones, those H's become L when preceded by one of the prefixes *né-*, *sé-* and *ché*.

(21)

N	with N	like N	of N	
mbwá	né-mbwà	sé-mbwà	ché-mbwà	'dog'
hóvé	né-hòvè	sé-hòvè	ché-hòvè	'fish'
mbúndúdzí	né-mbùndùdzì	sé-mbùndùdzì	ché-mbùndùdzì	'army worm'
hákátà	né-hàkàtà	sé-hàkàtà	ché-hàkàtà	'bones'
bénzíbvùnzá	né-bènzìbvùnzá	sé-bènzìbvùnzá	ché-bènzìbvùnzá	'fool'

As shown in (22) and by the last example of (21), an H tone which is not part of an initial string of H's will not undergo this lowering process.

(22)	N	with N	like N	of N	
	mùrúmé	né-mùrúmé	sé-mùrúmé	ché-mùrúmé	'man'
	bàdzá	né-bàdzá	sé-bàdzá	ché-bàdzá	'hoe'

The problem is that if we look at a word such as *mbúndúdzí* as having three H tones, then there is no way to apply the lowering rule to the word and get the right results. Suppose we apply the following rule to a standard segmental representation of this word.

(23)   V   → [−H] /   se, ne, che _
        [+H]   [+H]

Beginning from /né-mbúndúdzí/, this rule would apply to the first H-toned vowel giving *né-mbùndúndzí*. However, the rule could not apply again since the vowel of the second syllable is not immediately preceded by the prefix which triggers the rule. And recall from examples such as *né-mùrúmé* that the rule does not apply to noninitial H tones.

This problem has a simple solution in autosegmental theory, where we are not required to represent a string of *n* H-toned vowels as having *n* H tones. Instead, these words can have a single H tone which is associated with a number of vowels.

(24)

Given these representations, the tone-lowering process will only operate on a single tone, the initial tone of the noun, but this may be translated into an effect on a number of adjacent vowels.

(25)

There is a complication in this rule which gives further support to the autosegmental account of this process. Although this process lowers a string of H tones at the beginning of a noun, when one of these prefixes precedes a prefixed structure, lowering does not affect every initial H tone. When one prefix precedes another prefix which precedes a noun with initial H's, the second prefix has an L tone and the noun keeps its H tones.

(26)
N	of N	like of N	
mbúndúdzí	ché-mbùndùdzì	sé-chè-mbúndúdzí	'army worm'
hákátà	ché-hàkàtà	sé-chè-hákátà	'bones'

However, if there are three of these prefixes, the second prefix has an L tone, and lowering also affects the first (apparent) string of tones in the noun.

(27) sé-nè-ché-mbùndùdzì   'like with of army worm'
sé-nè-ché-hàkàtà   'like with of bones'

A simple statement like "lower a sequence of adjacent H's" after an H prefix would be wrong, as these data show. What we see here is an alternating pattern, which follows automatically from the rule that we have posited and the autosegmental theory of representations. Consider the derivation of a form with two prefixes.

(28) H H   H   H L   H
      | | /\ | | /\
   se-che-mbundudzi → se-che-mbundudzi

The lowering of H on *che* gives that prefix an L tone, and therefore that prefix cannot then cause lowering of the H's of the noun. On the other hand, if there are three such prefixes, the first H-toned prefix causes the second prefix to become L, and that prevents prefix 2 from lowering prefix 3. Since prefix 3 keeps its H tone, it therefore can cause lowering of H in the noun.

(29) H H H   H   H L H   L
      | | | /\ | | | /\
   se-ne-che-mbundudzi → se-ne-che-mbundudzi

Thus it is not simply a matter of lowering the tones of any number of vowels. Unlike the traditional segmental theory, the autosegmental model provides a very simple and principled characterization of these patterns of tone lowering.

10.1.5 Melodic patterns

Another phenomenon which supports the autonomy of tones and segments is the phenomenon of melodic tonal restriction. In some languages, there are restrictions on the possible tones of words, irrespective of the number of vowels in the word. Mende is an example of such a language. Although this language has H, L, rising, falling and rise–falling tones, the distribution of those tones in words is quite restricted. Words can be analyzed as falling into one of five tone melodies, illustrated in (30).

(30) H   pέlέ 'house,' kɔ́ 'war'
      L   bὲlὲ 'trousers,' kpà 'debt'
      HL   kényà, mbû 'owl'
      LH   nìká, mbǎ 'rice'
      LHL   nìkílì 'groundnut,' nyàhâ 'woman,' mbǎ 'companion'

If tones were completely unrestricted, then given five surface tones, one would predict twenty-five patterns for bisyllabic words and 125 patterns for trisyllabic words. Instead, one finds five patterns no matter how many vowels there are.

This distribution can be explained if the restriction is simply stated at the level of the tonal representation: the tone pattern must be one of H, L, LH, HL or LHL. As seen in (31), given an autosegmental representation of tone, *nìkílì, nyàhâ,* and *mbǎ* all have the same tonal representation.

(31)   LHL   L H L   L H L
       | | | | \/   \|/
      nikili   nyaha   mba

10.1.6 Floating tones

Another tonal phenomenon which confounds the segmental approach to tone, but is handled quite easily with autosegmental representations, is the phenomenon of floating tones, which are tones not linked to a vowel.

Anlo tone. The Anlo dialect of Ewe provides one example. The data in (32) illustrate some general tone rules of Ewe. Underlyingly, the noun 'buffalo' is /ētō/. However, it surfaces as [ètò] either phrase-finally or when the following word has an L tone.

(32) ètò   'buffalo'   ètò mè   'in a buffalo'
      ētō ɸēɸlē   'buffalo-buying'   ētō dyí   'on a buffalo'
      ētō mēgbé   'behind a buffalo'

These alternations are explained by two rules; one rule lowers M (mid) to L at the end of a phrase, and the second assimilates M to a following L.

(33)   M → L / __ ##   M → L / __ L

Thus in the citation form, /ētō/ first becomes ētò, then [ètò].

Two other tone rules are exemplified by the data in (34).

(34) ètó   'mountain'   ètó dyí   'on a mountain'
     ètő mégbé   'behind a mountain'

Here, we see a process which raises M to Superhigh tone (SH) when it is surrounded by H tones; subsequently a nonfinal H tone assimilates to a preceding or following SH tone.

(35) M → SH / H _ H   H → SH% SH _

We know from *ētō mēgbé* 'behind a buffalo' that *mēgbé* has the tones MH. Therefore, the underlying form of *ètő mégbé* 'behind a mortar' is *ètó mēgbé*. The underlying form is subject to the rule raising M to SH since the M is surrounded by H tones, giving *ètó mégbé*. This then undergoes the SH assimilation rule. Another set of examples illustrating these tone processes is (36), where the noun /àtyíkē/ ends in the underlying sequence HM. When followed by /mēgbé/, the sequence HMMH results, so this cannot undergo the M-raising rule. However, when followed by /dyí/, the M-raising rule applies to /kē/, giving a SH tone, and the preceding syllable then assimilates this SH.

(36) àtyíkè   'root'   àtyíkē φēφφlē 'root-buying'
     àtyíkē mēgbé   'behind a root'   àtyíkế dyí   'on a root'

There are some apparently problematic nouns which seem to have a very different surface pattern. In the citation form, the final M tone does not lower; when followed by the MM-toned participle /φēφφlē/, the initial tone of the participle mysteriously changes to H; the following L-toned postposition *mè* inexplicably has a falling tone; the postposition /mēgbé/ mysteriously has an initial SH tone.

(37) ētō   'mortar'   ētō φēφφlē 'mortar-buying'
     ētō mê   'in a mortar'   ētō dyí   'on a mortar'
     ētō mégbé   'behind a mortar'

All of these mysteries are resolved, once we recognize that this noun actually does not end with an M tone, but rather ends with a H tone that is not associated with a vowel, thus the underlying form of the noun 'mortar' is (38).

(38) e t   o
     | |
     M   M H

Because the noun ends in a (floating) H tone and not an M tone, the rule lowering prepausal M to L does not apply, which explains why the final tone does not lower. The floating H associates with the next vowel if possible, which explains the appearance of an H on the following postposition as a falling tone (when the postposition is monosyllabic) or level H (when the next word is polysyllabic). Finally, the floating H serves as one of the triggering tones for the rule turning M into SH, as seen in *ētō mĕgbé*. The hypothesis that this word (and others which behave like it) ends in a floating H tone thus provides a unified explanation for a range of facts that would otherwise be inexplicable. However, the postulation of such a thing as a "floating tone" is possible only assuming the autosegmental framework.

Mixtec.   Another example of floating tones can be seen in the language Mixtec. As (39) indicates, some words such as *kēē* 'will eat' have no effect on the tone of the following word, but other words such as the apparently homophonous verb meaning 'will go away' cause the initial tone to become H.

(39) sùčí   'child'   kēē   'will go away'
      kōò   'snake'
      kēē   'will eat'
      kēē sùčí 'the child will eat'   kēē súčí 'the child will go away'
      kēē kōò   'the snake will eat'   kēē kóò   'the snake will go away'

A similar effect is seen in (40), where *tàká* 'all' has no effect on the following word, but *máá* 'that' causes raising of the initial tone of the next word.

(40) tàká sùčí   'all the children'   máá súčí   'that child'
      tàká bē?ē   'all the houses'   máá bé?ē   'that house'
      tàká kōò   'all the snakes'   máá kóò   'that snake'
      tàká mìnī   'all the puddles'   máá mínī   'that puddle'

These data can be explained very easily if we assume the following underlying representations.

(41)   MM   MMH   L H   HH H
        || || | | ||
        k e e   k e e   t a k a   m a a

Gã.   Other evidence for floating tones comes from Gã. In this language, there is a rule changing the tone sequence HL at the end of a phrase into H'H. The operation of this rule can be seen in the data of (42), where the presence of the future tense prefix *baá* causes a change in the tone of final L-toned verbs with the shape CV.

(42) *3sg past*   *3sg future*
      e-ča   e-baá-'čá   'dig'
      e-ǰo   e-baá-'ǰó   'dance'
      e-gbe   e-baá-'gbé   'kill'
      e-kpɛ   e-baá-'kpɛ́   'sew'
      e-šɔ̃   e-baá-'šɔ̃́   'pull'
      e-tū   e-baá-'tū́   'jump'
      e-wo   e-baá-'wó   'wear'

The necessity of restricting this rule to an HL sequence which is at the end of a phrase is demonstrated by examples such as *ebaágbe Ako* 'he will kill Ako,' *ebaákpɛ ataadé* 'he will sew a shirt,' *ebaášɔ kpaŋ* 'he will pull a rope,' where the sequence is not prepausal. This restriction also explains why verbs with long vowels or two syllables do not undergo this alternation: the L-toned syllable that comes after the H is not also at the end of the phrase

(43) *3sg past*   *3sg future*

    e-gbɔɔ   e-baá-gbɔɔ   'hunt'

    e-hao   e-baá-hao   'worry'

    e-sɔɔ   e-baá-sɔɔ   'catch'

    e-sɔle   e-baá-sɔle   'pray'

    e-hala   e-baá-hala   'chose'

This rule does not apply to tense-inflections on verbs, for example the plural imperative *-a* (*nyɛ̃-hé-a* 'buy (pl)!') or the habitual *-ɔ* (*e-mãjé-ɔ* 'he sends').

A second relevant rule is Plateauing, whereby HLH becomes H¹HH. This can be seen in (44) involving verbs with final HL. When the following object begins with a H tone, the resulting HLH sequence becomes H¹HH.

(44) nyɛ̃-hé-a   'buy (pl)!'

    nyɛ̃-hé-¹á tũ   'buy (pl) a gun!'

    nyɛ̃-hé-a fɔ   'buy (pl) oil!'

    e-mãjé-ɔ ako   'he sends Ako'

    e-mãjé¹ɔ́ ákú   'he sends Aku'

    mĩ́ŋgbe kwakwé   'I am killing a mouse'

    mĩ́ŋ¹gbé fóte   'I am killing a termite'

This rule also applies within words, when the verb stem has the underlying tone pattern LH and is preceded by an H-toned prefix.

(45) *3sg past*   *3sg future*

    e-hulú   e-baá¹-húlú   'jump'

    e-kasé   e-baá¹-kásé   'learn'

    e-kojó   e-baá¹-kójó   'judge'

    e-mãjé   e-baá¹-mãjé   'send'

> In these examples, the rule changing prepausal HL to H¹H does not apply to the verb in citation form because the L tone is in a tense suffix.

There are a number of areas in the language where floating tones can be motivated. The perfective tense provides one relevant example. Consider the data in (46), which contrasts the form of the subjunctive and the perfective. Segmentally these forms are identical: their difference lies in their tone. In both tenses the subject prefix has an H tone. In the perfective, the rule affecting prepausal HL exceptionally fails to apply to an L toned CV stem, but in the subjunctive that rule applies as expected.

(46) *3sg subjunctive*   *3sg perfective*

    é-¹čá   é-ča   'dig'

    é-¹ǰó   é-ǰo   'dance'

é-ˈgbé	é-gbe	'kill'
é-ˈkpé	é-kpɛ	'sew'
é-ˈšɔ̃́	é-šɔ̃	'pull'
é-ˈwó	é-wo	'wear

You might think that the perfective is an exception, but there is more to it.

Another anomaly of these verbs forms is that the Plateauing rule fails to apply between the verbs of (46) and an initial H tone, even though the requisite tone sequence is found.

(47) é-gbe ákú   'he has killed Aku'
      é-šɔ̃ gúˈgɔ̃́   'he has pulled a nose'
      é-wo ǰwɛ́ˈɛ́   'he has worn grass'

The failure of both the HL → HˈH rule and the Plateauing rule can be explained by positing that the perfective tense is marked by a floating L tone which comes between the subject prefix and the verb stem; thus the phonological representation of perfective é-wo would be (48).

(48) H L L
      | |
      e – wo

The floating L between the H and the L of the root means that the H is not next to the prepausal L, which we have already seen is a crucial condition for the change of HL to HˈH. In addition, the presence of this floating L explains why this verb form does not undergo Plateauing. Thus two anomalies are explained by the postulation of a floating tone.

Other examples of the failure of the Plateauing rule in this tense can be seen below. The examples from the simple past show that these verbs underlyingly have the tone pattern LH, which surfaces unchanged after the L-toned subject prefix used in the simple past. The subjunctive data show that these stems do otherwise undergo Plateauing after an H-toned prefix; the perfective data show that in the perfective tense, Plateauing fails to apply within the word.

(49) | 3sg past | 3sg subjunctive | 3sg perfective | |
      |---|---|---|---|
      | e-hulú | éˈ-húlú | é-hulú | 'jump' |
      | e-kasé | éˈ-kásé | é-kasé | 'learn' |
      | e-kojó | éˈ-kójó | é-kojó | 'judge' |
      | e-mãjé | éˈ-mã́jé | é-mãjé | 'send' |

Again, these facts can be explained by positing a floating tone in the perfective tense: that L means that the actual tone sequence is HLLH, not HLH, so Plateauing would simply not be applicable to that tone sequence.

(50)   H L L H
       | | |
       e – hulu

Finally, the postulation of a floating L as the marker of the perfective explains why a downstep spontaneously emerges between the subject prefix and a stem-initial H tone.

(51) | *3sg past* | *3sg subjunctive* | *3sg perfective* | |
       |------------|-------------------|------------------|--|
       | e-bé | é-bé | é^l-bé | 'quarrel' |
       | e-chṹ | é-chṹ | é^l-chṹ | 'send' |
       | e-dṹ | é-dṹ | é^l-dṹ | 'cultivate' |
       | e-fó | é-fó | é^l-fó | 'weep' |
       | e-fóté | é-fóté | é^l-fóté | 'pour' |
       | e-jálé | é-jálé | é^l-jálé | 'rinse' |

Thus the postulation of a floating tone as the marker of the perfective explains a number of anomalies: insofar as floating tones have a coherent theoretical status in autosegmental phonology but not in the linear theory, they provide strong support for the correctness of the autosegmental model.

10.1.7 Tonal morphemes

Another example of the kind of dissynchrony between tones and vowels which is explained by the autosegmental model is the tonal morpheme, where a particular morpheme is expressed solely as a tone – this is a variant of the problem of floating tones. One such example is the expression of case marking and the marking of modified nouns in Angas. When a noun is case marked in Angas (when it is at the end of the subject or object NP, for example), case marking is indicated with a suffixed floating H which links to the final vowel, forming a rising tone if the final tone of the noun is M or L. When a noun is followed by an adjective in its phrase, that fact is marked by the suffixation of a floating L tone, which forms a falling contour tone when the last tone is M or H.

(52) | | | | | | |
       |--|--|--|--|--|--|
       | téŋ | 'rope' | téŋ | 'rope (case)' | têŋ | 'rope (modified)' |
       | mús | 'cat' | mús | 'cat (case)' | mûs | 'cat (mod.)' |
       | čén | 'hoe' | čén | 'hoe (case)' | čên | 'hoe (mod.)' |
       | nyí | 'elephant' | nyí | 'elephant (case)' | nyî | 'elephant (mod.)' |
       | ʔās | 'dog' | ʔǎs | 'dog (case)' | ʔās | 'dog (mod.)' |
       | žwāl | 'boy' | zwǎl | 'boy (case)' | žwāl | 'boy (mod.)' |
       | ɟēm | 'child' | ɟēm | 'child (case)' | ɟēm | 'child (mod.)' |
       | màs | 'locust bean' | mǎs | 'bean (case)' | màs | 'bean (mod.)' |
       | pùk | 'soup' | pǔk | 'soup (case)' | pùk | 'soup (mod.)' |
       | ʔàs | 'tooth' | ʔǎs | 'tooth (case)' | ʔàs | 'tooth (mod.)' |
       | jólì | 'ape' | jólǐ | 'ape (case)' | jólì | 'ape (mod.)' |

Tiv is another language with morphemes being marked by tone, in this case verbal tense-aspect. Verb roots in Tiv lexically have either an H tone or an L tone on the first syllable of the root. The general past tense is marked with a floating L tone; the past habitual with a H; the recent past with the tone sequence HL.

(53) H verbs   L verbs
      General past (L)
      vá   'come'   dzà   'go'
      úngwà   'hear'   vèndè   'refuse'
      yévèsè   'flee'   ngòhòrò   'accept'

      Past habitual (H)
      vá   dzá
      úngwá   vèndé
      yévésé   ngòhóró

      Recent past (HL)
      vá   dzá
      úngwá   vèndé
      yévèsè   ngòhórò

In addition to showing the effects of various floating tone morphemes which mark tense-aspect, these data illustrate the application of a contour-simplification rule. We now consider how representative forms are actually derived. The concatenation of the L root *ngohoro* and the recent past morpheme gives the following underlying form:

(54)   L   HL
          |
       ngohor

These tones must be assigned to the vowels of the stem: we can see that the first tone links to the first free vowel and the second tone links to the second free vowel. This is an instance of one-to-one left-to-right mapping.

(55)   Link free tones to free vowels, one-to-one, from left to right

This process is so common that it had been thought that it is actually a universal convention on free tones – we now know, since languages have been discovered which do not obey this condition – that it is a language-specific rule, though a very common one. Application of this rule to (54) gives the surface form.

Now consider the disyllabic L root *vèndé*. This root has two vowels but three tones. If all of the tones were to be associated with the vowels of the root, this would force the final syllable to bear the tone sequence HL, i.e. it would have a falling tone. We can see that there are no contour tones in the data. This leaves us with two possibilities in accounting for *vèndé*: either the rule associating floating tones with vowels simply does not link a floating tone with a vowel that already has a tone, or floating tones do associate with vowels that already bear a H and then some later rule eliminates tonal contour tones. If we assume that floating tones are all initially associated with a vowel and contours are later eliminated, we will require the following rule, which deletes the L-tone component of a falling tone.

(56) H L → ∅
       \ /
        V

Finally, we come to /dzà/, which has H if one of the floating tone patterns H or HL is added to the root. This can be explained if floating tones are associated with root vowels even when this would result in a contour tone. Linking the melodic tones to this root would result in the following representation:

(57)   L H L
        \|/
        dza

Rule (56) applies in a mirror-image fashion: it deletes L in combination with an H on one vowel, standing before or after the H. This explains why the lexical L is replaced with an H. Under the alternative account, that floating tones only link to vowels which do not have any other tone, we would be unable to explain why the lexical L is replaced by H when a melodic pattern with an H tone is added.

10.1.8 Toneless vowels

Another phenomenon demonstrating the independence of tones and vowels is the existence of underlyingly toneless vowels. This can be illustrated with data from Margyi. There are two tones in Margyi, H and L, but there are three underlying types of vowels in terms of tonal behavior, namely H, L, and toneless. Examples of underlyingly toneless morphemes are /ɗəl/ 'buy,' /skə/ 'wait' and /na/ 'away.' When two morphemes with underlying tones are combined, there are no surface tone changes. However, when one of the toneless morphemes is combined with a morpheme with tone, the toneless morpheme takes on the tone of the tone-bearing morpheme.

(58) tá + bá → tábá   'to cook all'
      ndàl + bá → ndàlbá   'to throw out'
      ɗəl + bá → ɗə́lbá   'to buy'

      ná + ɗà → náɗà   'give me'
      hə̀rì + ɗà → hə̀rɗà   'bring me'
      skə + ɗà → skə̀ɗà   'wait for me'

      tá + na → táná   'to cook and put aside'
      ndàl + na → ndàlnà   'to throw away'
      ɗəl + na → ɗə̀lnà   'to sell'

As (59) indicates, this can be accounted for by spreading tone (i.e. adding associations between tone and vowels) to toneless vowels.

(59)
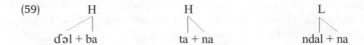

The form *ɗə̀l-nà* 'to sell,' which combines two toneless morphemes, illustrates another property of tone systems. Since all vowels must on the surface have some tonal specification, the following question arises: if there is no tone present in the string which could spread to toneless vowels, how do toneless vowels get their surface tone? The answer is that there are also rules of **default tone assignment**, which guarantee that if a vowel does not otherwise have a tone value, one is automatically assigned. Such a rule can be formalized as (60).

(60)
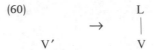

Generally, in languages with two levels of tone, the default value assigned to otherwise toneless vowels is L; in languages with three tone levels, the default tone specification is usually M tone. Yoruba is a language with three tone levels, where it can be argued that M-toned vowels are actually underlyingly toneless, and M tones are assigned by a default tone-assignment rule. The examples in (61) illustrate a very general tone-spreading rule whereby L tone becomes falling after H, and H tone becomes rising after L. However, M is unchanged after either L or H, and M also has no effect on a following L or H.

(61) kò pɔ̀   'it is not plentiful'   kò dùn   'it is not sweet'
      ó pɔ̂   'it is plentiful'   ó dûn   'it is sweet'
      ɛ̀kɔ̌   'lesson'   ɔ̀bɔ̌   'monkey'
      ɔ̀fɔ̀   'mourning'   gígā   'height'
      īṣé   'work'   ējò   'snake'

The question is how to exclude M tone from being targetted by this rule, and how to prevent M tone from spreading. If we assume that tonally unspecified vowels are assigned an M tone by default, and that M tones in Yoruba derive only from application of this default specification rule, then we can explain these patterns rather simply. We can assume the following tone-spreading rule, where T represents any tone.

(62)   T   T

       V   V

The fact that contours are not formed with M tone follows from the fact that a contour is two tone specifications on one vowel, plus the hypothesis that M tone is only assigned if there is no tonal specification on a vowel.

10.1.9 Tonal mobility

The final demonstration of the autonomy of tone from segments is the tone mobility, which is the fact that tones can move about from vowel to vowel quite easily, in a fashion not shared with segmental properties. One example of tonal mobility comes from Nkore, seen in (63). This language has an underlying contrast between words whose last syllable is H toned, and those whose penultimate syllable is H toned. In prepausal position, underlyingly final H tones shift to the penultimate syllable, thus neutralizing with nouns having an underlyingly penult H. When some word follows the noun, the underlying position of the H tone is clearly revealed.

(63)   *Nouns with penult H*

òkùgúrù	'leg'	òkùgúrù kùrùùnjì	'good leg'
òmùkózì	'worker'	òmùkózì mùrùùnjì	'good worker'
èmbúzì	'goat'	èmbúzì nùùnjì	'good goat'
èchìkópò	'cup'	èchìkópò chìrùùnjì	'good cup'
èmbíbò	'seeds'	èmbíbò nùùnjì	'good seeds'

   Nouns with final H

òmùgúzì	'buyer'	òmùgùzí mùrùùnjì	'good buyer'
òmùkámà	'chief'	òmùkàmá mùrùùnjì	'good chief'
èémbwà	'dog'	èèmbwá nùùnjì	'good dog'
òbúrò	'millet'	òbùró bùrùùnjì	'good millet'
kàsúkù	'parrot'	kàsùkú nùùnjì	'good parrot'

There are a number of reasons internal to the grammar of Nkore for treating L tone as the default tone, and for only specifying H tones in the phonology so that phonetically L-toned vowels are actually toneless. This alternation can be accounted for by the following rule of tone-throwback.

(64)

$$
\begin{array}{c}
\mathrm{H} \\
\diagdown \!\! \downarrow \\
\mathrm{V\ C_0V\ \#\#}
\end{array}
$$

Another example of tone shift can be seen in Kikuyu. Like Nkore, there are good reasons to analyze this language phonologically solely in terms of the position of H tones, with vowels not otherwise specified as H being realized phonetically with a default L tone. We will follow the convention adopted in such cases as marking H-toned vowels with an acute accent, and not marking toneless (default L) vowels.

Consider the Kikuyu data in (65) from the current habitual tense. The first two examples in (65a) would indicate that the morphemes *to-*, *-rɔr-*, *-aγ-*, and *-a* are all toneless. The third example, however, shows the root *rɔr* with an H tone: this happens only when the root is preceded by the object prefix *ma*. In (65b), we see that – in contrast to what we see in (65a) – the habitual suffix

-aγ- has an H tone when it is preceded by the root *tom* (which is itself tone-less on the surface). As with (65a), the syllable that follows *ma* has an H tone.

(65)   a.   to -rɔr   -aγ -a   'we look at'
             we-look at-hab-tense
             to -mo -rɔr   -aγ -a   'we look at him'
             we-him-look at-hab-tense
             to -ma   -rɔ́r -aγ -a   'we look at them'
             we-them-look at-hab-tense
    b.   to-tom-áγ-a   'we send'
             to-mo-tom-áγ-a   'we send him'
             to-ma-tóm-áγ-a   'we send them'

It is clear, then, that certain syllables have the property of causing the following syllable to have a surface H tone. This is further demonstrated in (66), where the derivational suffixes -er- and -an- follow the roots -rɔr- and -tom-: we can see that the syllable after -tom always receives an H tone.

(66)   to-rɔr-er-aγ-a   'we look for'
       to-tom-ér-aγ-a   'we send for'
       to-rɔr-an-aγ-a   'we look at each other'
       to-tom-án-aγ-a   'we send each other'
       to-rɔr-er-an-aγ-a   'we look for each other'
       to-tom-ér-an-aγ-a   'we send for each other'

Further examples of this phenomenon are seen in the examples of the recent past in (67). In (67a), the root *rɔr* (which generally has no H tone) has an H tone when it stands immediately after the recent-past-tense prefix -a-; or, the object prefix that follows -a- will have a surface H tone. The examples in (67b) show the same thing with the root -tom- which we have seen has the property of assigning an H tone to the following vowel.

(67)   a.   to-a-rɔ́r-a   'we looked at'
           to-a-mó-rɔr-a   'we looked at him'
           to-a-má-rɔ́r-a   'we looked at them'
    b.   to-a-tóm-á   'we sent'
           to-a-mó-tom-á   'we sent him'
           to-a-má-tóm-á   'we sent them'

We would assume that the root -tóm- has an H, as do the object prefix -má- and the tense prefix -a-, and this H tone is subject to the following rule of tone shift, which moves every H tone one vowel to the right.

(68)   H
        ⌇
        V C_0 V

Thus, /to-tóm-er-aγ-a/ becomes *totoméraγa*, /to-má-rɔr-aγ-a/ becomes *tomarɔ́raγa*, and /to-á-má-tóm-a/ becomes *toamátómá*.

(69)
```
      H  II II
       ╲   ╲╲ ╲
      t o a m a t o m a
```

An even more dramatic example of tone shifting comes from Digo. In this language, the last H tone of a word shifts to the end of the word. The root *vugura* is toneless, as is the object prefix *ni*, but the object prefix *a* 'them' has an underlying H tone, which is phonetically realized on the last vowel of the word. Similarly, the root *togora* is toneless, as is the subject prefix *ni*, but the third-singular subject prefix *a* has an H tone, which shifts to the end of the word. Lastly, the root *tsukura* is toneless, as is the tense-aspect prefix *-na-*, but the perfective prefix *ka* has an H tone which shifts to the last vowel of the word.

(70) a. ku-vugura   'to untie'   ku-vugurira   'to untie for'
      ku-ni-vugurira 'to untie for me' ku-a-vugurirá 'to untie for them'
   b. ku-togora   'to praise'   ni-na-togora   'I'm praising'
      a-na-togorá   'he's praising'
   c. ku-tsukura   'to carry'   ni-na-tsukura 'I'm carrying'
      a-na-tsukurá   'he's carrying' ni-ka-tsukurá 'I have carried'

These data can be accounted for by a rule of tone shift which is essentially the same as the Kikuyu rule, differing only in that the tone shifts all the way to the end of the word.

(71)
```
      H
       ╲
      V  ...      V#
```

10.2 Extension to the segmental domain

The foregoing modification of phonological theory had the obvious good consequence that tonal phenomena could be accounted for very nicely, whereas previously tone was largely outside the grasp of the theory. The impact of autosegmental phonology was much more profound than that, however. The obvious thing to wonder is, if tones are separate from the rest of the segment, then perhaps segments themselves are not such monolithic, unstructured entities. And so investigators looked for evidence for a similar separation of segmental features.

10.2.1 The autonomy of all features

An example of segmental phenomena which are reminiscent of autosegmental tonal properties are floating segmental features as morphemes. One such case is seen in Vata, there the past-tense marker can be argued to be simply the specification [+hi], which is suffixed to the stem and is realized phonetically on the last vowel.

(72)   n le   'I eat'   n li   'I ate'
      n plɛ   'I pass'   n plɪ   'I passed'

n mlɛ	'I go'	n mlɪ	'I went'
n no	'I hear'	n nu	'I heard'
n zɔ	'I place'	n zʊ	'I placed'
n wɔlɔ	'I wash'	n wɔlʊ	'I washed'

A second example comes from Fula, where a particular agreement pattern ("pattern B" below) is marked by a prefix composed of the segmental specification [−continuant] which causes an initial continuant to become a stop.

(73) *Pattern A*   *Pattern B*

wecco	becce	'rib'
wibjo	bibje	'wing'
ruulde	duule	'cloud'
sekko	cekke	'mat'
hello	kelle	'slap'
yeɓre	jeɓel	'seed'
yimre	jimel	'poem'
yontere	jonte	'week'

> CP has been proposed as a feature used to describe pharyngealization.

Aramaic CP.   Azerbaijani Aramaic provides evidence for treating the feature [constricted pharynx] ([CP]) autosegmentally. This dialect has a contrast between pharyngealized or emphatic vowels (A E I U O) specified as [+CP], and plain vowels (a e i u o). In most words, either all of the vowels are emphatic, or none of them is.

(74)

AmrA	'wool'	brata	'daughter'
zArʔA	'seed'	bela	'house'
qUlOx	'stand up!'	nŭjum	'sorcery'

Some words may have nonemphatic vowels followed by emphatic vowels. In such a case, the first emphatic vowel is always a low vowel.

(75)

šarAw	'corn growing wild'	riswAy	'unmannerly speech'
seyfullAh	'a great deal'	fandbAz	'trickster'
nišAn	'sign'	peštAmAl	'towel'
milAqE	'hung grapes'	eliyAhU	'name'
galimbAjI	'brother's wife'	silAhlAmIš	'supplied with weapons'

These distributional properties will play an important role in arguing for an autosegmental treatment of [CP].

In line with the fact that all vowels in a word generally agree in the feature [CP], (76) shows that suffixes harmonize in [CP] with the preceding vowel.

(76)

lixm-a	'bread'	lixm-e	pl
pirčaxwar-a	'old woman'	pirčaxwar-e	pl
nOhr-A	'mirror'	nOhr-E	pl
dIqnAxwAr-A	'old man'	dIqnAxwAr-E	pl

klu	'write! (sg)'	klu-mun	pl
bilbul	'seek!'	bilbul-un	pl
qU	'rise!'	. qU-mUn	pl
mIšltUn	'make a king!'	mIšltUn-Un	pl

[CP] will spread through a whole sequence of suffixes.

(77)
mĭr-a	'she said'	xIt-lAx	'you (fem sg) sewed'
mir-wa-la	'she had said'	xIt-wA-lAx	'you had sewn'
mir-wa-la-la	'she had said it'	xIt-wA-lAx-U	'you had sewn them'

We will assume that the only value underlyingly marked for this feature is [+CP], and that [+CP] spreads to the right by the following rule:

(78)   [+CP]

        V   V

This rule thus explains why [+CP] vowels are always followed by [+CP] vowels. However, we also need to explain why roots with a [+CP] specification (generally) have [+CP] beginning with the first vowel. We can assume that, in the general case, the specification [+CP] is not associated to any particular vowel, but is just floating, and an unassociated [+CP] specification is associated with the first vowel of the word by the following rule:

(79) $[+CP]'$

        # C$_0$V

The derivation of *mIšltUn-Un* 'make a king (pl)!' shows these rules.

(80)   [+CP]   (rule (79))   [+CP]   (rule (78))   [+CP]
                 →   →
        mišitun-un   mišitun-un   mišitun-un

There are some suffixes whose vowels are invariably emphatic; that vowel is always the vowel [A]. No suffixes are invariably plain.

(81)
qalăma	'pen'	qalam-dAn	'case for scribe's utensils'
qand	'sugar'	qand-dAn	'sugarbowl'
šakăr	'sugar'	šakăr-dAn	'sugarbowl'
dukana	'store'	dukan-dAr	'shopkeeper'
mewana	'guest'	mewan-dAr	'hospitable'
jut	'plow'	jut-kAr	'plower'
nŭjum	'sorcery'	nŭjum-kAr	'sorcerer'
naqš	'engraving'	naqš-kAr	'engraver'

These suffixes will be assumed to have underlying [CP] specifications, in contrast to most other suffixes which are unspecified for [CP]. Since the suffix vowel is lexically associated with [+CP], it does not associate with the first vowel of the word, and since it does not associate with the first vowel of the word, [+CP] does not spread to any vowels before that of the suffix.

We also find spreading of [+CP] between members of a compound. In the examples of (82), [+CP] spreads from the first compound to the second.

(82)	tAhA	'3'	imme	'100'
	tAhA-mmE	'300'		
	dIqnA	'beard'	xwara	'white'
	dIqnA-xwArA	'old man'		

This is the expected pattern: [+CP] spreads rightward from the first member of the compound to the second.

If the second member of the compound has [+CP] vowels, [+CP] spreads through the second member of the compound.

(83)	xwara	'white'	dIqnA	'beard'
	xwArA-dIqnA	'old man'		
	be	'without'	hAd	'limit'
	bEhAd	'exceedingly'		
	qahwa	'coffee'	xAnA	'shelter'
	qAhwA-xAnA	'coffee-room'		

This apparent exceptional leftward spreading of [+CP] is nothing of the sort. Rather, the second member of the compound has a floating [+CP] specification; in a compound, that feature links to the first vowel of the word by rule (79), and then spreads to the right.

(84)

Another case of [+CP] appearing to the left of the morpheme where it originates is seen in (85), where a prefix is added to a root with a floating [+CP] specification.

(85)	xoš	'good'	na-xoš	'ill'
	hAq	'right'	nA-hAq	'wrong'
	rAzI	'satisfied'	nA-rAzI	'unsatisfied'
	pyala	'fall'	ma-pole	'cause to fall'
	šatoe	'drink'	ma-stoe	'give drink'
	myAsA	'suck'	mA-mOsE	'give the suck'
	rAdOxE	'boil (intr.)'	mA-rdOxE	'boil (tr.)'

Given the assumption that a root specification of [+CP] is not generally associated in the underlying form (except in roots such as (75) where [+CP] is unpredictably associated with a noninitial low vowel), our analysis predicts that the [+CP] specification will link to the first vowel of the word, which will be the prefix vowel in this case, and spreads to the right thereafter.

The locational suffix -*istan* has the interesting property that it causes all vowels in the word to which it is attached to become [+CP].

(86)   xaraba   'ruined'   xArAb-IstAn   'ruined place'
        čol   'uninhabited land'   čOl-IstAn   'wilderness'
        hind   'India'   hInd-IstAn   'India'

This makes sense if the suffix -*istan* also has a floating specification [+CP], which automatically associates with the first vowel of the stem and then spreads rightward.

(87)   [+CP]   [+CP]   [+CP]
                        $\rightarrow$ | $\rightarrow$
      xarab - istan   xarab - istan   xarab - istan

10.2.2 Feature geometry

It was realized that all features are autonomous from all other features, and exhibit the kind of behavior which motivated the autosegmental treatment of tone. The question then arises as to exactly how features are arranged, and what they associate with, if the "segment" has had all of its features removed. The generally accepted theory of how features relate to each other is expressed in terms of a feature-tree such as (88). This tree – known as a feature geometry – expresses the idea that while all features express a degree of autonomy, certain subsets of the features form coherent phonological groups, as expressed by their being grouped together into constituents such as "Laryngeal" and "Place."

(88)

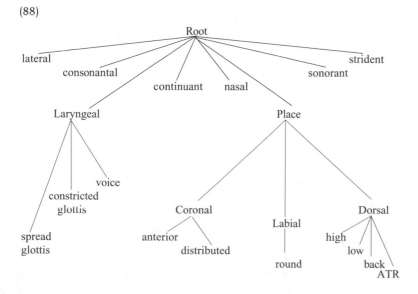

The organization of features into such a structure went hand-in-hand with the realization that the theory of rules could be constrained in very important ways. A long-standing problem in phonological theory was the question of how to express rules of multiple-feature assimilation. We have discussed rules of nasal place assimilation in previous chapters, and noted in chapter 6 that such rules necessitate a special notation, the feature variable notation using α, β, γ and so on. The notation makes some very bad predictions. First, notice that complete place assimilation requires specification of ten features in total.

$$(89) \quad C \rightarrow \begin{bmatrix} \alpha coronal \\ \beta anterior \\ \gamma back \\ \delta high \\ \theta distributed \end{bmatrix} / \underline{\quad} \begin{bmatrix} \alpha coronal \\ \beta anterior \\ \gamma back \\ \delta high \\ \theta distributed \end{bmatrix}$$

This is less simple and, by the simplicity metric used in that theory, should occur less frequently than (90).

$$(90) \quad C \rightarrow [\alpha coronal] / \underline{\quad} [\alpha coronal]$$

This prediction is totally wrong: (90) is not just uncommon, it is completely unattested. Were there to be such a rule that assimilates only the specification of coronal, we would expect to find sets of assimilations such as the following:

$$(91) \quad
\begin{array}{ll}
\text{mč} \rightarrow \text{nč (not ñč)} & \text{ŋč} \rightarrow \text{ñč} \\
\text{ñp} \rightarrow \text{ŋp} & \text{np} \rightarrow \text{mp} \\
\text{ñk} \rightarrow \text{ŋk} & \text{nk} \rightarrow \text{mk} \\
\text{ñt} \rightarrow \text{ñt} & \text{nč} \rightarrow \text{nč}
\end{array}$$

The fact that the feature-variable theory allows us to formulate such an unnatural process at all, and assigns a much higher probability of occurrence to such a rule, is a sign that something is wrong with the theory.

The theory says that there is only a minor difference in naturalness between (92) and (89), since the rules are the same except that (92) does not include assimilation of the feature [anterior].

$$(92) \quad C \rightarrow \begin{bmatrix} \alpha coronal \\ \gamma back \\ \delta high \\ \theta distributed \end{bmatrix} \underline{\quad} \begin{bmatrix} \alpha coronal \\ \gamma back \\ \delta high \\ \theta distributed \end{bmatrix}$$

There is a huge empirical difference between these rules: (89) is very common, (92) is unattested. Rule (92) is almost complete place assimilation, but [anterior] is not assimilated, so /np/, /ñk/, and /mt/ become [mp], [ŋk], and [nt] as expected, but /ñt/ and /nč/ do not assimilate (as they would under complete place assimilation); similarly, /ŋč/ becomes [ñč] as expected (and as well attested), but /ŋp/ and /ŋt/ become [np] and [nt], since the underlying value [−anterior] from /ŋ/ would not be changed. Thus the inclusion of feature variables in the theory incorrectly predicts the possibility of many types of rules which do not exist in human language.

The variable-feature theory gives no special status to a rule where both occurrences of α occur on the same feature.

$$(93) \quad C \rightarrow \begin{bmatrix} \alpha\text{coronal} \\ \beta\text{anterior} \\ \gamma\text{back} \\ \delta\text{high} \\ \theta\text{distributed} \end{bmatrix} \Big/ \underline{\quad} \begin{bmatrix} \theta\text{coronal} \\ \alpha\text{anterior} \\ \beta\text{back} \\ \gamma\text{high} \\ \delta\text{distributed} \end{bmatrix}$$

This rule describes an equally unnatural and unattested process whereby a consonant becomes [t] before [pʸ], [p] before [q], and [pʸ] before [k]. Rules such as (93) do not exist in human language, which indicates that the linear theory which uses this notation as a means of expressing assimilations makes poor predictions regarding the nature of phonological rules.

The variable notation allows us to refer to legions of unnatural classes by randomly linking two unrelated features with a single variable:

$$(94) \quad \text{a.} \begin{bmatrix} \alpha\text{high} \\ \alpha\text{round} \end{bmatrix} \quad \text{b.} \begin{bmatrix} \alpha\text{distributed} \\ \alpha\text{nasal} \end{bmatrix} \quad \text{c.} \begin{bmatrix} \alpha\text{coronal} \\ \alpha\text{anterior} \end{bmatrix} \quad \text{d.} \begin{bmatrix} \alpha\text{voice} \\ \alpha\text{lateral} \end{bmatrix}$$

Class (a) applied to vowels refers to [ü, u, e, ə, a]; (b) refers to [n̪, ñ, p, t̪, k] but excludes [m, n̪, t̪, č, ŋ]; (c) groups together [t, k] and excludes [p, č]; (d) refers to [l] plus voiceless consonants. Such groupings are not attested in any language.

With the advent of a theory of feature geometry such as in (88), this problem disappeared. In that theory, the process of place assimilation is formulated not as the change of one feature value into another, but is expressed as the spreading of one node – in this case the Place node – at the expense of another Place node. Thus the change /ñ/ → [m] / _ [p] is seen as working as in (95):

(95)

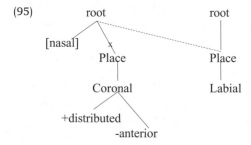

Just as tone assimilation is the rightward or leftward expansion of the domain of a tone feature, this process of place assimilation is expansion of the domain of one set of place specifications, to the exclusion of another. When one Place node spreads and replaces the Place node of a neighboring segment, that means that all of the original place features are deleted, and the segment then comes to bear the entire set of place features that the neighboring segment has.

What the feature-variable notation was able to do was express multiple-feature assimilations, but given this alternative theory, multiple feature assimilations will be recast as spreading some node such as Place. The feature-variable notation can be entirely eliminated since its one useful function is expressed by different means. The theory of feature geometry enables a simple hypothesis regarding the form of phonological rules, which radically constrains the power of phonological theory. This hypothesis is that phonological rules can perform one simple operation (such as spreading, inserting or deletion) on a single element (a feature or organizing node in the feature tree).

The thrust of much work on the organization of phonological representations has been to show that this theory indeed predicts all and only the kinds of assimilations found in human languages (specific details of the structure of the feature tree have been refined so that we now know, for example, that the features which characterize vowel height form a node in the feature tree, as do the features for the front/back distinction in vowels). The nonlinear account of assimilations precludes the unnatural classes constructed by the expressions in (94), since the theory has no way to tie a specific value for a feature to the value of another feature. The theory does not allow a rule like (92), which involves spreading of only some features under the place node. The nature of a tree like (88) dictates that when a rule operates on a higher node, all nodes underneath it are affected equally. Unattested "assimilations" typified by (93) cannot be described at all in the feature geometric theory, since in that theory the concept "assimilation" necessarily means "of the same unit," which was not the case in the variable-feature theory.

The theory of features in (88) makes other claims, pertaining to how place of articulation is specified, which has some interesting consequences. In the linear model of features, every segment had a complete set of plus or minus values for all features at all levels. This is not the case with the theory of (88). In this theory, a well-formed consonant simply requires specification of one of the articulator nodes, Labial, Coronal or Dorsal. While a coronal consonant may have a specification under the Dorsal node for a secondary vocalic articulation such as palatalization or velarization, plain coronals will not have any specification for [back] or [high]; similarly, consonants have no specification for [round] or Labial unless they are labial consonants, or secondarily rounded. In other words, segments are specified in terms of positive, characteristic properties.

Laryngeal consonants like h and ʔ, however, may lack any place specifications: the feature structure of laryngeals remains a topic for investigation.

This has a significant implication in terms of natural classes. Whereas labials, coronals, and dorsals are natural classes in this theory (each has a common property) – and, in actual phonological processes, these segments do function as natural classes – the complements of these sets do not function as units in processes, and the theory in (88) provides no way to refer to the complement of those classes. Thus there is no natural class of [−coronal] segments ([p, k] excluding [t, č]) in this theory. Coronal is not seen as a binary feature in the theory, but is a single-valued or privative property, and thus there is no way to refer to the noncoronals since natural classes are defined in terms of properties which they share, not properties that they don't share (just as one would not class rocks and insects together as a natural group, to the exclusion of flowers, by terming the group "the class of nonflowers"). Importantly, phonological rules do not ever seem to refer to the group [−coronal], even though the class [+coronal] is well attested as a phonological class. The model in (88) explains why we do not find languages referring to the set [p, k]. It also explains something that was unexplained in the earlier model: the consonantal groupings [p, t] versus [č, k] are unattested in phonological rules. The earlier model predicted these classes, which are based on assignment of the feature [±anterior]. In the model (88) the feature [anterior] is a dependent of the Coronal node, and thus labials and velars do not have a specification of [anterior], so there is no basis for grouping [p, t] or [č, k] together.

Summary

A simple problem, how to represent contour tones, led to ideas which not only solved the problem of contours, but also solved a whole array of problems related to tone. Since there is no reason to think that there should be a special theory just for tone, a natural development of these changes applied to tone was a general application of the autosegmental idea to all of phonology. This resulted in sweeping changes to the theory of phonology, and has resolved many earlier problems in how to state rules in a constrained manner. This generalization of the results in one area to an entire subdiscipline is typical of the progression of scientific theories.

Exercises

1 Lulubo

Note on tone marks: [v̌] = rising from L to M, [v̂] = falling from M to L, [v́] = rising from M to H and [v̂] = falling from H to M. Give the underlying form of the noun roots and whatever morphemes mark the four case forms in the following data; briefly discuss what theoretically interesting property these data illustrate.

Subject object	Unfocused object	Focused object	Proper name	
èbì	ándɛ̀ èbì	ándɛ̀ èbǐ	ándɛ̀ èbî	'lion'
àrī	ándɛ̀ àrî	ándɛ̀ àrī	ándɛ̀ àrī	'bird'
tí	ándɛ̀ tî	ándɛ̀ tí	ándɛ̀ tǐ	'cow'

2 Holoholo

Verbs have an infinitive prefix or a subject marker, an optional negative prefix, then an optional object pronoun, and lastly the verb stem. The stem is composed of a root, a number of optional derivational suffixes, plus the morpheme *-a* which means 'nonpast verb' or *-ile* meaning 'past.' Consonant mutation rules can be ignored (e.g. *il → in*), as well as some of the segmental allomorphs (*kuhuulééna* from /kuhuulilana/, or *kumweenâ* from /kumonila/). What is important is tone and rules relating to vowel sequences. Assume a principle of compensatory lengthening for the language where glide formation and vowel fusion applying to an underlying V+V sequence lengthen the vowel –/i+o/ becomes [yoo].

There are regularities regarding vowel length to consider. There are no surface representations such as *[kuponka], with a short vowel followed by the sequence nasal plus consonant, also no forms like *[kufyaka], with short vowel after a glide. Furthermore, no words end in a long vowel.

The data are divided into conceptually related groups illustrating a particular point such as a rule, a particular restriction on a rule, or the surface tone pattern of words of a particular syllabic structure. It is important to integrate the whole data set, and for example to relate *kumonánâ* 'to see other' to *kumoná* 'to see,' and also to *kulolana* 'to look at e.o,' since *kumonánâ* has morphemes in common with both words.

kumoná	'to see'	kusilá	'to forge'
kulola	'to look at'	kubula	'to draw'
kumonánâ	'to see e.o.'	kusilílâ	'to forge for'
kulolana	'to look at e.o.'	kubulila	'to draw for'
kusilílána	'to forge for e.o.'	kubulilana	'to draw for e.o.'
kutegéléla	'to listen'	kutegélésya	'to make listen'
kutegélélana	'to listen to e.o.'	kusololana	'to choose e.o.'
kulyá	'to eat'	kuhyá	'to carry'
kuliilâ	'to eat for'	kuhiilâ	'to carry for'
kubuusyâ	'to ask'	kukwaatâ	'to own'
kubiihâ	'to be bad'	kuhiita	'to be black'
kutuuta	'to hit'	kusyiika	'to bury'
kubiikâ	'to put'	kubiikílila	'to put for'
kuliilíla	'to eat for s.t. for s.t. else'	kukwaatána	'to own e.o.'
kusyiikana	'to bury e.o.'	kutuutila	'to hit for'
kwiitá	'to call'	kwiitánâ	'to call e.o.'
kweema	'to suffer'	kwaatíkâ	'to split'
kweelélâ	'to clean up'	kweelélána	'to clean e.o. up'
kwiihaga	'to kill'	kwiihagana	'to kill e.o.'
kooja	'to rest'	kuula	'to buy'
koogá	'to wash'	koogélâ	'to wash for'
koogéléla	'to wash for s.t. for s.t. else'	koogélélana	'to wash for e.o.'
kutoontá	'to fill'	kutoontámána	'to be full'
kuloombá	'to request'	kuloombélâ	'to request for'
kuloombélána	'to request for e.o.'	kusiindálâ	'to make disappear'
kusiingínâ	'to put across'	kusiingínína	'to put across for'

kwiimbá	'to sing'	kwiimbílâ	'to sing for'
kunywiisâ	'to make drink'	kunywiisííbwa	'to be made to drink'
kuhuulééna	'to hit for e.o.'	kutimwíína	'to break for'
kuhimá	'to leave'	kuhimyâ	'to make leave'
kukwaatâ	'to own'	kukwaatyâ	'to make own'
koonká	'to suck'	koonkyâ	'to make suck'
kubusá	'to miss'	kubusyâ	'to make miss'
kukoloma	'to irritate'	kumukoloma	'to irritate him'
kubakólóma	'to irritate them'	kulola	'to look at'
kumulola	'to look at him'	kubalólâ	'to look at them'
kumumoná	'to see him'	kubamóná	'to see them'
kutegéléla	'to listen to'	kumutegélóla	'to listen to him'
kubatégéléla	'to listen to them'		
kusimóná	'to not see'	kulola	'to look at'
kusilólâ	'to not look at'	kusikólóma	'to not irritate'
kusimúlóla	'to not look at him'	kusibálólâ	'to not look at them'
kusimúmóná	'to not see him'	kusibámóná	'to not see them'
kutiinína	'to worry'	kusitíínína	'to not worry'
kwiitíínína	'to worry oneself'	kumutıinína	'to worry him'
kwiilólâ	'to look at oneself'	kwiimóná	'to see oneself'
kuula	'to buy'	kusyuulâ	'to not buy'
kusyuulána	'to not buy e.o.'	kusimúúla	'to not buy him'
kwiitá	'to call'	kusiitá	'to not call'
kusiilólâ	'to not look at self'	kusiimóná	'to not see self'
ulolilé	'you (sg) looked'	usilílé	'you (sg) forged'
tulolilé	'we looked'	tusilílé	'we forged'
mulolilé	'you (pl) looked'	musılílé	'you (pl) forged'
úlólilé	'he looked'	úsílílé	'he forged'
bálólilé	'they looked'	básílílé	'they forged'

Further reading
Clements and Hume 1995; Goldsmith 1990; Hayes 1986; Odden 1995.

Glossary

absolute neutralization	The elimination of an underlying phoneme in all contexts, so that is always merges with some other phoneme.
acoustics	The study of physical vibrations (sounds).
affricate	A stop with a homorganic fricative release.
allomorphs	Different surface realizations of a single morpheme, traditionally only considering nonallophonic differences, e.g. the three variants of the English plural [-s], [-z] and [-ɨz]
allophone	A contentually determined variant of a phoneme: the realization of a phoneme in a specific environment, e.g. [k], [kʰ], [kʸ] [kʰʸ] in English are allophones of the phoneme /k/.
alveolar ridge	The ridge between the back of the teeth and the hard palate.
alveopalatal	A consonant produced by placing the tongue on the hard palate behind the alveolar ridge.
APA	Americanist Phonetic Alphabet (an unofficial name given to a particular set of transcription symbols).
approximant	A sound made with very little constriction, where articulators approximate but do not touch, which produces no turbulence in the airflow.
archiphoneme	A theoretical segment which is only partially specified for phonetic properties, omitting some properties such as voicing or nasality which may be determined by rule.
articulation	The contact of two speech organs, such as the tongue tip and the hard palate.
aspiration	Noise produced by air rushing through the open glottis at the release of a consonant.
assimilation	Making segments be more similar along some dimension.
association lines	Lines which indicate that two autosegments are in an association relation, thus are produced at the same time.
bilabial	A sound produced with both lips.
blade	The flat surface of the tongue, behind the tip and in front of the root.
breathy	A sound produced with abducted vocal folds and a high rate of airflow through the glottis.
central	A vowel formed with the tongue horizontally positioned in the center of the space for vowel articulation, between front and back (compare mid for the vertical axis).
click	A stop consonant produced by creating a vacuum inside the mouth with a raised back of the tongue and tongue tip or closed lips. Employed in a limited number of African, especially Khoisan, languages.
close	A higher variant of a vowel, as in mid-close [e] as opposed to mid-open [ɛ]. Comparable to tense; contrast open.

compensatory lengthening	The lengthening of a segment, caused by the deletion or desyllabification of an adjacent segment.
complementary distribution	Distribution of two or more sounds where the context in which one sound appears is the complement of the contexts where the other sounds appear.
complex wave	A waveform built from more than one sine wave.
contour tone	A tone produced by movement from one pitch level to another.
contrast	A property of pairs of sounds: two sounds contrast if they can form the sole difference between different words in a language.
coronalization	The change of a noncoronal sound (p, k) to a coronal sound (t, $č$), usually in the environment of a front vowel or glide.
creaky	An irregular mode of vocal fold vibration where only the front portion vibrates.
decibel	A logarithmic measure of sound power connection to the notion of "loudness." The decibel is the minimum difference in sound power necessary for the average human to hear a difference
dental	A consonant produced by contact with the teeth.
determinant	The segment in the environment which causes a phonological change (also **trigger**).
diphthong	A combination of two vocoids within the syllable nucleus.
dissimilation	Making two segments become less alike.
distinctive features	A set of phonetic properties, hypothesized to be universal and the basis for all human language sounds.
downstep	A contrastive lowering of tone register, notated with a raised exclamation mark or down-arrow. See **upstep**.
ejective	A stop consonant produced by raising the larynx with the glottis constricted, which creates pressure in the oral cavity.
environment	The sounds preceding and following some other sound.
epenthesis	Insertion of a segment.
flap	A consonant produced by rapidly striking one articulator with another. Flaps are usually produced with the tongue.
floating tone	A tone which is not associated with a segment.
focus	In a rule, the segment which undergoes the change.
foot	A prosodic, rhythmic unit constructed on syllables.
formant	An overtone caused by the resonance frequency of the vocal tract; a frequency band where there is a concentration of acoustic energy.
free variation	A pair of pronunciations, either of which can be used: the choice is not governed by grammatical factors.
frequency	Rate of repetition of a (semi-)periodic function.
fricative	A sound produced by forcing air through a narrow constriction, which creates turbulence.
front	A vowel formed with the tongue horizontally positioned in front of of the space for vowel articulation, closest to the mouth opening.
glide	A vowel-like consonant produced with minimal constriction.
glottis	The opening in the larynx between the vocal folds, through which air passes.
hacek	The diacritic symbol ˘ used to indicate rising tone on vowels and alveopalatal articulation on consonants.

hardening	The change of a less constricted consonant to a more constricted one, such as the change of a glide to a fricative or a stop.
Hertz	The unit of frequency measure: 1 cycle per second.
high	Sounds produced with a raised tongue body. For vowels, [i, u] as contrasted with [e, o].
homorganic	Having the same place of articulation.
implicational relation	The relation where presence of one property in a language is a necessary precondition for the presence of some other property.
implosive	A stop consonant formed by creating a vacuum within the mouth, by constricting and lowering the larynx.
IPA	International Phonetic Association or International Phonetic Alphabet.
labial	A segment involving the lips as an articulator.
larynx	The cartilaginous structure that houses the vocal folds.
lax	Vowel produced with a less deliberate, more central or lower articulation. Comparable to open; contrast tense.
lenition	A change of a consonant to reduce the degree of constriction, e.g. the change from a stop to a fricative or glide.
lexicon	The collection of morphemes which must be memorized: a mental dictionary.
lingual	Pertaining to the tongue.
liquids	Consonants of the type [r, l].
low	Sounds produced with a lowered tongue: vowels like [a, æ] and pharyngeals [ħ, ʕ]
major class	The set of features [sonorant], [syllabic], [consonantal], or their equivalents.
manner of articulation	Traditionally, the properties of a consonant other than the place of articulation and its laryngeal properties.
markedness	An abstract property refering to the "unusualness" or difficulty of a sound or process.
mid	Vowel sounds such as [e, o] produced with the tongue around the midpoint on the vertical axis: compare central which pertains to the midpoint along the horizontal axis.
minimal pair	A pair of distinct words differing solely in the choice of a single segment.
mora	A unit of prosodic weight, related to length: a long vowel has two moras and a short vowel has one. The mora may be a property of both a particular segment and an entire syllable.
morpheme	The smallest unit of word-analysis, such as a root or affix. Supposedly the smallest meaning-bearing unit, but not all morphemes have identifiable meanings.
morpheme structure rules, conditions	Rules that state the nature of possible underlying forms of morphemes.
morphophonemics	Phonological alternations, especially nonallophonic changes.
nasal	A sound produced with air flowing through the nasal passages.
natural class	A set of segments defined by a particular combination of feature specifications, which act as a group in phonological rules.

neutral position	The position which the tongue assumes prior to speaking, approximately that of [ɛ]. Used as the reference point to define relative movements of the tongue.
neutralization	Eliminating an underlying distinction between phonemes in some context.
obstruents	Nonsonorant consonants, such as stops and fricatives.
onset	The consonants at the beginning of the syllable which precede the vowel.
open	A lower variant of a vowel, as in mid-open [ɛ] as opposed to mid-close [e]. Comparable to lax; contrast close.
palatal	Referring to the hard or soft palate. As a primary articulation, a consonant produced at the boundary between the hard and soft palate.
palatalization	Either a secondary articulation made by superimposing a *y*-like articulation on a consonant, or a wholesale change of a consonant's place of articulation to alveopalatal (see coronalization).
periodic	A physical sound whose (approximate) pattern repeats.
pharynx	The lower part of the throat.
phonation	The manner of vibration of the vocal folds (modal, breathy, creaky).
phoneme	A mental integration of the different physical properties of the sounds used in a language, abstracting away from specific phonetic properties which are due to the context where the sound appears.
pitch	The percept of rate of vibration.
prenasalization	A sound produced with an initial interval of nasal airflow ~ often treated as a homorganic cluster of nasal plus consonant.
privative	A feature having only one value: either the feature is present, or not present.
prosody	Properties "above" the segment which pertain to syllabification, length, stress, and rhythm.
resonance	Periodic transfer of energy, in speech related to the size of a vocal tract cavity.
retroflex	Consonant articulation involving the tip of the tongue and the back of the alveolar ridge or palate.
reversal of sound change	The historical loss of a phonological rule, which leads to the (partial) restoration of earlier sounds – Yiddish and Ukrainian provide classic examples.
round	A sound produced with protruded lips.
segment	A mental division of the continuous stream of speech into significant permutable units.
semi-vowels	See glide.
sine wave	A pure tone which is described by the sine function.
spectrogram	A continuous analytic display of acoustic properties of sound over time, showing which frequencies are emphasized at each moment.
spectrum	An analytic display of the amplitude of sound at all frequencies, taken at a single point in time.
spontaneous voicing	Passive vibration of the vocal folds which results from breathing, a characteristic of sonorants. This is brought about by a particular positioning of the vocal folds combined with a relatively unconstricted air passage.

stop	A sound where the flow of air is completely obstructed.
stress	A form of prosodic prominence typically resulting in greater length and higher pitch within the syllable.
structural change	That part of a rule which states in what way a given sound changes.
structure preserving	The property of rules that outputs are modified to preserve the nature of underlying forms, especially in terms of what phonemes exist in the language.
syllable	A unit of speech claimed to be relevant for the organization of words, a grouping of consonants and vowels into a $C_0V_1C_0$ constituent.
syllable peak	The span within the syllable perceived as (capable of) bearing stress.
syncope	Deletion of a vowel in a medial syllable, especially in a fashion that affects alternating syllables.
target	See *focus*.
tense	Vowel produced with a more deliberate and higher. Comparable to **close**; contrast **lax**.
tone	A property based on the contrastive use of pitch.
translaryngeal harmony	Assimilation of vowels which applies only across laryngeal consonants.
trigger	See **determinant**.
typology	The parametric study of crosslinguistic variation in grammatical structure.
underlying	Pertaining to the initial state in a phonological derivation; the phonological facts holding of a word or morpheme before phonological rules affect changes.
upstep	A contrastive raising of tone register, notated with a raised inverted exclamation mark or an up-arrow. See **downstep**.
uvular	A consonant formed by constricting the back of the throat near the uvula with the back of the tongue.
velar	A consonant formed by bringing together the back of the tongue and the soft palate.
velarized	A secondary articulation formed by approximating the back of the tongue towards the soft palate.
velum	The soft palate.
vocal folds	Two membranes in the larynx, whose vibration provides voicing and most of the sound energy of speech.
vocal tract	The air passages above the glottis, including the oral tract and the nasal passages.
vocoid	A vowel-like sound with no major obstruction: the class of vowels and glides.
voicing	The presence of vocal fold vibrations during the production of a sound produces voicing.
vowel harmony	An assimilation between vowels where one vowel takes on the properties of a neighboring vowel.
waveform	A display of the time-varying amplitude of sound pressure.
weakening	See **lenition**.
weight	A property of syllables which may be divided into light and heavy syllables: heavy syllables typically have a long vowel or diphthong, or sometimes a short vowel plus consonant. See **mora**.

References

Abaev, V. I. 1964. *A Grammatical Sketch of Ossetic*. Bloomington: Indiana University Press.

Akinlabi, Akin. 1984. Tonal Underspecification and Yoruba Tone. Ibadan: University of Ibadan, doctoral dissertation.

Al-Mozainy, Hamza Q. 1981. Vowel Alternations in a Bedouin Hijazi Arabic Dialect: Abstractness and Stress. Austin: University of Texas, doctoral dissertation.

Allen, Joseph and J. B. Greenough. 1983. *Allen and Greenough's New Latin Grammar for Schools and Colleges, Founded on Comparative Grammar*. New Rochelle, NY: A.D. Caratzas.

Ambrazas, Vytautas. 1997. *Lithuanian Grammar*. Vilnius Baltos: Lankos.

Andersen, Torben. 1987. "An outline of Lulubo phonology." *Studies in African Linguistics* 18: 39–65.

Anderson, Stephen. 1974. *The Organization of Phonology*. New York: Academic Press.

Andrzejewski, B. 1964. *The Declensions of Somali Nouns*. London: School of Oriental and African Studies.

Aquilina, J. 1965. *Maltese*. London: Teach Yourself Books.

Ariste, Paul. 1968. *A Grammar of the Votic Language*. Bloomington: Indiana University Press.

Arnott, David W. 1964. "Downstep in the Tiv verbal system." *African Language Studies* 5: 34–51.

Barker, Muhammad A. R. 1963. *Klamath Dictionary*. University of California Publications in Linguistics 31. Los Angeles and Berkeley: University of California Press.

1964. *Klamath Grammar*. University of California Publications in Linguistics 32. Los Angeles and Berkeley: University of California Press.

Beatty, John. 1974. *Mohawk Morphology*. Occasional Publications in Anthropology, Linguistic Series 2. Greeley, Colorado: Museum of Anthropology, University of Northern Colorado.

Bhat, D. N. S. and M. S. Ningomba. 1997. *Manipuri Grammar*. Munich: Lincom Europa.

Bills, Garland, Bernardo Vallejo and Rudolph Troike. 1969. *An Introduction to Spoken Quechua*. Austin: University of Texas Press.

Borg, Albert and Marie Azzopardi-Alexandre. 1997. *Maltese*. London: Routledge.

Boxwell, Helen and Maurice Boxwell. 1966. "Weri phonemes." In S. A. Wurm (ed.), *Papers in New Guinea Linguistics*, 5: 77–93. Australian National University, Canberra.

Brame, Michael. 1972. "On the abstractness of phonology: Maltese ʕ." In M. Brame (ed.), *Contributions to Generative Phonology*, 22–61. University of Texas Press: Austin.

Bright, William. 1957. *The Karok Language*. University of California Publications in Linguistics 13. Los Angeles and Berkeley: University of California Press.

Bulatova, Nadezhda Ja. and Lenore Grenoble. 1999. *Evenki*. Munich: Lincom Europa.

Campbell, Lyle. 1974. "Phonological features: problems and proposals." *Language* 50: 52–65.

Carlton, Terence. 1971. *The Declension of Nouns in Ukrainian: a Student's Reference*. Edmonton: Department of Slavic Languages, University of Alberta.

Chomsky, Noam. 1967. "Some general properties of phonological rules." *Language* 43: 102–28.

Chomsky, Noam and Morris Halle. 1968. *The Sound Pattern of English*. New York: Harper and Row.

Chung, Sandra. 1983. "Transderivational relations in Chamorro phonology." *Language* 59: 35–66.

Clements, G. N. 1978. "Tone and syntax in Ewe." In D. J. Napoli (ed.), *Elements of Tone, Stress, and Intonation*, 21–99. Washington: Georgetown University Press.

1984. "Principles of tone assignment in Kikuyu." In G. N. Clements and J. Goldsmith (eds.), *Autosegmental Studies in Bantu Tonology*, 281–340. Dordrecht: Foris.

Clements, G. N. and Elizabeth Hume. 1995. "The internal organization of speech sounds." In J. Goldsmith (ed.), *Handbook of Phonological Theory*, 245–306. Oxford: Blackwell.

Cohn, Abigail. 1993. "Nasalization in English: phonology or phonetics." *Phonology* 10: 43–81.

Cole, Desmond. 1955. *An Introduction to Tswana*. Capetown: Longman.

1967. *Some Features of Ganda Linguistic Structure*. Johannesburg: Witwatersrand Press.

Coupez, André. 1955. *Esquisse de la langue holoholo*. Terveuren: Musée royale de l'afrique centrale.

Cowan, William and Jaromira Rakušan. 1998. *Source Book for Linguistics*. 3rd edition. Amsterdam and Philadelphia: John Benjamins.

Cowell, Mark. 1964. *Reference Grammar of Syrian Arabic*. Washington: Georgetown University Press.

Cusihuamán, Antonio. 1976. *Diccionario Quechua Cuzco-Collao*. Lima: Ministerio de educacion / instituto de estudios peruanos.

Dambriunas, Leonardas, Antanas Klimas and William Schmalstieg. 1966. *Introduction to Modern Lithuanian*. Brooklyn: Franciscan Fathers Press.

Doke, Clement. 1938. *Textbook of Lamba Grammar*. Johannesburg: Witwaterstrand Press.

Dolphyne, Florence Abena. 1988. *The Akan (Twi-Fante) Language*. Accra: Ghana Universities Press.

Downing, Laura. 1996. *The Tonal Phonology of Jita*. Munich: Lincom Europa.

Ebert, Karen. 1975. *Sprache und Tradition der Kera (Tschad)*. Marburger Studien zur Afrika und Asienkunde, Serie A, Bd. 6. Berlin: Reimer.

Echeverría, Max and Heles Contreras. 1965. "Araucanian phonemics." *International Journal of American Linguistics* 31: 132–5.

Einarsson, Stefán. 1945. *Icelandic: Grammar, Texts, Glossary*. Baltimore: Johns Hopkins Press.

Elimelech, Baruch. 1978. *A Tonal Grammar of Etsako*. University of California Press: Berkeley.

Emeneau, Murray. 1961. *Kolami: a Dravidian Language*. Annamalainagar: Annamalai University Press.

Flora, Marie Jo-Ann. 1974. "Palauan Phonology and Morphology." San Diego: University of California, doctoral dissertation.

Foster, Joseph. 1969. "On Some Phonological Rules in Turkish." Champaign: University of Illinois, doctoral dissertation.

Fry, Dennis B. 1979. *The Physics of Speech*. Cambridge: Cambridge University Press.

Gerfen, Chip. 1999. *Phonology and Phonetics of Coatzospan Mixtec*. Dordrecht: Kluwer.

Gleason, Henry. 1955. *An Introduction to Descriptive Linguistics*. New York: Holt.

Goldsmith, John. 1976. "Autosegmental Phonology." Cambridge, Mass.: MIT, doctoral dissertation. Distributed by Indiana University Linguistics Club, Bloomington

1990a. *Autosegmental and Metrical Phonology*. Oxford: Blackwell.

1990b. "Harmonic phonology." In J. Goldsmith (ed.), *The Last Phonological Rule*, 21–60. Chicago: University of Chicago Press.

Greenberg, Joseph. 1978. *Universals of Human Language*. Stanford: Stanford University Press.

Hale, Mark and Charles Reiss. 2000. "Phonology as cognition." In N. Burton-Roberts, P. Carr and G. Docherty (eds.), *Phonological Knowledge: Conceptual and Empirical Issues*, 161–84. Oxford: Oxford University Press.

Hale, William Gardner and Carl Darling Buck. 1966. *A Latin Grammar*. Tuscaloosa: University of Alabama Press.

Halle, Morris. 1959. *The Sound Pattern of Russian*. Mouton: The Hague.

Halle, Morris and George N. Clements. 1983. *Problem Book of Phonology: A Workbook for Courses in Introductory Linguistics and Modern Phonology*. Cambridge, MA: MIT Press.

Hangin, John. 1968. *Basic Course in Mongolian*. Bloomington: Indiana University Press.

Harris, John. 1994. *English Sound Structure*. Oxford: Blackwell.

Hayes, Bruce. 1986. "Assimilation as spreading in Toba Batak." *Linguistic Inquiry* 17: 467–99.

1995. *Metrical Stress Theory: Principles and Case Studies*. Chicago: University of Chicago Press.

Hoberman, Robert. 1988. "Emphasis harmony in a Modern Aramaic dialect." *Language* 64: 1–26.

Hoffmann, Carl. 1963. *A Grammar of the Margi Language*. London: Oxford University Press.

Hoijer, Harry. 1933. *Tonkawa, an Indian Language of Texas*. Handbook of American Indian Languages III. Washington: Smithsonian Institutes.

Hualde, Jose. 1999. *Catalan: a Comprehensive Grammar*. London: Routledge.

Hudson, Grover. 1974. "The role of SPC's in Natural Generative Phonology." In A. Bruck, R. Fox and M. LaGaly (eds.), *Papers from the Parasession on Natural Phonology*, 171–83. Chicago: Chicago Linguistics Society.

Hulstaert, Gustav. 1961. *Grammaire du lomóngo*. Terveuren: Musée royale de l'Afrique centrale.

Hume, Elizabeth. 1996. "Coronal consonant, front vowel parallels in Maltese." *Natural Language and Linguistic Theory* 14: 163–203.

Hume, Elizabeth and Keith Johnson. 2001. "A model of the interplay of speech perception and phonology." In Hume and Johnson (eds.), *The Role of Speech Perception in Phonology*, 3–26. New York: Academic Press.

Hyman, Larry. 1970. 'How concrete is phonology?' *Language* 46: 58–76.

Hyman, Larry and Russell Schuh. 1974. "Universals of tone rules: evidence from West Africa." *Linguistic Inquiry* 5: 81–115.

Inkelas, Sharon. 1989. "Prosodic Constituency in the Lexicon." Stanford: Stanford University, doctoral dissertation.

International Phonetic Association. 1999. *Handbook of the International Phonetic Association*. Cambridge: Cambridge University Press.

Jakobson, Roman and Morris Halle. 1956. *Fundamentals of Language*. The Hague: Mouton.

Jakobson, Roman, Gunnar Fant, and Morris Halle 1952. *Preliminaries to Speech Analysis*. Cambridge, Mass.: MIT Press.

Johnson, Keith. 1997. *Acoustic and Auditory Phonetics*. Oxford: Blackwell.

Jónsson, Snæbjörn. 1966. *A Primer of Modern Icelandic*. London: Oxford University Press.

Josephs, Lewis. 1975. *Palauan Reference Grammar*. Honolulu: University of Hawaii Press.

Kahn, Daniel. 1976. "Syllable Based Generalizations in English Phonology." Cambridge: MIT, doctoral dissertation. Distributed by Indiana University Linguistics club: Bloomington.

Kaisse, Ellen and Patricia Shaw. 1985. "On the theory of lexical phonology." *Phonology* 2: 1–30.

Kaye, Jonathan. 1982. "Harmony processes in Vata." In N. Smith and H. van der Hulst (eds.), *Structure of Phonological Representations, part II*, 385–452. Foris: Dordrecht.

Kelly, John and John Local. 1989. *Doing Phonology*. Manchester and New York: Manchester University Press.

Kenesei, István, Robert M. Vago and Anna Fenyvesi. 1998. *Hungarian*. London and New York: Routledge.

Kenstowicz, Michael. 1972. "Lithuanian phonology." *Studies in the Linguistic Sciences* 2,2: 1–85.

1972. "The morphophonemics of the Slovak noun." *Papers in Linguistics* 5: 550–67.

1994. *Phonology in Generative Grammar*. Oxford: Blackwell.

Kenstowicz, Michael and Charles Kisseberth. 1977. *Topics in Phonological Theory*. New York: Academic Press.

1979. *Generative Phonology: Description and Theory*. New York: Academic Press.

Kimball, Geoffrey D. 1991. *Koasati Grammar*. Lincoln: University of Nebraska Press.

Kiparsky, Paul. 1968a. "Linguistic universals and linguistic change." In E. Bach and R. Harms (eds.), *Universals of Linguistic Theory*, 171–202. New York: Holt.

Kiparsky, Paul. 1968b. "How abstract is phonology?" Distributed by Indiana University Linguistics Club, Bloomington. Reprinted in P. Kiparsky, *Explanation in Phonology*. Dordrecht: Foris, 1982.

Kisseberth, Charles. 1969. "On the abstractness of phonology: the evidence from Yawelmani." *Papers in Linguistics* 1: 248–82.

1984. "Digo tonology." In G. N. Clements and J. Goldsmith (eds.), *Autosegmental Studies in Bantu Tonology*, 105–82. Dordrecht: Foris.

Klokeid, Terrence. 1976. "Topics in Lardil Grammar." Cambridge, Mass.: MIT, doctoral dissertation.

Konstantinova, Olga A. 1964. *Evenkijskij Jazyk: Fonetika, Morfologija*. Moscow: Nauka.

Koutsoudas, Andreas, Gerald Sanders and Craig Noll. 1974. "On the application of phonological rules." *Language* 50: 1–28.

Krauss, Scott. 1981. Topics in Chukchee Phonology and Morphology. Urbana: University of Illinois, doctoral dissertation.

Krueger, John. 1962. *Yakut Manual; Area Handbook, Grammar, Graded Reader and Glossary*. Bloomington: Indiana University Press.

Ladefoged, Peter. 2001a. *A Course in Phonetics*. Orlando: Harcourt.

2001b. *Vowels and Consonants*. Oxford: Blackwell.

Ladefoged, Peter and Ian Maddieson. 1996. *The Sounds of the World's Languages*. Oxford: Blackwell.

Leben, William. 1978. "The representation of tone." In V. Fromkin (ed.), *Tone: a Linguistic Survey*, 177–219. New York: Academic Press.

Lees, Robert. 1961. *The Phonology of Modern Standard Turkish*. Uralic and Altaic Series 6. Bloomington: Indiana University Press.

Lehtinen, Meri. 1963. *Basic Course in Finnish*. Bloomington: Indiana University Press.

Levelt, Willem. 1989. *Speaking: from Intention to Articulation*. Cambridge, Mass.: MIT Press.

Liberman, Mark. 1983. "Uncommon approaches to the study of speech." In P. MacNeilage (ed.), *The Production of Speech*, 265–74. New York and Berlin: Springer.

Lleo, Concepción. 1970. *Problems of Catalan Phonology*. Studies in Linguistics and Language Learning 8. Seattle: University of Washington.

Maddieson, Ian. 1984. *Patterns of Sounds*. Cambridge: Cambridge University Press.

Martin, Samuel. 1975. *A Reference Grammar of Japanese*. New Haven: Yale University Press.

Martin, Samuel. 1992. *A Reference Grammar of Korean*. Rutland, VT: C. E. Tuttle.

Mathiassen, Terje. 1996. *A Short Grammar of Lithuanian*. Columbus: Slavica.

Michelson, Karin. 1988. *A Comparative Study of Lake Iroquoian Accent*. Dordrecht: Reidel.

Milner, G. B. 1966. *Samoan Dictionary*. London: Oxford University Press.

Nedjalkov, Igor. 1997. *Evenki*. Routledge: London.

Newman, Paul. 1968. "The reality of morphophonemics." *Language* 44: 507–15.

Newman, Stanley. 1944. *Yokuts Language of California*. New York: Viking Fund Publications in Anthropology 2.

Obolensky, Serge, Debebow Zelelie and Mulugeta Andualem. 1964. *Amharic*. Washington: Foreign Service Institute.

Obolensky, Serge, Kambiz Panah and Fereidoun Nouri. 1963. *Persian Basic Course Units 1–12*. Foreign Service Institute, reprinted by Center for Applied Linguistics:Washington.

Odden, David. 1995. "Tone: African languages." In J. Goldsmith (ed.), *The Handbook of Phonological Theory*, 444–75. Oxford: Blackwell.

Ohala, John. 1978. "Southern Bantu vs. the world: the case of palatalization of labials." *Proceedings of the Annual Meeting of the Berkeley Linguistic Society* 4: 370–86.

Oresnik, Janez. 1985. *Studies in the Phonology and Morphology of Modern Icelandic : a Selection of Essays*, ed. Magnús Pétursson. Hamburg: Buske.

Osborn, Henry. 1966. "Warao I: phonology and morphophonemics." *International Journal of American Linguistics* 32: 108–23.

Paradis, Carole. 1992. *Lexical Phonology and Morphology: the Nominal Classes in Fula*. New York and London: Garland.

Payne, David L. 1981. *The Phonology and Morphology of Axininca Campa*. Arlington: Summer Institute of Linguistics.

Pike, Kenneth. 1947. *Phonemics*. Ann Arbor: University of Michigan Press.

1948. *Tone Languages: a Technique for Determining the Number and Type of Pitch Contrasts in a Language*. Ann Arbor: University of Michigan Press.

Pitkin, Harvey. 1984. *Wintu Grammar*. Berkeley and Los Angeles: University of California Press.

Popova, Tatiana V. 1972. "Paradigmatičeskije konsonantyje rjady čeredovany v jugo-zapadnyx ukrainskix dialektax (na materiale govora s. sadžava)." In G. Klepikova (ed.), *Karpatskaja Dialektologia i Onomastika*, 179–239. Moscow: Nauka.

Postal, Paul. 1968. *Aspects of Phonological Theory*. New York: Harper & Row.

Press, Ian and Stefan Pugh. 1994. *Colloquial Ukrainian*. London and New York: Routledge.

Pullum, Geoff. 1976. "The Duke of York gambit." *Journal of Linguistics* 12: 83–102.

Pullum, Geoff and William Ladusaw. 1986. *Phonetic Symbol Guide*. Chicago: University of Chicago Press.

Rennison, John. 1997. *Koromfe*. London and New York: Routledge.

Rice, Keren. 1989. *A Grammar of Slave*. Berlin: De Gruyter.

Rich, Furne. 1963. "Arabela phonemes and high-level phonology." In B. Elson (ed.), *Studies in Peruvian Indian Languages*, 193–206. Norman, OK: Summer Institute of Linguistics.

Rubach, Jerzy. 1993. *The Lexical Phonology of Slovak*. Oxford: Clarendon Press.

Saeed, John. 1993. *Somali Reference Grammar*. Kensington, MD: Dunwoody.

1999. *Somali*. Amsterdam and Philadelphia: Benjamins.

Sapir, Edward. 1925. "Sound patterns in language." *Language* 1: 37–51.

1933. "The psychological reality of phonemes." In David Mandelbaum (ed.), *Selected Writings of Edward Sapir*, 46–60. Berkeley and Los Angeles: University of California Press.

Saxton, Dean. 1963. "Papago phonemes." *International Journal of American Linguistics* 29: 29–35.

Saxton, Dean and Lucille Saxton. 1969. *Papago and Pima to English Dictionary*. Tucson: University of Arizona Press.

Schadeberg, Thilo. 1982. "Nasalisation in Umbundu." *Journal of African Languages and Linguistics* 4: 109–32.

Siptár, Péter and Miklós Törkenczy. 2000. *The Phonology of Hungarian*. Oxford: Clarendon Press.

Smalley, William. 1963. *Manual of Articulatory Phonetics*. Tarrytown, NJ: Practical Anthropology.

Snoxall, R. A. 1967. *Luganda–English Dictionary*. Oxford: Oxford University Press.

Snider, Keith. 1990. "Tonal Upstep in Krachi: evidence for register tier." *Language* 66.3:453–74.

Snyman, J., J. Shole, and J. Le Roux. 1990. *Dikišinare ya Setswana, English, Afrikaans*. Pretoria: Via Afrika.

Sohn, Hoh-min. 1975. *Woleaian Reference Grammar*. Honolulu: University of Hawaii Press.

Stanley, Richard. 1967. "Redundancy rules in phonology." *Language* 43: 393–436.

Stevens, Kenneth 1998. *Acoustic Phonetics*. Cambridge, Mass.: MIT Press.

Topping, Donald. 1968. "Chamorro vowel harmony." *Oceanic Linguistics* 7: 67–79.

Topping, Donald and Bernadita Dungca. 1973. *Chamorro Reference Grammar*. Honolulu: University of Hawaii Press.

Trubetzkoy, Nicholas. S. 1939. *Principles of Phonology*. Translated by C. Baltaxe, 1969, Berkeley and Los Angeles: University of California Press.

Tryon, James. 1970. *An Introduction to Maranungku*. Pacific Linguistics B15. Canberra: Australian National University.

Vago, Robert. 1980. *The Sound Pattern of Hungarian*. Washington: Georgetown University Press.

Vaux, Bert. 1998. *The Phonology of Armenian*. Oxford: Oxford University Press.

Vennemann, Theo. 1974. "Words and syllables in Natural Generative Grammar." In A. Bruck, R. Fox and M. LaGaly (eds.), *Papers from the Parasession on Natural Phonology*, 346–74. Chicago: Chicago Linguistics Society.

Wheeler, Max. 1979. *Phonology of Catalan*. Oxford: Blackwell.

Whitley, M. Stanley. 1978. *Generative Phonology Workbook*. Madison: University of Wisconsin Press.

Whitney, Arthur. 1956. *Teach Yourself Finnish*. Kent: Hodder & Stoughton.

Zemlin, Willard. 1981. *Speech and Hearing Science: Anatomy and Physiology*. Englewood Cliffs: Prentice-Hall.

Zwicky, Arnold. 1973. "The analytic leap: from 'some Xs are Ys' to 'All Xs are Ys'." *Chicago Linguistic Society* 9: 700–9.

1974. "Taking a false step." *Language* 50: 215–24.

1975. "The strategy of generative phonology." In W. Dressler and F. V. Mareš (eds.), *Phonologica 1972*, 151–68. Munich: Fink.

Index of languages

General Index